Dismantling the Dream Factory

Film Europa: German Cinema in an International Context
Series Editors: **Hans-Michael Bock** (CineGraph Hamburg);
Tim Bergfelder (University of Southampton); **Sabine Hake**
(University of Texas, Austin)

German cinema is normally seen as a distinct form, but this new series emphasizes connections, influences, and exchanges of German cinema across national borders, as well as its links with other media and art forms. Individual titles present traditional historical research (archival work, industry studies) as well as new critical approaches in film and media studies (theories of the transnational), with a special emphasis on the continuities associated with popular traditions and local perspectives.

The Concise Cinegraph: An Encyclopedia of German Cinema
General Editor: Hans-Michael Bock
Associate Editor: Tim Bergfelder

International Adventures: German Popular Cinema and European Co-Productions in the 1960s
Tim Bergfelder

Between Two Worlds: The Jewish Presence in German and Austrian Film, 1910–1933
S.S. Prawer

Framing the Fifties: Cinema in a Divided Germany
Edited by John Davidson and Sabine Hake

A Foreign Affair: Billy Wilder's American Films
Gerd Gemünden

Destination London: German-speaking Emigrés and British Cinema, 1925–1950
Edited by Tim Bergfelder and Christian Cargnelli

Michael Haneke's Cinema: The Ethic of the Image
Catherine Wheatley

Willing Seduction: *The Blue Angel*, **Marlene Dietrich and Mass Culture**
Barbara Kosta

Dismantling the Dream Factory: Gender, German Cinema, and the Postwar Quest for a New Film Language
Hester Baer

DISMANTLING THE DREAM FACTORY

FACTORY

Gender, German Cinema, and the Postwar
Quest for a New Film Language

Hester Baer

Berghahn Books
New York • Oxford

Published in 2009 by

Berghahn Books

www.berghahnbooks.com

© 2009, 2012 Hester Baer
First paperback edition published in 2012

Library of Congress Cataloging-in-Publication Data

Baer, Hester.
   Dismantling the dreamfactory: gender, German cinema, and the
postwar quest for a new film language / Hester Baer.
      p. cm. -- (Film Europa; v. 9)
   Includes bibliographical references and index.
   ISBN 978-1-84545-605-4 (hbk.) -- ISBN 978-0-85745-617-5 (pbk.)
   1. Motion pictures--Germany--History--20th century. 2. Motion pictures-
-Social aspects--Germany. 3. Motion pictures for women--Germany. 4.
Motion picture audiences--Germany. 5. Women in motion pictures. I. Title.
   PN1993.5.G3B275 2009
   791.430943'09044--dc22

                              2009032996

British Library Cataloguing in Publication Data

A catalogue record for this book is available from the British Library
Printed in the United States on acid-free paper.

ISBN: 978-0-85745-617-5 (paperback)   ISBN: 978-0-85745-618-2 (ebook)

For Ryan Long
and in loving memory of our son
Ansel Rees Baer

CONTENTS

Part III. Towards the New Wave: Gender and the Critique of Popular Cinema

LIST OF ILLUSTRATIONS

ACKNOWLEDGMENTS

This book would not exist without the guidance, encouragement, and generosity of many teachers, colleagues, and friends who contributed substantially to its research and writing. Without Leslie Morris, I would not have become a Germanist, and I am grateful for her mentorship over many years. Rick McCormick first taught me about German cinema, and his friendship and encouragement during the writing of this book have been crucial. Lutz Koepnick supported this project from the earliest stages of its development, and his influence as a teacher and friend has been profound. Mike Lützeler has been a wonderful adviser, both during my years as a graduate student at Washington University and especially since.

I would like to thank Stephan Schindler, Lynne Tatlock, Jennifer Jenkins, and Erin Mackie for their thoughtful comments on the earliest version of this project. Jennifer Askey, Sonja Fritzsche, Dick Langston, Jed Mayer, Beth Muellner, and Christina White also read early versions of various chapters, and their insightful comments helped set me in the right direction. I am grateful for the advice and guidance of Jean Fox O'Barr, Peter McIsaac, and Ann Marie Rasmussen during my year at Duke University, where I also benefited from presenting my research to audiences in the Women's Studies and German departments. The German Film Institute led by Eric Rentschler and Anton Kaes in 2002, "After the War, Before the Wall," helped take my thinking about postwar German cinema in new directions. Earlier versions of chapters 9 and 10 were published in *Sound Matters: Essays on the Acoustics of German Culture* (Berghahn Books, 2004) and *Light Motives: German Popular Film in Perspective* (Wayne State University Press, 2003). The comments of the editors of those volumes, Nora Alter and Lutz Koepnick, and Randall Halle and Maggie McCarthy, shaped my writing in valuable ways.

My initial work on this project was supported by a grant from the German Academic Exchange Service (DAAD), which allowed me to live and conduct research in Berlin. I have returned repeatedly to the Filmmuseum Berlin-Deutsche Kinemathek, where I am especially grateful for the assistance of Regina Hoffmann and Peter Latta. All of the photographs in this book appear courtesy of the Deutsche Kinemathek. I began writing this book with the generous support of the Lisa Lee and Marc Ewing Postdoctoral Fellowship in German Studies and Women's Studies at Duke University. My research also benefited from a Fulbright travel grant to participate in the 2004 seminar "Visual Culture in Germany."

At the University of Oklahoma, I have been fortunate to enjoy both generous research funding and the support of many good friends, which has made the completion of this book possible. Grants from the College of Arts and Sciences, the Vice President of Research, and the Department of Modern Languages, Literatures, and Linguistics allowed me to make several research trips to Berlin. I owe a particular debt of gratitude to Helga Madland and Pamela Genova for their support, and to Kathy Peters for her incredible efficiency and administrative skills. At OU's Bizzell Library, Calvin Byre has answered my research questions with astonishing speed and accuracy, and the staff of the Interlibrary Loan department has pulled out all the stops to get me rare materials. Thanks also to Ray Canoy, Joe Sullivan, and especially Karin Schutjer, whose encouragement and collegiality have made OU such a hospitable place.

I am grateful to the editors of the Film Europa Series, Tim Bergfelder, Hans-Michael Bock, and especially Sabine Hake, for their enthusiasm about my project and their help in developing the manuscript. Thanks to Ann Przyzycki, Mark Stanton, and Noa Vázquez Barreiro at Berghahn, who have shepherded this book through production skilfully and graciously, and to Caroline Richards for her meticulous copyediting. I would also like to thank Marion Berghahn for her personal attentiveness throughout the publication process. I owe special thanks to the anonymous reader whose incredibly thorough and well-taken critique of the manuscript helped me to avoid several key mistakes, clarify my argument, and significantly improve the final book.

Throughout the writing of this book, Bob Shandley has been both a good friend and an invaluable source of hard-to-find movies and information. Without Elizabeth Birdsall, I might never have discovered my passion for German cinema. The friendship of Stacy Lewis and Kiersten Figurski has sustained me for two decades. Jennifer Askey, Lisa Hock, and Katja Altpeter-Jones are great friends, whose support after my son's death made a return to work on this book seem possible again. Thanks also to Nathaniel Baer and Karen Smith for essential conversation, nourishment, and distraction. My in-laws, Donna and Fred Long, provided sustenance and caffeine. Because of Rachel and Luis Cortest, Susan and Michael Winston, and Susan Beaty, I am happy to call Oklahoma home. I am also very grateful to Shanah Ahmadi and Thom Rose for their amazing devotion to my daughter's development and well-being.

My parents, Clint and Elizabeth Baer, have challenged me intellectually and encouraged me in all my pursuits, and they continue to be an incomparable source of support, good humor, conversation, and perspective on a daily basis. They each read large portions of this book in its various incarnations, and their perceptive comments about the book and about German culture at large have proved especially valuable. As Paco and Gaga, they also provided urgently needed childcare at several key stages in the research and writing process.

Ryan Long has read every page of this book several times, and it would not exist without his keen intellect, unwavering patience, and steadfast support. Not only has he contributed as my best critic and editor, but he has also accompanied me on numerous research trips and willingly watched and discussed an incredible number of German films, most without subtitles. He has also given me the time, space, and fortitude to write, even though both of our children were born during the gestation of this book. I thank him for inspiring me every single day.

Finally, my biggest and best thanks go to Della, who makes everything I do more fun.

Introduction

DISMANTLING THE DREAM FACTORY:
GENDER AND SPECTATORSHIP IN
POSTWAR GERMAN CINEMA

In 1947, Helmut Käutner, one of postwar cinema's key players, published a programmatic essay in the journal *Film-Echo* entitled "Demontage der Traumfabrik." In his essay, Käutner detailed the positive developments in the German cinematic landscape since the end of World War II. Filmmakers and technicians had overcome personal privation and want in their first attempts to create a new artistic postwar cinema, and they had also received a great deal of beneficial assistance from economic development agencies, cultural funds, and the occupation military governments. Yet despite the best efforts of individual artists and technicians and the help of so many agencies, German filmmakers had still failed to realize their common goal of "dismantling the dream factory," and for Käutner the reason was clear: "One decisive group has failed to join in the effort: the German audience."[1]

Käutner's essay introduced already in 1947 what was to become a commonplace in analyses of early postwar film: the cinema of the reconstruction and Adenauer eras ultimately failed to break with the Nazi past, offering little but generic entertainment fare in order to cater to the demands of a mass public that wanted "relaxation, conflicts instead of problems, superficial plot instead of experience, and … a world whose pleasant aspects belong just as unequivocally to the past as its unpleasant aspects."[2] In sum, how could filmmakers create a new German cinema when audiences demanded nothing short of escapist kitsch conforming to the dictates of Goebbels' Nazi filmmaking apparatus?

The history of postwar German cinema has most often been told as a story of failure, a failure paradoxically epitomized by the remarkable popularity of film throughout the late 1940s and 1950s.[3] According to this narrative, West German cinema only succeeded in breaking with the past and creating a new aesthetically legitimate cinema with the emergence of the Young German Film and then the New German Cinema in the 1960s and 1970s.[4] It was only when a new generation of postwar filmmakers was liberated from the commercial restrictions of studio filmmaking and, more significantly, from the necessity of appealing to a popular audience, that this new cinema could emerge, enabled in large part by the generous and diversified subvention system established in the Federal Republic in the aftermath of the "Oberhausen Manifesto."[5] In this sense, then, the New German Cinema appeared not only to confirm but, indeed, to emerge directly out of the critique of the German audience articulated by Käutner and others throughout the early postwar period.[6]

However, this strategy of blaming postwar cinema's failures on its audience is at once symptomatic and disingenuous. Not only do Käutner and his followers resort to tired clichés and scapegoating mechanisms in order to explain the postwar failure to produce a newly legitimate cinematic language, but their accounts mask the complex reasons for this ostensible failure. In the wake of Nazism's exploitation of the cinematic apparatus, as well as the total collapse of German society at the end of World War II, postwar filmmakers faced not only a crisis in cinematic representation but also a social crisis of epic proportions. After the delegitimation of many conventional filmmaking practices and traditional social formations, it was necessary for filmmakers to reimagine both film form and content, a task that continued to occupy the emergent film production organs in both the Federal Republic and the German Democratic Republic throughout the 1950s and beyond. As they sought to relegitimate cinema amidst the reconstruction of German society in the postwar period, filmmakers experimented with a wide array of genres, styles, plot structures, and star types in their attempt to address both issues of film form and contemporary social problems, while also appealing to postwar viewers.

Indeed, in a very short period of time, West German filmmakers (and not least Helmut Käutner himself) succeeded in creating a vital new cinema that was wildly popular with domestic audiences. By the 1950s, West Germany was the fifth largest producer of films in the world, and domestic receipts reached an all-time German high in 1956, when 818 million movie tickets were sold in the Federal Republic. Moreover, although the West German market was flooded with Hollywood films in the postwar period, German-language productions (including Austrian films) held a high market share throughout the 1950s, earning an average 75.4 percent of the revenue from the top ten films each year (compared to only 14.7 percent for Hollywood films).[7]

Yet from the beginning of the postwar period, the troubled question of spectatorship has vexed the critical reception of this immensely popular body of films. Writing about postwar viewers in his 1947 article, Käutner noted, "The *economic* help that comes from them is certainly significant, for never has attendance at the movie theaters been greater than it is today, but the *fundamental* help, the real genuine interest in the intellectual reformulation of the German film, has not yet materialized."[8] Käutner's argument is predicated on the notion that postwar German audiences failed to support the project of dismantling the dream factory, a project that filmmakers could swiftly and readily complete were it not for the demands of the mass public. This tension between the artistic, and indeed *auteurist*, impulses of filmmakers and the retrograde tastes of an uninformed and unengaged public is certainly a staple of cinema debates dating back to the birth of film.[9] Yet the fact that it was articulated with a new currency in postwar Germany is no accident. For what implicitly underpins not only Käutner's characterization of the postwar public but also the many debates about film form and spectatorship that typified the postwar era is the fact that this postwar audience consisted largely of female viewers.

Indeed, well into the 1950s, women comprised 70 percent of cinema audiences in postwar Germany.[10] This gender disproportion resulted not only from the fact that women dramatically outnumbered men in the aftermath of World War II,[11] but also from the centrality of cinema to postwar women's lives: cinema constituted the primary leisure activity of the day and presented a public space where women could spend time unaccompanied.[12] Already a subject of public attention in the late 1940s and 1950s, when the iconic figure of "Lieschen Müller" became a stand-in for the average cinema spectator,[13] the association of early postwar German cinema with largely female audiences has continued to play a role in the denigration and exclusion of this body of films ever since the 1950s.[14] As Tassilo Schneider has perceptively argued, it is no accident that until recently, the early postwar period has been systematically marginalized by film scholars in the U.S. and Germany alike:

> On the textual level, it is noteworthy that the period of German film history that … is the most maligned and ridiculed (if it is not simply ignored), the 1950s and 1960s, is, at the same time, the period whose genres and films arguably afforded German women the most prominent roles and voices. Very possibly, the fact that the "feminine" genres that dominated German theater screens during the immediate postwar decades—the domestic melodrama and the *Heimatfilm*—have thus far failed to attract much critical attention, is not exclusively a function of institutional and methodological constraints.[15]

Indeed, Schneider points out that the symptomatic exclusion of popular cinema from German film historiography goes hand in hand with the failure of film scholars to investigate adequately questions of spectatorship and address, despite the propensity, born from the influence of Siegfried Kracauer, to draw sweeping conclusions about German national identity and social psychology.[16] Yet questions of spectatorship proved pivotal for the reconstruction and eventual boom of postwar German cinema. Filmmakers engaged in an ongoing quest to redefine both filmic representation and modes of audience perception in the wake of cinema's thorough delegitimation in the Third Reich, and the renewal of cinema was the subject of intensive public debate. Far from remaining a speculative debate, however, the struggle to relegitimate cinema found its way into postwar films themselves. As a result, these films often exhibit clashing codes, disparate styles, generic inconsistencies, and metacinematic moments resulting from experiments with new narrative styles and formal languages. Given the centrality of formal concerns to postwar films, it is striking how little attention questions of form have received from those scholars (often historians or sociologists) who have published groundbreaking work on early postwar West German cinema.[17]

At the same time, the search for legitimate aesthetic forms in postwar cinema was inseparable from the narrative attempt to imagine solutions for social problems.[18] Notably, both of these pursuits crystallized around issues of gender and sexuality. Not only were gender and sexuality implicated in many of the social problems facing reconstruction Germany, but issues of representation were charged with gender politics during the postwar period as well. Writing about the postwar United States, Kaja Silverman has argued that Hollywood films from the late 1940s attest to a crisis of masculinity occasioned by the historical trauma of World War II. According to Silverman's influential psychoanalytic reading, certain historical moments mark a collapse of the phallic authority that normally compensates for the fundamental lack or castration of all (male) subjects. At these moments of historical trauma, there is a loss of collective belief in ideal masculinity (usually figured by the equation of the phallus with the penis), as well as a concomitant loss of belief in the "dominant fiction" that underpins and sustains all social formations.

Silverman demonstrates how, in postwar films, "the 'hero' returns from World War II with a physical or psychic wound which marks him as somehow deficient, and which renders him incapable of functioning smoothly in civilian life. Sometimes the veteran also finds himself strangely superfluous to the society he ostensibly protected during the war; his functions have been assumed by other men, or—much more disturbingly—by women."[19] Moreover, these films not only overturn or invert conventional specular relations (in which the man is typically the subject of the gaze and the woman is the object), but also depart in other ways as well from the standard codes of classical cinema. While Silverman finds examples in postwar Hollywood films of inverted gender roles that are also reflected by inverted cinematic codes, she argues that the Hollywood films largely work to reestablish male authority. They do so in part through mechanisms of fetishism and disavowal that require female characters to "uphold the male subject in his phallic identification by seeing him with her 'imagination' rather than with her eyes."[20] Despite the return to order ultimately demonstrated by these films, Silverman sees the examination of the marginal, nonphallic masculinities they exhibit as "an urgent feminist project": "To effect a large-scale reconfiguration of male identification and desire would, at the very least, permit female subjectivity to be lived differently than it is at present."[21] Nonetheless, she stops short of examining the effects of such marginal male subjects on the filmic representation of or appeal to women.

Much like the Hollywood films analyzed by Silverman, postwar German films also exhibit marginal male subjectivities and attest to a loss of faith in the dominant fiction, as a number of important studies have documented. Drawing directly on Silverman's work, Jaimey Fisher has argued that the rubble films of the early postwar era exhibit "the ruins of the German male" by decentering the male protagonist (often a *Heimkehrer*, or soldier returning home from war) and demonstrating his loss of authority and privilege:

> The films are infused with the sense that the Heimkehrer is now superfluous to the society whose center he once occupied—and without this traditional center, the films depict a kind of dephalliation, a weakening of traditional social relations that generally privilege the male. Such a sociocinematic shift requires a rethinking of key differences regarding the male protagonist, which should include both generational and gender differences.[22]

Fisher's work focuses particularly on the former, arguing that, in the rubble films, youth (especially male children) often come to occupy the central position held by the male protagonist in classical cinema. Because the films reflect a weakening of both social relations and filmic codes as a result of the decentering of male authority, Fisher terms early postwar German film a "cinema of dispersion."[23]

While Robert Shandley primarily focuses on the representation of the Nazi past in his important study *Rubble Films*, the conspicuously passive, marginal male protagonist also emerges as a central character in his taxonomy of the genre. As Shandley concludes, rubble films ultimately addressed the problems of postwar life, most particularly troubled gender relations, at the expense of adequately confronting the heritage of the Holocaust and the Third Reich: "Rather than question the very foundations of subjectivity upon which Germans' understandings of themselves were based, rubble filmmakers attempted to rapidly recoup traditional gender positions."[24] According to Shandley, they did so by aggressively seeking to reestablish male authority and to redomesticate women, often via the genre conventions of the love story, "one of the most common tropes for integrating people, usually men, into the social order."[25] In so doing, they laid the groundwork not only for the popular genre cinema of the 1950s— which so often appears to erase all traces of recent German history—but also for the more critical attempts to engage cinematically with the troubled German past that emerged in the 1960s and beyond.

Gender roles and especially the "crisis of masculinity" also figure as a central facet of postwar German reconstruction in Heide Fehrenbach's comprehensive account of the renewal of the West German film industry after World War II, *Cinema in Democratizing Germany*. Fehrenbach recounts the ways in which masculinity was implicated in the devastating destruction of traditional culture and social ideologies as well as in the reconstruction of national identity after Hitler, and her analysis emphasizes both the instability of masculinity and the search for stable male figures to lead Germany into the future in postwar films from the rubble period well into the 1950s. Her invaluable historical account attends to "the redefinition of social (and gender) identities and the role cinematic representation and film spectatorship were assumed to play in this process" together with extensive discussions of Allied film policies and of German debates about the regulation and development of postwar culture.[26] Importantly, Fehrenbach does note the significance of female spectatorship for understanding the popularity of postwar cinema, and she emphasizes both the appeal to the female consumer and the restoration of the bourgeois family as important tropes of 1950s films, in particular those of the *Heimatfilm* genre.

The 1950s incarnation of the *Heimatfilm* dominates Johannes von Moltke's history of the genre, which emphasizes the dialectical processes of modernization and nostalgia at play in these films. As von Moltke suggests, the *Heimatfilme* became so popular in part due to their deployment of a "cinema of attractions" that treated the viewer to an array of visual and aural pleasures. At the same time, the genre of the *Heimatfilm* represented a key site for negotiating the contradictions and ambivalences of the 1950s, a decade that saw both a restoration of conservative values and a rapid modernization of the economy, culture, and society. In many ways the most emblematic films of the Adenauer Era, the *Heimatfilme* exhibit qualities shared by other postwar German films, not least the tendency to cast women "as agents of modernization" who must "overcome entrenched expectations about gender, which invariably results in a partial restoration of gender norms by the film's end."[27] Thus, to the extent that he addresses postwar gender trouble, von Moltke's analysis focuses far less on the crisis of masculinity than on the dynamic but often ambivalent representation of femininity found in the *Heimatfilme*, thereby laying the groundwork for a reexamination of women in postwar German cinema.

In *Dismantling the Dream Factory*, I draw from the extensive scholarship documenting marginal masculinity in postwar film, while taking a cue from the compelling but brief forays into postwar cinematic femininity offered by Fisher, Fehrenbach, Shandley, and von Moltke. While marginal male protagonists are conspicuous and indeed ubiquitous in postwar German films, they have attracted scholarly attention far more often than the troublingly ambivalent but intriguing female characters with whom they share screen space.[28] Thus, I shift the focus of my analysis away from the decentered males of postwar German film and towards the women who emerge as the new focal point both in the stories and formal codes of the films themselves and, extradiegetically, in the cinema audiences. As I suggest, postwar filmmakers seeking a new cinematic language after the delegitimation of film in the Third Reich often experimented with cinematic conventions in making films that addressed female experience. On the one hand, female experience offered a seemingly less problematic alternative to male experience, which was contaminated by its links to fascism, militarism, and Germany's defeat.[29] On the other hand, the attempt to address female experience arose from the concerted effort to create a commercial appeal to the largely female viewing public of the postwar era.

Focusing on the centrality of spectatorship in the quest for a new film language after Nazism, this book proposes a new history of West German popular cinema from the end of World War II through the early 1960s, arguing along with Frank Stern that, "the New German Cinema began in 1946 and not in the late 1960s."[30] While the history of postwar film has often been told as a series of ruptures and breaks, the version I offer here emphasizes continuities, not only retrospective continuities between postwar filmmaking and Third Reich cinema, but, more importantly for this project, prospective continuities between the popular cinema of the late 1940s and 1950s and the emergent Young German Cinema of the 1960s.[31]

Representing themselves as part of an Oedipal struggle against the "grandfather's generation" responsible for producing the *Papas Kino* (Daddy's cinema) of the early postwar period, the young filmmakers and critics responsible for the "Oberhausen Manifesto" made explicit the extent to which the search for a new language of cinema in postwar Germany was cast in familial and gendered terms.[32] Yet the patriarchal and masculinist metaphors proposed by so many postwar commentators—which situated men as active, embattled producers of cinema, while resorting to age-old clichés of a feminized mass audience of passive consumers—have too often conditioned the way film scholars have continued to apprehend this period ever since the 1950s.

By contrast, this book re-reads postwar West German cinema as a women's cinema, understood in the broadest terms as a filmmaking practice seeking to appeal to female spectators. Not simply a gesture of turning the tables on the master narrative, my argument here accords with the notion that national cinema—particularly in the German context—may be productively redefined and understood at the site of consumption rather than exclusively at the site of production.[33] Thus I return here to the original context of early postwar cinema's consumption, deploying the notion of women's cinema both as a means of examining the contested status of popular film during the immediate postwar period and of explaining the lacuna in film history that this era still represents.

While I argue that the turn to female experience and the appeal to female spectators was a conscious strategy on the part of postwar filmmakers, which served the function of relegitimating the cinema at large while also contributing to the popularity of individual movies, I do not suggest that the popular cinema of the postwar period was feminist in intention or result. As we have seen, Johannes von Moltke proposes that postwar cinema was characterized by a dialectics of restoration and modernization, which, I would add, applies as much to ideologies of gender as it does to the representation of space.[34] While this book therefore contributes to the project of writing postwar cinema back into German film history, it does not seek to recuperate this cinema as a good object of feminist analysis. Rather, I also read postwar cinema as a site of conflict and contradiction. Following Tassilo Schneider, I seek to establish the heterogeneity of this cinema, including its often incongruous and ambivalent qualities, in order to reinscribe "into the historical scenario those discourses (of marginalized social groups, of contradictory ideological positions, and so forth) that <the> historical reconstruction <of German film history> has thus far succeeded in writing out of it."[35]

Postwar German cinema is characterized by incongruity and conflict at the level of both form and content, and nowhere are its contradictory qualities more evident than in its encoding of gender roles and ideologies. As Erica Carter has noted, many early West German films "are directed toward the transformation of feminine identity" in the postwar period.[36] Indeed, most of the films I discuss point toward the reconstruction of traditional gender roles and the increasing prominence of the public/private divide in postwar German society, suggesting that personal happiness is ultimately to be found in the private sphere. Notably, however, these films virtually always stop short of portraying that harmonious domestic sphere, revoking the fulfillment of private desires by failing to provide the "happy end" promised by marriage and family (and thereby avoiding mention of the repressive consequences of this return to the private sphere as well). Over the course of the late 1940s and 1950s, West German films chart the ambivalent—though central— positions occupied by women during the restoration period and in the *Wirtschaftswunder*.

As I argue in this study, it is in this sense above all that the popular West German cinema of the postwar period closely resembles the mid-century Hollywood "woman's film." A catalyst for much important scholarship in feminist film theory during the 1970s and 1980s, the woman's film is characterized by genre and star choices meant to appeal to female viewers, but also, more importantly, by its emphasis on ambivalence and contradiction surrounding gender roles.[37] In her influential study of the 1940s Hollywood woman's film, Mary Ann Doane defines the genre thus:

> The films deal with a female protagonist and often appear to allow her significant access to point of view structures and the enunciative level of

filmic discourse. They treat problems defined as "female" (problems revolving around domestic life, the family, children, self-sacrifice, and the relationship between women and production vs. that between women and reproduction), and, most crucially, are directed toward a female audience.[38]

In contrast to some readings of the genre that seek to recuperate the woman's film as a positive locus for the unfolding of female subjectivity, however, Doane emphasizes the "difficulties and blockages" confronted by the genre's "attempts to trace the contours of female subjectivity and desire within the traditional forms and conventions of Hollywood narrative," which produce "perturbations and contradictions within the narrative economy" of the woman's film.[39] Such blockages and contradictions, a result of the attempt to represent women's subjectivity and desire within dominant cinematic conventions and also of the related attempt to create a new postwar cinematic language, are a primary characteristic of West German films of the late 1940s and 1950s.

Undertaken several decades ago, the work of Doane and others contributed to a productive rethinking of women's genres and questions of spectatorship and address in dominant Hollywood cinema, which has proved crucial to subsequent scholarship in film studies. Feminist film theories of women's cinema have been productive for this book as well, for several reasons. First, much of this theoretical work emerged from the project of rediscovering women's cinema as a central genre of mid-century Hollywood cinema. In returning to the same period of cinematic production in postwar Germany, I have participated in a similar project of rediscovery surrounding this understudied body of films. While the social and historical context that shaped German film production after Nazism differed substantially from that in the United States, nonetheless the insights of Anglo-American feminist film theory about genre, spectatorship, and address in particular shed light on the ambiguities and contradictions, successes and failures of postwar German filmmaking strategies.

Second, as Alison Butler has argued, women's cinema may be said to constitute a "minor cinema" that is "not 'at home' in any of the host cinematic or national discourses it inhabits, but … is always an inflected mode, incorporating, reworking and contesting the conventions of established traditions. <Woman's films> can be situated within at least one other context (such as a national cinema or an international mode of representation) besides that of women's cinema; few of them, however, are fully comprehended by their other contexts."[40] In as much as women's cinema presents a hybrid formation drawing on transnational influences, the return to influential theories of women's cinema that emerged from other cultural contexts proves essential to understanding this "minor cinema."

As I have argued elsewhere, women's cinema also constitutes one of the primary genres of German national cinema across the twentieth century; despite different historical inflections, the turn to women's genres and the address to female spectators represents a moment of continuity in a filmmaking practice that has otherwise followed the vicissitudes of political and social change.[41] Thus this study relies not only on the insights of feminist scholarship about mid-century cinema in the Anglo-American context, but also on the important contributions of feminist scholars of German cinema to reconstructing the history of women's genres in the German context.[42]

Building on theories of women's cinema, feminist film theorists in the 1980s and 1990s turned to the study of cinema spectatorship, proposing various paradigms for apprehending the process of spectatorship that seek to bridge the gap between the imagined spectator constructed by the text, the interpellated subject of ideology, and the sociohistorical subject in the audience.[43] Particularly useful for this study is Christine Gledhill's conception of spectatorship as a process of negotiation among texts, institutions, and audiences. As Gledhill suggests,

> <T>he term negotiation implies the holding together of opposite sides in an ongoing process of give-and-take. As a model of meaning production, negotiation conceives of cultural exchange as the intersection of processes of production and reception, in which overlapping but non-matching determinations operate. Meaning is neither imposed, nor passively imbibed, but arises out of a struggle or negotiation between competing frames of reference, motivation, and experience.[44]

Similarly, my understanding of spectatorship focuses on the complex interactions of textual address, institutional contexts, and audience reception in reconstructing the relationship between viewer and film. Reading postwar West German cinema as women's cinema, I trace the history of this cinema through close readings of ten emblematic films, which all sought to appeal to female spectators through genre and star choices, narrative content, and formal language, as well as through extratextual effects such as promotional and publicity materials, film programs, spreads in fan magazines, and advertising campaigns. These films are emblematic in a larger sense as well, for all of them clearly exhibit the ongoing postwar search for legitimate aesthetic forms, coupled with a narrative attempt to imagine solutions for postwar social problems such as the pervasive anxiety surrounding gender.

As I suggest in the first part of the book, the quest to solve representational and social problems began with the very first postwar German films. The so-called *Filmpause* following the end of World War II, when German film production ceased for over a year, provided an opportunity for filmmakers and critics alike to debate about the shape the new cinema should take. Thus commenced a discussion that would last for years to come, encompassing virtually every aspect of cinematic production and consumption as well as the connections between film aesthetics and social issues. The postwar cinema debates proved quite influential in the reconstruction of postwar cinema, even finding their way into the films themselves.

In the four chapters that comprise part I, I address different facets of these debates over cinema in order to shed light on the larger social and representational context out of which postwar filmmaking emerged. The films I address in this section all respond explicitly to these debates; at the same time they all display a clear appeal to female experience, which is a central facet of their search for a new cinematic language. Already during the *Filmpause*, commentators on cinema expressed concern about the ability of postwar cinema to break with the past and adequately represent the social problems of the present day. Wolfgang Staudte's *Die Mörder sind unter uns* (The Murderers Are Among Us, 1946), the movie that ended the *Filmpause*, responded to these concerns, addressing the different war experiences of men and women and the strained gender relations of the postwar period by endowing its male and female protagonists with different generic codes, visual styles, and formal qualities.

As the *Filmpause* came to an end, critics and filmmakers turned their attention to the *Filmdichter*, or artistic screenwriter, who was cast as the potential savior of postwar filmmaking, a figure who would break with the styles and ideologies of Third Reich cinema and assist in the creation of a newly legitimate German cinema that could contend with contemporary realities. Rudolf Jugert's *Film ohne Titel* (Film Without a Title, 1948) uses a metacinematic frame story featuring a director, writer, and actor engaged in the process of making a film to comment on the problem of writing scripts that will appeal to female film viewers; at the same time, the film within a film addresses changing class and gender roles from the Weimar Republic through the Third Reich and into the period of occupation.

Taking up the challenge of postwar demands for a new, socially responsible and aesthetically progressive film practice, production companies such as Filmaufbau Göttingen experimented with new styles and forms of address. Their first production, Wolfgang Liebeneiner's *Liebe '47* (Love '47, 1949), based on Wolfgang Borchert's famous drama about soldiers returning from war, *Draussen vor der Tür* (The Man Outside), alters the narrative structure of the play to incorporate a female perspective and expands Borchert's focus on male subjectivity to address female experience and the problematic gender relations of the postwar period. A colossal failure with postwar audiences, *Love '47* tells us as much about the state of popular filmmaking in the postwar period as do many of the box office smashes considered in this study.

The return to conventional genre cinema was one strategy adopted by filmmakers seeking to appeal to audiences while also addressing the complex social and representational problems at stake in postwar cinema. One of the few early postwar films to address issues of race and ethnicity, Helmut Käutner's *Epilog* (Epilogue, 1950) is an elaborate allegory of the political situation as well as the status of image making and story telling in postwar Germany; gender plays a central role in the film's explication of political responsibility, authorship, and spectatorship.

In the second part of the book, I turn to a series of films from the 1950s that construct metacinematic narratives surrounding visual artists, who are omnipresent protagonists in German films from this era. Beginning with characters like Susanne in *The Murderers Are Among Us* and Leata in *Epilogue*, painters, graphic artists, and fashion designers appear again and again across genres, in rubble films, suspense thrillers, *Heimatfilme*, problem films, and melodramas. Often invested with special visionary abilities or plagued by disturbances of vision, these characters generally set in motion metacinematic narratives that explicitly address questions of representation, perception, and difference. The device of the visual artist allows films to inscribe a series of diegetic spectator positions through which characters in the films look at and respond to varying kinds of visual representations.

As Angela Dalle Vacche has written, "<T>he history of art is *in* film, even though, by evoking high art and creativity, rather than technology and mass culture, painting for the cinema constitutes a forbidden object of desire."[45] It should perhaps come as no surprise, however, that this forbidden object of desire returns with a vengeance in the West German cinema of the early postwar period. After fascism, the relationships among high art, mass culture, creativity, and technology were both overdetermined and in flux. These relationships were implicated in any attempt to create a new visual culture, including a relegitimated cinema, yet a direct theoretical or representational apprehension of the political and ideological complexities at stake in these relationships only began to emerge slowly.

The most straightforward attempt in the early postwar era to address the heritage of Nazi art and cultural policies was the extensive public debate about abstract painting that took place in the Federal Republic in the late 1940s and 1950s, a debate that took place under the sign of Cold War anti-communism. This debate found its echo in the films of the era. By incorporating painting and other visual arts into their narratives and *mise en scène*, films commented on and attempted to come to terms with cinema's disputed status.[46] Thus the explicit visual and narrative thematization of other arts was another step in the ongoing attempt of postwar filmmakers to relegitimate the cinema and find a new film language.

The three chapters of part II address popular films that engage questions of representation and perception through the metacinematic introduction of visual art—in particular abstract art—into the filmic narrative. Like the early postwar films discussed in the first section of this book, these films from the heyday of the 1950s cinema boom continue to address postwar representational problems in tandem with contemporary social problems, in particular ongoing anxieties surrounding gender and sexuality. In these films, abstract artists are imagined as representatives of a perverse, disturbed mode of vision that must be retrained, cleansed, even cured. In each instance, the subsumption of the abstract artistic gaze into a healthy realist gaze is accomplished in tandem with the artist's reintroduction into a normative, bourgeois, heterosexual economy. However, this narrative trajectory is not achieved without producing larger tensions in the films. These tensions are reflected in the ambiguity of closure offered by the films, but also in a certain ambivalence at the metacinematic site of enunciation: the milieu in which modern, abstract art is produced is discursively figured as perverse, but its *mise en scène* is often reproduced in such dense detail that it becomes at the same time the site of visual and aural pleasure for the spectator of the film.

Like many postwar films beginning with *The Murderers Are Among Us*, Willi Forst's *Die Sünderin* (The Sinner, 1951) endows its male and female protagonists with different modes of vision that figure the ongoing gender trouble in postwar Germany. In this case, the male artist's tendency to paint abstractly is explained by the fact that he has a brain tumor that impairs his ability to see clearly, while his lover, who sees things "as they are," seeks to cure him so that he may paint in a realist mode again. Alfons Stummer's 1955 Austrian film *Der Förster vom Silberwald* (The Forester of the Silver Wood), which was one of the most popular *Heimatfilme* of the decade in West Germany, represents an exception to dominant trends by telling the story of a *female* abstract artist. Her turn to realist painting parallels her return from Vienna to her native town in rural Austria and her rejection of decadent, modern urban life (embodied by her Viennese boyfriend), in favor of the natural landscapes and traditional culture of rural Austria (embodied by her new boyfriend, the local forest ranger). Veit Harlan's 1957 *Anders als du und ich* (Different from You and Me) is a social problem film about homosexuality, which tells the story of a teenage boy whose abstract paintings are linked to his attraction to homosexual men. His parents seek to "cure" him of homosexuality by encouraging their maid to sleep with their son; after drawing a realist portrait of the maid, the son makes aggressive sexual advances towards her. All of these films employ abstract art in order to investigate questions of representation, perception, and difference, and their connections to gender roles, sexuality, and family politics. Recent German history, though rarely addressed head on, is also implicated in each narrative, as the extradiegetic production and reception contexts of these films also reveal.

The final part of the book examines the shifting status of cinema in the late 1950s and early 1960s, as the popular genre films of the previous decade gave way to a new filmmaking practice that was more explicitly critical on both political and aesthetic levels. As I argue, issues of gender continued to be strongly implicated in the production and reception of cinema during this period, when ticket sales began to decline sharply and the postwar cinema entered a new phase of transition in its thematization of both formal concerns and social problems.

Helmut Käutner's 1957 film *Die Zürcher Verlobung* (Engagement in Zurich) is a romantic comedy and self-critical spoof of the film industry.

A transitional film, *Engagement in Zurich* resuscitates many tropes of *Film Without a Title*, which Käutner co-wrote and produced ten years earlier. *Engagement in Zurich* addresses the status of filmmaking in 1957 through a metacinematic story about a female screenwriter; gender plays a central role in its explication of questions of authorship and spectatorship, representation and perception. Rolf Thiele's blockbuster 1958 film *Das Mädchen Rosemarie* (The Girl Rosemarie) was one of the most popular *and* most socially critical films of the decade. *The Girl Rosemarie* appeals to audiences by blending familiar strategies of popular 1950s genre cinema with new innovations in the deployment of image and especially of sound. Based on the sensational true story of the murdered prostitute Rosemarie Nitribitt, Thiele's film articulates a biting critique of the West German consensus culture of the *Wirtschaftswunder* years through an analysis of gender relations at the level of both social problems and cinematic representation. In the final chapter of this book, I turn to Herbert Vesely's *Das Brot der frühen Jahre* (The Bread of Those Early Years). Released in 1962, Vesely's film is situated historically and aesthetically between the popular West German cinema of the 1950s and the emergent European avant-garde cinema of the 1960s. *The Bread of Those Early Years* was the first new wave film to be released after the "Oberhausen Manifesto," which was signed not only by Vesely, the film's director, but also by its producer Hansjürgen Pohland, its cameraman Wolf Wirth, and its male lead Christian Doermer. Anxiously awaited by audiences and critics alike, the film was ultimately deemed a resounding popular and critical failure. As I suggest, the extensive public discourse surrounding this film presents a useful case study for unpacking not only the gendered anxieties surrounding the transition from popular to avant-garde filmmaking, but also the larger social and political anxieties at stake in West Germany during this period of intense economic and social transformation. Finally, my analysis of Vesely's film and the anxieties it unleashed sheds light on larger issues of German film history, in particular on the vexed relation of the New German Cinema to its more popular precursors.

All of the films I examine seek to address female spectators not only through conventional textual effects, but also by departing from dominant cinematic conventions in ways designed explicitly to appeal to women. At the same time, all of them deal metacinematically with the dilemmas of filmmaking in the early postwar period. By attending closely to the formal issues at stake in these films—and the ways in which they closely mirror social problems—I seek to add another dimension to the important work on German popular cinema that has commenced in recent years, fusing the insights of German studies and cultural studies.[47] At the same time, by articulating an explicitly feminist analysis of early postwar cinema, I hope to revitalize attention to issues of gender in the "new film history" out of which much of this work on popular cinema has emerged.[48]

Notes

1. Helmut Käutner, "Demontage der Traumfabrik," *Film-Echo* 5 (June 1947). Rpt. in *Käutner*, ed. Wolfgang Jacobsen and Hans Helmut Prinzler (Berlin, 1992), 113. All translations from the German are my own unless otherwise noted.
2. Käutner, "Demontage der Traumfabrik," 113.
3. For a comprehensive survey of film history texts that represent early postwar West German cinema as a failure, or overlook this cinema entirely, see Tassilo Schneider, "Reading Against the Grain: German Cinema and Film Historiography," in *Perspectives on German Cinema*, ed. Terri Ginsberg and Kirsten Moana Thompson (New York, 1996), 32–37. Particularly noteworthy texts in this regard include Roger Manvell and Heinrich Fraenkel, *The German Cinema* (New York, 1971); Hans Günther Pflaum and Hans Helmut Prinzler, *Film in der Bundesrepublik Deutschland* (Munich, 1979); John Sandford, *The New German Cinema* (London, 1980); Timothy Corrigan, *New German Film: The Displaced Image* (Austin, 1983); James Franklin, *New German Cinema: From Oberhausen to Hamburg* (Boston, 1983); Eric Rentschler, *West German Film in the Course of Time* (Bedford Hills, NY, 1984); and Julia Knight, *Women and the New German Cinema* (New York, 1992).
4. For a history of the rise of the New German Cinema, and for the distinction between Young German Film and New German Cinema, see Thomas Elsaesser, *New German Cinema: A History* (New Brunswick, NJ, 1989). Although Elsaesser suggests that the "Oberhausen Manifesto" "belongs at least as much to the 1950s as it does to the 1970s" (2), his argument is primarily economic, and his discussion of continuities does not include issues of representation, perception, or intellectual tradition. In general, Elsaesser gives short shrift to West German cinema of the pre-Oberhausen era, though he does praise certain technically proficient and socially critical directors (he mentions Helmut Käutner, Wolfgang Staudte, Kurt Hoffmann, Gerhard Lamprecht, and Rolf Thiele) (14). He also concedes that, "some films from the 1950s are due for a reevaluation" (17).
5. On the development and finer points of film subsidies in the Federal Republic, see Elsaesser, *New German Cinema*, esp. 18–46.
6. Enno Patalas and the other students who founded the important journal *Filmkritik* in 1957 took up the critique of the German audience and the demand for a new *Autorenkino* beginning with their earliest publication, *film 56: Internationale Zeitschrift für Filmkunst und Gesellschaft*. The economic and psychological arguments articulated in the Oberhausen Manifesto have their origins in the publications of the *Filmkritik* collective. In their influential history of film, first published in 1962, *Filmkritik* writers Patalas and Ulrich Gregor devoted a mere two pages out of nearly 500 to the West German cinema of the 1950s, which they portrayed in devastating terms. See Gregor and Patalas, *Geschichte des Films* (Gütersloh, 1962). Other well-known writers from this period who indicted postwar cinema, blaming the audience for the poor quality of German films and demanding a new *auteur* cinema, include Wolfdietrich Schnurre, *Rettung des deutschen Films: Eine Streitschrift* (Stuttgart, 1950); Walther Schmieding, *Kunst oder Kasse: Der Ärger mit dem deutschen Film* (Hamburg, 1961); and Joe Hembus, *Der deutsche Film kann gar nicht besser sein* (Munich, 1981 <1961>).
7. Joseph Garncarz, "Hollywood in Germany. Die Rolle des amerikanischen Films in Deutschland: 1925–1990," in *Der Deutsche Film: Aspekte seiner Geschichte von den Anfängen bis zur Gegenwart*, ed. Uli Jung (Trier, 1993), 173.
8. Käutner, "Demontage der Traumfabrik," 113.
9. See for example Anton Kaes, ed., *Kino-Debatte: Texte zum Verhältnis von Literatur und Film 1909–1929* (Munich, 1978).
10. The statistic of 70 percent is commonly quoted in many sources from the late 1940s and 1950s, although it is not attributed to confirmed survey data. See for example "Die Mörder sind unter uns. Der erste deutsche Film der Nachkriegszeit," *Film Revue*

Sonderablage <n.d., probably 1947>, photocopy in file on *Die Mörder sind unter uns*, Schriftgutarchiv, Stiftung Deutsche Kinemathek, Berlin. See also Kurt Wortig, *Ihre Hoheit Lieschen Müller: Hof- und Hinterhofgespräche um Film und Fernsehen* (Munich, 1961), 15.

11. On the "surplus of women" and the public anxieties and discourses that surrounded this notion, see Elizabeth Heineman, "The Hour of the Woman: Memories of Germany's 'Crisis Years' and West German National Identity," *American Historical Review* 101.2 (1996): 354–95; Robert G. Moeller, ed., *West Germany Under Construction: Politics, Society, and Culture in the Adenauer Era* (Ann Arbor, 1997); and Moeller, *Protecting Motherhood: Women and the Family in the Politics of Postwar West Germany* (Berkeley, 1993).

12. See Angela Delille and Andrea Grohn, *Blick zurück aufs Glück: Frauenleben und Familienpolitik in den 50er Jahren* (Berlin, 1985), 90; see also Erica Carter, *How German Is She?: Postwar West German Reconstruction and the Consuming Woman* (Ann Arbor, 1997), 175. The key theorization of the role of cinema spectatorship in the changing status of women in the public sphere can be found in the work of Miriam Hansen. See for example "Adventures of Goldilocks: Spectatorship, Consumerism, and Public Life," *Camera Obscura* 22 (1990): 51–71, and *Babel & Babylon: Spectatorship in American Silent Film* (Cambridge, 1991).

13. For further discussion of "Lieschen Müller," see chapter 8.

14. Tim Bergfelder also asserts that it is "suggestive to read the critical decline of the German cinema from the late 1940s onwards in connection with its perceived 'feminisation.'" Bergfelder, *International Adventures: German Popular Cinema and European Co-Productions in the 1960s* (New York, 2005), 35.

15. Schneider, "Reading Against the Grain," 43.

16. Siegfried Kracauer, *From Caligari to Hitler: A Psychological History of the German Film* (Princeton, 1947).

17. See for example Gerhard Bliersbach, *So grün war die Heide ... Die gar nicht so heile Welt im Nachkriegsfilm*, abridged ed. (Weinheim and Basel, 1989); Bärbel Westermann, *Nationale Identität im Spielfilm der fünfziger Jahre* (Frankfurt, 1990); Barbara Bongartz, *Von Caligari zu Hitler – von Hitler zu Dr. Mabuse? Eine "psychologische" Geschichte des deutschen Films von 1946 bis 1960* (Münster, 1992); Heide Fehrenbach, *Cinema in Democratizing Germany: Reconstructing National Identity After Hitler* (Chapel Hill, 1995); and Bettina Greffrath, *Gesellschaftsbilder der Nachkriegszeit: Deutsche Spielfilme 1945–1949* (Pfaffenweiler, 1995). On the lack of attention to questions of methodology and film form in scholarship on the early postwar period, see also Johannes von Moltke, *No Place Like Home: Locations of Heimat in German Cinema* (Berkeley, 2005), 82–83.

18. Jaimey Fisher notes this imbrication of social and cinematic crises in his study of youth in postwar Germany, emphasizing the way that children and young people were deployed to help resolve social and representational problems in many postwar cultural contexts, including rubble films. See Fisher, *Disciplining Germany: Youth, Reeducation, and Reconstruction after the Second World War* (Detroit, 2007), esp. 175–80.

19. Kaja Silverman, *Male Subjectivity at the Margins* (New York, 1992), 53.

20. Silverman, *Male Subjectivity at the Margins*, 47.

21. Silverman, *Male Subjectivity at the Margins*, 2–3.

22. Jaimey Fisher, "On the Ruins of Masculinity: The Figure of the Child in Italian Neorealism and the German Rubble-Film," in *Italian Neorealism and Global Cinema*, ed. Laura E. Ruberto and Kristi M. Wilson (Detroit, 2007), 30. See also Fisher, "Deleuze in a Ruinous Context: German Rubble-Film and Italian Neorealism," *iris* 23 (1997): 53–74; and Fisher, *Disciplining Germany*, 178–85.

23. Fisher, *Disciplining Germany*, 179.

24. Shandley, *Rubble Films: German Cinema in the Shadow of the Third Reich* (Philadelphia, 2001), 186.

25. Shandley, *Rubble Films*, 187.

26. Fehrenbach, *Cinema in Democratizing Germany*, 6.
27. Von Moltke, *No Place Like Home*, 26.
28. The scholarly emphasis on the trope of "male subjectivity in crisis" in German cinema can also be attributed in part to the influence of Kracauer, who extensively analyzes the centrality of this trope in Weimar cinema in *From Caligari to Hitler*.
29. See Heineman, "The Hour of the Woman."
30. Frank Stern, "Film in the 1950s: Passing Images of Guilt and Responsibility," in *Miracle Years: A Cultural History of West Germany, 1949–1968*, ed. Hanna Schissler (Princeton, 2001), 267.
31. A number of important studies have contributed to the reevaluation and rediscovery of postwar German cinema, while also emphasizing its continuities with the past and future. In addition to the work of Fisher, Fehrenbach, Shandley, and von Moltke outlined above, see also Hilmar Hoffmann and Walter Schobert, eds., *Zwischen Gestern und Morgen. Westdeutscher Nachkriegsfilm 1946–1962* (Frankfurt am Main, 1989); John Davidson and Sabine Hake, eds., *Framing the Fifties: Cinema in a Divided Germany* (New York, 2007); and Bergfelder, *International Adventures*. Bergfelder rightly emphasizes the ongoing popularity of mainstream commercial genres in the 1960s, pointing out that the German art cinema never took hold with domestic audiences.
32. The journal *Filmkritik* first imported the phrase *Papas Kino* from the French journal *Arts*, which ran a review of Alain Resnais's *Last Year at Marienbad* (1961) under the title "Le cinéma de papa est mort." See Hans Dieter Roos, "Papas Kino ist tot," *Filmkritik* 1 (1962): 7–11. Originally a catchphrase for the French New Wave, *Filmkritik* adopted the term as part of its call for a new German cinema that would break with the past, and the term quickly came to symbolize everything that was wrong with German film, historically and in the 1950s. Although it responded to the journal's call for a break from *Papas Kino*, the "Oberhausen Manifesto" itself does not use the term. However, its declaration, "The old film is dead. We believe in the new one," partakes of the same Oedipal language that informs the notion of *Papas Kino*, and the Oberhausen movement was repeatedly associated with the break from *Papas Kino* in public discourse. The "Oberhausen Manifesto" is reprinted in German in *Augenzeugen. 100 Texte neuer deutscher Filmemacher*, ed. Hans Helmut Prinzler and Eric Rentschler (Frankfurt am Main, 1988) and in English in *West German Filmmakers on Film*, ed. Eric Rentschler (New York, 1988).
33. See the classic essays on national cinema: Andrew Higson, "The Concept of National Cinema," *Screen* 30.4 (1989): 36–46; and Stephen Crofts, "Concepts of National Cinema," in *The Oxford Guide to Film Studies*, ed. John Hill and Pamela Church Gibson (Oxford, 1998), 385–94. See also Schneider, "Reading Against the Grain."
34. Von Moltke, *No Place Like Home*, esp. 115–21.
35. Schneider, "Reading Against the Grain," 44.
36. Erica Carter, "Deviant Pleasures? Women, Melodrama, and Consumer Nationalism in West Germany," in *The Sex of Things: Gender and Consumption in Historical Perspective*, ed. Victoria de Grazia and Ellen Furlough (Berkeley, 1996), 361. Carter also calls for further investigation of questions of form and spectatorship in postwar films in order to examine the inscription of feminine identity transformations: "Entirely absent from my discussion here, for instance, is the important question of textual positioning of the female spectator via the organization of point-of-view and the female gaze in postwar popular cinema. If, as I have implied, these films are directed toward the transformation of feminine identity, then we need an analysis of the mechanisms of identification and/or of the organization of visual perception that engage the attention of the female audience" (361).
37. For important contributions to the theorization of women's cinema, see for example Claire Johnston, "Women's Cinema as Counter Cinema," *Movies and Methods I*, ed. Bill Nichols (Berkeley, 1976), 208–17; Annette Kuhn, *Women's Pictures: Feminism and Cinema* (1982), 2nd ed. (London and New York, 1994); E. Ann Kaplan, *Women & Film:*

Both Sides of the Camera (New York, 1983); *Re-Vision: Essays in Feminist Film Criticism*, ed. Mary Ann Doane, et al. (Los Angeles, 1984), esp. contributions by Judith Mayne, Doane, and Linda Williams; Mary Ann Doane, *The Desire to Desire: The Woman's Film of the 1940s* (Bloomington, 1987); Constance Penley, *Feminism and Film Theory* (New York, 1988); Laura Mulvey, *Visual and Other Pleasures* (Bloomington, 1989); Teresa de Lauretis, "Rethinking Women's Cinema: Aesthetic and Feminist Theory," *Issues in Feminist Film Criticism*, ed. Patricia Erens (Bloomington, 1990), 140–61. For a useful recent contribution, see Alison Butler, *Women's Cinema: The Contested Screen* (London and New York, 2002). On the definition of the woman's film in the German context, see Christiane Riecke, *Feministische Filmtheorie in der Bundesrepublik Deutschland* (Frankfurt am Main, 1998), 71–76.

38. Doane, *The Desire to Desire*, 3.
39. Doane, *The Desire to Desire*, 13.
40. Butler, *Women's Cinema*, 22.
41. Hester Baer, "From Riefenstahl to Riemann: Revisiting the Question of Women's Cinema in the German Context," *The Cosmopolitan Screen: German Cinema and the Global Imaginary, 1945 to the Present*, ed. Lutz Koepnick and Stephan Schindler (Ann Arbor, 2007), 193–202.
42. See for example Patrice Petro, *Joyless Streets: Women and Melodramatic Representation in Weimar Germany* (Princeton, 1989); Richard W. McCormick, *Gender and Sexuality in Weimar Modernity: Film, Literature, and "New Objectivity"* (New York, 2001); Antje Ascheid, *Hitler's Heroines: Stardom and Womanhood in Nazi Cinema* (Philadelphia, 2003); and Susan E. Linville, *Feminism, Film, Fascism: Women's Auto/ Biographical Film in Postwar Germany* (Austin, 1998).
43. Important studies of spectatorship that have influenced my conceptualization of this project include Judith Mayne, *Cinema and Spectatorship* (New York, 1993) and Jackie Stacey, *Star Gazing: Hollywood Cinema and Female Spectatorship* (New York, 1994). See also a number of essays collected in Linda Williams, ed., *Viewing Positions: Ways of Seeing Film* (New Brunswick, NJ, 1995).
44. Christine Gledhill, "Pleasurable Negotiations," in *Female Spectators: Looking at Film and Television*, ed. E. Deidre Pribram (London and New York, 1988), 67–68.
45. Angela Dalle Vacche, *Cinema and Painting: How Art Is Used in Film* (Austin, 1996), 1.
46. See Brigitte Peucker, *Incorporating Images: Film and the Rival Arts* (Princeton, 1995).
47. See Randal Halle and Margaret McCarthy, eds., *Light Motives: German Popular Film in Perspective* (Detroit, 2003); see also Bergfelder et al., eds., *The German Cinema Book* (London, 2002).
48. See Thomas Elsaesser, "The New Film History," *Sight & Sound* 55.4 (1986): 246–51; Anton Kaes, "German Cultural History and the Study of Film: Ten Theses and a Postscript," *New German Critique* 65 (1995): 47–58; and Bergfelder et al., "Introduction," *The German Cinema Book*, 1–12

Part I

RELEGITIMATING CINEMA: FEMALE SPECTATORS AND THE PROBLEM OF REPRESENTATION

Chapter 1

HOW DO YOU SOLVE A PROBLEM LIKE SUSANNE?: THE FEMALE GAZE IN WOLFGANG STAUDTE'S *THE MURDERERS ARE AMONG US* (1946)

At the end of World War II, only 1,150 cinemas remained standing in Germany, a mere fraction of the 7,000 cinemas operating at the height of the Third Reich. By 1946, there were already 2,125 movie theaters in the Western zones, which sold tickets to approximately 300 million spectators that year (an average of 6.5 visits to the movies for every Western German).[1] Though the Allies at first banned all German films, mandating that cinemas screen dubbed or subtitled foreign productions from the Allied countries instead, a large number of popular films from the Third Reich were approved for exhibition beginning in the autumn of 1945.[2] According to one American military survey, among the most popular films of the years 1945–46 were the Ufa color melodramas *Die goldene Stadt* (The Golden City, 1942) and *Immensee* (1943), both directed by Veit Harlan; the Marika Rökk vehicle *Die Frau meiner Träume* (The Woman of My Dreams, 1944), directed by Georg Jacobi; and the Viennese musical *Der weisse Traum* (The White Dream, 1943), directed by Geza von Cziffra.[3] As this list makes clear, moviegoers preferred German films to foreign imports in the immediate postwar period. Indeed, they continued to do so throughout the 1940s and 1950s. The popular cinema of the Third Reich clearly represented a familiar and conservative choice for postwar spectators seeking escape from the hardships of everyday life. However, audiences and critics alike anxiously anticipated the first postwar German film, and their high expectations were not disappointed.

Wolfgang Staudte's *Die Mörder sind unter uns* premiered on October 15, 1946, in East Berlin. The premiere took place in the provisional home of the German State Opera, which was outfitted with projection equipment for the festive event, since there was no standing movie theater in the Eastern zone that could accommodate the world premiere of a newly released film. Despite technical difficulties and the poor quality of the print that was shown, critics noted that spontaneous applause broke out during the screening in response to particularly artistic sequences of the film. After the premiere and at subsequent screenings, audience members engaged in lengthy discussions of the film's representation of contemporary life and the dilemmas of recent German history.[4]

A spread on the film in the fan magazine *Film Revue* recorded several viewer responses to *The Murderers Are Among Us* soon after its premiere. Notably, the magazine chose to focus exclusively on the responses of female viewers, in a section entitled "Seen Through the Eyes of Woman." As the magazine explained, "More than 70 percent of all cinema-goers in Germany are—women and girls. It is said that they just want to see entertainment in the film theater: pictures of fashion, heroes, and sentimental love scenes. Is that the truth?"[5] In contrast to the common attitude that held female viewers (and their "retrograde" tastes) responsible for the failure of early postwar films to gain popularity with audiences, *Film Revue* suggested through its collection of testimonials about *The Murderers Are Among Us* that female viewers responded positively both to the social and political implications of the film's narrative and to its formal and artistic qualities. In the article's lead-off quote, viewer Hilde Nowack creates an explicit link between the film's representation of German history and her own wartime experiences, focusing both on guilt for Nazi crimes and on the suffering caused by the war:

> In its simplicity and objectivity, the film has such a strong impact on the viewer that one leaves the cinema deeply affected, asking the question: how did such barbaric deeds ever befall humanity? By the end of the film, we feel responsible <mitschuldig> for the cruel acts that were performed, because we did not have the strength and were too cowardly to fight against such barbaric deeds ... I personally can only give expression to my wish that every German see this film. My happiness was also destroyed: my child no longer has a father. For that reason, I will be engaged with all my strength my whole life long, especially in order to make young people understand that a Hitler dictatorship will never again overtake Germany, and therefore that a war will never again overtake Germany either.[6]

Drawing parallels between her own life and the images of personal and collective history portrayed in the film, this viewer emphasizes the film's moral tone and its indictment of the postwar atmosphere of reconstruction.

Reviewers of *The Murderers Are Among Us* generally expressed positive responses to the film as well. However, while they heaped praise on Staudte's contribution to the renewal of German filmmaking, they were also critical of the film's often muddled narrative and overblown symbolism. As critic Friedrich Luft put it, "One would have hoped that a film about this theme <guilt, responsibility, and retribution for the crimes of the Nazi past> would have conveyed clarity and energy rather than getting lost in the depths of imagistic symbolism. Finding the new form for the new film is difficult." [7]

Indeed, *The Murderers Are Among Us* showcases, at the levels of both form and content, the representational problems faced by postwar filmmakers. At the same time, the film foregrounds postwar social problems, in particular the pervasive problem of gender relations and the incompatibility of the sexes in the aftermath of the war. While *The Murderers Are Among Us* was ultimately unsuccessful in developing solutions for either set of problems, the traces that it leaves behind provide a useful starting point for understanding the reconstruction of popular cinema in the postwar period.

I

Following the end of the war, German film production ceased entirely for over a year. Caused by a combination of political, technical, and aesthetic factors (including the initial total ban on filmmaking by the Allies), this *Filmpause*, as it came to be known, provided the opportunity for critics and filmmakers to take stock of the current state of German cinema and begin planning for the future, thereby initiating a critical discussion that would last for years to come. Commenting on the *Filmpause* in November 1945, director Harald Braun highlighted the necessity of such a hiatus, arguing that before new films could be made, "The legitimacy of both the personnel and the artistic qualities <of filmmaking> must be completely assured."[8]

While the discussion that emerged from the *Filmpause* explicitly addressed the problem of German cinema's legitimacy in the aftermath of National Socialism, developing new and newly legitimate artistic qualities for the postwar cinema proved much more difficult than filmmakers at first anticipated, and this problem would continue to vex German filmmaking throughout the 1950s. As Robert Shandley explains, "Whether because German filmmakers had abused the power of the image so egregiously during the Third Reich or simply because they lost the war, many of cinema's generic and narrative codes had been thoroughly delegitimated. It was unclear what cinematic language filmmakers would be able to call upon once they were able to resume production."[9] Should filmmakers return to the legacy of German cinema before 1933, in particular the language of the Weimar art cinema? Should they look abroad to discover new trends and styles that had been suppressed in the Third Reich during the war years? What elements of Third Reich cinema could or should be salvaged?

Of course it was neither possible nor desirable for postwar filmmakers seeking to appeal to German audiences to break entirely with the conventions of German cinema as it had developed during the 1930s and 1940s. However, within certain boundaries they did seek to establish new formal conventions, focus on the social and political problems of postwar life, and address changing audiences in new ways. Of central importance here was the quest to redefine the language of cinematic realism, and, by extension, to redefine the role of illusionism in cinema as well. While postwar films rarely departed from a realist idiom, they borrowed from a range of realist styles, including classical forms associated with both Hollywood and Third Reich cinema, as well as Italian neo-realism.[10]

The struggle to endow narrative cinema with a new legitimacy was a topic of debate among filmmakers and critics alike throughout the postwar period. Moreover, this struggle was often reproduced in the films themselves, resulting in narrative ambivalence, clashing codes and styles, and metacinematic elements that derived from experiments with film form and content. The representational eclecticism (or indecision) of these films was often cause for alarm among commentators and has contributed to the longstanding view of postwar cinema as aesthetically problematic. However, a closer look at the films suggests that they were not simply the result of confusion or entropy, but that they telescope the postwar representational crisis in ways that can prove instructive for film history. Demonstrating a concern with the formal language of cinema, these films also sought to find new narrative means to address the problems of postwar life. The search for legitimate aesthetic forms was thus inseparable from the narrative attempt to imagine solutions for social problems in postwar cinema. Both of these pursuits converged around issues of gender and sexuality, a process that begins already with the paradigmatic postwar film, *The Murderers Are Among Us.*

Clearly, gender and sexuality were implicated in many of the social problems faced by postwar Germans. Men and women had very different experiences of the war years, which led both to strained relations between the sexes and to the need to reformulate gender roles and gender relations in the postwar period. The emasculation of men after the military and political defeat of Nazi Germany was accompanied by a "masculinization" of women in public discourse, as epitomized by the figures of the passive, marginal *Heimkehrer* (soldier returning from war) and the active, central *Trümmerfrau* (rubble woman). Returning home, men often had a hard time rejoining changed families and finding a place in society, while women, who had gained independence during the war years, now played a central role in the reconstruction of Germany and the reformulation of society after 1945. That year, German women outnumbered men by at least 7.3 million; four million German men had been killed in World War II and 11.7 million German soldiers were held in prisoner-of-war camps.[11] According to one account of this so-called *Frauenüberschuß* (surplus of women), "For every 100 men between the ages of 20 and 40 there are 158 women; for men between the ages of 20 and 30 there are actually 168 women. In Leipzig, according to one count last fall, there were 211 women for every 100 men between the ages of 19 and 50. In the British zone, the population increased through resettlement by 2 million women and only by 90,000 men."[12] The period between 1945 and 1948 soon became known as the "hour of the woman," a term that reflected the gender imbalance in the population and the prominent role of women not only in the everyday work of reconstruction but also in the national imaginary during this time. Staple characters of early postwar cinema such as the *Heimkehrer* and the *Trümmerfrau* symbolized the inverted gender roles and strained gender relations of the postwar period, while also pointing to the gendered conceptions of memory and responsibility for Nazi crimes that shaped public discourse about the past.

Problems relating to sexuality were less visible but nonetheless central in postwar society. In particular, public debates focused on the perception of women's widespread adultery, prostitution, and fraternization. On the one hand, this perception masked the reality of rape by Allied soldiers and held women responsible for their own sexual victimization. On the other hand, by labeling sexually independent women as sexual aggressors, commentators blamed women for the moral degradation of wartime and postwar life and for a wide array of social, economic, and political problems that began with and emerged from Germany's defeat. Finally, in postwar social discourse and in the movies, problems of gender and sexuality often functioned as a cipher for the sublimated issues of race, ethnicity, and national identity.

Just as gender and sexuality were central to the social problems of the postwar period, issues of representation were also charged with gender politics during this era. As Kaja Silverman suggests in her study of male subjectivity, Hollywood films from the late 1940s, much like their German counterparts, reflect a preoccupation with problems of gender and sexuality stemming from the historical trauma of World War II. Silverman argues that these films, "attest to a massive loss of faith in traditional masculinity, and … dramatize the implications of that dissolution not only for gender and the family, but for the larger society."[13] According to Silverman, in the aftermath of the war, a historical moment ensued when the equation of the penis and the phallus collapsed, leading to a recognition of male lack and a concomitant "collective loss of belief in the whole of the dominant fiction."[14] That is, the impaired masculinity so evident in the postwar period contributed to a destabilization of the psychic and ideological structures that sustain conventional social formations, including sexual difference, the family, the nation, and, indeed, the perception of "reality" itself. Silverman demonstrates how certain films respond to this crisis of male subjectivity by departing from the conventions of classical cinema, and even, at times, by investing female characters with functions typically assumed by men. As her analysis shows, however, Hollywood films also developed compensatory mechanisms—primarily fetishism—in order to disavow the loss of masculine adequacy and mastery.

In the German context, the crisis of masculinity and the "ideological fatigue" it produced were, if anything, more acute than the American phenomenon analyzed by Silverman. In the Hollywood films, "the hero no longer feels 'at home' in the house or town where he grew up, and resists cultural (re-)assimilation; he has been dislodged from the narratives and subject-positions which make up the dominant fiction, and he returns to them only under duress."[15] While the same can generally be said of postwar German cinema, in these films the houses and towns where the heroes grew up have often been decimated in the war, while the narratives and subject-positions that comprised Nazi ideology have been thoroughly discredited, leading to an even more radical ideological fatigue and loss of belief in the dominant fiction. Moreover, while Hollywood cinema certainly underwent a number of transformations at mid-century in part resulting from the caesura of World War II, filmmakers in Hollywood did not confront the dramatic necessity faced by German filmmakers of thoroughly redefining and relegitimating cinema in the postwar period.

Adapting Silverman's argument for the German context, Jaimey Fisher puts it this way:

> In postwar Germany, ... historians have documented how the domestic/familial sphere became uncannily alien for the returning man, and rubble-films depict how marginal males fail to reassume the roles allotted to them by the dominant fiction. In certain historical moments, then, the discourse of masculinity can operate differently; it can expose male lack, introduce it as alterity, and invert the normal specular relations that underpin it.[16]

As Fisher shows, this inversion of normal specular relations often leads to a transformation of "the traditional male *subject* of the gaze into a humiliated *object* of the gaze"; because of the concomitant "decentering of the male protagonist," these films often offer strong figures beyond the male protagonist with whom spectators can identify.[17] Fisher's analysis demonstrates how women and male children come to occupy central positions in many rubble films, replacing or standing in for the marginal males no longer able to function as active protagonists or figures of identification.

As Elizabeth Heineman has argued, the extremity of the crisis of masculinity in postwar Germany led not only to a discrediting of male experience, but indeed to an overwhelming turn to female experience in German narratives and identity constructions. Writing about "the hour of the woman," Heineman has argued that women's experience in the second half of the 1940s became emblematic for a whole generation of Germans, and was thus universalized into constructions of postwar national identity. Heineman suggests that the total defeat of the Third Reich and its militaristic ideologies made male experience utterly problematic, thus creating a "representational vacuum" of national symbolism that was filled in part by new symbols drawing on prototypically female experiences. According to Heineman, victimization, rebuilding, and sexual promiscuity constituted three particularly female experiences that were generalized in public (and private) discourse to describe the German nation as a whole after 1945.[18]

Thus postwar filmmakers seeking to fill the "representational vacuum" caused by the crisis of masculinity often experimented with the conventions of dominant cinema in making films that addressed female experience. The films that resulted often emphasized the female gaze and female voiceovers in unusual ways, and they often featured strong female protagonists and stories relevant to women's lives. As we shall see, postwar German cinema well into the 1950s continued to place women in central positions, creating active female characters with whom spectators could identify by vesting them with narrative authority, allowing them to possess the gaze, and turning them into the subject rather than exclusively the object of formal and narrative codes. The turn to female experience thus constituted one central aspect of the search for a new cinematic language and the struggle to relegitimate cinema in the postwar period.

Of course, films that addressed female experience often appealed to female audiences as well, making this strategy doubly effective in a period when women comprised 70 percent of film audiences. Filmmakers were certainly conscious of the demographics and demands of their audiences, and the necessity of appealing to viewers was often remarked upon in debates about the new form cinema should take, though often in a negative register. In particular, filmmakers often blamed a feminized mass audience for the failure of postwar cinema to find a new language; if audiences rejected unconventional postwar films it was because of their conservative preference for conventional genre cinema (and not because of the postwar crisis in cinematic representation). For example, in his contribution to debates about postwar cinema, "Dismantling the Dream Factory," Helmut Käutner stressed the role of the audience in determining the content of postwar films:

> It is clear to most German filmmakers that it is not possible or even advisable to lie about the things that have happened and their consequences. They are of the opinion that the dream factory must finally be dismantled. The problems of Germany yesterday, today, and tomorrow—in as much as they have begun to appear—must become the primary themes of our work. Various attempts of this type have been made. German audiences have so far failed to react to these attempts. They ostentatiously turn away from any focus on contemporary issues, which, as a result of bad habits, they understand as tendentious or as propaganda.[19]

According to Käutner, postwar audiences, accustomed to the escapist fare of Third Reich cinema, were unwilling to adjust their expectations to "the intellectual reformation of the German film" to which postwar filmmakers aspired. Given that his own first postwar effort, *In jenen Tagen* (In Those Days, 1947), a film that addresses German history and contemporary issues through the device of an omniscient automobile, debuted to a resounding popular and critical success in the same month that the above statement was published, perhaps Käutner's evaluation of postwar audiences was a bit hasty.[20] Nonetheless, his sentiment was often repeated by filmmakers and critics alike who purported to view postwar audiences, which consisted largely of women, as an uneducated, unengaged, lazy, and residually fascist mass.

These commentators represent yet another instance of the longstanding tendency to impose gendered metaphors on debates about modern art and mass culture, whereby art is associated with masculinity and activity, while mass culture and its "passive" consumers are feminized. Following Patrice Petro, this tendency to resort to gendered oppositions appears to be heightened at moments of transition, when the legitimacy of new forms hangs in the balance.[21] What is striking in contemplating these oppositions in postwar Germany, however, is the extent to which the films themselves tend to both thematize and undermine them, regardless of the filmmakers' assertions. Again and again, postwar films invoke and complicate gendered oppositions such as active/passive, modern art/mass culture, and abstract/realist, pointing once more to the imbrication of the postwar gender crisis and the postwar representational crisis.

I have suggested above that postwar German cinema turned to female experience as a representational strategy, as a means of addressing social problems, and as a way of appealing to audiences consisting largely of women. Because of the crisis of representation and the struggle to relegitimate cinema, postwar films often exhibited clashing codes and styles. Beginning with *The Murderers Are Among Us*, these films were characterized by a further ambivalence as well: narrative aporia and formal inconsistencies generated by the attempt to represent women's experience and female desire within the dominant conventions of popular cinema.

II

A "test of the medium"[22] of cinema in 1946, *The Murderers Are Among Us* has also constituted a test case for histories and theories of postwar German cinema ever since its debut. The film has thus served as an example, on the one hand, of postwar cinema's continuities with Third Reich cinema and its failure to adequately tackle the Nazi past, and, on the other, of the early rubble film's break with the dominant styles of recent German cinema and its groundbreaking attempt to address German history and contemporary reality.[23] Whether the film is perceived as representing continuity with the Nazi past or a decisive break from it, however, most analyses share two things in common: a preoccupation with the film's clashing codes and generic confusion and irritation at its troubling representation of gender roles.[24] As I will suggest, *The Murderers Are Among Us* addresses postwar problems of representation and gender at the levels of both form and content, and the film's inconsistencies result in part from its attempt to imagine solutions to these problems. Considering the film's appeal to spectators suggests some new answers not only to the film's formal discrepancies, but also to its gender trouble. Indeed, female viewers responded very positively to the film, despite its inconsistencies, a response that can be attributed in part to the remarkable attractions of Hildegard Knef, the first star of postwar German cinema, who played the film's female lead, Susanne Wallner.

A 1946 reviewer summarized the plot of *The Murderers Are Among Us* as follows:

> The destiny that unwinds is so true to contemporary reality that we could have experienced it yesterday or the day before: upon her arrival home, the young girl returning from a concentration camp finds her apartment occupied by Dr. Mertens, who, haunted by bloody visions of the war, feels himself incapable of returning to work, and instead spends his days at the bar. In these close quarters, love grows out of mutual sympathy, and the man finds his way back to the land of the living. First, though, he believes he must fulfill a duty by exacting revenge on his former captain Brückner, now a well regarded industrialist and pater familias, for the slaughter of Polish women and children that he ordered on Christmas Eve in 1942.[25]

As this review emphasizes, the narrative of Staudte's film is set in motion by Susanne, a young graphic artist who returns home to Berlin after her release from an unnamed concentration camp. Not only does Susanne's return to her apartment trigger the central conflict of the film, but Susanne herself structures the quest for knowledge about Hans Mertens and the causes of his bad behavior. Our interest in Hans's story is configured through Susanne's perspective. Despite the fact that Susanne Wallner is at the center of the film's narrative and identificatory structures, however, the film's story focuses largely on Hans Mertens, and this is one reason the film has proved so puzzling in terms of both gender and representation.

Mertens, a *Heimkehrer* who is plagued by a traumatic wartime experience that prevents him from reintegrating into postwar society, is the first in a long line of conspicuous passive male protagonists in postwar German cinema. Mertens's marginal masculinity, which is central to the film's narrative and aesthetic problems, has long been a primary focus of criticism about the film. Deliberately echoing Siegfried Kracauer's reading of masculinity in Weimar cinema, Theodor Kotulla, writing in *Filmkritik* in 1960, noted that: "Staudte's script can be traced back to particularly questionable clichés of the German film tradition: above all, to that of the passive hero, who is only able to muster powers of the soul in the face of the blows dealt him by fate."[26] Indeed, it is no surprise that the portrayal of Mertens has long disturbed critics. As Jaimey Fisher notes, the film radically foregrounds the postwar crisis of masculinity: "For its first twenty-six minutes, Wolfgang Staudte's *The Murderers Are Among Us* deliberately portrays male lack, male loss of control over specularity, and male alterity."[27]

Like the problem of masculinity, the "Susanne problem" in *The Murderers Are Among Us* has also been the subject of much attention. In particular, the film has been criticized for relegating Susanne's story to the background of the plot: while we do find out that Susanne's father was a political dissident, we never learn the precise cause of *her* imprisonment in the camps, nor are we privy to her thoughts or emotions about this experience. While the film presents several subjective flashbacks that grant us insight into the internal tumult of Hans's life, Susanne remains a one-dimensional character who selflessly and inexplicably devotes herself to the healing of Hans's damaged masculinity.[28] This type of reading emphasizes that, although the film seems to point to a more critical vision of contemporary social problems, it ultimately disregards female experience and resorts to retrograde gender roles in its superficial characterization of Susanne Wallner.

In his convincing gendered analysis of the film, Fisher suggests that *The Murderers Are Among Us* inverts the specular relations between the sexes: "This is not love at first sight; nor is it the normal, boy-spots-girl, boy-gets-girl formula of most specular sequences. From the first scene in which Mertens looks at Susanne, his gaze is not desiring; it is unhealthy and inadequate. Her presence humiliates and tortures him: he buries his head on his arm at the moment she looks lovingly at him."[29] By contrast, Susanne exhibits a steadfast "desire for male lack": she pursues Mertens from the moment she meets him, disavowing his status as a passive, castrated man, and working tirelessly to restore his agency, authority, and desiring masculinity. Fisher argues that the film ultimately rights the gender inversion it has staged, containing female desire and reestablishing the dominant fiction by reconstructing male subjectivity. Yet for Fisher, *The Murderers Are Among Us*, like other rubble films, remains ambivalent, leaving traces of the postwar crisis in masculinity through the highly ambivalent characters of Brückner and Mondschein, troubling figures who both complicate the film's seemingly neat restoration of the dominant fiction.[30] Though Fisher notes the film's inversion of gender roles and its remarkable (albeit brief) portrayal of Susanne with narrative and cinematic codes usually reserved for male characters, the ultimate focus of his analysis remains marginal masculinity. As I will propose, however, far from attaining an unproblematic closure vis-à-vis female gender roles and the structure of the gaze, the film also leaves traces of an active, authoritative, and desiring femininity figured by Hildegard Knef's mastery of the gaze, which cannot simply be contained by the healing of Mertens.

In considering the representation of gender in *The Murderers Are Among Us*, Robert Shandley points out that Hans Mertens and Susanne Wallner are "like characters in different films that have been forcibly merged."[31] Indeed, these two characters are troubling not only in their embodiment of problematic gender roles, but also because they epitomize the clashing codes and generic inconsistencies—the representational problems—of the film. One common explanation for these inconsistencies invokes the production history of Staudte's film, particularly the censorship to which it was subjected by the Soviet occupation authorities. As is by now well known, Wolfgang Staudte completed a script in the final months of the war for a film entitled "Der Mann, den ich töten werde" (The man I will kill), which eventually would become *The Murderers Are Among Us*.[32] Immediately after the war ended, Staudte sought a license and financing for the film.[33] When the Soviets, alone among the Allies, expressed interest in making the film, they demanded a number of changes to the script, most prominently to its ending. In the original script, Hans Mertens seeks to avenge the war crimes of his commanding officer, Ferdinand Brückner, who is now a wealthy industrialist profiting from the postwar boom. Taking justice into his own hands, Hans shoots and kills Brückner, and the final third of the film portrays Hans's trial for this vigilante-style killing.[34]

Due to the changes demanded by the Soviet censors, however, neither the shootout nor the trial takes place; in *The Murderers Are Among Us*, Susanne stops Hans from shooting Brückner, and the film ends instead with Brückner behind bars. Staudte recalled the objections of the Soviet censors to his original ending: "One thing is naturally impossible, and that is the ending. If the film is a success, people will come out of the cinemas and there will be shooting in the streets, and of course that is out of the question. We can understand the wish for revenge, but it must be said that that is precisely the wrong way to go about it."[35] The censorship of *The Murderers Are Among Us* certainly accounts for some of the film's peculiarities, in particular its unsatisfactory ending. But the film's censored ending does not provide an explanation for the clash of codes that marks *The Murderers Are Among Us* from its very first sequence and that is especially visible in the characterization of Hans and Susanne.

Shandley has convincingly argued that the film can be read as a western lacking the final shootout; it also contains elements of a domestic melodrama, but similarly lacks the explosive catharsis typical of that genre. Indeed, Staudte's film can be read as a sort of postwar proving ground for filmic codes, styles, and genres, which the film plays off against one another from the outset. Moreover, this clash of codes is clearly gendered in ways that both recall previous moments of stylistic differentiation in German film history and anticipate future tensions in postwar cinema. Beginning with the opening sequence, the film endows its male and female protagonists with two discrete visual styles, two discrete sets of genre characteristics, and two discrete structures of looking.

This strategy encodes in *The Murderers Are Among Us* a commonplace of everyday life in postwar Germany: the fact that, like Hans Mertens and Susanne Wallner, men and women had very different war experiences and very different outlooks on life in the aftermath of Germany's defeat.

After a black and white credit sequence that culminates in the words "Berlin 1945 – The city has capitulated," *The Murderers Are Among Us* begins with a close-up of hastily created graves on the side of a road. Accompanied by an upbeat soundtrack, the camera pans up from the graves to reveal a busy city street in decimated postwar Berlin: we see children playing, but also the shell of a tank, a rusting car, and the smoking rubble of bombed-out buildings. In a long take, Hans Mertens (Ernst Wilhelm Borchert) slowly walks down the street, moving towards the camera until he occupies the entire frame. Hans literally emerges from the rubble; like the rubble, he is also smoking.[36] Hans's association with the rubble introduces him as a defeated man; the camera's canted angle further suggests that Hans's world is askew, tumultuous, out of order. As Hans turns away from the camera, it follows his gaze upward to reveal a bar in the background, whose sign reads "Dance – Atmosphere – Humor." This incongruous shot establishes both Hans Mertens's own cynicism and the contradictory world that he inhabits.

A dissolve and an abrupt change in music accompany the film's transition to the next scene, which introduces Susanne Wallner (Hildegard Knef). This scene is visually marked through its diametrical opposition to the previous scene: the camera is positioned on the right instead of the left, and motion within the frame tracks from left to right instead of from right to left. The long take of the opening scene is replaced by quick shot/reverse shot editing, and the canted angles disappear. This marked shift in cinematography and editing indicates a concomitant shift in perspective between the first two scenes of the film. Indeed, the smoking rubble and bombed-out vehicles of the first scene are contrasted in the second scene with a train arriving at a station—a symbol of progress and hope. Like Hans Mertens, Susanne Wallner moves toward the camera until she is framed in medium close-up; but unlike the isolated figure of Hans, Susanne approaches as part of a crowd and she is consistently centered in the frame. In a further parallelism to the previous scene, the introduction of Susanne ends with a shot that follows her gaze to reveal a sign: a travel poster in the train station advertising "Beautiful Germany," now damaged, hanging crooked, and surrounded by wounded war veterans. Like the bar sign Hans sees, this poster presents a visual irony, but one that points to Susanne's critical (rather than cynical) evaluation of the postwar situation. While the drunken Hans's gaze at the bar sign is marked by a canted angle, Susanne's gaze is not impaired—it is the poster itself that hangs askew.

The second sequence of *The Murderers Are Among Us* begins with a dissolve from the train station to scenes of rubble-strewn Berlin, as

Susanne Wallner makes her way home.[37] Walking through the rubble, she passes a large statue of a mother holding a child: this pietà stands out as the only intact object in a landscape of destruction. After establishing a visual connection between Susanne and the pietà, the camera lingers on the statue. In an example of the overblown symbolism for which it was criticized, the film furthers the metonymic link between Susanne and the idealized mother figure with a dissolve to the interior of Susanne's apartment building, where a drunken Hans climbs the stairs, thus foreshadowing Susanne's eventual role in his domestication. Immediately, the style of the film shifts again, and we see the stairwell engulfed in ominous shadows, as the residents of the building gossip about their drunken neighbor. A pan across the exterior of the building now reveals its many broken windows (as well as a large sign reading "Optics"), before the camera comes to rest on a broken mirror, in which the figure of Susanne Wallner is reflected. Strikingly, though the mirror is broken, Susanne's image is reflected whole in an intact piece of the mirror, and as she hears the bells of the optician's door ring, we see her smile in the mirror.[38]

 Just after this important shot, which emphasizes her control of the gaze and establishes her subjective integrity, Susanne enters the optician Mondschein's store. In the store, a woman pleads, "I'm desperate, I've broken my glasses," and Mondschein promises to fix them. In the next scene, we see Hans, who now occupies Susanne's apartment, rummaging through one of her old drawers and pulling out her camera, which he hopes to sell on the black market. As Susanne enters the apartment, however, he returns the camera to its drawer, and subsequently decides not to sell it after all. In both of these scenes, Susanne is linked to the repair or preservation of optical signifiers, an association that will be maintained throughout the film. As its focus on cameras, screens, and spectatorship demonstrates, not only is *The Murderers Are Among Us* quite literally concerned with repairing the "broken" filmic apparatus, but it suggests that women play a fundamental role in its repair.

III

From the outset, then, *The Murderers Are Among Us* establishes a metacinematic discourse on gender and representation that is central to the film's appeal to its spectators. At the levels of both form and content, the film explores the different roles that men and women play in shaping postwar discourse and in repairing postwar society. Through its obsessive focus on the damage to and repair of optical signifiers such as windows, mirrors, glasses, and cameras, as well as its further thematization of vision and sight through the characters of Mondschein, the optician, and Timm, the *Hellseher* (fortune teller or visionary), the film attends to contemporary debates about visual representation and cinematic legitimacy emerging from the *Filmpause*, which *The Murderers Are Among Us* helped to end. In the case of Staudte's film, this attention results in a radical breakdown of the conventional cinematic codes of gaze, spectacle, and spectatorship, codes that no longer appear legitimate in the postwar period. Beginning with the introduction of Hans and Susanne—both of whom are represented in establishing shots followed by subjective shots that track their gazes—*The Murderers Are Among Us* links its protagonists to two distinctly different modes of vision, two different gendered gazes, which suggest alternative ways of remembering the past and confronting the present. Hans never exhibits mastery of the gaze, while Susanne demonstrates an unusual level of agency in the film that is figured by her control of the gaze.[39] Like many later male characters in postwar German films, Hans's vision is constantly blurred and disturbed, while Susanne is virtually the only character in the film who can see things for what they are, both literally and figuratively.

Indeed, Hans Mertens evidences a disturbed mode of vision throughout the film that is emblematic of his fragmented subjectivity. He literally cannot "see clearly," a fact that is narrativized through his blurred vision when he is in an alcoholic stupor; his inability to look at blood despite his training as a doctor; and his flashbacks to his war experiences, over which he has no control, and which are passively triggered by various visual signifiers in the present day. Subjective shots from Hans's perspective are often highly abstract—they are blurred or skewed, and they are marked as being somehow "impaired." Because of his troubled past, Hans's present life is disturbed, and his disturbed vision is the clearest marker of this fact in the film.

By contrast, Susanne Wallner repeatedly evidences a clear, active mode of vision that figures her active relationship to dealing with the past and present, as well as her narrative authority in the film. Susanne is one of the few characters in the film not linked to metaphors of broken or disturbed vision, like the many broken mirrors, windows, and glasses that recur throughout the film. Rather, as in the film's opening sequence, she is consistently able to see herself clearly reflected, and is often metonymically linked to the repair of broken optical signifiers. A graphic artist, Susanne creates posters for social causes. We see her at work at her drafting table on a poster for a campaign to fight hunger and help feed children: her drawing is an evocation of a starving child rendered in the manner of Käthe Kollwitz (see figure 1.1). Unlike Hans, who is so haunted by his visions of the past that he cannot function in society, let alone work, Susanne seeks to channel her troubles into visual expressions to aid the greater good. Susanne's artwork suggests that visual representation is an integral part of the process of repairing postwar society.[40] Her role as an artist and her mastery of the gaze not only complicate conventional codes, but also move her beyond a mere figure of objectification or spectacle to a producer of meaning in the film.

Figure 1.1 The female gaze: Susanne at her drafting table in *The Murderers Are Among Us*. Source: Deutsche Kinemathek.

In dominant cinema, the male character is typically the subject of the gaze, while the female character is its object—in Laura Mulvey's words, "Woman as Image, Man as Bearer of the Look."[41] As feminist film theorists have argued, within this conventional structure, the woman represents not only the source of pleasure in looking for the male gaze (both within the diegesis and for the spectator watching the film) but also a potential danger to male subjectivity, through her erotic attractions and the threat of castration she invokes. Thus, the male gaze not only objectifies the woman, but in so doing attempts to neutralize the threat that she poses. For this reason, classical film narrative often punishes the woman, particularly when she attempts to assume a dominant role by taking ownership of the gaze. Analyzing the gendered structures of vision and the gaze in classical cinema, Linda Williams writes:

> <T>he female protagonist often fails to look, to return the gaze of the male who desires her. In the classical narrative cinema, to see is to desire. It comes as no surprise, then, that many of the "good girl" heroines of the silent screen were often figuratively, or even literally, blind. Blindness in this context signifies a perfect absence of desire, allowing the look of the male protagonist to regard the woman at the requisite safe distance necessary to the voyeur's pleasure, with no danger that she will return that look and in so doing express desires of her own. ... <E>ven when the heroine is not literally blind, the failure and frustration of her vision can be the most important mark of her sexual purity.[42]

In *The Murderers Are Among Us,* as in many postwar German films, then, this relation is quite markedly inverted, so that the male protagonist is characterized by a failure of vision, while the female protagonist is "a woman who looks."

As Silverman and Fisher argue, this gendered inversion of conventional cinematic codes arises from the postwar crisis of masculinity, which resulted in the decentering of male protagonists and the dispersion of narrative authority and identificatory structures onto other characters, often women. However, as *The Murderers Are Among Us* and many of the films that followed it also demonstrate, it was neither unproblematic nor entirely desirable to reestablish these codes in postwar Germany. Instead, the dismantling of filmic conventions and the gender inversions and dispersions exhibited by Staudte's film and its successors came to function as a response not only to the crisis of masculinity but also to the postwar crisis of representation, and as a strategy for appealing to female spectators. The narrative of *The Murderers Are Among Us* aims toward a closure that will reinstate traditional gender roles, reconcile the troubled relations between the sexes, and resolve the ideological tensions that the film has exposed. Yet the film's formal codes tell a different story, creating a supplemental set of meanings and opening up new viewing positions, which the film's highly ambivalent ending is unable to foreclose.

Even in women's films, which address a female spectator and therefore manipulate conventional structures of the gaze to some degree, the woman is still generally punished for possessing agency and owning the gaze. Thus, female spectators of dominant cinema are often forced into a masochistic identification with the female character that ultimately functions to reaffirm traditional roles and relations between the sexes. E. Ann Kaplan sums up this point: "The idealized male screen heroes give back to the male spectator his more perfect mirror self, together with a sense of mastery and control. In contrast, the female is given only powerless, victimized figures who, far from perfect, reinforce the basic sense of worthlessness that already exists."[43] Aside from masochistic identification, to gain pleasure in viewing a film the female spectator may adopt the masculine viewing position through "masquerade" or "transvestism," which allow her to identify with the male character and partake in his mastery of the gaze.[44] According to Sabine Hake, the "conventional dynamics of image and gaze" identified by feminist film theorists was very much in play in women's films of the Third Reich, "which partook of negative investments that made femininity the center of great anxieties and ambiguities, especially for the female spectator who had no choice but to adopt the male point of view."[45] By contrast, in *The Murderers Are Among Us,* the inversion of conventionally gendered codes had some different consequences for the representation of and appeal to women.

Despite the fact that, for at least the first third of the film's narrative, she is clearly in control of the gaze, a control that figures her active desire as she pursues the emasculated Hans, Susanne is never punished for possessing this degree of agency. In addition, while Susanne gets the guy—winning a declaration of love from Hans toward the end of the narrative—she is not fully redomesticated, forced to give up her work, or relegated to the role of wife and mother by the film's ending. Instead, for female spectators, Susanne remains a compelling figure of identification, forcing neither masochistic recognition of the female victim, nor a masquerading affinity with the male protagonist. Ultimately, Susanne's character remains too underdeveloped to allow her to fully transcend conventional codes and function as a figure of feminist identification. Nonetheless, as Fisher suggests of the rubble films in general, "While they reject a more radical gender and cinematic stance, they also incorporate or acknowledge the gender and cinematic alternative, making these films much more nuanced and ambivalent than has been noted in previous accounts."[46]

This point is underscored by a number of sequences in *The Murderers Are Among Us* that problematize spectacle and spectatorship through the figure of the screen. Judith Mayne has analyzed the ambivalent function of the screen in both classical Hollywood cinema and feminist cinema, arguing that symbols of the screen often complicate the role of spectacle in narrative film as well as the privileged boundaries between spectator and spectacle, male and female, subject and object that structure cinematic representation. Mayne notes that, in classical Hollywood films that manifest "a trouble in the realm of heterosexual desire and resolution," the screen becomes "a nodal point in the representation of the difficulty of closure in any simplistic sense."[47] And in feminist cinema, "the figure of the screen emerges as the embodiment of ambivalence, as the site at which cinema both resists and gives support to the representation of female agency and female desire."[48]

Indeed, screen surfaces in *The Murderers Are Among Us* crystallize the gender trouble that the film manifests. One of the film's most famous shots occurs during the scene in which Susanne and Hans first meet, when they are shown together in a reverse shot through the apartment's broken windows. This shot foregrounds the incommensurability of these two characters and the fractured state of relations between the sexes in general. As a stand-in for the cinema screen, this wall of broken windows is also a metaphor for the disturbance of representational codes in the postwar period. At other times, screen surfaces reflect Susanne alone, often pointing to female agency and desire (as in the shot of Susanne smiling in the mirror discussed above) and the limitations in the film's ability to represent them.

Screen surfaces in *The Murderers Are Among Us* are virtually always broken; as the threshold between the spectator and the filmic apparatus, the symbol of the fractured screen points to the upheaval in spectatorial relations to postwar German cinema. Throughout the film, the broken windows continue to function as a screen onto the conflicted domestic space of the apartment as well as the rubble of the wrecked cityscape outside the building, and thus as a constant reminder of the decimation of private and public life resulting from Nazism and the war. Lacking panes, the broken windows constitute a threshold between private and public spaces that highlights the erosion of any distinction between the two. At the end of the film, however, Hans and Susanne repair the broken windowpanes with x-rays from Hans's prewar medical practice. On Christmas Eve, just before Hans sets out to shoot his former commander Brückner, the empty panes are suddenly filled by a series of body parts, exposed to the naked eye through the optics of x-ray technology (see figure 1.2). Symbols of a mode of vision that penetrates an external shell and unmasks that which is hidden, the x-rays suggest that the film's characters, and its spectators too, must look deeper than the postwar wreckage to uncover the effects of history. The repair of the window panes with x-rays further emphasizes the quality of the windows as screen, implying that a relegitimated and "repaired" cinema—one that is not merely concerned with surface spectacle—might help spectators examine that history.

Figure 1.2 Repairing screens and relegitimating the cinema: Susanne Wallner (Hildegard Knef) and Hans Mertens (Ernst Wilhelm Borchert). Source: Deutsche Kinemathek.

IV

The Murderers Are Among Us tackled the postwar problems of disturbed gender relations and delegitimated cinematic representation by proposing that men and women literally *see* differently. Through its encoding of differently gendered gazes and its portrayal of discretely gendered modes of dealing with the present and past, the film also opened up new spaces for reception by female spectators. On a formal level, the film's complication of conventional cinematic codes of gaze and spectacle favored the female spectator, as did the story of Susanne Wallner, a strong and competent woman who is the agent of the transformations charted by the film. A closer look at several extradiegetic factors that influenced spectatorship underscores the film's appeal to female viewers in the late 1940s.

Most central to this appeal was the star aura of Hildegard Knef, the actress who played Susanne Wallner. Knef, postwar German cinema's first star, was wildly popular among early postwar audiences, and her performance in her first starring role set the stage for this popularity.[49] In their focus on the film's diegetic narrative and visual sophistication, critics have tended to neglect the nondiegetic appeal of *The Murderers Are Among Us* to spectators, in particular the significant role Hildegard Knef played in establishing this appeal. Playing her first major screen role here, Knef presented a fresh face and a fresh acting style, both of which distinguished her not only from the film's other actors, but from the familiar female stars of Third Reich cinema as well.

As we will see in subsequent chapters, female stars in the early postwar period functioned, in Richard Dyer's sense, as sites for the resolution of the many ideological tensions and social conflicts that pervaded postwar Germany.[50] In particular, postwar female stars presented spaces for the negotiation of new notions of femininity and national identity. For spectators, female stars were a fulcrum between tradition and modernity, between the Nazi past and an uncertain future. In practical and ideological terms, they were situated at the interstices of competing political structures that shaped film production and reception in the period of Allied occupation.

Jaimey Fisher has noted the irreconcilability of stars and rubble films, arguing that well-known male stars seemed inappropriate for representing the stock male character of the rubble film, the *Heimkehrer*, a figure "based on a complicated, compromised masculinity who has an altogether different relationship to his social environment than is usually the case with a star. The compromised masculinity of the Heimkehrer prevents him from fulfilling conventional social roles: he fails to play the traditional male, a struggle that threatens to destabilize the social order that the star invariably upholds."[51] It is true that the rubble film neither produced new male stars nor resuscitated the careers of well-known stars from the past. Female stars, however, were crucial to cinema's quest for renewal and legitimacy in the postwar period. This was true of no star more than Hildegard Knef, whose debut in *The Murderers Are Among Us* presented a new kind of femininity and a new image of Germanness.

Regardless of the specific characters they are playing, stars typically bring to their roles a certain residue or supplement, a set of traits that consistently exemplify their star aura from movie to movie. The famous emigré producer and Allied film officer Erich Pommer, who was instrumental in Staudte's discovery of Knef and Knef's decision to take the role of Susanne in his film, characterized her star aura this way: "She is simply ... almost one hundred percent a product of the times, of our times. She comes closest to representing the type that we call 'the girl of today.'"[52] As Pommer's statement suggests, Knef broke with the glamorous, diva image of Third Reich stars to embody the more practical, everyday qualities that made her an image of identification for so many postwar women. As Ursula Bessen describes her, "She shows us women, eclectic and complex, just as they are in reality: practical, capable, courageous women."[53]

Writing about Knef's star aura, Georg Seeßlen has also noted that she represented "the history of the woman in Germany after the war." He attributes her remarkable impact to her ability to inhabit contradictory qualities of inhibition and freedom, to combine the virgin and the vamp in one performance. As Seeßlen's characterization of Knef's stardom suggests, the actress herself embodied the ambivalent dialectic of restoration and progress that was so characteristic of postwar Germany. Thus she could play characters who superficially appear to help restore order, while at the same time delineating "an image of woman that contradicted not only the postwar attempts at restoration—the new, cozy, neurotic, and silly patriarchy—but also every desire for harmony and security."[54] For Seeßlen, Knef's role in *The Murderers Are Among Us* is an emblematic one for her star image: Susanne is a figure of redemption, but Knef lends her an air of sovereignty, a certain aplomb that exceeds the apparent flatness of the character. In analyzing the immense power of Knef as Susanne, Seeßlen notably focuses on the central role of her gaze:

> This actress was able to bring to the screen all the terror of the past years, all the crimes, the bombings, the losses, the fear, but at the same time the power to overcome them. As is so often the case with Staudte's films, the dance goes on despite the corpses, but Hildegard Knef has something else in her gaze—call it love or democracy—through which she communicates hope to the spectator.[55]

As Seeßlen's analysis suggests, Knef's performance exceeded the limitations of Susanne's characterization to communicate with the audience at an extradiegetic level that transcends the film's narrative, supplementing the conventional gender ideology that the story works toward reestablishing. Here, too, the despecularization and active gaze of Susanne/Knef figure the film's ultimate failure to right its gender inversions or establish closure.

The publicity documents used in the marketing of *The Murderers Are Among Us* similarly underscore this unconventional representation of femininity by failing to present Susanne as the eroticized object of the male gaze, just as the film avoids this type of specularization.[56] Rather, as in the film, these images depict Susanne Wallner actively looking at other characters or gazing directly into the camera. For example, the invitation to the premiere of the film underscores the centrality of Susanne (and the decentering of Hans) by portraying a large blow-up of Susanne in the middle of the card, surrounded by smaller still images: a contemplative Susanne, Susanne at her drafting table, the industrialist and war criminal Brückner surrounded by cabaret dancers, the repairman and optician Mondschein with Susanne, a bombed-out church, and, at bottom center, a rubble-strewn landscape with two tiny figures whose identity can hardly be discerned (they are Susanne and Hans). Thus the press materials for the film emphasize an explicit appeal to female spectators, drawing them into the film through the character of the actively gazing Susanne Wallner.

It is noteworthy that these press materials are focused almost exclusively on Susanne Wallner, while the image of Hans Mertens is virtually absent. This can be attributed in large part to the fact that the actor who played Hans, Ernst Wilhelm Borchert, was arrested by American authorities shortly before the premiere of the film because he had lied about his membership in the Nazi Party on a denazification questionnaire. As a result, Borchert's name and picture were erased from advertising materials for the film.[57] However, the outcome of Borchert's disputed status in 1946 is that the press kit for the film presents Susanne Wallner as the central character in *The Murderers Are Among Us*, highlighting her role in shaping the narrative of the film as well as her status as a figure of identification for the film's spectators. For viewers who eagerly anticipated the first postwar German film, these documents created a set of expectations about the role of Knef's character that was met by the remarkable star aura of the actress herself.

<h2 style="text-align:center">V</h2>

Susanne Wallner was central to the appeal of *The Murderers Are Among Us* in numerous ways, from the publicity campaigns surrounding the film to the identificatory structures produced by the film's narrative and formal language to the star status of Hildegard Knef. Attention to her centrality—particularly in formal and extradiegetic terms—for female spectators in the 1940s helps provide an explanation for some of the internal contradictions of the film. This is particularly the case if we return to the idea that social and representational problems are often imbricated in early postwar films, and that attempts to find solutions for these problems often crystallize around gender and sexuality.

The Murderers Are Among Us is a story about guilt, responsibility, and retribution for Nazi crimes, and about the traumas experienced by individual Germans and by postwar German society as a result of Nazism and World War II. At every turn, however, this story is embedded in a narrative that focuses on gender roles and (hetero)sexuality. Hans Mertens's feelings of guilt and his experience of trauma are nothing more than the subject of gossip among neighbors until Susanne Wallner shows up, bringing along the promise of a heterosexual relationship. Hans cannot "be a man" unless he is able to overcome his inability to look at blood, which will allow him to become a provider in the relationship by practicing his profession again; he must also exact retribution from Brückner, whom he sees as responsible for the crimes he was forced to help commit, in order to establish a new moral order that will create a basis for this relationship.

Yet in each case, it is the agency not of Hans Mertens, but of the film's female characters that is responsible for inaugurating Hans's transformation. Susanne first initiates contact with Brückner (by bringing Frau Brückner a letter her husband wrote to her at the height of the war), thus forcing Hans's confrontation with him. When Hans sets out to kill Brückner, women stop him from doing so twice, demanding a moral transformation in Hans that will cause him to reject violence, and at the same time facilitating his development into healthy masculinity and his ability to occupy traditional male roles. In the first instance, a mother stops Hans from shooting Brückner by demanding his help for her dying child; when he literally saves a life rather than taking one, Hans is once again able to perform as a surgeon—and as a man. In the second instance, Susanne Wallner stops Hans from shooting Brückner once again, this time ensuring that Hans will reject vigilantism for good, embracing the legal system and finally embracing her as well. Notably, however, the film stops short of bringing together this legal discourse with the reestablishment of heteronormative social order by uniting the two characters in marriage. The film ends, not with a wedding, but with images of a graveyard. Thus, despite the righting of the gender inversions staged by the film, it ultimately fails to attain the kind of closure that would ensure the restoration of traditional gender ideology.

We are left with several unresolved questions about Susanne Wallner: Why does she devote herself to healing the damaged Hans, and why does she fall in love with him to begin with? Why do we learn that she was imprisoned in a concentration camp, although she appears quite healthy and well-nourished, and why does the film not present us with more information about her past? In contemplating the first question, it is noteworthy that, for all its emphasis on normative gender roles and closure built around the reunion of the heterosexual couple, *The Murderers Are Among Us* also presents a slightly more complicated view of the family as the key institution of postwar reconstruction. The tentative relationship between Hans and Susanne is contrasted with the rock-solid bourgeois stability of the Brückner family, where the patriarch Brückner rules over his wife and children with the same mixture of artificial joviality and authoritative force that he exercised as the commander of Hans Mertens's army unit. The film's indictment of Brückner as patriarch (only too happily supported by his fawning wife) goes hand-in-hand with its condemnation of his economic opportunism (he owns a factory that converts steel army helmets into cooking pots). Altogether, this portrait of Brückner produces the film's clear critique of the climate of restoration in postwar Germany, which was predicated on continuities with the past and a failure to confront history. In his script treatment for *The Murderers Are Among Us*, Staudte explains Susanne Wallner's choice of Hans Mertens: "To her, this man appears more valuable in his brokenness than the man upon whom the horrible experiences of history passed by without a trace, leaving no effect."[58] Indeed, Hans appears infinitely preferable to the other type of man imagined by the film, the unrepentant Nazi embodied by Brückner.

The question of Susanne's concentration camp background and her underdeveloped history (in a film that emphasizes the necessity of coming to terms with the past) is more difficult to answer adequately. Robert Shandley suggests that, "Because of the discourse of guilt that included all Germans in 1946, the film needs to find a position of innocence from which it can civilize Hans. Any ordinary woman who had been living in Germany at the time would have been burdened with a morally questionable past."[59] Furthermore, as Elizabeth Heineman shows, occupation authorities assigned former Nazis and their families to clear away rubble in the immediate aftermath of the war; thus, the first *Trümmerfrauen* were associated with Nazis in the public imagination.[60] Since Susanne Wallner comes to epitomize the *Trümmerfrau* in *The Murderers Are Among Us*, perhaps the easiest way to avoid the implication that she might be a Nazi was to invest her with an obvious victim status.

Susanne Wallner's history as a concentration camp victim introduces the subject of the camps (and therefore the Holocaust) into the film, only to sublimate it immediately by transforming the conflict raised by Susanne's past—the conflict between an innocent concentration camp victim and a guilty *Wehrmacht* soldier—into the more benign dilemma of Hans's and Susanne's domestic and sexual incompatibility. In so doing, *The Murderers Are Among Us* engages in a typical tactic of German cinema: to sublimate issues of race, ethnicity, and nationality into more easily digested conflicts of gender and sexuality.

However, the decision to endow Susanne Wallner with a history, albeit one that is only hinted at, does not simply invest her with innocence and virtue. Susanne's background also gives her knowledge—of Nazi crimes, of the world of the camps, of the truth of history—that permits her to be the center of moral judgment in the film. Like Hans, Susanne returns home after the war with hopes for a new beginning, only to clash with the new domestic (dis)order that has been established in her absence. In imagining both characters' struggle for integration into postwar society, the film suggests that the solution for postwar problems—from personal trauma to guilt and responsibility for Nazi crimes—lies in the reestablishment of a heteronormative social order and the return to traditional gender roles.

Yet this solution fails to satisfy the expectations that the film has created on a representational level. By setting Susanne Wallner up as the film's source of narrative authority and moral goodness, and by granting her, especially on a formal level, a degree of agency and subjective integrity not shared by other characters in the film, *The Murderers Are Among Us* tried to deploy its female protagonist as one means of filling the "representational vacuum" in the postwar period. Susanne Wallner has always proved irritating to critics of the film because she is not merely a spectacle or object—she demands further explanation. Though the film itself creates this demand, it is ultimately unable to represent adequately Susanne's desire or subjectivity.

Writing about Hollywood woman's films of the 1940s, Mary Ann Doane asserts, "It is as though the insistent attempt at an inscription of female subjectivity and desire, within a phallocentrically organized discourse such as the classical Hollywood text, produced gaps and incoherences which the films can barely contain."[61] As I have argued, many of the "gaps and incoherences" that have plagued critics of *The Murderers Are Among Us* condense around Susanne and the film's difficulties in accommodating the formal and thematic excesses generated by her character. The woman's film, according to Doane, is an "impure" genre that crosses a variety of filmic styles to address a female audience; as such, it is defined largely by this address, rather than by a shared set of generic traits or characteristics. Rereading *The Murderers Are Among Us* as a woman's film, as I have done in this chapter, not only provides some new explanations for the well-known gaps and incoherences of the film, but also lays the groundwork for understanding subsequent popular cinematic productions in postwar Germany. As the quest for a new cinematic language continued to dovetail with the goal of addressing a largely female audience, postwar filmmakers took up where *The Murderers Are Among Us* left off, investing the "woman's film" with new styles and representational strategies.

Notes

1. Between 1942 and 1944, over one billion movie tickets were sold each year in the Third Reich. For comparative statistics on cinemas and ticket sales, see Hans Helmut Prinzler, *Chronik des deutschen Films 1895–1994* (Stuttgart, 1995), 147, 151, 156, 165; Johannes Hauser, *Neuaufbau der westdeutschen Filmwirtschaft 1945–1955 und der Einfluß der US-amerikanischen Filmpolitik. Vom reichseigenen Filmmonopolkonzern (UFI) zur privatwirtschaftlichen Konkurrenzwirtschaft* (Pfaffenweiler, 1989), 367–68, 376, 673–77; and Elizabeth Prommer, *Kinobesuch im Lebenslauf. Eine historische und medienbiographische Studie* (Konstanz, 1999), 93. Comparable statistics about cinemas and ticket sales in the Eastern zone are not available for most years. According to Prinzler, in 1947 there were 460 million tickets sold in the Western zones and 180 million tickets sold in the Eastern Zones; these numbers remain almost constant in 1949. Prinzler, *Chronik des deutschen Films*, 169, 177.
2. For informative accounts of Allied film policy in postwar Germany, see Hauser, *Neuaufbau der westdeutschen Filmwirtschaft*; Heide Fehrenbach, *Cinema in Democratizing Germany: Reconstructing National Identity After Hitler* (Chapel Hill, 1995); and Robert Shandley, *Rubble Films: German Cinema in the Shadow of the Third Reich* (Philadelphia, 2001).
3. See Bettina Greffrath, *Gesellschaftsbilder der Nachkriegszeit. Deutsche Spielfilme 1945–1949* (Pfaffenweiler, 1995), 122.
4. By most accounts, *The Murderers Are Among Us* was very popular with viewers, though accurate statistics about distribution and ticket sales before 1949 are rare. Based on archival research and information culled from the contemporary press, Elizabeth Prommer qualifies *The Murderers Are Among Us* as a "hit," but she was unable to locate precise attendance records. Prommer, *Kinobesuch im Lebenslauf*, 349. According to Bettina Greffrath, DEFA's own statistics suggest that over five million viewers saw the film, but Greffrath does not qualify these statistics, and it remains unclear to which time frame and which zone(s) the statistics refer. See Greffrath, *Gesellschaftsbilder der Nachkriegszeit*, 129.
5. "Die Mörder sind unter uns. Der erste deutsche Film der Nachkriegszeit," *Film Revue Sonderablage* <n.d., probably 1947>, photocopy in file on *Die Mörder sind unter uns*, Schriftgutarchiv, Stiftung Deutsche Kinemathek, Berlin.
6. "Die Mörder sind unter uns," *Film Revue Sonderablage*.
7. See Friedrich Luft, "Der erste deutsche Film nach dem Kriege," rev. of *Die Mörder sind unter uns, Der Tagesspiegel*, October 16, 1946, rpt. in *Staudte*, ed. Eva Orbanz and Hans Helmut Prinzler (Berlin, 1991), 176. See also rev. of *Die Mörder sind unter uns, Die Neue Zeitung* (Munich), October 18, 1946. On the popular and critical reception of the film, see Christiane Mückenberger and Günter Jordan, *"Sie sehen selbst, Sie hören selbst …" Eine Geschichte der DEFA von ihren Anfängen bis 1949* (Marburg, 1994), 41–52.
8. Harald Braun, "Die Bedeutung der 'Filmpause'," *Die Neue Zeitung*, November 12, 1945. Rpt. in *Das Jahr 1945: Filme aus fünfzehn Ländern*, ed. Hans Helmut Prinzler (Berlin, 1990), 117–20.
9. Shandley, *Rubble Films*, 26. See also Shandley's discussion of the *Filmpause*, 20–24.
10. On the call to redefine German cinematic realism in relation to Italian neo realism, see Jaimey Fisher, "Deleuze in a Ruinous Context: German Rubble-Film and Italian Neorealism," *iris* 23 (1997): 53–74; and Fisher, "On the Ruins of Masculinity: The Figure of the Child in Italian Neorealism and the German Rubble-Film," in *Italian Neorealism and Global Cinema*, ed. Laura E. Ruberto and Kristi M. Wilson (Detroit, 2007), 25–53.
11. Statistics quoted in Fehrenbach, *Cinema in Democratizing Germany*, 95.
12. Herman Nohl, "Die heutige Aufgabe der Frau," *Die Sammlung* 2.7 (1947): 353.
13. Kaja Silverman, *Male Subjectivity at the Margins* (New York, 1992), 8.
14. Silverman, *Male Subjectivity at the Margins*, 2.
15. Silverman, *Male Subjectivity at the Margins*, 53.
16. Fisher, "On the Ruins of Masculinity," 29.
17. Fisher, "On the Ruins of Masculinity," 36, 34.

18. See Elizabeth Heineman, "The Hour of the Woman: Memories of Germany's 'Crisis Years' and West German National Identity," *American Historical Review* 101.2 (1996): 354–95.

19. Helmut Käutner, "Demontage der Traumfabrik," *Film-Echo* 5 (June 1947). Rpt. in *Käutner*, ed. Wolfgang Jacobsen and Hans Helmut Prinzler (Berlin, 1992), 113–14.

20. On the popular and critical success of *In Those Days*, see "Das erlösende Wort," rev. of *In jenen Tagen, Die Gegenwart* 17 (March 1948), rpt. in Jacobsen and Prinzler, *Käutner*, 197–200; Wolfdietrich Schnurre, "Erfindungsgabe und Improvisationstalent," *Der neue Film* 4 (July 7, 1947), rpt. in Jacobsen and Prinzler, *Käutner*, 201–203; and Helmut Käutner, "Kunst im Film ist Schmuggelware," Interview with Edmund Luft, 1973–74, rpt. in Jacobsen and Prinzler, *Käutner*, 120–71, esp. 140.

21. See Patrice Petro, "Mass Culture and the Feminine: The 'Place' of Television in Film Studies," *Cinema Journal* 25.3 (Spring 1986), rpt. in Petro, *Aftershocks of the New: Feminism and Film History* (New Brunswick, NJ, 2002), 13–30. Petro compares Weimar debates about art cinema and popular cinema with 1980s U.S. debates about the role of television in academic film studies. On gendered oppositions in debates about art and mass culture in the German context, see also Andreas Huyssen, "Mass Culture as Woman: Modernism's Other," in *After the Great Divide: Modernism, Mass Culture, Postmodernism* (Bloomington, 1986), 44–62.

22. Shandley, *Rubble Films*, 25.

23. For example, Eric Rentschler argues that *The Murderers Are Among Us* and its successors "failed to explore the sociopolitical factors that furthered fascism" and expressed optimism about the possibility of a new beginning rather than a convincing critique of history. Rentschler, "Germany: The Past That Would Not Go Away," in *World Cinema Since 1945*, ed. William Luhr (New York, 1987), 212. By contrast, Robert and Carol Reimer posit Staudte's film as a highly successful example of what they call "Nazi-retro film," arguing that it creates spectator positions that encourage engagement with German history and the Holocaust. Robert C. Reimer and Carol J. Reimer, *Nazi-Retro Film: How German Narrative Cinema Remembers the Past* (New York, 1992). Both positions can also be found in early reviews of the film. See for example Luft, "Der erste deutsche Film," and Walter Lennig, "Ein Film der deutschen Wirklichkeit," rev. of *Die Mörder sind unter uns, Berliner Zeitung*, October 17, 1946.

24. One major exception to this tendency is Jaimey Fisher's convincing reading of *The Murderers Are Among Us* in "Deleuze in a Ruinous Context." Here, Fisher argues that the film represents "the replacement of the masculine action-image by a less-than-ideally masculine pure optical-sound situation, and by more active agencies in nontraditional, dispersive centers" (62). That is, in Staudte's film, the male authority evacuated from the marginal protagonist Mertens is dispersed onto the female protagonist, Susanne, who "fills in for the man in the dominant fiction of sexual pursuer, patriarchal family, and domestic bliss" (63). While *The Murderers Are Among Us* and rubble films more generally thus represent the transition, in Deleuzean terms, from a cinema of agency to a cinema of passivity, Fisher argues that they ultimately work to restore male authority and the "masculine action-image." However, this restoration does not fully succeed, for by exhibiting a proliferation of marginal masculinities the films acknowledge alternative gender constructions, thereby remaining highly ambivalent.

25. "'Die Mörder sind unter uns': Premiere des deutschen Films," rev. in *Sonntag*, October 20, 1946.

26. Theodor Kotulla, rev. of *Die Mörder sind unter uns, Filmkritik* 1 (1960): 28. This review addressed a West German revival of the film.

27. Fisher, "Deleuze in a Ruinous Context," 63.

28. For example, Anton Kaes writes, "From today's perspective it is striking how strongly the film emphasizes male heroes. Women seem to have no history of their own; they are only projections of male fantasies. Not until the late 1970s was the female perspective of history addressed." See Kaes, *From Hitler to Heimat: The Return of History as Film* (Cambridge, 1989), 216, n. 21. For a more nuanced analysis of the "Susanne problem," see Shandley, *Rubble Films*, 44–45.

29. Fisher, "Deleuze in a Ruinous Context," 64.
30. Fisher suggests that the film problematizes Brückner's far too easy restoration of ideal masculinity as well as Mondschein's far too perfect faith in the dominant fiction, condemning "not only Brückner's high bourgeois values, but also Mondschein's petty-bourgeois ones." Fisher, "Deleuze in a Ruinous Context," 66.
31. Shandley, *Rubble Films*, 44.
32. Staudte, who was born in 1906, began his career as a film and theater actor in the Weimar Republic. At first banned from theater acting in the Third Reich, Staudte went on to work in the film industry during the 1930s as a sound synchronizer and actor, mostly in small roles, including one in the notorious propaganda film *Jud Süss* (Veit Harlan, 1940). Staudte began his directorial career making advertising and industrial films, and went on to direct several feature films in the early 1940s, including *Akrobat Schö-ö-ö-n* (1943), which some scholars have seen as one of the few examples of critical filmmaking during the Third Reich. After *The Murderers Are Among Us*, Staudte went on to direct a number of successful films for both DEFA and Western German production companies throughout the 1940s and 1950s, gaining a reputation for his ability to combine social-critical narratives and aesthetic experimentation with popular styles.
33. According to Staudte, although he was already licensed to make films by the British (he lived in the British sector of Berlin), the British were not interested in helping him finance the film, nor were the French or the Americans. See Wolfgang Staudte, Interview with Heinz Kersten et al., May 13, 1974, rpt. in *Staudte*, 133. The production of Staudte's film in the Soviet zone led to the foundation of the Deutsche Film-AG (DEFA) on May 17, 1946, in Babelsberg, under the control of the Soviet military administration. *The Murderers Are Among Us* is the only DEFA film I discuss in this study, as my focus is on films that were produced in the Western part of Germany. I have chosen to make an exception in the case of this important film because it was made so early, and because it was eventually shown in all sectors of occupied Germany. Nonetheless, it is extremely relevant that the film was rejected by the Western Allies, and the fact that it was made for DEFA certainly has a bearing on the production and reception contexts of the film.
34. See Wolfgang Staudte, "Ein Exposé. Arbeitstitel: Die Mörder sind unter uns" (1946), in Orbanz and Prinzler, *Staudte*, 155–57. In this treatment of the film, the outcome of the trial is not made clear: the film ends, just as the court convenes to determine the verdict, with an image of the wall of the courtroom "where a picture of the bloodiest tyrant of history once hung and where now the goddess of justice stands, waiting and weighing, with blindfolded eyes" (157).
35. Staudte, Interview, *Staudte*, 133.
36. I would like to thank Adam Hurst for pointing out this connection to me.
37. Fisher points out that, "One of the film's most conspicuous gender inversions locates Mertens as the one waiting in the house and Susanne as the one returning to it, deliberately reversing the cliché of the waiting wife and the reintegrating husband" (63).
38. Fisher also notes that the film "dwells on Susanne as the subject of wholeness, agency, and unity," in contrast to its conspicuous representation of male lack and passivity in the figure of Mertens (64).
39. "The gaze" refers to the system of looks encoded by the cinematic apparatus through the alignment of camera shots with the perspectives of individual characters within the filmic narrative. "The gaze" functions also to inscribe a textual address to an implied or ideal spectator, which may (or may not) function to align the gaze of real viewers in the audience with the gaze of characters within the film—and by extension with the camera itself—through mechanisms of identification and conventions of viewing. Because it helps to structure and provides perspective for what is and is not seen on screen, "the gaze" is a primary tool through which knowledge, authority, identity, and subjectivity are constructed and attributed within the filmic text, as well as for the implied spectator and, potentially, the real viewer of the film. For a productive reconsideration of the gaze (in particular as it was articulated in 1970s apparatus theory) and of larger issues

surrounding the theorization of spectatorship, see Judith Mayne, *Cinema and Spectatorship* (New York, 1993).

40. Ursula Bessen notes that the slogan illustrated by Susanne's drawing, "Rettet die Kinder" <Save the children> was the slogan of the first campaign launched by the government Committees on Women's Issues after the war, and thus had a direct political connotation for viewers in 1946. See Bessen, *Trümmer und Träume: Nachkriegszeit und fünfziger Jahre auf Zelluloid—Deutsche Spielfilme als Zeugnisse ihrer Zeit* (Bochum, 1989), 226, n. 3.

41. The classic analysis of the gendered structure of the gaze in dominant cinema is Laura Mulvey's 1975 essay "Visual Pleasure and Narrative Cinema," rpt. in *Visual and Other Pleasures* (Bloomington, 1989), 14–26. See also E. Ann Kaplan, "Is the Gaze Male?," in *Women & Film: Both Sides of the Camera* (New York, 1983), 23–35.

42. Linda Williams, "When the Woman Looks," in *Re-Vision: Essays in Feminist Film Criticism*, ed. Mary Ann Doane et al. (Los Angeles, 1984), 83.

43. Kaplan, *Women & Film*, 28.

44. Mulvey suggests the term "transvestism" to describe the process in which female spectators must engage, while Mary Ann Doane proposes the trope of the masquerade. See Mulvey, "Afterthoughts on 'Visual Pleasure and Narrative Cinema' Inspired by *Duel in the Sun*," rpt. in *Visual and Other Pleasures*, 29–38; and Doane, "Film and the Masquerade: Theorizing the Female Spectator," rpt. in *Femmes Fatales: Feminism, Film Theory, Psychoanalysis* (New York, 1991), 17–32. On the idea that female spectators must adopt a masculine position to view mainstream films, see also Kaplan, "Is the Gaze Male?," *Women & Film*.

45. Sabine Hake, *Popular Cinema of the Third Reich* (Austin, 2001), 193.

46. Fisher, "Deleuze in a Ruinous Context," 62.

47. Judith Mayne, *The Woman at the Keyhole: Feminism and Women's Cinema* (Bloomington, 1990), 43.

48. Mayne, *The Woman at the Keyhole*, 51.

49. For further discussion of Knef's stardom, see chapter 2 and chapter 5.

50. Dyer reads stars as semiotic texts that produce social meaning for spectators. In particular, Dyer argues that stars serve as privileged sites for the negotiation of ideological dilemmas, instabilities, and contradictions that cannot be resolved in the dominant culture. See for example Dyer, *Stars* (London, 1979) and *Heavenly Bodies: Film Stars and Society* (New York, 1986).

51. Jaimey Fisher, *Disciplining Germany: Youth, Reeducation, and Reconstruction after the Second World War* (Detroit, 2007), 220.

52. Erich Pommer, "Der natürliche Lebenshunger," *Spiegel* (May 7, 1952), 28, qtd. in Bessen, *Trümmer und Träume*, 204.

53. Bessen, *Trümmer und Träume*, 205.

54. Georg Seeßlen, "Die andere Frau: Hildegard Knef," *EPD Film* 8.1 (1991): 16.

55. Seeßlen, "Die andere Frau," 17.

56. See for example the invitation to the film premiere and the press booklet in the file on *Die Mörder sind unter uns*, Schriftgutarchiv, Stiftung Deutsche Kinemathek, Berlin.

57. F.-B. Habel suggests that Borchert was ultimately classified as a *Mitläufer* for having played a limited role in the Nazi Party and released from Allied custody in time to attend the film's premiere. However, Christa Bandmann claims that the Soviets, fearing for the fate of the film, put up bail to ensure Borchert's release in time for the premiere; afterwards he spent three months in prison for lying on his denazification questionnaire. See Habel, *Das grosse Lexikon der DEFA-Spielfilme* (Berlin, 2000), 414; and Bandmann, *Es leuchten die Sterne: Aus der Glanzzeit des deutschen Films* (Munich, 1979), 115–16.

58. Wolfgang Staudte, "Ein Exposé," in Orbanz and Prinzler, *Staudte*, 155.

59. Shandley, *Rubble Films*, 44.

60. See Heineman, "The Hour of the Woman," 375–76.

61. Mary Ann Doane, "The 'Woman's Film': Possession and Address," in *Re-Vision: Essays in Feminist Film Criticism*, 69.

Chapter 2

WHEN FANTASY MEETS REALITY:
AUTHORSHIP AND STARDOM IN RUDOLF JUGERT'S *FILM WITHOUT A TITLE* (1948)

The consumption and production of movies was gaining momentum in all zones of Germany by the third postwar year. In the Western zones, 850 new cinemas opened between 1946 and 1948, and ticket sales continued to increase to a total of 443 million in 1948, an average of nine visits to the cinema for every Western German that year.[1] Cinemas continued to rely on foreign productions, particularly from the Allied countries, to fill their screens, but they could now include increasing numbers of new German movies as well. Thirty feature films were produced in 1948 (twenty-three in the Western zones and seven by DEFA), up from a total of four features only two years before. These films were marked by an increasing range of styles and genres, a fact that helped make German films more successful than ever among postwar audiences. The most successful German film of 1948 and the winner of the first ever "Bambi" film prize for its popularity with audiences, Rudolf Jugert's *Film ohne Titel* reflected on the status of filmmaking three years into the period of occupation.[2]

Film Without a Title premiered on January 23, 1948, in West Berlin. The premiere took place at the Marmorhaus, the venerable cinema on the Kurfürstendamm where *The Cabinet of Dr. Caligari* had premiered nearly thirty years before. Remarkably, the Marmorhaus had survived the war largely unscathed. Writing about the premiere of *Film Without a Title*, a reviewer for the *Neue Zeit Berlin* dryly noted, "There was much applause. One had the impression that with this film we have finally achieved international caliber. At least in the elaborate production of its 'Gala Premiere.'"[3] With its glamorous Berlin premiere and unrivaled popularity, *Film Without a Title* signaled a benchmark in postwar filmmaking as well as the beginning of a transition away from the rubble film genre, whose conventions it both invokes and parodies.[4]

The triumphant Berlin premiere of *Film Without a Title* was followed very quickly by highly successful runs in Cologne, Essen, and Hamburg. Reviewers were overwhelmingly positive in their assessment of the film, lauding its comedic and parodic elements as well as the productive spectatorship it encouraged: "In that the filmmakers themselves put their working process on display for the spectators, and thereby put up for discussion all their possible choices in treating the material in words and images—they even leave the choice of a title up to us—they have given preference to a vital method, which rejects anything schematic and makes the spectator the judge."[5]

Indeed, *Film Without a Title* achieved popularity with viewers by acknowledging directly the problems that filmmakers had faced so far in developing legitimate forms of cinematic representation and in meeting audience expectations of postwar cinema. By incorporating into the film a frame narrative in which a director, an actor, and a screenwriter argue about the form and content their film should take, *Film Without a Title* emphasized the difficulties of writing quality scripts for postwar audiences and thereby responded to contemporary debates about the central role of authorship in creating a new postwar cinema. As one reviewer wrote of screenwriters Helmut Käutner, Ellen Fechner, and Rudolf Jugert: "They had the idea of projecting the difficult business of authorship right up onto the screen."[6] This point was underscored already by the publicity campaign for *Film Without a Title*, which included a contest asking viewers to come up with a good title for the film. A cute marketing device, this campaign dovetailed with an idea that was quickly gaining currency in postwar Germany: that common people—everyday film viewers—might do a better job of creating a legitimate new cinema than the compromised filmmakers who had so far failed at the task.

If *The Murderers Are Among Us* is marked by gaps and inconsistencies that emerged from its attempt to imagine solutions for both representational and social problems in the postwar period, *Film Without a Title* makes such gaps and inconsistencies the explicit subject of its narrative. The film humorously interweaves the story of three filmmakers trying to write a "light-hearted but realistic contemporary comedy" with the unlikely love story of a farm girl and a Berlin antiques dealer, whose relationship is set in motion but also constantly challenged by changing class and gender roles during the Third Reich, wartime, and the period of occupation. As the filmmakers come up against the limitations of filmic conventions while attempting to envision a possible ending for this "real-life" love story, the film quite literally shows how the processes of solving social and representational problems are inextricably intertwined. Yet in contrast to contemporary discourse suggesting that the "artistic screenwriter" could imagine successful solutions to these problems, *Film Without a Title* presents a more complicated picture of the collaborative, compromising—and indeed, compromised—process of popular filmmaking, in which authorship is revealed to be just one of many important factors, including genre, stardom, the creative vision of the director, and the expectations and imaginations of spectators.

I

As filmmaking resumed in Germany and the *Filmpause* slowly came to an end, the debate about cinema was recast in new terms: critics began to focus on the central role of the *Filmdichter*, or artistic screenwriter, in creating a new postwar film. The search for the *Filmdichter* went hand in hand with the postwar call to deconstruct Goebbels's aesthetic program and to move beyond the industrial studio production style of Third Reich cinema. Helmut Käutner, one of the screenwriters of *Film Without a Title*, had laid out the terms for this call in his 1947 essay "Dismantling the Dream Factory," and other commentators on postwar cinema eagerly took up his terms.[7] But while Käutner was quick to blame German audiences for what he saw as an unwillingness to adjust their expectations to the postwar context, subsequent observers turned their attention to the role of the screenwriter in creating a new cinematic form and content that would break with the past.

Indeed, the *Filmdichter* came to be seen as the savior who would bring authenticity, vitality, originality, and *Geist* back to the German cinema. Most importantly, the *Filmdichter* would help to create the balance among popular appeal, artistic form, and social-critical content that would finally ensure the legitimacy of postwar cinema. In 1947, a full-scale debate about the role of the *Filmdichter* emerged in the *feuilleton* pages of newspapers and in film periodicals.[8] Several popular magazines even sponsored contests to discover new screenwriting talents.[9]

One contribution to the debate published in *Der Rheinische Merkur* summed up the hope for German cinema that the *Filmdichter* represented:

> We are all experiencing the grotesque situation that the demands of the public and the hunger for film among the masses are growing steadily, while the acquisition of new material and the search for great screenwriters <*Film-Dichtern*> are causing ever greater difficulties. Not to mention that the experience of reality in the past few years—especially in Germany—has been more penetrating, stronger, and more dramatic than the most intensely moving images. Even the most explicit newsreels devoted to representing images of horror were hardly able to touch the souls of spectators. This must somehow come to an end. It is at this point that the long anticipated *Filmdichter* must step in.[10]

As this contribution suggests, spectators had become thoroughly desensitized to cinematic images during the Third Reich, a dilemma for postwar filmmakers seeking a new cinematic language that could address postwar social problems and appeal to audiences at the same time. This disconnect between filmmakers and audiences could only be solved by the mediating figure of the *Filmdichter*, who would address contemporary subject matter in new terms, thus facilitating the invention of a formal language that would revive the power of cinematic imagery while also responding to spectators' demands for entertainment.

In 1947, the film journal *Der neue Film* solicited contributions about the state of filmmaking and the role of the screenwriter from "young people and practitioners … but above all from authors, the originators of all film material."[11] According to the journal's call for contributions:

> The dramaturgical conversation about the intellectual standpoint of the German film has entered a decisive phase. This debate has found a lively echo not only in the active participation of the public, but also already in the press. No wonder—German film is facing a decision as to whether or not it will be able successfully to assert its claim to cultural legitimacy before the world. Much has been tried since the collapse—some has been achieved—little that is decisive has happened. We know the difficulties of a new beginning and value the fumbling attempts of the first postwar films accordingly. However, we also know about the singular opportunity represented by this moment, into which, from an official standpoint, the export possibilities for German film must also be calculated. That is one side of things. On the other side, zonal borders have thus far hindered any long-range work. Now it seems that an interzonal film exchange will be introduced. As a result it has become necessary to move from this situation of fragmentary coexistence to a planned cooperation of production companies—above all in regard to content. This process must begin with the author![12]

The editors of *Der neue Film* thus imagine the "film author" as someone who is capable not only of creating newly legitimate film content and therefore of ensuring the export value of German cinema, but also of serving as a mediator who will be able to overcome the fragmentary state of postwar film production and promote cooperation among production companies in spite of political, material, and structural hurdles.

The responses to this call printed in *Der neue Film* are instructive in that they address the role of the screenwriter within the larger context of German cinema's future. In particular, these contributions focus on two primary and interlinked questions: Must the postwar German film take the form of the *Zeitfilm*, that is, a film that addresses contemporary reality? And must the dream factory be dismantled, or does escapist entertainment fare have a place in postwar German cinema?

As Thomas Brandlmeier points out, respondents to the forum in *Der neue Film* and to the *Filmdichter* debate generally answered these questions in one of two ways. While one camp argued that the new German film must respond to the problems and conflicts of contemporary reality, the other camp suggested that real life was so full of problems and conflicts that no one wanted to see them replayed on screen. Similarly, one group argued that postwar cinema could only achieve success in representing contemporary reality if filmmakers broke with the conventions associated with the dream factory, while the other group argued that to dismantle the dream factory would be to forsake the fantastic, idealistic (and implicitly the escapist) elements of the cinema altogether.[13]

The 1947 debate about the *Filmdichter* proved prophetic in several respects. First, contributors to the debate articulated a persistent feeling of unease with popular entertainment cinema that would continue to characterize discussions about German film well into the 1960s. It is particularly noteworthy that their preferred solution to this feeling of unease was the film author, the creative genius who would instill film with authenticity and originality. The figure of the absent author would continue to haunt postwar German cinema throughout the 1950s; it is in this context that the emergence of the *Autorenfilm* (*auteur* cinema) of the 1960s and 1970s can best be understood.[14]

Second, the debate foreshadowed the rise—at the expense of the social-critical *Zeitfilm*— of precisely the sort of popular cinema critics most feared, which would in fact come to dominate the German cinematic landscape in the 1950s. One contributor to the debate even predicted the emergence of the *Heimatfilm* as the most popular genre of the new entertainment cinema, a prediction that is echoed, as we shall see, in *Film Without a Title*.[15] In sum, then, the *Filmdichter* debate laid out the polarizing terms in which critics would continue to debate German cinema throughout the postwar period.

One contributor to *Der neue Film* did move beyond these polarities to offer a closer examination of the unique situation of postwar German filmmaking. A prominent theater director during the Weimar Republic, Jacob Geis went on to become a successful screenwriter during the Third Reich. His screenwriting career continued into the postwar period, when he also became a producer.[16] Notably, Geis's contribution to *Der neue Film* focuses on the changing conditions of spectatorship in the postwar period and the concomitant imperative to adjust screenwriting and filmmaking to meet the new needs of postwar spectators. According to Geis:

> <T>he turbulence and the irrationality of the course of history <*Weltlauf*> have made dramaturgically "correct," logically constructed narratives questionable. Everyone can relate such an abundant number of improbable narrative events from his or her own experience that the "dramaturgical," with its logical interconnections, must in the best case scenario seem like an isolated coincidence, not at all engaging. A new feeling has emerged for an illogical and erratic mode of being, which cannot be connected to any greater purpose nor steered through particular intentions. … If one admits the fleeting and questionable quality of human relations, then it seems obvious to derive ideas for content precisely from this situation. That means first and foremost a compulsion to address *current* subject matter. Only through current subject matter can this altered basis of human activity be made comprehensible.[17]

Addressing the debate about the dream factory, Geis goes on in his piece to suggest the legitimacy and indeed the psychological importance for postwar audiences of including fantastic, dreamlike, and utopian elements in a cinema that would not, however, resort to the clichés and conventions of Third Reich studio productions. This "third way" that Geis suggests did not become the predominant mode of representation for postwar cinema, which in many ways continued to echo the polarities so clearly articulated by the *Filmdichter* debate. However, it did find expression here and there, particularly in the transitional years 1947–50, as the rubble film began to give way to the entertainment cinema of the following decade.

In many ways, *Film Without a Title* is emblematic of Geis's cinematic third way. While the film dismantles the logic of the conventional cinematic narrative, it also caters to spectatorial fantasies and desires. In its emphasis on the vexed creative process and its open-ended narrative, the film encourages productive spectatorship and addresses the changing needs of postwar film viewers. At the same time, its self-reflexive satire and comedic elements also make light of the heavy-handed attempts of many postwar filmmakers to address the dilemmas of postwar society and cinematic representation.

II

An emblematic transitional film, *Film Without a Title* uses the device of a frame story to thematize, metacinematically, questions of authorship and spectatorship that were central to the problems of representation faced by postwar filmmakers trying to develop a newly legitimate German cinema. *Film Without a Title* never explicitly addresses Nazi crimes or the Holocaust; in this sense, as Robert Shandley has noted, it is an "amnesic film."[18] Eschewing an explicit engagement with the past while parodying the political discourse present in many of its postwar precursor films, *Film Without a Title* signals a shift towards the more ahistorical filmmaking that came to dominate the West German cinematic landscape in the 1950s.

While it parodies both the *Zeitfilm* and the typical dream factory genre film, though, *Film Without a Title* also addresses contemporary social problems by focusing on changing class and gender roles during wartime and the period of occupation. Like many of its precursors and successors, *Film Without a Title* also displays a marked fixation on problems of form and representation that have their origins in the Nazi past. And as in those other films, problems with form in *Film Without a Title* are inextricably linked to social problems. Like *The Murderers Are Among Us*, *Film Without a Title* tells a story about the postwar crisis of masculinity, but this time the crisis is implicated not only in the film's narrative, but also in its frame story, which exhibits a (rather playful) metacinematic critique of the limitations of male authors as producers of postwar cinema, not least when it comes to representing women.

One 1948 reviewer described *Film Without a Title* as follows:

Film Without a Title is not without a certain something. It gets laughs by making fun of itself. It circumvents the misery of lacking subject matter by taking precisely this misery as its subject matter. And it neutralizes all possible objections by strongly articulating these objections itself. This, then, is the joke: three people are looking for a film subject—a screenwriter <*Autor*> as well as a director and an actor. They want in all seriousness to make a light-hearted contemporary film <*Zeitfilm*>, although they are well aware of the difficulties and dangers present in this contemporary time period. But they don't have any ideas. … Helmut Käutner, however, had a good one: He has the filmmakers literally pick an idea up off the street. A returning soldier comes along, and his story, which begins as an aside, becomes the basis of the film. It is the story of a well-to-do man (Hans Söhnker) who falls in love with a simple maid (Hildegard Knef). However, they cannot come together because their class differences run too deep. After the collapse, everything is turned around: now he is the poor, homeless man while she, as the daughter of a farmer who quickly hustles his way to wealth, is a desirable match. Just as his prejudiced sister had done before, now her father turns up his nose at a partner from an inferior social class. How will all this end? Spellbound by the story, the filmmakers begin spinning their own yarn out of it. Each of them shows how he imagines the story's ending: the director in a tragically avant-garde manner with fat cats in a night club and hollow-cheeked agony in a rubble world shot with canted angles; and the actor (Willy Fritsch) optimistically, through rose-colored glasses, with a happy choreographed dance scene at the end. As a third possible ending, "real life" is shown (which in reality is of course also made up). It is a simple, plausible happy end, straight off the rack of real life.[19]

As this reviewer suggests, it is the screenwriter who rescues the film from tired clichés—the binary choices of *Zeitfilm* (here advocated by the director) or dream factory entertainment (advocated by the actor Willy Fritsch) that were so vociferously debated in contemporary discussions of the *Filmdichter*—by insisting on the precedence of "reality."[20] Yet as we shall see, in the end even the author cannot save the cinema, and *Film Without a Title* ultimately leaves it up to the viewer to decide not only on the film's title, but also on how its story will turn out. Thus spectatorship trumps authorship in the search for a new film language in postwar German cinema.

From the title sequence onward, *Film Without a Title* consistently thematizes the difficulties faced by postwar filmmakers, while also encouraging reflection on the process of filmmaking. After an opening card announcing the film's distributor, Herzog Verleih, the title sequence presents the logo of the production company, a movie camera that is shown rotating in close-up. The printed words "Camera Film Production – Artistic Director Helmut Käutner" appear on screen, as a disembodied voiceover speaks directly to the viewer: "Presenting to you a light-hearted film without a title." Already in this title sequence, the role of the film author is at once asserted and undermined.

Though we do not see the name of the film's director here, we do see the name of one of its screenwriters, Helmut Käutner, well known to audiences in the late 1940s and credited here for his creative contributions to the film. Käutner, born in 1908, was among the most influential filmmakers of the postwar period. Active as a director during the Third Reich, Käutner made a number of films in the late 1930s and early 1940s that were lauded for their artistic qualities. Critics have often viewed him as one of only a few exceptional figures who managed to retain some degree of autonomy from the Nazi filmmaking apparatus. In the postwar period, Käutner founded his own production company, Camera Film-Produktion, in order to retain a degree of artistic control over his films. His first postwar film *In jenen Tagen* (In Those Days, 1947) consolidated Käutner's reputation as an *auteur* who made artistic yet popular movies, a reputation he continued to enjoy throughout the 1950s. Käutner surrounded himself with a creative team of filmmakers with whom he consistently worked, often in differing capacities—not only as a screenwriter, director, and producer, but also as an actor. Among these was his longtime directorial assistant Rudolf Jugert, who made his directorial debut with *Film Without a Title*. Jugert subsequently made his name as a successful director of numerous films in the Federal Republic during the 1950s. Though Käutner did not direct, but only co-wrote the screenplay for *Film Without a Title* with director Jugert and Ellen Fechner, the film was consistently billed as a "Käutner Film" in publicity documents and in the press. In particular, Fechner's creative role in the film was quickly erased, a point I will return to below.

At the same time that the film foregrounds Käutner's authorship through title cards, a nondiegetic voiceover that accompanies the title sequence stresses the author's inability to find a title for his film—a point that will be made again in the film's closing sequence. The voiceover alerts viewers that they are about to watch a cheerful, light-hearted film, something that is problematized immediately in the subsequent opening scene, when the filmmakers in the film's frame story discuss precisely the impossibility of making a cheerful, light-hearted film in the troubled climate of postwar Germany. By displaying a film camera and placing the artistic process of authorship in question, the title sequence of *Film Without a Title* already asks viewers both to contemplate and to participate in the process of filmmaking.

An iris shot begins the film proper, emphasizing the indeterminacy of the narrative we are about to watch: it focuses our attention on a piece of paper covered with film ideas, suggestions, and doodles, including the words "Film Without a Title." The camera pulls back over the shoulder of the doodler—the film director (Peter Hamel)—and pans across a pastoral landscape before settling on the central couple Martin Delius (Hans Söhnker) and Christine Fleming (Hildegard Knef), who have come to visit the screenwriter (Fritz Odemar). Seeing that he is embroiled in conversation, Martin wishes to leave, but Christine insists that they stick around so that she can meet the famous actor Willy Fritsch, whom she has instantly recognized.

It is through Martin's and Christine's perspective that we witness the filmmakers' heated conversation about the film they wish to make. Their conversation revolves around the difficulties of making a film "set against the desolate backdrop" of postwar Germany.[21] Rejecting the gamut of postwar films up until now ("No rubble film … No coming-home film … No fraternizing film … No anti-Nazi film … No political film … No film for or against something"), the filmmakers settle on the necessity of making "a contemporary comedy" despite the inherent difficulties of doing so in a time of economic and political crisis. Ironically, *Film Without a Title* manages to incorporate all of the elements the filmmakers reject, while also making light of them. As one contemporary reviewer wrote, "The film evidently takes nothing seriously. And yet it does not shy away from confronting contemporary questions: the black market and the refugees, the shortage of space, the world of the rubble, the city dwellers in the country, and the greediness of farmers."[22]

The filmmakers are ultimately interrupted in their discussion by Martin and Christine. A stand-in for the average female spectator to whom the filmmakers hoped to appeal with their new film, Christine asks Willy Fritsch whether screen kisses are real. "It depends on the partner," Fritsch replies, "If I were playing opposite you, then they most certainly would be!" Not only does the film send up Fritsch, one of the Third Reich's biggest stars, but its satire of postwar stardom also derives from the contrastive casting of popular Third Reich stars Hans Söhnker and Irene von Meyendorff (Angelika Rösch) opposite postwar cinema's first and biggest star, Hildegard Knef. As part of the "dream couple" of Third Reich cinema, Willy Fritsch played opposite Lillian Harvey as the most popular male romantic lead of the era. Hans Söhnker, a Käutner standby, was known for his portrayal of the aristocratic *bon vivant*; Irene von Meyendorff was similarly typecast as a well-bred aristocrat after her famous turn as Octavia in Veit Harlan's immensely popular *Opfergang* (The Sacrifice, 1943). All of these actors contrasted sharply in both star aura and acting style with Hildegard Knef, who made her screen debut in *The Murderers Are Among Us*, and who became an emblem of postwar femininity. The opening sequence of *Film Without a Title*, then, already illustrates the changing discourses not only of authorship and genre, but also of stardom within postwar German filmmaking.

As Martin and Christine leave the scene, both Fritsch and the film director express curiosity about this unlikely couple, and the screenwriter begins to narrate their story. The rest of the film is told in a series of flashbacks that are structured through the omniscient voiceover of the screenwriter, with intermittent interruptions that return to the present day, when the filmmakers debate the possibilities for turning Martin's and Christine's story into a film.

The first of these flashbacks begins with an image of Martin's most beloved possession, an antique statue of his namesake St. Martin, which, the voiceover explains, will play a large role in the story of Martin and Christine. It is wartime, and Martin stubbornly refuses to relinquish his bourgeois life in his villa in the Grünewald section of Berlin, where he has surrounded himself with beautiful objects. Sitting at the dinner table with his sister Viktoria Luise, his business partner and sometime lover Angelika Rösch, and several guests, Martin declares, "I don't believe that a life without culture would have any meaning for me. … For me, form and content are inseparable. If the form is shattered, then the content is ruined for me too." "Those are just theories," Angelika presciently declares, "After this is all over, praxis will look much different."

If the frame story of *Film Without a Title* centers on the search for a new form for postwar cinema, this exchange between Martin and Angelika during the first flashback sequence signals that the framed narrative will also address the destruction of aesthetic value and in particular the problematic relation of form and content that was the cultural legacy of National Socialism. Throughout the film, the disturbed relation between form and content serves as a metaphor for social relations in the postwar period, and the quest to mend both sets of relations ultimately revolves around developing new aesthetic and social categories to accommodate them—as Angelika's comment suggests, new theories must be developed to explain a very different postwar praxis.

The filmmakers foreground problematic class and gender relations resulting from the Third Reich and World War II primarily through the relationship between Martin and Christine. At the beginning of *Film Without a Title*, Christine is a maid in the service of the beautiful and affluent Angelika, who runs an antiques business with Martin. When Angelika's apartment is bombed, she and Christine go to live with Martin and his sister, where Christine takes over as maid. In one of the film's famous jokes about aesthetic judgment, Christine undertakes a careful cleaning of the entire Delius household, including a scrub down with a brush and scouring powder of the beloved statue of St. Martin (see figure 2.1). Of course, her scrubbing virtually ruins the statue's antique aura; as Angelika explains, "Centuries-old dirt is called patina!" Christine, a devotee of the cinema, has no understanding or appreciation of antique art, a clear sign of her working-class status. By the same token, Martin's obsession with antiques is a mark of his fixation on the old and his inability to adapt to the new. As the film suggests, both positions will become untenable in the new social and aesthetic regime of the postwar period.

Despite their differences, Martin is immediately taken with Christine, comparing her to an antiquity: a fourteenth-century Madonna from the Upper Rhine area reproduced in one of his art books. When the two find themselves alone in the house during an air raid, they end up spending the night together, "et cetera, et cetera, et cetera," as the screenwriter's

Figure 2.1 "Centuries-old dirt is called patina!": Christine Fleming (Hildegard Knef) exhibits poor aesthetic judgment in *Film Without a Title*. Source: Deutsche Kinemathek.

voiceover returns to tell us. "Don't be so hasty and imprecise—are you afraid of censorship?," asks Willy Fritsch, but the screenwriter simply resumes his flashback narration with an account of the next morning's events. Martin's and Christine's tryst is discovered, much to the chagrin of Viktoria Luise and much to the amusement of Angelika, who utters one of the film's funniest lines for viewers in the late 1940s: "You can't think I'm going to waste my time worrying about the lost innocence of a young girl. All sorts of other values are going to ruin these days <*es gehen heutzutage ganz andere Werte zugrunde*>!"[23] With its references to postwar censorship codes and the loss of moral values in the Nazi period, *Film Without a Title* appealed here to the sophistication of jaded German audiences familiar with the limitations of representational practices when it came to reflecting adequately the reality of social relations.

The flashback narrative informs us that the inexorable class differences between Martin and Christine stand in the way of their developing relationship. As the pretentious Viktoria Luise informs Christine, "I only want to say this much: a respectable girl does not give herself to a relationship with a man whose social position basically excludes the thought of marriage. Perhaps you'll think about that." Unsure if Martin's intentions are entirely honorable, Christine hitches a ride out of Berlin, stopping only to save the St. Martin statue from the berubbled Delius house along the way. Her decision to rescue the statue suggests not only Christine's devotion to Martin, but also her new appreciation for the value of his beloved antiques. Christine returns to her family's farm, where she is not only protected from Allied bombs, but also well fed. Martin, meanwhile, who has lost his home and his possessions in an air raid, is ultimately drafted into military service and ends up as a soldier at the front, despite an injury that had kept him out of the army before.

In the final months of the war and in the early postwar period, the class roles of Martin and Christine are completely reversed. Introducing the trope of the *Heimkehrer* into *Film Without a Title*, Martin returns from the war a penniless soldier with nothing but the clothes on his back and a Persil laundry soap box containing his few meager possessions.[24] By contrast, the Fleming family farm is flourishing. The farm itself has become a haven for refugees from the East, and Christine's ruthless father acquires luxury goods such as a silver samovar for the price of an egg or two. When Martin arrives at the farm and eventually asks for Christine's hand in marriage, Christine's father refuses. Echoing Viktoria Luise's objection to the relationship, albeit in reverse, he now sees Martin as a gold digger and a social climber.

At the beginning of the film, the impossibility of the relationship between Martin and Christine was symbolized by Christine's misapprehension of patina—the essential formal quality that endowed the statue of St. Martin with its auratic aesthetic value. While Christine's rescue of the statue during wartime indicates her adjustment to Martin's aesthetic framework, now it is Martin who must adjust his aesthetic values in order to conform to the new social order. Ultimately, it is the resolution of a disturbed relation between form and content and the formulation of new aesthetic values that will pave the way for a resolution of the relationship between Martin and Christine.

III

From the outset of the film, the filmmakers in the metacinematic frame story discuss the unlikely nature of the relationship between Martin and Christine and its resultant incompatibility with the conventions of dominant cinema. Above all, they are concerned about how the story will end, a concern that escalates over the course of the film. In a lengthy sequence that comprises much of the last half of *Film Without a Title*, the author, the director, and the actor Willy Fritsch debate about the dramaturgical possibilities of adapting Martin's and Christine's relationship for the screen. Each man imagines a possible ending to the film, and each of these very different visions is enacted in an imagined scene. A lampoon of early postwar German cinema, this sequence clearly pillories the dichotomous choices of *Zeitfilm* and dream factory confection that were so strongly debated in film discourse in the late 1940s. At the same time, the sequence takes exception to the much-vaunted solution of the author as savior of cinematic legitimacy in the postwar period. Poking fun at the limitations of fiction film to represent social relations adequately, in this sequence *Film Without a Title* undermines the idea that the screenwriter has a more privileged relation to reality than other filmmakers. Ultimately the film suggests that it is up to the spectator to decide on the direction that German cinema should take, though the film does not harbor any illusions about the desires of most spectators around 1948.

The sequence begins when the author admits that he does not know how things ultimately turned out for the couple after Christine's father rejected Martin's proposal of marriage. "That is impossible—dramaturgically and generally speaking!," exclaims the director, "Antiques—that should be the title of the film. On the one hand those are the objects that set the plot in motion, and on the other hand they are the attitudes that prevent the two from finding happiness—the same bourgeois prejudices today and yesterday, only today they are reversed. This must all be brought to a

Figure 2.2 Decadent femininity: The New Woman Angelika Rösch (Irene von Meyendorff). Source: Deutsche Kinemathek.

forceful conclusion, but how?" The director proceeds to imagine a prototypical rubble film, in the style of *The Murderers Are Among Us*, replete with canted angles, black market trading, and an illegal bar filled with decadent characters, where Angelika earns her living as a chanteuse in the style of Marlene Dietrich in Billy Wilder's *A Foreign Affair*, also from 1948 (see figure 2.2). A poor *Heimkehrer*, Martin makes his way on foot in the pouring rain to Christine's village, only to find her in the process of marrying another man. Dissolve to a desolate berubbled landscape, as the director explains: "Rubble, rubble, the music swells, rubble, rubble."

The screenwriter interrupts to remind the group that they are out to make a comedy. Now it is Willy Fritsch's turn to imagine an ending for the film. "In reality, the two got together in the end, so a happy ending is completely logical. Martin becomes a farmer," Fritsch proclaims. Tellingly, in his version, Fritsch himself plays Martin Delius, while Hildegard Knef continues to play Christine Fleming. Fritsch imagines happy, sun-dappled scenes of Martin working in the fields, until one day Angelika arrives to buy Martin out of his half of their business. With this windfall, Martin is able to buy his own farm, and now Christine's father wants him as a son-in-law. Fritsch imagines a huge double wedding for the Fleming siblings with folk costumes and traditional dancing; he envisions the consummate *Heimatfilm*, a harbinger of the blockbuster success of Hans Deppe's *Schwarzwaldmädel* (Black Forest Girl, 1950) only two years later. As Fritsch declares, "This will please the people, it's what they like to see at the movies, and it's right." The sequence ends with the following exchange among the three filmmakers, an exchange that again pokes fun at Fritsch's outmoded star status:

Director:	That's impossible!
Fritsch:	No, your suggestion is impossible. Imagine the movie poster: Willy Fritsch in *Antiques*! *The King's Children* – now that's a title. They couldn't come together, but then they did after all ...
Director:	That's kitsch, Herr Fritsch!
Fritsch:	Excuse me!
Screenwriter:	Gentlemen! He's right, it just doesn't work. But your suggestion doesn't work either. If you are already taking your material from real life, then you should stick to real life in the end. May I make a very original suggestion about how we might find a good ending? On Sunday a wedding will in fact take place, that of Christine's brother Jochen. ... Then you can ask Martin and Christine how they finally reached their Happy Ending.

A dissolve to the wedding introduces the final scene of the film, where the three filmmakers question Martin, Angelika, and Christine about their story.

As they learn, Martin has resolved to quit the antiques business because he is upset by the exploitative postwar trade in antiques that takes advantage of starving people by offering small sums in trade for valuable family heirlooms. Using his training as a carpenter, he has started a new business building functional but aesthetically pleasing modern furniture for everyday use. Thus Martin has rejected his investment in the auratic value of centuries-old patina—along with his allegiance to an antiquated class structure—while still adhering to his belief in the necessary relation of form and content. By adopting the idea that "form follows function," Martin endows his aesthetic value with use value, thus creating a new postwar praxis, just as Angelika had predicted. In the world of the film, it is this resolution of the disturbed relation between form and content upon which Martin's restored masculinity, and thus his ability to begin a romantic relationship, is predicated. A *Heimkehrer* like Hans Mertens in *The Murderers Are Among Us*, Martin represents once more the passive, marginal male who has trouble reintegrating into the postwar social order, which is conspicuously marked by an upheaval of traditional class and gender distinctions. Fully emasculated by his stint as a common soldier, the loss of his livelihood, and the end of his bourgeois lifestyle, Martin's attempts at contributing to farm work on the Fleming estate are generally ridiculed. By building modern furniture, however, Martin mediates between the past and the present and ultimately contributes to the development of new postwar social and aesthetic structures at the same time.

Yet the happy ending suggested by the restoration of Martin's masculinity does not take place as such. Just like *The Murderers Are Among Us*, *Film Without a Title* notably sets up the expectation of marriage between the central couple, only to revoke this promise by the end of the film. Indeed, *Film Without a Title* goes so far as to imagine several fantasy versions of this wedding, even picturing them on screen, before finally ending with a real wedding—*not* between Martin and Christine, but between Christine's brother Jochen and his fiancée Helene. The fact that *Film Without a Title* does not end in marriage between its central characters suggests that the relationship between the aesthetic and the social consistently foregrounded in the narrative has in fact not been resolved. This point is underscored by the filmmakers' inability to find a resolution to either set of problems in the film's narrative or formal structures, both in regard to *Film Without a Title* and within the film's metacinematic frame story.

Learning how anticlimactic Martin's and Christine's story really is, the screenwriter—previously so vested in the relevance of trusting reality—utters the last line of the film, "That may be a nice little story straight out of real life, but it will never be a film—the difficulties begin already with the title. I can't even think of a title." As the wedding guests dance and sing, the closing credits begin on screen with the words, "You saw a film without a title." A shot of the three filmmakers is accompanied by the superimposed credits, "It did not star Willy Fritsch, Fritz Odemar, and Peter Hamel." In this closing credit sequence, then, the filmmakers essentially erase themselves from the text of the film, suggesting the futility of their quest to determine the course of the new cinema, and ironically undermining the emphasis that public discourse around 1948 placed on the role of the author as the creative visionary who will legitimate postwar German cinematic production.

IV

In *Film Without a Title*, the creative genius of the single (male) author stands in tension with the collaborative nature of popular commercial filmmaking in general and the demands of postwar German filmmaking in particular. Specifically, the film posits and then evacuates the narrative control of each of the male authorial figures (screenwriter, director, actor), exhibiting the limitations of this control when it comes to representing female experience and appealing to female spectators. In the process, *Film Without a Title* both displays and self-consciously parodies the fissures in the filmic text caused by the irreconcilability of male authorship with the representation of female subjectivity and desire.

Writing about the question of female authorship in relation to dominant cinema, Judith Mayne notes the reluctance of film critics to identify a "female tradition" within the history of cinema that would correspond to the canon of female authors uncovered by feminist literary critics. Mayne suggests that this reluctance is the result not simply of an absence of women in the history of filmmaking (though certainly women have had markedly less access to the means of film production), but also of "the peculiar status of authorship in the cinema":

> Particularly insofar as the classical Hollywood cinema is concerned, the conventional equation of authorship with the role of the film director can repress or negate the significant ways in which female signatures *do* appear on film. For instance, consideration of the role of the oft-forgotten, often-female screenwriter might suggest more of a female imprint on the film text; and the role of the actress does not always conform to common feminist wisdom about the controlling male gaze located in the persona of the male director ...[25]

Indeed, *Film Without a Title* presents a case in point. Notably, one of the film's screenwriters, Ellen Fechner, was female, a fact that was erased not only by the film's metacinematic narrative about authorship, but also in most of the publicity documents and the production history of the film.[26] As Mayne suggests, Fechner's imprint as screenwriter on *Film Without a Title* may account in part for the critique of male authorship developed by the film. Moreover, the film's female actresses also generally resist the controlling male gaze of the directors, both within the metacinematic narrative and in the film's main story. The fact that the female figures do not conform entirely to the fantasies of the male authorial figures within the film provides the substance of the narrative of *Film Without a Title*: it is thus the tension between "real-life experience" and male fantasy upon which the "failure" of male authorship is predicated.

This tension is articulated from the beginning of the film onward in several discrete ways. As we have seen, the male film authors in the diegesis struggle throughout the film to imagine the motivations and desires of the story's female characters, in particular Christine. In sequences such as the one analyzed above, the male authors attempt unsuccessfully to predict an ending for the story, in the process deploying an arsenal of filmic clichés and gendered stereotypes, male fantasies that fail to do justice to the ostensible "real life story" that *Film Without a Title* seeks to represent. Not only does the film lampoon conventional structures of cinematic objectification here, but, through its episodic and fragmentary narrative, it denies identification with any dominant male perspective or cohesive male gaze. Far from controlling the gaze, the authorial figures within the film's diegesis demonstrate, through their fantasy sequences, not only the constructed nature of objectified images of women in the cinema in general, but also their inability to imagine more appropriate modes of representation for the postwar period. In this sense, *Film Without a Title* bears witness both to the disintegration of outmoded genres and styles of filmmaking and to the problematization of conventional gendered structures of the gaze in the postwar period.

Second, the discourse of stardom parodied within the film's narrative provides a space through which to examine new star paradigms and new notions of gender embodied by postwar stars such as Hildegard Knef, in contrast to the prevailing fantasies attached to male and female stars in the Third Reich.[27] Willy Fritsch, himself a huge star under the Nazi filmmaking apparatus, is the film's primary mouthpiece for this discourse. Imagining himself into the role of Martin at several junctures in *Film Without a Title*, Fritsch envisions scenes between himself and Hildegard Knef/Christine that are comedic precisely because they wrench Knef out of her identification as the consummate star of rubble films into a paradigm of musical comedy and/or melodrama associated with the immensely popular Ufa style of the Third Reich's dream factory.

Indeed, it is Fritsch who first remarks on the potential of Martin's and Christine's story as material for a film. Caught within this old paradigm, however, he does so by remarking, "Could you imagine Söderbaum as Christine?," referring to one of the biggest stars of Third Reich melodrama, Kristina Söderbaum.[28] While Söderbaum represented the embodiment of Nazi womanhood, Knef was associated with a postwar split from Nazi ideals of femininity—as such, these two actresses seem to epitomize two irreconcilable star types, if not, in the final analysis, truly different gender types.

While much of its metacinematic narrative focuses on questions of authorship that pervaded public discourse on film in 1948, the subtext of *Film*

Without a Title addresses changing notions of stardom in the postwar period. Because stardom is so closely tied to both spectatorial desires and gender constructs, an analysis of postwar star discourse in *Film Without a Title* reveals much about the film's often conflicted representation of femininity.

V

Antje Ascheid has argued that female stars of Third Reich cinema rarely conformed to the Nazi ideology that situated woman as the Aryan ideal of wife and mother. Rather, "more often than not Nazi films featured actresses whose star images and screen characters struggled to incorporate National Socialist doctrine. In contrast, they referred back to those discourses operative in international cinema and Weimar traditions."[29] Ascheid shows that the most popular and successful female stars of Third Reich cinema in many ways directly contradicted Nazi ideals of femininity. Far from promoting "natural," Germanic femininity or motherly values, these stars were glamorous and cosmopolitan; moreover, many of them were not even German.

While postwar audiences continued to adore many of the biggest stars of the Third Reich,[30] they also began to look for new models of female stardom. Film viewers increasingly expressed a clear desire for new film actresses and film roles for women that would depart from the typical fare of Nazi cinema and prove more relevant to the concerns of the postwar period and the emergent postwar cinema. In the first year of its publication, 1949, the popular West German women's magazine *Film und Frau* published an article that addressed postwar spectators' identifications with and fantasies about film stars. Entitled "If You Were a Film Star …," the article begins:

> No doubt, dear reader, even if you have only been to the movies a dozen times in your life, as long as you liked the films and their actors, you have certainly asked yourself the secret question: If I were a film star, what role would I want to play? It is likely that you have asked yourself even more frequently (and even more secretly): If I could be a film actor, how or which one would I want to be? Would I want to be like Garbo, beautiful, fascinating, burning under ice? Like Marlene, crackling with sex appeal, or like Marika, a magical dancer and singer with paprika in her blood? Would I want to be a man like Clark Gable, the daredevil pursued by success, or a comedian like Rühmann, full of shy impudence? Or a grand nobleman like Birgel? Or, or, or?[31]

This passage is striking not for its construction of stardom or spectator identification per se, which follows a conventional model, but for the particular stars that are mentioned: a mixture of Hollywood stars (Greta Garbo, Marlene Dietrich, Clark Gable), two of whom are closely associated with German cinema of the Weimar period, and of Nazi cinema stars (Marika Rökk, Heinz Rühmann, Willy Birgel), none of whom had yet established strong careers in the postwar period. Absent from this textual catalog of famous stars are any of the new stars of postwar cinema.

However, as the article goes on to explain, it is precisely a new model of star that contemporary German audiences desired, a fact revealed by a 1949 survey conducted by the Allensbach Institute, which asked young German film spectators: "If you were a film actor, which roles would you most like to play?" According to *Film und Frau*, "The results are enlightening, even astonishing. Or shouldn't one be surprised that the top fantasy roles of girls and women were 'doctor' and 'farm girl,' while 'famous women,' 'society women,' 'demimondaines' and 'comedy roles' fell to the end of the list?"[32]

The desires and fantasy projections of female spectators expressed in the Allensbach poll and recounted in the *Film und Frau* article shed light on developments in the West German film industry in the early 1950s, when new female stars such as Marianne Hoppe and Sonja Ziemann were introduced and the doctor film and the *Heimatfilm* became two of the decade's most popular and top-grossing genres (a trend that is also foreshadowed in *Film Without a Title*). More importantly, the fact that doctors and farm girls constituted the most desirable film roles for German women in 1949 clearly implies the desire for a practical and unglamorous feminine cinematic ideal that breaks with both Nazi and Hollywood models of femininity. The traditional association of film stardom with these latter models is foregrounded in the text of the article, which, as mentioned above, lumps Nazi and Hollywood stars together, failing to name any new German stars of the postwar period.

The *Film und Frau* article is accompanied by images of stars Mae West and Rita Hayworth, paradigmatic for the model of stardom now rejected by postwar female spectators. It is also accompanied by several images portraying contemporary stars that female spectators might embrace, including a still of Hildegard Knef playing Christine in *Film Without a Title*. The caption of the photo reads, "Strangely, many women long to play a girl from the country these days. Does this reflect the desire to escape the misery of temporary housing and the rubble of our major cities? Although this role appears to be easy, it demands not only grace, but also capability and empathy."[33] *Film und Frau* suggests here one convincing and often repeated explanation for the shifting desires of postwar female spectators that ultimately led to the demise of the rubble film and the rise of the *Heimatfilm*—the demand for escapism in the cinema. In discussing Hildegard Knef's performance in the role of Christine in *Film Without a Title*, reviewers offered another interesting explanation for the new model of stardom that she epitomized:

> The actors in our postwar films are confronted with a strange psychological situation. Based on their earlier work <i.e. in Nazi cinema>, they have been typecast in certain ways, and now they are supposed to play completely new social types—soldiers returning from war, refugees, people who have

been bombed out, the destitute. However, the slightest bit of bad acting in playing these types will be painfully disruptive, because every viewer either is or was one of these types, or knows one of them very well. ... In this film, this kind of consideration mainly applies to Hans Söhnker. ... One has the feeling that he is always a few strikes behind the role, that he never really inhabits it. Though one actually believes his transformation from an aesthete art dealer into a practical carpenter, he is always somehow burdened by the nice, likeable young men he was accustomed to playing. All of this does not apply to Hildegard Knef. She has immersed herself in and internalized this Christine in such a natural way that her acting and her face remain unforgettable.[34]

Notably, this reviewer suggests that male stars of Third Reich cinema are out of place in postwar German cinema, because their star images are burdened with associations that taint their ability to portray new kinds of postwar characters. Jaimey Fisher has similarly analyzed the difficulty of casting male stars in rubble films, since the crisis of masculinity embodied by the *Heimkehrer* is irreconcilable with the "transcendent individuality" of the star, who generally upholds the social order.[35] By contrast, the 1948 reviewer compliments Hildegard Knef's natural and convincing portrayal of Christine as a character who embodied postwar femininity, echoing the ringing endorsements of Knef in postwar discourse as a star who breaks with the social types common to Third Reich cinema.

In its reimagination of postwar cinema for a new, largely female, postwar audience, *Film Without a Title* playfully comments on changing conceptions of femininity from the Weimar Republic through the Third Reich and into the early postwar period through the characters of Christine and Angelika and the two well-known stars who played them. In many ways a typical "New Woman," Angelika is a sexually and financially independent person, who, like her business partner Martin, has managed to hang on during the Third Reich to a lifestyle and livelihood begun during the Weimar period. Angelika wears pants, smokes and drinks, and possesses an irreverent sense of humor that is reflected in her pointed, witty comments throughout the film. By contrast, Christine represents a very different gender type. A domestic servant and farm girl, she is consistently associated with the home, the hearth, and the land, an association confirmed by Martin's comparison of Christine to a medieval Madonna representation.

While Angelika is in some ways the film's most likeable character, she is also represented as decadent and profligate, particularly during the postwar period, when she ruthlessly exploits not only the system, painting her car to give the impression that she works for the Allies, but also those selling goods on the black market, where she acquires antiques for a fraction of their worth. Clearly, Angelika represents a mode of femininity that is associated with the Weimar Republic and thus with the past, a point that is underscored not only by her continuing association with antiques, but also by Martin's final rejection of her. It is of course the woman Martin embraces instead, Christine, who embodies the new femininity, a gender profile that, paradoxically, looks suspiciously close to Nazi ideals of womanhood.

If Angelika is the film's New Woman, Christine represents the more traditional values of *Kinder, Küche, Kirche*—indeed, numerous scenes in the film depict Christine working in the kitchen, and she is also shown attending church. It should be noted, however, that Christine is not entirely the angel of the house, nor does *Film Without a Title* efface female sexuality altogether. As we have seen, several humorous lines in the film in fact make fun of emergent postwar sexual morality and the censorship codes that sought to control representations of female sexuality on screen. Not only does the film clearly depict Christine's overnight tryst with Martin as a sexual liaison, but we also learn over the course of the film that she has a sexual history as well: she came to Berlin to work as a maid after a scandalous relationship forced her to leave her hometown.

Just like *The Murderers Are Among Us, Film Without a Title* thus introduces a complicated female protagonist with a history and then fails to elaborate on that history, instead lapsing into tired gender stereotypes. Both films raise the specter of female experience, only to renege on the promise to enunciate it. In *Film Without a Title*, as in *The Murderers Are Among Us*, then, the limits of dominant cinema are reached in the attempt to represent female desire and subjectivity. While on the one hand *Film Without a Title* comments on these limits through its metacinematic narrative on film authorship, on the other hand it seeks to appeal to a contemporary female audience by catering to spectatorial desires, particularly in its choice of female stars.

Indeed, it is no accident that the complicated female protagonists in both *The Murderers Are Among Us* and *Film Without a Title* are played by Hildegard Knef. Even if Christine appears to embody Nazi ideals of womanhood in *Film Without a Title*, Knef, as we have seen, could not have been more different from the popular stars of Third Reich cinema. *Film Without a Title* depends on the contradictory femininity embodied by Knef's star aura and her strong identificatory appeal to postwar audiences in order to lend Christine a more multifaceted persona than is evident from the seeming flatness of this character.

A transitional film, *Film Without a Title* presents a metacinematic discourse on authorship that comments on the difficulties of creating new modes of cinematic representation in the postwar period. By employing a mixture of Third Reich stars (one of whom even plays himself) and postwar stars, the film presents a further commentary on changing styles of representation as well as changing gender ideals and social roles. At the same time, the film exploits both the humorous frame story and especially its mixture of stars to appeal to the widest possible postwar audience—a strategy that was apparently quite successful, given the immense popularity of *Film Without a Title* in 1948. In all respects, *Film Without a Title* seeks to have it both ways; as such, the film leaves virtually everything up to the audience: with a paradoxical title and an open-ended conclusion, the film presents a spectrum of star choices, representational possibilities, and social formations that cater to a wide range of spectatorial desires and expectations. Thus, *Film Without a Title* ultimately admits that spectatorship trumps authorship as a provisional solution to the problems of postwar cinematic representation.

Indeed, despite his well-known bluster about the failures of postwar spectators to adapt to new styles of cinematic production, writer-producer and artistic director Helmut Käutner continued to make films throughout the late 1940s and 1950s that were immensely popular with the largely female viewing public of postwar West Germany. As we shall see, these films catered to female audiences not only with popular star and genre choices, but also by continuing to explore questions of (female) authorship and spectatorship in often complex and interesting ways.[36] Nonetheless, many of the films Käutner had a hand in, like *Film Without a Title*, reached the limits of popular cinematic representation when it came to portraying female experience on screen. Meanwhile, in the transitional period of the late 1940s, other filmmakers continued to experiment with new strategies for solving the representational dilemmas of German cinema while also addressing the irreconcilability of male and female experiences during wartime and the early postwar period.

Notes

1. See Hans Helmut Prinzler, *Chronik des deutschen Films 1895–1994* (Stuttgart, 1995), 165–73. For statistics relating the number of ticket sales to population figures, see Elizabeth Prommer, *Kinobesuch im Lebenslauf. Eine historische und medienbiographische Studie* (Konstanz, 1999), 350–52. Statistics about number of cinemas and ticket sales do not exist for the Soviet zone for the year 1948.
2. The Bambi Film Prize (later renamed Media Prize) was founded in Karlsruhe in 1948 by the publisher Karl Fritz. In its early years, the prize was awarded each year to the most successful film of the year and to the public's most beloved stars. In 1948, in addition to *Film Without a Title*, film stars Marika Rökk and Stewart Granger were awarded Bambis.
3. "Spiel mit der Wirklichkeit. Der 'Film ohne Titel' im Marmorhaus," rev. of *Film ohne Titel, Neue Zeit Berlin*, January 25, 1948.
4. *Film Without a Title* was also successful abroad, winning second prize after Roberto Rossellini's *Germania Anno Zero* at the Locarno International Film Festival (the precursor to the Cannes film festival) in 1948, where Hildegard Knef won the best actress award for her role in the film.
5. Homo Ludens, rev. of *Film ohne Titel, Berlin am Mittag*, January 27, 1948.
6. Rev. of *Film ohne Titel, Rheinische Zeitung* (Köln), February 11, 1948.
7. Helmut Käutner, "Demontage der Traumfabrik," *Film-Echo* 5 (June 1947). Rpt. in *Käutner*, ed. Wolfgang Jacobsen and Hans Helmut Prinzler (Berlin, 1992), 113–14.
8. On the *Filmdichter* debate, see Thomas Brandlmeier, "Und wieder Caligari ... Deutsche Nachkriegsfilme 1946–1951," in *Der deutsche Film. Aspekte seiner Geschichte von den Anfängen bis zur Gegenwart*, ed. Uli Jung (Trier, 1993), 139–66.

9. For a discussion of one such contest, co-sponsored by the Berlin Film Club and the magazine *Revue*, see "Ernste Liebe im Preisausschreiben: Happy end wenig gefragt," *Der Spiegel* (June 19, 1948): 23. For another article advocating the participation of lay screenwriters in film production, see "Der Schrei nach dem Filmdichter," *Film und Frau* 1.11 (1949): 6.

10. *Rheinischer Merkur*, January 25, 1947, qtd. in Brandlmeier in Jung, *Der deutsche Film*, 148.

11. Several contributions to the forum on film authorship in *Der neue Film*, as well as the journal's original call for contributions, are reprinted in Johannes Hauser, *Neuaufbau der westdeutschen Filmwirtschaft 1945–1955 und der Einfluß der US-amerikanischen Filmpolitik. Vom reichseigenen Filmmonopolkonzern (UFI) zur privatwirtschaftlichen Konkurrenzwirtschaft* (Pfaffenweiler, 1989), 740–44.

12. "Um den deutschen Film. Ein Aufruf an alle Autoren!," *Der neue Film* 6 (1947): 1. Rpt. in Hauser, *Neuaufbau der westdeutschen Filmwirtschaft*, 740.

13. See Brandlmeier in Jung, *Der deutsche Film*, 155–56.

14. On the question of authorship, the *Autorenfilm*, and the New German Cinema, see Thomas Elsaesser, *New German Cinema: A History* (New Brunswick, NJ, 1989), esp. chapter 2, "The Old, the Young, and the New: Commerce, Art Cinema, and *Autorenfilm*?," and chapter 3, "The Author in the Film: Self-expression as Self-representation."

15. See Leonhard Fürst, "Was sollen wir drehen? Zur Frage der Stoffwahl im heutigen Filmschaffen," *Der neue Film* 9 (1947): 2. Rpt. in Hauser, *Neuaufbau der westdeutschen Filmwirtschaft*, 743.

16. According to Brandlmeier, Geis was a friend and associate of Bertolt Brecht during the 1920s, and he also worked closely with Karl Valentin and Marieluise Fleißer. See Brandlmeier in Jung, *Der deutsche Film*, 156. During the Third Reich, Geis wrote screenplays for such prominent films as *Der Mustergatte* (The Model Husband, 1938) and *Der Meineidbauer* (The Farmer's Perjury, 1941). In 1947, Geis achieved success with *Zwischen gestern und morgen* (Between Yesterday and Tomorrow).

17. Jacob Geis, "Zur Frage der heute möglichen Filmstoffe," *Der Neue Film* 7 (1947): 1. Rpt. in Hauser, *Neuaufbau der westdeutschen Filmwirtschaft*, 741. See also Brandlmeier, who discusses this passage in some detail. Brandlmeier in Jung, *Der deutsche Film*, 156–57.

18. Robert Shandley, *Rubble Films: German Cinema in the Shadow of the Third Reich* (Philadelphia, 2001), 159.

19. Wolfgang W. Parth, rev. of *Film ohne Titel*, sie, February 1, 1948.

20. On *Film ohne Titel* and its "renewed commitment to cinematic realism," see also Johannes von Moltke, *No Place Like Home: Locations of Heimat in German Cinema* (Berkeley, 2005), 73–78.

21. This conversation is quoted in its entirety by Shandley, *Rubble Films*, 153.

22. Hedwig Traub-von Grolman, rev. of *Film ohne Titel*, *Rheinischer Merkur*, February 7, 1948. Qtd. in Shandley, *Rubble Films*, 157.

23. Reviews mention the audience laughing uproariously at this line. See for example rev. of *Film ohne Titel*, *Film-Dienst* 1:4 (1948): n.p.

24. The Persil box suggests (quite satirically) that Martin has emerged from the war uncorrupted by Nazi values. Persil was the most famous brand of laundry detergent in the postwar period and an infamous sign of postwar reconstruction, both literally and figuratively. During the denazification period of the late 1940s, formal statements by known opponents of the Nazis vouching for an accused person's innocence were nicknamed "Persil certificates," indicating that the individual could be "cleansed" of any association with the Nazis. A virtual black market trade in such certificates arose during this period, perpetuating the already complex relation between victims and perpetrators in the postwar period and casting a problematic light on denazification procedures.

25. Judith Mayne, *The Woman at the Keyhole: Feminism and Women's Cinema* (Bloomington, 1990), 93. On the question of female authorship and women's cinema, see

also Kaja Silverman, "The Female Authorial Voice," in *The Acoustic Mirror: The Female Voice in Psychoanalysis and Cinema* (Bloomington, 1988), 187–234; and Anneke Smelik, "In Pursuit of the Author: On Cinematic Directorship," in *And the Mirror Cracked: Feminist Cinema and Film Theory* (New York, 1998), 28–55.

26. Fechner, who was born in 1895, was a successful author of popular novels, children's stories, and magazine and newspaper feature articles during the late 1930s and 1940s. She also co-wrote several successful screenplays during the Third Reich, including two Arthur Maria Rabenalt films, *Meine Frau Teresa* (My Wife Teresa, 1942), based on her own novel, and *Liebespremiere* (Love Premiere, 1943). Both films starred Hans Söhnker, who went on to play Martin in *Film Without a Title*. Fechner's last film in the postwar period was the comedy *Artistenblut* (Artists' Blood, 1949), which she co-wrote with Peter Hamel, who played the director in *Film Without a Title*. Fechner died in 1951. Not only has Fechner largely been written out of the production history of *Film Without a Title*, she is virtually absent in reference works on German film history.

27. For more on the postwar discourse about stardom, in particular the problematic transition of male stars from Third Reich cinema to postwar cinema, see Jaimey Fisher, *Disciplining Germany: Youth, Reeducation, and Reconstruction after the Second World War* (Detroit, 2007), 213–58.

28. As Antje Ascheid points out, Söderbaum has often been seen as the "quintessential Nazi star," and she was deployed by the Nazis as "the incarnation of German womanhood." The wife of notorious film director Veit Harlan, Söderbaum was particularly famous for her roles in Harlan's Ufa color melodramas *Die Goldene Stadt* (The Golden City, 1942), *Immensee* (1943), and *Opfergang* (The Sacrifice, 1944). See Ascheid, "Kristina Söderbaum: The Myth of Naturalness, Sacrifice, and the 'Reich's Water Corpse,'" in *Hitler's Heroines: Stardom and Womanhood in Nazi Cinema* (Philadelphia, 2003), 42–97.

29. Ascheid, *Hitler's Heroines*, 7.

30. For example, the winner of the 1948 Bambi for most beloved actress was, as noted above, the Third Reich star Marika Rökk.

31. "Wenn Sie ein Filmstar wären," *Film und Frau* 1.15 (1949): 10.

32. "Wenn Sie ein Filmstar wären," 10.

33. While naming Knef's ability as an actress, the text of this caption, oddly, fails to name either the film or Knef herself, who, despite being pictured, is in fact never mentioned anywhere in this two-page *Film und Frau* spread. Why, in an article that examines the changing status of stardom in the postwar period, is postwar Germany's biggest star—a star who so clearly embodied the qualities desired by contemporary female spectators—never discussed, but presented only as a surface image? In 1948, Knef had moved to Hollywood after negotiating a contract with David O. Selznick through the help of the famous Weimar producer and American émigré Erich Pommer, who had returned to Germany after the war as the chief film officer for the American occupation forces. That same year, Knef married Kurt Hirsch, an American film officer under Pommer, who was also Jewish. By 1949, Knef was represented in the German press at best as a Hollywood star, embodying the postwar desire for integration into the West, and at worst as a fraternizer and gold digger who had forsaken the German cinema. Thus it is not entirely surprising that *Film und Frau* would choose not to name Knef in this 1949 spread. For more on Knef's conflicted star sign, see my discussion of her in Wolfgang Staudte's *The Murderers Are Among Us* (1946) in chapter 1 and in Willi Forst's *The Sinner* (1951) in chapter 5.

34. "Spiel mit der Wirklichkeit," *Neue Zeit Berlin*.

35. Jaimey Fisher, *Disciplining Germany*, 220–21.

36. See my chapter 4, on Käutner's *Epilogue* (1950), and chapter 8, on his *Engagement in Zurich* (1957).

Chapter 3

GENDERED VISIONS OF THE GERMAN PAST: WOLFGANG LIEBENEINER'S *LOVE '47* (1949) AS WOMAN'S FILM

The final two years of the decade brought a new period of transition to the postwar German film industry. Economic and political developments such as the currency reform and the founding of the two postwar German states exerted a strong influence on the changing industry and on audience responses to contemporary cinema. As the licensing period ended and the deprivations of the immediate postwar years gave way to a new consumerism, viewers rejected the realism of the contemporary *Zeitfilm* and demanded more escapist fare. Despite the challenges presented by the new economy, the film industry continued to expand. Another 385 cinemas opened in the emergent Federal Republic in 1949, bringing the total number of movie theaters in the country to 3,360. Ticket sales increased to 467 million that year, an average of 9.5 visits to the movies for each West German. Perhaps most notably, domestic film production almost tripled, with sixty-two new features made in Western Germany in 1949.[1]

The swansong of rubble filmmaking and the first feature of the new Göttingen-based Filmaufbau production company, Wolfgang Liebeneiner's *Liebe 47*, premiered on March 7, 1949, at the Capitol-Lichtspiele cinema in Göttingen. *Love '47* was hailed by critics as one of the best and most profound postwar films.[2] Writing in *Die Zeit*, critic Gertrud Runge proclaimed, "There is no other film to date in which the postwar reality of Germany is evoked in such a merciless and thoroughgoing fashion. Filmaufbau Göttingen had the courage to reject radically the dream factory. ... The artistic seriousness and the uncompromising stance that underpin this film deserve high regard and elevate the film far above the average production."[3] The magazine *Der neue Film* declared, "When all of the so-called *Zeitfilm* productions have been long forgotten ... this film will still be current like hardly any other of the new German films. It is a masterpiece."[4]

Based on the first big postwar German literary sensation, Wolfgang Borchert's play *Draußen vor der Tür* (The Man Outside, 1947), *Love '47* tells the story of the soldier Beckmann, who is plagued by guilt for his actions on the front, and who returns from war and imprisonment to discover that his son is dead and his wife has left him for another man. In adapting *The Man Outside* for the screen, Wolfgang Liebeneiner, who had also directed the premiere run of the stage play, made substantial changes to Borchert's work. Foremost among these was the addition of a female character, Anna Gehrke, who exists in the original play only in nascent form as an unnamed figure called simply "the Fräulein." Drawing on a story by his co-writer Kurt Joachim Fischer, Liebeneiner transformed Borchert's classic work about male subjectivity in crisis to focus in equal measure on female subjectivity. *Love '47* features a new plotline, not part of the original play, that focuses on Anna's experiences on the home front, including the death of her husband and child, her life as a refugee, and the liaisons with various men that she carries on to maintain the material conditions necessary for her survival. Using an elaborate flashback structure, *Love '47* contrasts the stories of Anna and Beckmann in order to emphasize the radically different experiences of German women and men during World War II and the early postwar period.

Like *The Murderers Are Among Us*, *Love '47* endows its male and female characters with different visual languages and generic characteristics in order to explore their differently gendered histories.[5] A similar film in many ways, *Love '47* functions almost as a corrective to *The Murderers Are Among Us*: in contrast to the earlier film's Susanne Wallner, about whose history we learn virtually nothing, Anna Gehrke not only has a clearly delineated history, but she also narrates it herself. *Love '47*, like many of its predecessors, turned to female experience as a representational strategy, in this case as a way of adapting a well-known drama for the screen. The introduction of the character Anna Gehrke brought a new dimension to a play that had perhaps run its course in the public imagination.[6] This strategy, of expanding the play's narrow focus on male experience to address the larger issue of strained gender roles in the postwar period, was also certainly calculated to appeal to the still largely female cinema audiences of the day. However, while *Love '47* was a critical success, these audiences for the most part rejected it. In some ways both ahead of and behind the times, the film exhibited a certain non-synchronism with the demands placed on cinema around 1949.

The Göttingen premiere of *Love '47* was a gala event, which gave no indication that audiences would later come to reject the film. The premiere was attended not only by the film's cast and crew, but also by prominent politicians, by representatives of the Allied occupation, and by the mother of deceased playwright Wolfgang Borchert.[7] According to the periodical *Film-Echo*, "The audience at the premiere followed the film with rare attention. When it ended, there was a poignant silence followed by unanimous and sustained applause."[8] In the first week of its run in Göttingen, 18,000 viewers saw *Love '47* at the Capitol-Lichtspiele cinema, and two weeks after its premiere the highly acclaimed film was presented to politicians in a special screening at the parliament of Schleswig-Holstein.[9] In the next months, the film opened in other German cities to continued acclaim from critics.[10] However, by early April, cinemas were already beginning to limit their screenings of the film due to strong audience reactions against it.[11] Within a year, Love '47 was deemed a colossal flop, rejected by audiences and considered a total financial loss for Filmaufbau, which was forced to declare bankruptcy and reorganize its operations as a result.[12]

Explanations for the failure of Love '47 reveal much about the status of postwar filmmaking and changing audience tastes around 1949. While critics were virtually unanimous in their early praise of the film, several already predicted soon after the premiere that the film would not do well with audiences. The Catholic periodical Filmdienst der Jugend, which sought to rescue the film from commercial failure by devoting an unprecedented three pages to a detailed analysis of Love '47, noted just one month after the film's debut:

> "Love '47" is without a doubt in every regard the boldest, deepest, most stirring and ambitious postwar German film. Perhaps it even reaches toward the peak achievements of the French. Unfortunately the hesitant bookings of the cinema owners give cause to worry that it will find a more grateful audience abroad than at home, where we are so oversaturated with the pathetic stories of soldiers returning from war that the taste buds of the masses are too dulled to respond even to such a valid work of art, particularly with the hard realism of this plotline, which, after all, demands an attention span of two hours and twelve minutes (!)[13]

As this commentator suggests, the "hard realism" of Love '47, which emphasized not only the crisis of masculinity exemplified by the Heimkehrer, but also the theme of female sexual victimization during wartime and the postwar period, proved crucial to the film's popular failure with contemporary audiences.

I

Filmaufbau Göttingen was established with the eponymous program of building up the new postwar German film. Its founders, Hans Abich and Rolf Thiele, were both twenty-eight years old when their new production company received a license to begin operations from the British military government on October 12, 1946. Neither Abich nor Thiele had a background in filmmaking, but they saw this lack of experience as an asset that would allow them to bring a fresh perspective to the German cinema. Their lack of affiliation with the Nazi film industry, along with their youth and enthusiasm, helped them to receive not only a British license, but also the cooperation of the military government and the state cultural authority in constructing their new company. These qualities were also likely instrumental in Abich and Thiele's ability to secure the financing they needed to build from scratch a film studio with all the necessary infrastructure to begin producing films (including costumes and sets as well as technical equipment such as cameras and editing machines), a facility for sound synchronization and film duplication, and a marketing and distribution department.[14]

Eschewing the commercial aspirations of many of their contemporaries, Abich and Thiele hoped to produce challenging and artistic films that would address the problems of the day. In particular, they wanted to tap into film's capacity as an educational medium that could provide a critique of the Nazi past as well as a new image of German national identity for the future. In fact, they chose Göttingen as the site for their experiment in filmmaking not only because it had emerged from the war largely unscathed, but also because, as a university town, it boasted a successful theater and a cultural and intellectual environment that Abich and Thiele hoped to draw on.

Anticipating the manifestos that would shape the course of German cinema in the 1960s and 1970s, Abich and Thiele formulated several theoretical platforms that informed their filmmaking practice. The first of these, known as "Die Starnberger Denkschrift" (The Starnberg Exposé), was written shortly after the end of the war. Under the subheading "Film Against Film," the "Exposé" lays out the philosophy behind Abich and Thiele's proposal to help rebuild German cinema:

> The films that are produced in Göttingen must consciously turn away from the dishonesty of the dream factory and elevate to the subject of their art the real human being as a document of this world. The future belongs only to films that in this way become influential instruments of the time. This insight should be taken into account particularly in regard to foreign countries, since new German films are often seen there as the standard bearer of what is German par excellence. The new German film must make palpable the fact that the basic principles of our existence have been transformed. It must break through from appearance to reality. The self-purification of the German people can by all means be brought to expression through the medium of the film camera. To unleash its magical powers is the task of the new German film. Our Aufbau Film Production Company must place its work in the service of truth. We are not calling for the filmic representation of the bleak tragedy of the ruins, but rather it is imperative that we make clear that film, like any other art form, can and should follow intellectual, religious, and ethical imperatives. The contemporary film must seek answers to the pressing questions of our day: It must search for the reality of truth and the meaning of responsibility.[15]

Like other commentators who addressed the problem of postwar cinema at the time of the *Filmpause*, Abich and Thiele outlined their goals for postwar filmmaking in opposition to the deceptive qualities of Third Reich cinema, the "dishonesty of the dream factory."[16] Although their emphasis on film as an "influential instrument of its time" and on the "magical powers of the film camera" may paradoxically recall nothing so much as Nazi ideology, Abich and Thiele do seek to differentiate their program by stressing a humanist vision of cinema as a realist rather than illusionary medium that should be shaped by an ethical vision. Strikingly, they are immensely concerned in the "Exposé" with harnessing film as a means of improving the reputation of Germany abroad, a goal that Filmaufbau would continue to pursue throughout its existence and one that also looks forward to the New German Cinema.[17] While they appear to reject the trajectory of the rubble film explicitly, Abich and Thiele do propose to make films that address contemporary reality, putting on display the "transformation" of Germany during the reconstruction era and examining the question of responsibility for the crimes of the Nazi period.

In a second manifesto formulated in 1948, after Filmaufbau had finally been established, Abich and Thiele refined the goals outlined in the "Exposé." Their second platform maintains the humanistic emphasis of the earlier manifesto, while demonstrating a somewhat more sophisticated apprehension of the stakes of postwar filmmaking:

1. Devoting oneself to an artistically, culturally, and politically responsible film production today means undertaking the attempt to apply competently contemporary means to tame dangers born of our time.
2. Although this word has been overused to the point of distortion in the phraseology of the epoch that now lies behind us, it is precisely the image <das Bildhafte> that appears best suited to address people at their most pliable <bildsamste> moments.
3. We expect of the new film that it will open the playing field in regard to cosmopolitanism, which must be won back, albeit without doing away with the specificity of the German character. In this respect, we believe that the preparation of our production plans for the German initiative in Göttingen is consistent with the concerns of the re-education program of the occupation forces.
4. We do not want any paternalism vis-à-vis the audience in our films, but rather would like to cede the possibility of an individual resolution of the situation to each person as he leaves the movie theater, rather than sticking to the usual convention of majority rule.
5. The polyphonic formal qualities of film go against any artistic dogma, against any doctrine of cultural policy, and against the primacy of generic content. In the broad field between problem films and entertainment, the film of today can in our opinion be most ethically effective when it strikes a subtle tone. The obeisance to the so-called contemporary film <Gegenwartsfilm> that is so typical today generally overlooks the fact that we need not limit ourselves to our own times,

although we certainly must have knowledge of these times if we are to be qualified to make an artistic statement.[18]

Echoing many of the concerns addressed by commentators in the *Filmdichter* debate, Abich and Thiele stress here the necessity of finding a cinematic happy medium between the polarized options of the dogmatic contemporary film, obsessed with the problems of the day, and the generic confection that forsakes contemporary problems entirely.[19] Abich and Thiele emphasize both the influential power of film and the need to relegitimate cinema after its "distortion" by the Nazis; they point to film's didactic potential while also suggesting that the most effective films will accomplish pedagogical goals through subtle means. Finally, they maintain the objective of creating films that will promote productive spectatorship rather than "paternalistically" manipulating audiences, yet at the same time they declare their intention to help establish a new cosmopolitanism among audiences, an aim that they see as consistent with Allied re-education policy.

These lofty goals set the course for Filmaufbau's initial production schedule. The fact that the goals are contradictory should perhaps come as no surprise. Abich and Thiele were educated at university during the Third Reich, and though they had not been party members, neither had they expressed any particular opposition to the Nazi regime. They approached filmmaking in the postwar period as idealistic dilettantes who embraced the can-do spirit of the reconstruction period. At the same time, both men were devoted to the prospect of establishing a new critical filmmaking tradition in postwar Germany. Developing a vision of what this new film might look like, Abich and Thiele drew on often incongruous ideas. Of course, this kind of incongruity was quite characteristic of German filmmaking during the reconstruction period, which, as we have seen, was marked by a representational crisis that generated numerous inconsistencies and disparities, contradictions that also found their way into Filmaufbau's first production, *Love '47.*

II

As they began to plan their first production, Abich and Thiele needed to find experienced personnel who could help them to convey their nascent film program into practice. Wolfgang Liebeneiner, one of the most entrenched figures of the Third Reich film industry and a favorite of Goebbels, presented an odd choice for two young men eager to distance themselves from the cinema of the Third Reich and produce a film that would confront the Nazi past. Ironically, it was precisely their interest in contending with the Nazi past that Abich and Thiele used to justify their choice of Liebeneiner as the director for the first Filmaufbau production.

As Hans Abich recalled, "I suspect that as contemporaries of the time, we were all of the opinion that anyone who had the wherewithal to do it should be allowed to work off his share of the Third Reich, to pay his debt, and it was interesting for us to see how a man like him would deal with this topic."[20]

Liebeneiner had been the Head of Production at the Ufa studios during the final years of the Third Reich and one of only two filmmakers upon whom Goebbels bestowed the distinguished title "Professor of Film Arts" (the other was Veit Harlan). Originally a celebrated actor, Liebeneiner was most notorious for directing the 1941 film *Ich klage an* (I Accuse), which helped to make a case for the Nazi euthanasia program that aimed to murder disabled people and thereby to "purify" the Aryan race. Liebeneiner made entertainment films in a variety of genres throughout the Nazi period, and he became one of the Reich's most consistent and prolific directors.[21]

Over objections by the American military government, Liebeneiner was cleared by the British authorities in 1945 and granted a denazification certificate along with a license to work in the British zone.[22] In 1947, he was invited by the artistic director of the Hamburger Kammerspiele, Ida Ehre, to stage the premiere of Borchert's *The Man Outside*, an invitation that further cemented his postwar credentials.[23] Wolfgang Borchert himself was apparently pleased with the choice of Liebeneiner to direct the first stage performance of his drama, which had already met with great success as a radio play.[24] The two men consulted not only about the shape the stage play should take, but also about the possibility of a film version of the drama. Liebeneiner's stage production opened on November 21, 1947, one day after Borchert died of liver disease, at the age of twenty-six.[25] Like the radio play, the stage play was immensely successful. According to Gordon Burgess, "It was *the* overwhelming success of the postwar German theater. Between 21 November and the end of 1947, it was produced four times, and this was followed by thirty-two productions in 1948 and eleven new productions in 1949."[26]

Hans Abich and Rolf Thiele had already begun negotiations with Wolfgang Liebeneiner in 1946, when they embarked on a search for expert talent to help them execute their plans for Filmaufbau, and in 1947 he was engaged to direct their first production. Despite Abich and Thiele's determination to produce a new type of picture that would break with the mainstream, a determination captured by Filmaufbau's motto "Film Against Film," Liebeneiner seems to have had a free hand in determining the content of the movie he would direct. After his first screenplay, based on the true story of a Nazi soldier turned resistance fighter, was rejected by the British film office,[27] Liebeneiner sought permission to make a film version of *The Marquise von O.*[28] While he hoped that a film based on a classic literary text predating the Nazi period would pass the film censors more easily, Liebeneiner also chose Kleist's famous story precisely because of its connections to contemporary reality. In notes on his conversation with the British film officer in charge of the case about the contemporary implications of the project, Liebeneiner recalled, "I <told him> that the desire for peace, the necessity of coming to terms with rape, and the internal conduct of families all bear a strong connection to contemporary reality and would have a very important didactic function—above all the question of rape must finally be addressed in Germany."[29] When this project was also rejected by the British film office, Liebeneiner returned to the idea of filming Borchert's drama, and an adaptation originally titled *Love '48* was given the green light.[30] As we shall see, however, Liebeneiner did not entirely give up on the idea of making a film that addressed the problem of sexual victimization.

The turn to literary adaptation was an obvious strategy for a company like Filmaufbau, which was interested in prestige productions that might address the contemporary situation and appeal to sophisticated, middle-class audiences, while also contributing to the legitimation of cinema in the aftermath of National Socialism.[31] While literary adaptations had made up a large proportion of Third Reich productions, postwar filmmakers were slow to return to literature as a basis for the new cinema.[32] The very first postwar adaptation was a DEFA production, Georg C. Klaren's 1947 *Wozzeck*, based on Georg Büchner's drama. According to Jan-Christopher Horak, "Klaren's adaptation had much to offer, for it not only explored explanations for the Nazi-created debacle, but also positive traditions for the creation of a non-fascist, German national identity."[33] Adaptations of classic literary texts eventually became an important feature of postwar cinema in both East and West Germany, because, like *Wozzeck*, they allowed filmmakers to explore alternative traditions in German history, and because literary texts often gave sanction to allegorical statements about the contemporary situation.

Liebeneiner's *Love '47* was one of the first postwar films to adapt a contemporary German text to the screen. According to one commentator from the period, Kurt Lothar Tank, there were simply too few accomplished texts to adapt:

> The German film is lacking a <formal> language . ... There are a few German directors who know that. In a few postwar German films it flares up: in Käutner's films, in Barlog's *Where the Trains Travel*, in Liebeneiner's *Love '47*—but it isn't wholly there. The right language for the right film is missing, and it is missing because it can't be had without literature. It is for this reason that the contemporary German novel is so important. But precisely in the area of the contemporary novel, we have not moved beyond the rudiments.[34]

As Tank suggests, contemporary literature might provide the basis for a new filmic language, saving the German cinema from its representational crisis and thus offering a solution to the problem of the missing *Filmdichter*. Notably, Tank presents *Love '47* as an exception to this general crisis in filmmaking, an exception that is not coincidentally also a literary adaptation. Like Tank, most critics in the late 1940s hailed *Love '47* as an exceptional film.[35] Perhaps contrary to expectations, these critics did not balk at the extensive changes Liebeneiner made to Borchert's drama. In fact, Liebeneiner's interventions were generally praised as artistically successful and politically necessary, given the historical moment at which the film was produced.

III

Love '47 explores the legacy of Nazism in gendered terms. Like *The Murderers Are Among Us*, Liebeneiner's film situates its characters' quest to come to terms with their own guilt and responsibility for wartime deeds in a narrative that revolves around problems of gender and sexuality. Counterposing the female experience of the home front with the soldier's experience of war and the return from battle, Liebeneiner conveys Borchert's play about male subjectivity into a woman's film (see figure 3.1). Invoking female experience in order to critique male narratives, the film also features an unusual use of female voiceover and foregrounds the female gaze. At the levels of both form and content then, *Love '47* employs female experience and female agency as a strategy of

Figure 3.1 *Love '47* as woman's film: Anna Gehrke (Hilde Krahl) at the center and Beckmann (Karl John) on the margins. Source: Deutsche Kinemathek.

adaptation, thereby problematizing not only the limitations of Borchert's drama, but also the conventions of dominant cinema. The character of Anna Gehrke thus reveals the connections between the postwar gender crisis and the postwar representational crisis once again: she functions both as a conduit for introducing gender conflicts into the film and as a mechanism for relegitimating German cinema.

A kind of tour de force of postwar filmmaking strategies, *Love '47* unequivocally brings to the surface both the social problems and the representational problems that underpin so many early postwar films. The film's narrative addresses head on the incommensurability of male and female experiences of the war, the strained gender relations of the postwar period, the emasculation of men and the "masculinization" of women, the decimation of the family in the Third Reich, and the need to reformulate gender roles and family structures for a new postwar social order. Importantly, the film also tackles the problems of adultery, prostitution, and sexual victimization. At the same time, *Love '47* addresses Nazism much more explicitly than other films of the period, with direct mentions of "Hitler," the "Führer," the "Nazis" and their "six million" innocent victims, as well as myriad references to the consequences for various characters of subscribing to Nazi ideology.[36]

While *Love '47* displays neither the same degree of formal gaps and inconsistencies as *The Murderers Are Among Us* nor the same metacinematic thematization of these inconsistencies as *Film Without a Title*, the dilemmas of artistic representation in postwar Germany are nonetheless very evident in the film. Like *The Murderers Are Among Us*, *Love '47* endows its male and female protagonists with different generic codes, and their stories are presented using very different formal and stylistic devices. Like *Film Without a Title*, *Love '47* is told through a complicated series of flashbacks, and it contains at least one key metacinematic moment that sheds light on the film's own construction. While *The Murderers Are Among Us* neglects the history of its female protagonist and *Film Without a Title* portrays the failure of male narrative authority, *Love '47* attempts to correct both of these problems by allowing its female lead to speak for herself and to narrate her own history.

One 1949 reviewer described the premise of *Love '47* this way:

> A man and a woman who had never met during their lives coincidentally end up at the same place on the riverbank, planning to jump in the water … Strangely, the voice of conscience has not been fully silenced yet in either of them; both still hold onto an image of the human being as he ought to be. Behind their backs, however, Death grins. A portly victor of war, he is already sure of his sumptuous prey. Liebeneiner's artistic concept opposes these two fates using film flashbacks: first, the war and its aftermath shown completely from the woman's perspective, and then from the viewpoint of the man, both of whom are entangled in guilt and suffering, and both of whom are conscious of personal responsibility.[37]

As this reviewer suggests, the film literally presents a "She Said, He Said" account of the war and its aftermath. The first hour of the film encompasses Anna Gehrke's narrative, while the second hour, which hews closely to Borchert's drama, features Beckmann's story.

A largely dialogue-driven film, Love '47 is for the most part visually unremarkable. The film begins with a close-up of Death, embodied by a corpulent man in a tuxedo and top hat. Death observes a man and a woman, standing a short distance apart on the riverbank, and comments that they are a timely pair of lovers, "two water corpses." Walking through a field of huge bells, all of them broken and silenced by bombs, God now arrives on the scene, an old man dressed in black. God introduces himself to Death ("I am the God that no one believes in any more"), and Death presents himself in turn, explaining that he has gotten fat as a result of brisk business from all the recent wars. A shot of the swirling waters of the Elbe brings us to the river's edge, where the film's protagonists meet and reveal their mutual intention to jump in and commit suicide. God and Death, seeing that the two have found one another, retreat through the berubbled landscape of Hamburg, agreeing to give them some time to carry out their intentions or change their minds (Death: "Together, death is easier"; God: "Together, life is easier").

A medium shot now frames the film's protagonists. Repeating the words of Death, "Together, death is easier," Beckmann (Karl John) begins a conversation with Anna (Hilde Krahl) that sets the plot of the film in motion. "Together, everything is easier," Anna responds. "During the war, one was never alone," says Beckmann. "But we were!" retorts Anna, whose point is underlined by a close-up that reveals her angry gaze at Beckmann. "We?" says Beckmann meekly. "We women, I mean," replies Anna, emphasizing already in the film's opening sequence the differences in men's and women's experiences of the war.

Following this opening sequence, Anna begins to narrate her own personal history in an extended voiceover that sutures together a lengthy series of flashbacks to the past. These are regularly punctuated by shots returning us to the present time at the river's edge, and then to Anna's apartment, where she and Beckmann repair to smoke and eat as they listen to one another's stories. Triggered by the sound of bells ringing in the distance, a dissolve ushers in the first flashback of the film, which creates a parallel between Anna's suicide pact with Beckmann in 1947 and her wedding to Jürgen Gehrke eight years earlier. Looking back on the wedding, which took place shortly before Germany's invasion of Poland, Anna characterizes herself as very "naïve and stupid" to have believed in the future and not to have questioned or criticized the direction the Nazis were taking the country under the rubric of "German values."

Describing how devastated she was when her husband was called up for military service, Anna recalls: "I was so miserable. And then I heard him talking <to a neighbor in the garden> and he wasn't miserable at all. He was even a little bit happy about it. *A typical man! ...* That's when I realized it. It may be true that women worshipped the Führer, but the war was definitely made by men. The world is ruled by men, and they have left their mark on it." While Anna was absorbed in love, marriage, and happiness in the private sphere, her husband saw the war as an adventure, a chance to climb mountains in new parts of the world. Thus, Anna portrays herself and her friends and family as *Mitläufer*—fellow travelers who paid little attention to political events and whose ingenuousness regarding the rise of fascism led to widespread suffering and pointless deaths. To be sure, Anna's story focuses solely on the suffering and death of ethnic Germans, while Jewish victims of the Nazis remain faceless in the film. However, though Anna's version of history emphasizes gendered experience and blames men for the ravages of war, she also acknowledges women's role in the rise of fascism by pointing to their adoring worship of Hitler.

Beckmann responds to Anna's narrative by telling her that he suffered too—not only did he lose his knee in Russia, but he missed the birth of his son, an event that we see portrayed in flashback. "You see! And your wife was left completely alone," Anna replies. Here, in a remarkable display of narrative and visual authority, Anna's vision literally takes over Beckmann's flashback. As her voiceover recalls the uniquely difficult female experience of giving birth during wartime, a dissolve replaces the image of Beckmann's wife in the hospital with one of Anna after the birth of her daughter. Universalizing women's wartime experiences, this dissolve also foregrounds Anna's discursive control of the film's visual language, which she wrenches away from Beckmann. *Love '47* thus gives primacy to Anna's version of history, situating her as the subject of the gaze and also as the enunciator of the film's narrative at both the thematic and the formal level of the film.

Like the postwar Hollywood films discussed by Kaja Silverman and the rubble films analyzed by Jaimey Fisher, *Love '47* presents another example of the "cinema of dispersion," which decenters the marginal male protagonist (notably a *Heimkehrer* once again) and displaces his authority onto the female character.[38] Liebeneiner's film thus reflects both the inverted gender roles and the inverted cinematic codes resulting from the crisis of masculinity and loss of belief in the dominant fiction that characterized society and cinema after the historical trauma of World War II. However, the film does not just strive toward re-establishing male authority and righting the gender inversions it stages. Rather, *Love '47* radically foregrounds both the limitations of male experience and the turn to female experience as a strategy through which to recover the ability to tell stories in postwar cinema.

When Anna explains that her husband went missing and that it took two years for her finally to learn that he was dead, Beckmann tries again to compare his experience to hers. Telling Anna that some men returned home only to wish they were back in Russia, after seeing the berubbled home front and realizing how futile the war had been, Beckmann reveals the outlines of his own story as a *Heimkehrer*: he returned from two years in a Siberian prisoner-of-war camp to discover that his house was destroyed, his son had been killed, and his wife, falsely believing that Beckmann was dead, had left him for another man. Again, Anna, who lost her own daughter in a train accident during the war, has little sympathy for Beckmann and insists on the incomparability of male and female experiences of the war: "And who was there for your wife when the house collapsed and your son was killed? Who was with her when the bombs fell?"

Delving deeper into her personal history, Anna further accounts for women's unique experience of suffering during wartime and the postwar period by detailing their difficult and multifarious experiences of adultery, prostitution, and sexual victimization. In a series of flashbacks, she describes her liaisons with men upon whom she was forced to rely for her own physical and psychological survival. A refugee from the East, Anna received help along the way from a series of men in return for sexual favors, which she recalls with a mixture of shame and defiance. While the end of the war brought her some hope, Anna was again forced to rely on sexual relationships with men during the postwar period in order to find work, food, and housing. Although she asserts her own agency in entering into these relationships, some of which even brought her pleasure, the fact remains that, as a woman, Anna must rely on selling her body in order to survive. Utterly disillusioned by how little things have changed in postwar Germany, Anna explains to Beckmann how she came to the brink of suicide:

> As I've already told you, I'm fed up with life. No hope, no goal, no prospect that things will get better. You see, it's hell being here alone ... and feeling useless, because there are too many people here ... and futile, because no one knows why we're here, no one can use us women, because there are too many of us, except when they can use us after all—to *abuse* us. But that's no life. And getting married in order to be provided for—how is that any different? I'm familiar with that kind of misery—no thanks! And I lack the belief to become a nun ...

Commenting on the postwar "surplus of women" and locating marriage along with prostitution on a continuum of sexual exchange, Anna articulates here the utter degradation of women through sexual victimization and their inability—even in the postwar period—to achieve economic independence. A dissolve from Anna's face to a shot of the Elbe's swirling waters, which emphasizes the equation of sex and Anna's suicidal impulse, brings us to the end of her narrative and back to the present day. Alluding to the therapeutic value of narrating traumatic events, Anna thanks Beckmann for listening to her story.

Telling her that he has "made a big mistake" by focusing exclusively on his own (male) trauma, Beckmann thanks Anna in return, and begins to narrate his own story. "I feel guilty. I have murdered and I was murdered,"

Beckmann declares, explaining that his command resulted in twelve unnecessary deaths of soldiers in his unit. Like Mertens in *The Murderers Are Among Us*, Beckmann is haunted by uncontrollable dreams and visions, including images of the wives and children of the dead soldiers on his conscience, demanding retribution for their husbands' and fathers' deaths. Beckmann's visions are made worse by the fact that his commanding officer, who is prospering in postwar Berlin, refuses to acknowledge any guilt or responsibility for wartime events, instead laughing at Beckmann's "weakness" and questioning his masculinity.

While Anna's narrative is characterized by a clear-eyed and realistic portrayal of the traumas of war and the disappointments of the postwar period, relayed in a dramatic series of flashbacks that cover approximately eight years of time, Beckmann's story is conveyed in very different visual and generic terms. Focusing on only a few days after his return to Germany from Siberia in the present time of the narrative, 1947, Beckmann recalls his attempts to come to terms with his guilt and to find a place for himself in a vastly changed postwar society. Thus, Beckmann's story centers precisely on the postwar crisis of masculinity and the representational problems it occasioned. Unlike Anna's (melo)dramatic story, which is conveyed in a realist visual language, Beckmann's story is related primarily through a series of four contrived filmic devices, which draw on conventions from different moments of German cinematic tradition, in particular Expressionism and the fantastic. At times, *Love '47* almost seems like two different films strung together. The pronounced stylistic differences between the two halves of the film function not only as a way of highlighting gender differences, but also as a means of examining different strategies of cinematic representation at a moment when the traditions of German cinema had been so thoroughly delegitimated.

The first episode of Beckmann's story occurs when he visits his commanding officer in order to "return to him the responsibility" for wartime events, narrating to him and his family the guilt-induced traumatic dream-vision that he cannot shed. To the tones of the "Badenweiler Marsch" and other Nazi military music, Beckmann's vision is portrayed in an Expressionist visual language that recalls Fritz Lang's *Der müde Tod* (Destiny, 1921), and involves not only ghostly images of soldiers' wives and children and rows of graves, but also images of the officer himself banging with long, prosthetic arms on a xylophone made of bones (see figure 3.2). Unsure how to respond to Beckmann's grotesque vision, the officer finally breaks out in laughter, suggesting that Beckmann take this delectable "comedy routine" to the cabaret.

Following the officer's suggestion, Beckmann heads to a cabaret, where, after a few shots of schnapps, he musters up the courage to approach the director about an engagement. When the director gives Beckmann the chance to perform, this second scene develops into a metacinematic discourse on postwar entertainment. Beckmann's performance features a well-known popular song from the Third Reich,

Figure 3.2 Beckmann's grotesque vision of the German past. Source: Deutsche Kinemathek.

"Die tapfere kleine Soldatenfrau" (The Brave Little Soldier's Wife), sung with intense irony and inventive new lyrics as a comment on his own personal history. When the song is immediately rejected by the audience, the cabaret director escorts Beckmann offstage:

Director:	Not enough *esprit*—you're missing a certain discreet and intimate eroticism. At your age you still lack that certain carefree sangfroid … art needs to mature.
Beckmann:	Art … art?! This is the *truth*!
Director:	You see? That's the problem. It's the truth. But truth has nothing to do with art. You won't get too far with truth. You'll only make yourself unpopular that way. Where would we be if suddenly everyone wanted to tell the truth? Who wants to hear the truth these days?

The comments of the director could pertain directly to *Love '47*—itself an unabashedly head-on attempt at truth telling that foregoes any carefree "eroticism" in favor of a damning representation of men's emasculation and women's sexual victimization—and indeed, these comments were echoed by reviewers of the film when addressing its failure to find success with audiences.

Beckmann's postwar sojourn continues in a third episode when he sets out to visit his parents. Ringing at the door of their apartment, he is greeted by a strange woman who tells him that his parents now reside in "Chapel Five." In the darkly comic dialogue sequence that follows, the woman relates to Beckmann in highly critical terms the fact that his flag-waving parents have committed suicide: "You see, the old Beckmanns couldn't go on. They really went for broke during the Third Reich. Your father was a real fierce Nazi, as you must know. When it was over with the brown boys, it was like he was missing a tooth. And that tooth was rotten. I'll say that—it was really rotten to the core. … So <your parents> went ahead and de-Nazified themselves once and for all."

With this bitter discovery, Beckmann's flashback ends and we return to the present day. Refusing until the end to allow that Beckmann's suffering is worse than her own, Anna responds to his story:

> Why don't you do something about it? After all, you're a *man*! This is a challenge, a duty. … There's no reason to despair when <things go> a bit worse for a while. At least not for *a man*. But look at us! Are we still women? In such hopeless surplus? We're not women anymore, but numbers: Labor Deployment, Service Obligation, Women's Battalion. And those who don't want to participate must sell themselves—legally or illegally. But *you* have a duty. Make things better! Change the world.

Referring again to the film's themes—the crisis of masculinity, the surplus of women, women's economic dependence, and the pervasive problems of prostitution, adultery, and sexual victimization—Anna suggests that the hope for a new postwar social order must come from men, as she entreats Beckmann to overcome his marginal masculinity in order to work actively for change. Confirming the implication that women have little social or political agency in the public sphere, Anna retreats to the kitchen to cook Beckmann a meal and tells him to take a nap in her absence.

The final part of the film is comprised of a lengthy, fantastical dream sequence in which Beckmann's traumas are desublimated, allowing for a final resolution. Displaying an array of avant-garde symbols, including oversized clothing and figures, a giant chessboard, and the Elbe impersonated as a female figure with large eyes, as well as film techniques such as montage, split screen, and superimposition, this sequence focuses on Beckmann's emasculation through both his wife's desertion and Anna's aggressive attentions, as well as his rejection by God, Death, and the Elbe. While Anna works through the traumas of recent history by telling her story to Beckmann, it is striking that Beckmann's work of mourning is accomplished not through his narrative, but through his dream. *Love '47* thus exhibits not only competing male and female narratives about the traumas of the Nazi past and the struggles of the immediate postwar period, but also differently gendered means of working through those traumas.

IV

In *Love '47*, Anna Gehrke is granted a remarkable degree of access to the enunciative discourse of the filmic narrative. This access is made manifest, on a formal level, by her extended voiceover, mastery of the gaze, and authority in enunciating the film's elaborate flashback structure (she even wrenches away control of the diegesis from Beckmann at times), and, on a thematic level, by her narration of her own story and her constant disputation of Beckmann's version of events. Anna not only participates in the discursive production of meaning in the film, but she also uses her access to speech to articulate the truth about her experiences as a woman during the Third Reich and the postwar period, in particular her experiences of sexual victimization—and thereby to enunciate a critique of the patriarchal structures that have contributed to her oppression.

Like the postwar films analyzed by Silverman and Fisher, *Love '47* inverts traditional gender roles and overturns conventional aural and specular codes that situate man as subject and woman as object of discourse. Not merely a default dispersion of the narrative authority abdicated by the marginal male protagonist onto the female character, however, *Love '47* self-consciously deploys female experience as a strategy for investigating the Nazi past and the social and representational problems of the postwar present. While both Anna and Beckmann suffer from the traumas of history, their differently gendered modes of dealing with the past and present are figured by their different ways of speaking and seeing. Pitting female experience against problematic male experience, the film suggests that telling women's stories must constitute a central facet of the quest to relegitimate the cinema in postwar Germany.

As I have emphasized, Anna tells her own story in her own voice in *Love '47*. By placing her at the very center of its regimes of sound and image, Liebeneiner's film thus goes far beyond the inversions staged by other postwar films to foreground female agency and to grant spectators a unique degree of access to female subjectivity via female voice and gaze. Notably, Anna's narrative is predicated on the presence of a male listener: the rhetorical style of her story, which emphasizes the uniquely different experiences of men and women, requires a man whom she can convince of her standpoint. Anna virtually holds Beckmann captive, forcing him, and by extension the male spectator, to listen to her story, interrupting him when he tries to speak, and enforcing her interpretation of her story on him. This strategy yields success: by the end of Anna's narrative, both characters have achieved some degree of resolution. Anna acknowledges that her self-guided talking cure has been therapeutic, and thanks Beckmann for listening, while Beckmann thanks Anna in return for enlightening him about women's wartime and postwar experiences, admitting that he has "made a mistake" by focusing so much on male experience and failing to understand women. By contrast, as noted above, the resolution of

Beckmann's story comes not through his mastery of authoritative speech, but rather through his dream. To the extent that *Love '47* restores Beckmann's marginalized masculinity, then, it does so by moving outside the narrative codes of the film into a dream world, a gesture that underscores the film's inability to right the gender inversions it exhibits.

If *Love '47* displaces conventional structures of voice, its inversion of the traditionally gendered gaze is even more visible and explicit. Like Susanne and Hans in *The Murderers Are Among Us*, Anna and Beckmann in *Love '47* literally see differently, and the film employs several strategies to underscore this point. From the outset of the film, Beckmann wears a large pair of goggle-like glasses, which obscure his eyes almost entirely. In a pivotal scene, as Anna and Beckmann return to her apartment, she asks him why he wishes to commit suicide:

> Beckmann: It's because of my conscience—and my feelings of responsibility.
> Anna: You don't look like a murderer. What sort of strange glasses are those?
> Beckmann: My gasmask glasses—the lenses of the other pair were shot out.
> Anna: I hope you'll take them off when we get upstairs.
> Beckmann: I'm completely helpless without my glasses.
> Anna: Really? Well that makes me feel much better about things.

Beckmann's strange glasses are a symbol of his war wounds as well as a clear signifier of his conspicuous passivity and lack. If "to see is to desire" in the cinema, Beckmann's desire is already impaired by these glasses, which impede his mastery of the gaze.[39] When Anna and Beckmann enter her apartment, she removes the glasses, stripping Beckmann of the last vestiges of his masculinity and functionally castrating him (as the dialogue clearly suggests). As Beckmann strips to the waist and changes into the clean clothes Anna has offered, she watches him intently. Just then, the landlady knocks at the door, bursting into the apartment and catching Anna in the act of gazing at the half-naked Beckmann. Underlining the authority and eroticism of Anna's gaze, the landlady comments, "The situation is unambiguous!"

Love '47 clearly reverses the conventional structure of the gaze here: not only is Anna a "woman who looks," but hers is a sexualized gaze, and Beckmann is its object.[40] The reversal is underscored in this scene by the fact that Beckmann has been stripped of his glasses, and therefore of vision and the ability to desire altogether. Indeed, Beckmann's vision is problematized throughout the film, both through the device of his strange, gaze-obscuring glasses, which elicit repeated comments from all of the characters Beckmann encounters, and also through the fantastical dreams and visions that haunt him.

Notably, Anna does not return Beckmann's glasses to him until the final sequence of the film, after he has woken up from his lengthy bad dream. The film's closure is predicated on a return to traditional gender roles, suggesting like so many postwar films that the traumas and guilt produced by the war and the Nazi past can be overcome by "righting" the disturbed gender relations and solving the sexual problems of the present. As in other films of the period such as *The Murderers Are Among Us*, it is only through the agency of the woman that the man is "cured" of his problems, which are so often figured by his disturbed vision. Thus Anna returns to the kitchen to cook Beckmann a meal; by presenting him with the meal and with his glasses, Anna restores Beckmann's symbolic masculinity.

In this final scene, Anna and Beckmann decide to postpone their suicide pact. As Anna puts it, "We're both at rock bottom. But now you have someone and I have someone too. Why do we need to change the world? Let's start with ourselves. I'll help you and you help me." Just as the protagonists' individual stories have focused on the necessity of taking responsibility for the crimes and the suffering of the past, Anna and Beckmann now agree to take responsibility for one another in the present. When Beckmann grasps Anna's suggestion of a relationship, he utters the film's last line: "Thank you."

While the end of the film thus suggests a union between the two characters, *Love '47*, like *The Murderers Are Among Us* and *Film Without a Title* before it, does not end with a wedding. As Robert Shandley notes, "Even its 'happy ending' is unconvincing, after the film has revealed all of the burdens with which this relationship will have to deal."[41] Thus, *Love '47* ends with a literal and symbolic withdrawal into the private sphere, foreshadowing the renewed emphasis placed on domesticity and traditional gender roles in the Federal Republic in the 1950s, as well as the difficulties this return to family life caused for many men and particularly women.

Having returned Beckmann's glasses to him, and thereby restored his mastery of the gaze, Anna has only to renounce her own visual and auditory authority to ensure the film's closure, yet this does not entirely take place. In the film's final moments, Anna turns on the radio, authorizing a diegetic soundtrack that complicates our expectation of the swelling music that would indicate a happy ending. The film's final shot shows us Anna's face and look, while we see Beckmann only from behind, his face and eyes obscured from Anna's view and ours.

V

Love '47 represents one of the most sustained attempts in postwar filmmaking to examine the differences between male and female experiences of the Third Reich, World War II, and the postwar period. In terms of both form and content, the film sought to address the largely female audiences of the day by foregrounding the narrative authority of Anna Gehrke, who tells her own story while taking control of the visual and auditory codes of the film. Not surprisingly, the advertising campaign and publicity documents that accompanied the film emphasized Anna's role, an emphasis that was echoed by many reviewers.

Advertised as "Ein Film der Frauen unserer Zeit" (A Film of the Women of our Times), *Love '47* was presented by the production company Filmaufbau as a film about Anna Gehrke.[42] Not only do the press documents for the film downplay the fact that *Love '47* is an adaptation of Borchert's *The Man Outside* (a likely response to accusations of nihilism against the play), but they minimize references to Beckmann's role in the film altogether. The film program for *Love '47* is a case in point.[43] Its front cover features a blow-up of Anna Gehrke, with a much smaller image of Beckmann lurking in the background. The program's back cover presents a large head shot of Anna, while the inside photo spread contains six pictures of Anna and only two of Beckmann. Moreover, not only does the program recount the film's plot from Anna's perspective, but it also elides Beckmann's half of the story altogether, neglecting to even mention his name.

Female reviewers in particular also focused on the story of Anna Gehrke, lauding Liebeneiner's adaptation of Borchert's drama into a film that specifically addressed women. In *Die Zeit*, Gertrud Runge described *Love '47* as a kind of "musical counterpoint" of male and female voices, which "defuses the nihilism of Borchert's original, but remains very far from the erotic kitsch of the typical happy ending."[44] In the same newspaper, Erika Müller analyzed *Love '47* in the context of the growing anti-nuclear protest movement spearheaded by women, arguing that "it is a film which speaks specifically to women, for it is a clarion call against war and inhumanity."[45] The women's magazine *Film und Frau* agreed:

> "Love 1947" is, according to its original conception, an adaptation of Wolfgang Borchert's "The Man Outside"—and that is a man's play, bent on destruction from the first scene to the last. But Liebeneiner added a new component to the material, which is so strong that it became a woman's film: a woman outside, that is Anna Gehrke. To those who would condemn the women of today as soon as they err, she counters: You are also to blame for the fact that women could end up this way![46]

Like the publicity documents that doubtless shaped this article, *Film und Frau* relates the plot of *Love '47* in a lengthy two-page spread about Anna's story that dispenses entirely with Beckmann's half of the story; the article's plot summary also focuses specifically on the critique enunciated by Anna in the film.

The publicity documents for *Love '47* clearly reflect an attempt to appeal to female spectators, drawing them into the film through an identification with the character of Anna, and distancing the film from its literary precursor, Borchert's *The Man Outside*. Judging from the positive responses to the film articulated by female reviewers, the producers' aspiration to appeal to women found some resonance. Yet if *Love '47* made such an explicit appeal to female spectators, one that was lauded by female critics and women's magazines alike, then why did the film ultimately fail to meet those spectators' expectations?

VI

The failure of *Love '47* with audiences, which has been the subject of extensive critical treatment since the late 1940s, can be attributed to a combination of economic, political, social, and aesthetic factors.[47] A look at these factors can tell us much about the state of popular filmmaking at the end of the decade, when the postwar German cinema underwent a decisive series of transitions. These transitions came about in part as a result of the economic and political developments that brought an end to the initial period of occupation. Foremost among them was the currency reform, enacted on June 20, 1948, which introduced the new German Mark to the Western zones. Putting a symbolic end to the deprivations of the immediate postwar period, the currency reform surpassed all expectations when it succeeded in doing away with the black market and paving the way for the reintroduction of consumer goods that had not been seen in Germany for many years. What followed was not only a complete reorganization of the economy, but also a revaluation of all sectors of production, including artistic and cultural production.

According to historian Hermann Glaser, "By <June 22>, and for some time thereafter, culture was again an unsalable commodity. The concrete aesthetics of the new consumer goods was considered much more fascinating than art products. Because there was a longing to enjoy a better, happier, and more beautiful life at the basic level of existence, it was possible to dispense with the sublimation and projection of the superstructure."[48] In the aftermath of the currency reform, Germans chose to spend their new Marks on consumer durables rather than ephemeral cultural experiences like attending the cinema, the theater, or the opera, all of which became suddenly much more expensive in the new currency. But the "crisis of culture" ushered in by the currency reform did not result from the unsalability of culture alone. As Glaser notes, for many Germans in 1948, the crisis "showed that much of what had, during the rubble years, been perceived as great spiritual transformation and reflection, as moral renewal, in fact served only to compensate the materialism of which one had been deprived."[49]

The currency reform and the crisis in culture that ensued had a profound impact on all aspects of cinema in the emergent Federal Republic. According to Johannes Hauser, in the months following the currency reform, film attendance decreased by 63 percent in the American sector, 44 percent in the British sector, 40 percent in the French sector, and 53 percent in West Berlin.[50] Writing about the failure of *Love '47* and other "obsolete films," the *Wirtschaftszeitung* pinpointed the troubling effects of the currency reform on the film industry already in July 1949:

> Only now is it becoming fully clear how much the new monetary order has cost the German cinema. The crowds of viewers suddenly stopped coming, and the barely accumulated capital melted away, as did the bank loans. The studios, already few in number and small in capacity, are now for the most part standing empty. In this situation, it is especially depressing for the producers that the audiences have rejected almost every film that takes place in the years preceding the new monetary order.[51]

Indeed, while viewers soon began returning to the cinemas, they now sought out a different type of film altogether, definitively rejecting the rubble film and the *Zeitfilm*.[52]

Bettina Greffrath suggests that, following audience preferences, producers also rejected the moral imperatives and critical realism of the rubble films, and the collusion between audience demand and profit motive created fertile ground for a new type of popular entertainment cinema in the 1950s.[53] Despite its initial ill effects on the industry, the currency reform eventually paved the way for new types of capital to flow into film production through private banks and personal investment, and in the final year of the licensing period numerous new film production companies were founded as a result.[54] Nonetheless, the increased competition and the decline in cinema attendance combined to create an economic crisis for the German film industry in the late 1940s, of which *Love '47* was one casualty.[55]

However, the failure of *Love '47* cannot be attributed exclusively to the effects of the currency reform and the "crisis of culture" that ensued. Already in 1949, critics also explained the film's failure in social and aesthetic terms. While there is little evidence that audiences at the time rejected the film simply as a poor adaptation of Borchert, critics such as Gunter Groll did note the stylistic incongruity of the film's two halves as one reason for its failure:

> These two stories, told in flashback by a girl and a man respectively, both of them desperate narratives of misery, do not fit together: <screenwriter> Fischer's story is a naturalist document of contemporary times, while Borchert's story is stylized exaltation studded with dream visions. Here we have a mishmash of everything all at once: newsreel, documentary film, expressive theater, and fantastical surrealism. … Liebeneiner is sitting in the middle of two styles: what he has demonstrated, despite all his artistic desires and abilities, is once again the stylistic uncertainty of the German *Zeitfilm*.[56]

As Groll suggests, rather than demonstrating clear solutions to the representational problems of postwar German cinema, *Love '47* came across as yet another example of the clashing codes, disparate styles, and generic inconsistencies that characterized so many postwar films. While the film's producers, Hans Abich and Rolf Thiele, had hoped to revitalize the contemporary *Zeitfilm* with their first Filmaufbau production, their often contradictory aspirations for German cinema, as detailed in their manifestos, were mirrored in *Love '47*, a fragmentary film that did not attain closure.

Writing fifty years later about the film's failure with female audiences in particular, Massimo Perinelli argues that *Love '47* in fact failed because it offers *too much* closure, together with a retrograde solution to contemporary social problems that female audiences rejected. According to Perinelli, the film attempts to "reterritorialize women" by taming their sexuality and re-establishing patriarchal gender roles.[57] For Perinelli, *Love '47* is a transitional film not only aesthetically, but also ideologically, paving the way with its ending for the mass movement to redomesticate women in the 1950s. As he notes, male audiences responded much more favorably to *Love '47* than female audiences did, a statistic that supports Perinelli's argument that women rejected the film's solutions and its ideological tenor while men embraced them.[58]

While it is tempting to adopt Perinelli's argument that female viewers rejected Liebeneiner's film for protofeminist reasons, this argument focuses too neatly on the film's closure, and does not take into account issues of national myth making and of personal identification and fantasy that were also strongly implicated in the film's reception. At the heart of both these issues—and at the heart of Anna Gehrke's story—is the question of sexual victimization.

Elizabeth Heineman has shown how stories of female sexual victimization during World War II had a powerful currency in the emergent Federal Republic, allowing all Germans to identify as victims. Drained of its specificity, women's experience of rape came to stand in for the "rape" of Germany. As Heineman points out, "As the experience of rape was degendered to apply to the nation, the state refused to recognize a uniquely female experience of victimization by rape."[59] Thus, as men came to identify with stories of sexual victimization that allowed them to view Germans as victims rather than aggressors, paradoxically women's actual experiences of rape were denied by the larger culture. At the same time, as Heineman also demonstrates, women's sexual behavior during the postwar period—in particular their use of prostitution and fraternization as survival strategies—came to be seen as a potent symbol of the moral decline of the German nation. This second national myth surrounding female experience located Germany's downfall with the end of the war, allowing Germans to repress the role of Nazism and militarism in bringing about Germany's decline.

Wolfgang Liebeneiner intentionally set out to make a film that would address directly the difficult subject of women's sexual victimization and sexual behavior, an aim that resonated with Abich and Thiele's goals for Filmaufbau. Although granting Anna Gehrke the discursive authority to narrate her own story presented a compelling strategy for tackling the subject, in the context of national myth making that informed the film's reception, this strategy backfired for several reasons. First, although Anna tells her own story, this story, as I have argued, is articulated precisely for a male listener—and by extension a male spectator. In this sense, it is no accident that polls recorded men responding more positively to the film than women: dovetailing with larger social and national discourses, the film directly addressed male viewers, providing a fantasy space that allowed them to identify with the female victim. Second, and by the same token, female viewers found little to identify with in the character of Anna Gehrke, despite her mastery of the film's visual and auditory codes. This was due in part to casting: Hilde Krahl, the actress who played Anna (and the wife of director Liebeneiner), was familiar to audiences as a popular star of Third Reich cinema, and she did not present a new image of postwar femininity. More importantly, female audiences in 1949, seeking to escape their everyday reality, looked for female heroes on screen, rather than sexual victims like Anna. Not only was Anna's traumatic personal history all too familiar to female viewers, but her sexual behavior was so demonized in public discourse around 1949 that it is unsurprising that female viewers fled from the film. In this sense, it is precisely the film's success in representing contemporary reality that may account for its failure. As Shandley suggests, *Love '47* failed because of its "refusal to provide a fantasy space, in particular a romantic one" for postwar film audiences.[60]

Indeed, female audiences in 1949 were looking for movies that would provide them with escapist fantasies, especially in the aftermath of the currency reform, which proved especially devastating for women, who, due to new government policies, found it increasingly difficult not only to find employment, but also to collect unemployment benefits. At the same time, female viewers also continued to seek out movies that offered positive models of identification. Heineman details one further national myth drawing on female experience in the emergent Federal Republic, this one positive: the myth of the heroic and hard-working rubble woman, responsible for rebuilding Germany. Of course, the rubble woman found her cinematic embodiment in the actress Hildegard Knef, who provided a positive female role model who refused to be victimized in movies like *The Murderers Are Among Us* and *Film Without a Title*. It is no accident that those films, with their more expansive identificatory possibilities, were much more popular with female audiences than *Love '47*.

Liebeneiner's film addressed the traumas of World War II, the issue of guilt and responsibility for the crimes of the Nazi period, and differently gendered ways of experiencing and working through these problems. It did so not only at a moment when audiences had begun to reject the *Zeitfilm*, but during a period when the currency reform and the founding of the Federal Republic had begun to create a climate of national renewal and hope for the future, with a concomitant turning away from the past.

Love '47 demonstrates the limits of male narrative authority, employing female voiceover and the female gaze as a way of recovering the ability to tell a story, and thereby telling different stories at the same time—women's stories. Using similar strategies to *The Murderers Are Among Us* and *Film Without a Title*, Love '47 goes far beyond those films by featuring not only a complicated female protagonist, but also her detailed history. Anna's narrative, which supersedes Beckmann's story in relevance, currency, and authority throughout the film, provided a means of adapting Borchert's drama to the screen. By countering Beckmann's story with Anna's, Liebeneiner found a viable strategy for addressing postwar social problems like prostitution, adultery, and the incommensurability of men's and women's experiences of wartime and the postwar period. The introduction of Anna provided a way not only of problematizing male experience, but also of evaluating the relevance of different strategies of filmic representation in the quest to relegitimate cinema for the postwar period. In many ways a consummate woman's film, Love '47 also looks forward to the feminist reinvention of the *Frauenfilm* in the 1970s and 1980s, not only in terms of its formal strategies, but also in terms of its focus on women's sexual victimization.[61] Both as a film about coming to terms with the Nazi past and as a woman's film, Love '47 ultimately proved both too belated and too premature.

Notes

1. See Hans Helmut Prinzler, *Chronik des deutschen Films 1895–1994* (Stuttgart, 1995), 177; and Elizabeth Prommer, *Kinobesuch im Lebenslauf. Eine historische und medienbiographische Studie* (Konstanz, 1999), 350–52. In 1948, only twenty-three features were made in the Western zones.
2. The film was also praised abroad, for example at the 1949 Locarno International Film Festival, where lead actress Hilde Krahl won the prize for best acting.
3. Gertrud Runge, "Absage an die Traumfabrik. Göttinger Uraufführung von 'Liebe 47'," rev. of *Liebe 47*, *Die Zeit*, March 10, 1949.
4. Rev. of *Liebe 47*, *Der neue Film* 8 (1949). For a collection of reviews of *Liebe 47* from the late 1940s, including this one, see the section devoted to the film at *Film und Geschichte*, Lernwerkstatt Geschichte, Kulturarchiv der Fachhochschule Hannover and Historisches Seminar der Universität Hannover, May 27, 2005 <http://www.geschichte.uni-hannover.de/~kultarch/dnach45/zeitgen_spielfilme/filme/liebe47/film.htm>.
5. See Robert Shandley, *Rubble Films: German Cinema in the Shadow of the Third Reich* (Philadelphia, 2001), 71.
6. According to Gordon Burgess, the reception of Borchert's play changed dramatically along with the social and political situation in postwar Germany. The popularity of the play reached its apex in 1948, but by the end of that year the events of the escalating Cold War led to an increasing rejection of the play, which was now characterized as "'nihilism' with potentially dangerous consequences." See Burgess, *The Life and Works of Wolfgang Borchert* (Rochester, NY, 2003), 220.
7. See "'Liebe 47' uraufgeführt," rev. of *Liebe 47*, *Film-Echo*, March 20, 1949, and "Liebeneiners 'Liebe 47' in Göttingen," *Abendpost*, March 25, 1949.

8. "'Liebe 47' uraufgeführt," *Film-Echo*.
9. See "Liebeneiners 'Liebe 47' in Göttingen," *Abendpost*, and "'Liebe 47' läuft vor dem Landtag Schleswig-Holstein," *Film-Echo*, March 1, 1949.
10. See for example rev. of *Liebe 47, Rheinische Post* (Düsseldorf), July 6, 1949, and "Wall-Licht: 'Liebe 47'—ein Film, der Gültigkeit hat," rev. of *Liebe 47, Nordwest-Zeitung* (Oldenburg), August 27, 1949.
11. See for example rev. of *Liebe 47, Filmdienst der Jugend* 2: 13 (April 6, 1949).
12. On the film's financial failure, see the account offered by producer Hans Abich, "Die Göttinger Produktionen und der Film der fünfziger Jahre. Eine Ortsbeschreibung," *Zwischen Gestern und Morgen. Westdeutscher Nachkriegsfilm 1946–1962*, ed. Hilmar Hoffmann and Walter Schobert (Frankfurt am Main, 1989), 65–66.
13. Rev. of *Liebe 47, Filmdienst der Jugend*.
14. For an exhaustive account of the history and founding of Filmaufbau, see Gustav Meier, *Filmstadt Göttingen: Bilder für eine neue Welt? Zur Geschichte der Göttinger Spielfilmproduktion 1945 bis 1961* (Hannover, 1996). See also Jens U. Sobotka, "Die Filmwunderkinder: Hans Abich und die Filmaufbau GmbH Göttingen," Ph.D. diss. (Westfälische Wilhelms-Universität-Münster, 1997; Düsseldorf, 1999).
15. Qtd. in Sobotka, "Die Filmwunderkinder," 46. According to Sobotka, the original text of the "Starnberger Denkschrift" has been lost, and the version quoted here is a reconstruction taken from Andreas Gaw and H.P. Meyer, "Ein Hauch von Hollywood: Filmstadt Göttingen," *Lumiere. Zeitschrift der Film & Kino-Initiative Göttingen* 21 (April 30, 1991): 22. Meier quotes at length from a document he refers to as the "Denkschrift," but he does not credit his source. See Meier, *Filmstadt Göttingen*, 18–20.
16. See chapter 1 for a discussion of the *Filmpause*.
17. See John Davidson, *Deterritorializing the New German Cinema* (Minneapolis, 1999).
18. "Von den Absichten einer Göttinger Filmproduktion," April 27, 1948, Nachlaß der Filmaufbau GmbH Göttingen, 1. Qtd. in Sobotka, "Die Filmwunderkinder," 49–50.
19. See chapter 2 for a discussion of the *Filmdichter* debate.
20. Qtd. in Meier, *Filmstadt Göttingen*, 33.
21. For an overview of Liebeneiner's career, see John Davidson, "Working for the Man, Whoever That May Be: The Vocation of Wolfgang Liebeneiner," in *Cultural History through a National Socialist Lens: Essays on the Cinema of the Third Reich*, ed. Robert C. Reimer (Rochester, NY, 2000), 240–67.
22. Massimo Perinelli, *Liebe '47—Gesellschaft '49. Geschlechterverhältnisse in der deutschen Nachkriegszeit. Eine Analyse des Films* Liebe 47 (Hamburg, 1999), 14.
23. Accounts of the invitation suggest that Ehre, who was herself Jewish, vouched for Liebeneiner in the postwar period because he had offered help to various Jewish colleagues during the Third Reich. See Meier, *Filmstadt Göttingen*, 32, and Abich, in Hoffmann and Schobert, *Zwischen Gestern und Morgen*, 65.
24. The radio play debuted on February 13, 1947, and became an overnight sensation. It was subsequently rebroadcast numerous times in Germany and abroad. On the many permutations of Borchert's drama and their reception, as well as the relationship between Borchert and Liebeneiner, see Burgess, *Wolfgang Borchert*.
25. Although Borchert died of liver disease, his poor health also resulted from the period between 1943 and 1945, when he served as a soldier on the Eastern Front and was imprisoned by the Nazis numerous times. Borchert went to jail first on suspicion of wounding himself in order to be released from the military; later the Nazis imprisoned him again for defaming Josef Goebbels in a parody he wrote. During these years, Borchert was injured several times and suffered from frostbite, typhus, diphtheria, and jaundice.
26. Burgess, *Wolfgang Borchert*, 219.
27. The complicated story, which was widely told in newspapers during the immediate postwar years, concerned a man named Garden, who, though he was an enthusiastic Hitler Youth leader, was appalled by the murder of Jews and civilians that he witnessed as a soldier in the Soviet Union. After deserting and reporting on what he had witnessed

to friends back in Germany, he was sentenced to death by a Nazi tribunal. He eventually escaped from a Nazi prison by attacking the prison guard, who ultimately died from the attack. When he returned to Germany after the war from exile in Switzerland, he was put on trial and convicted of murdering the prison guard. For obvious reasons, the British film office did not see this story as appropriate film material for their efforts at re-education, and they refused to license the film. See Sobotka, "Die Filmwunderkinder," 76–77, and Meier, *Filmstadt Göttingen*, 52.

28. Accounts differ as to whether Liebeneiner wanted to film Kleist's novella or a modern adaptation of the story by Ferdinand Bruckner. See Meier, *Filmstadt Göttingen*, 52, and Sobotka, "Film Wunderkinder," 77–78.

29. Qtd. in Sobotka, "Filmwunderkinder," 77.

30. According to both Meier and Sobotka, the British film office objected to *The Marquise von O.* on the one hand because of its militaristic setting and on the other because they preferred to license (uncontroversial) films with contemporary German settings in order to keep the German market for costume dramas open to British productions. See Meier, *Filmstadt Göttingen*, 52, and Sobotka, "Die Filmwunderkinder," 77–78.

31. According to Meier, when Filmaufbau's studio opened in 1948, the company's upcoming production schedule included, in addition to *Love '47*, three further literary adaptations (including one of *Faust* planned for 1949, the 200th anniversary of Goethe's birth), as well as a biopic about E.T.A. Hoffmann and a film about modern dance (*Filmstadt Göttingen*, 53). In the 1950s, Filmaufbau went on to achieve great success with a series of Thomas Mann adaptations.

32. Eric Rentschler catalogs over one hundred adaptations in the years 1933–45. He counts only seven adaptations made in the Eastern and Western zones before the release of *Love '47* in 1949. See "Adaptations in German Film History: a Basic Guide (1913–85)," in *German Film and Literature: Adaptations and Transformations* (New York, 1986), 336–65.

33. Jan-Christopher Horak, "Postwar Traumas in Klaren's *Wozzeck* (1947)," in Rentschler, *German Film and Literature*, 133.

34. Kurt Lothar Tank, "Falsche Sprache zu den richtigen Bildern," *Hannoversche Allgemeine*, December 10, 1949, qtd. in Thomas Brandlmeier, "Und wieder Caligari … Deutsche Nachkriegsfilme 1946–1951," *Der deutsche Film. Aspekte seiner Geschichte von den Anfängen bis zur Gegenwart*, ed. Uli Jung (Trier, 1993), 150.

35. It is only in the years since the debut of the film that critics have come to reject Liebeneiner's adaptation. Focusing on the failure of *Love '47* with audiences, these critics have found one explanation in the fact that Liebeneiner's script is unfaithful to Borchert's original drama. The Borchert scholar Gordon Burgess is exemplary of this tendency. See his "The Failure of the Film of the Play. *Draussen vor der Tür* and *Liebe 47*," *German Life and Letters* 38.4 (1985): 155–64. Robert Shandley (*Rubble Films*, 75) also refers to the film as a critical failure; however, the reviews I have found suggest a generally positive reception of the film among critics.

36. On this point, see also Shandley, *Rubble Films*, 74–75.

37. Rev. of *Liebe 47*, *Evangelischer Film-Beobachter* 9 (May 2, 1949): 34.

38. See Kaja Silverman, *Male Subjectivity at the Margins* (New York, 1992), esp. 52–121, and Jaimey Fisher, *Disciplining Germany: Youth, Reeducation, and Reconstruction after the Second World War* (Detroit, 2007), esp. 175–80.

39. See Linda Williams, "When the Woman Looks," in *Re-Vision: Essays in Feminist Film Criticism*, ed. Mary Ann Doane et al. (Los Angeles, 1984), 83.

40. See Williams in Doane et al., *Re-Vision*, 83–99. See also my chapter 1 for a more detailed discussion of the gendered structure of the gaze in classical cinema. On the reversal of the gaze in this scene, see also Perinelli, *Liebe '47—Gesellschaft '49*, 145–49.

41. Shandley, *Rubble Films*, 75.

42. Press booklet in file on *Liebe 47*, Schriftgutarchiv, Stiftung Deutsche Kinemathek, Berlin.

43. "Liebe 47," *Illustrierte Film-Bühne* 327 (1949). The *Illustrierte Film-Bühne* printed film

programs for numerous German films. The programs, akin to theater programs, contained many stills from the film in addition to cast and credit information and a short summary of the film's plot. They were sold in cinemas, and many film fans collected the programs as mementos of the films they saw. These programs provide useful examples of how the films were advertised to contemporary audiences.

44. Runge, "Absage an die Traumfabrik."
45. Erika Müller, "'Liebe 47' und die Frauen," *Die Zeit*, May 19, 1949.
46. "Eine Frau, Draussen vor der Tür," *Film und Frau* 1.9 (1949): 4.
47. On the film's failure, see for example "Überholte Filme," *Wirtschaftszeitung*, July 16, 1949; Curt Riess, *Das gibt's nur einmal: Das Buch des deutschen Films nach 1945* (Hamburg, 1958), 204–208; Burgess, "The Failure of the Film of the Play"; Meier, *Filmstadt Göttingen*, 66–68; Sobotka, "Die Filmwunderkinder," 106–108; Perinelli, *Liebe '47—Gesellschaft '49*, 173–95.
48. Hermann Glaser, *The Rubble Years: The Cultural Roots of Postwar Germany, 1945–1948*, trans. Franz Feige and Patricia Gleason (New York, 1986), 326.
49. Glaser, *The Rubble Years*, 328.
50. Johannes Hauser, *Neuaufbau der westdeutschen Filmwirtschaft 1945–1955 und der Einfluß der US-amerikanischen Filmpolitik. Vom reichseigenen Filmmonopolkonzern (UFI) zur privatwirtschaftlichen Konkurrenzwirtschaft* (Pfaffenweiler, 1989), 374–75.
51. "Überholte Filme," *Wirtschaftszeitung*.
52. Perinelli notes that a summer 1948 poll found that 90 percent of film viewers in the Western zones did not want to see any more rubble films. See Perinelli, *Liebe '47—Gesellschaft '49*, 174.
53. Bettina Greffrath, *Gesellschaftsbilder der Nachkriegszeit. Deutsche Spielfilme 1945–1949* (Pfaffenweiler, 1995), 136.
54. Hauser, *Neuaufbau der westdeutschen Filmwirtschaft*, 452.
55. Hauser, *Neuaufbau der westdeutschen Filmwirtschaft*, 456.
56. Gunter Groll, "Borchert, Liebeneiner und der Zeitfilm. Der verlorene Maßstab/ Bemerkungen zu 'Liebe 47'," *Süddeutsche Zeitung*, May 28, 1949, rpt. in *Zwischen Gestern und Morgen. Westdeutscher Nachkriegsfilm 1946–1962*, ed. Hilmar Hoffmann and Walter Schobert (Frankfurt am Main, 1989), 348.
57. Perinelli, *Liebe '47—Gesellschaft '49*, 189.
58. A viewer poll from December 1949 revealed that audiences overwhelmingly rejected *Love '47*, although the poll also found that men were three times more likely to respond positively to the film than were women (Perinelli, *Liebe '47—Gesellschaft '49*, 190–91). See also Greffrath, *Gesellschaftsbilder der Nachkriegszeit*, 133.
59. Elizabeth Heineman, "The Hour of the Woman: Memories of Germany's 'Crisis Years' and West German National Identity," *American Historical Review* 101.2 (1996): 372.
60. Shandley, *Rubble Films*, 75.
61. Women's sexual victimization in the war and postwar years was a topic revisited by many feminist filmmakers, and proved central both to the formulation of West German feminism in the 1970s and 1980s and to the project of the feminist *Frauenfilm*. See for example Jutta Brückner's *Hungerjahre in einem reichen Land* (Hunger Years, 1980); Helma Sanders-Brahms' *Deutschland, bleiche Mutter* (Germany, Pale Mother, 1980); and Helke Sander's *BeFreier und BeFreite* (Liberators Take Liberties, 1992).

Chapter 4

UNSOLVED MYSTERIES: RACE, ETHNICITY, AND GENDER IN HELMUT KÄUTNER'S *EPILOGUE* (1950)

The film industry entered a new phase of consolidation in 1950, responding to the effects of the currency reform, which had initiated not only a series of economic and cultural transformations, but profound political changes as well. Signaling the first escalation of the emergent Cold War, the Soviet blockade of Berlin began only days after the currency reform in June 1948 and lasted until May 1949.[1] The division of Germany was cemented in 1949 by the founding of the Federal Republic on May 24, followed six months later by the founding of the German Democratic Republic on October 7. With the end of the licensing period, the film industry continued to expand and movie going continued to increase in popularity. A total of 602 new cinemas opened in the Federal Republic in 1950, and ticket sales increased to 487 million, an average of nearly ten visits to the movies for each West German that year. At the same time, domestic film production grew once again by a third, bringing to eighty the total number of West German features released in 1950.[2]

Along with the new West German state came a host of new institutions that bolstered its nascent film industry while also increasing government influence on film production. In 1949, the film industry introduced a series of measures for self-regulation and self-promotion, most notably the self-censorship code known as the *Freiwillige Selbstkontrolle der Filmwirtschaft* (FSK) and the lobbying group that controlled the FSK, the *Spitzenorganisation der Filmwirtschaft* (SPIO). In 1950, cinema owners came together to form their own association, the *Zentralverband der Deutschen Filmtheater*, a group responsible for publishing the important trade journal *Film-Echo*. Between 1949 and 1950, several federal states including Bavaria and West Berlin founded film credit programs that were designed to boost local economies while also helping the film industry out of financial crisis. In 1950, the federal government followed suit with its first film credit program, intended to help produce German films of international caliber. Such early film subsidy programs laid the groundwork for a network of government-backed loan guarantees that would shape the film industry throughout the 1950s. These diverse economic and regulatory measures ultimately led to a more standardized and circumscribed film production that favored traditional genres, accepted conventions, and popular stars as methods of ensuring commercial success. This strategy would come to dramatic fruition within the next several years, as cinema in West Germany began to experience an unparalleled boom.

Much maligned by critics, postwar German cinema's return to conventional genres began around 1950, when audiences had decisively rejected the rubble film, and film studios were seeking to recover from the impact of the currency reform. In a 1949 article about the effects of the currency reform on the film industry, the *Wirtschaftszeitung* summed up the situation:

> The great audience hits in the West Zones right now are the Austrian films, which serve up that old Viennese good nature in an artless but cozy fashion, with a pinch of Viennese humor. It is not surprising that German producers are drawing conclusions from this. … These days, when they plan a new film, they first eye the political and economic horizon with suspicion. What sudden change is on the way? … They are in the dark about the future, and these days nothing becomes outmoded more quickly than a *Zeitfilm*. No more of that. The rallying cry for the new beginning is to make suspense thrillers and something to laugh about, along with those beloved old derby and circus films. Those looking for artistic revelations, which could also help the German film win ground abroad, will have to wait.[3]

As this account makes clear, the consistent formula of genre cinema represented a more secure investment for the film industry in a period of economic uncertainty, and so German cinema began to turn away from its early postwar aspirations for political relevance and aesthetic experimentation. However, as we shall see, the move to genre cinema did not solve the representational problems that had plagued German film since the end of the war, and debates about cinematic legitimacy continued to be conducted in the press and to find their way into the films themselves.

Two popular films that premiered on the same night, September 7, 1950, illustrate the parallel trajectories of this new genre cinema, trajectories that would dominate German cinema throughout the 1950s and beyond: Hans Deppe's *Schwarzwaldmädel* (Black Forest Girl) and Helmut Käutner's *Epilog: Das Geheimnis der Orplid* (Epilogue: The Secret of the Orplid). What these two (in many ways very different) films have in common is that they both turned to genre cinema as a way out of the dilemmas presented by the *Zeitfilm*. Rather than tackling postwar social problems head on as rubble films such as *Love '47* had done, *Black Forest Girl* and *Epilogue* addressed these issues in veiled terms, through familiar conventions that drew on German cultural traditions. While both films offered new responses to the representational problems of postwar cinema, they continued to be marked by the kinds of tensions and inconsistencies that characterized so many postwar films.

Black Forest Girl celebrated its gala premiere at the Palast-Lichtspiele cinema in Stuttgart. Credited with reintroducing the *Heimatfilm* genre to postwar West Germany, *Black Forest Girl* went on to become the most popular film of the 1950–51 season.[4] A consummate genre film and the first postwar color picture, Deppe's film fueled the fire of postwar commentators who were eager to attack the waning artistic integrity of postwar cinema and the provincialism and traditional values that the *Heimatfilm* trumpeted. Yet *Black Forest Girl* was not merely a throwback. Combining elements of the *Heimat* tradition with trademarks of the Ufa style such as the musical revue number, *Black Forest Girl* set the stage for a new incarnation of popular cinema in the 1950s that sought to mediate between past and present on the levels of both form and content.[5] In this sense, *Black Forest Girl* can be seen as a precursor not only to subsequent *Heimatfilme*, but also to the *Arztfilme* <doctor films>, *Schlagerfilme* <popular music films>, and costume dramas that comprised some of the most popular successes of the decade.

Helmut Käutner's suspense thriller *Epilogue* premiered at the Venice International Film Festival to consistent acclaim from festival reviewers. The film's domestic premiere took place a few weeks later, at the Residenz Theater in Hamburg, on September 27, 1950. Chosen as an official West German submission to the Venice festival, Käutner's film represented the aspirations of the state and the film industry for the new West German cinema. Combining a star-studded cast with a suspenseful plot that caters to audience genre expectations while at the same time unraveling the conventions of that genre, *Epilogue* tries to have it both ways. A *Zeitfilm* that disguises itself as a political allegory, the film exhibits a pronounced artistry of form, especially editing, together with a sensationalist story and special effects designed for commercial appeal. With *Epilogue*, Käutner sought to copy the formula of Hollywood-style film noir, which so successfully combined the artistic heritage of Weimar cinema with the conventions of Hollywood genre cinema. While *Epilogue* did not go on to become a smash hit like *Black Forest Girl*, it did very well at the box office, despite mixed reviews from German critics.[6] More importantly, it laid the groundwork for a darker, more socially critical tradition of filmmaking, which, though not as ubiquitous as the *Heimatfilm* and its variations, produced some of the most popular films of the decade, from Willi Forst's *Die Sünderin* (The Sinner, 1951) to Rolf Thiele's *Das Mädchen Rosemarie* (That Girl Rosemarie, 1958).

Epilogue tells the story of a journalist, Peter Zabel, who tries (mostly in vain) to solve the mystery of the *Orplid*, a ship that sank in dubious circumstances in August 1949. A response to the demise of the *Zeitfilm*, *Epilogue* both indicts and reacts to the perceived incompatibility of politics with commercial entertainment in West Germany. Käutner avoids naming names or grounding the plot of his film in its historical context, and *Epilogue* is remarkably unspecific about the province of the political machinations that form the basis of its story. Nonetheless, the film does engage contemporary politics by addressing the controversial topic of rearmament, the profit motive of war, and the social ramifications produced by the threat of total annihilation. These subjects, which the film treats allegorically, clearly pertain to the Nazi past, but they also possessed new relevance in the Cold War climate of 1950. The outbreak of the Korean War in June hastened the Adenauer government's resolve to rearm and remilitarize the Federal Republic, while increasing public awareness of Germany's strategic value in the Cold War.

Not only a political allegory, *Epilogue* also treats the trauma and guilt of the Nazi period and the emerging Cold War climate of surveillance and paranoia on a formal level. As Yogini Joglekar argues, the film's interventions into the detective genre reflect the impossibility of epistemological certainty in Germany after the Holocaust and the Third Reich: "The politically motivated sub-text ... negates the authority of the detective figures and the efficacy of their search for certainties like knowledge or truth, and hence contains an anti-epiphanic, anti-epistemological impulse."[7] At the same time, the film's investigation into the status of image making in 1950 aligns *Epilogue* with other postwar productions that tackled debates about cinematic legitimacy in narratives about vision and visual artists.[8]

The journalist Zabel's primary source in reconstructing the events leading up to the shipwreck is a set of drawings made by the ship's sole survivor, a Malaysian servant named Leata. Due to the trauma of her experiences on board the ship, Leata has become mute, so only her drawings can bear witness to her tale. *Epilogue* thus presents a story about the production of images as a response to trauma—a story that certainly resonates with the project of postwar German filmmaking. Like other postwar films, *Epilogue* addresses the dilemmas of postwar cinematic representation in gendered terms, in a narrative that locates the origins of its images with a woman. In this allegory about image making, women create images that men appropriate and attempt to decode, never entirely successfully.

While in other postwar films like *The Murderers Are Among Us*, a narrative focus on gender often contributed to the sublimation of problems of race and ethnicity, *Epilogue* is notable for bearing traces of these problems on its surface. Indeed, issues of race and ethnicity are strongly implicated in *Epilogue* both at the level of production and at the level of narrative. The film was produced by Artur Brauner, one of the few Jewish filmmakers active in postwar Germany, and Brauner recruited a number of remigrant actors for the film, several of whom were Jewish. Race and ethnicity found their way into the diegesis of *Epilogue* not only through the remarkable and conflicted performances of Jewish remigrant actors Fritz Kortner and Camilla Spira, but also through the Malaysian character Leata, who serves as a cipher for the many unsolved and unsolvable mysteries presented by the film.

I

A central figure of postwar German filmmaking, producer Artur Brauner was a Polish Jew who escaped from the Lodz ghetto, fought with the partisans against the Nazis, and waited out the war in hiding in the Soviet Union.[9] While Brauner and his parents, who emigrated to Palestine, survived the Holocaust, forty-nine of their family members were murdered by the Nazis in ghettos and concentration camps. A film enthusiast since his youth, Brauner hoped to emigrate to Hollywood after the war and begin a career as a film producer. Like many Jewish DPs (displaced persons), however, Brauner ended up in Berlin while traveling westward, meeting his future wife Therese Albert along the way. Called Maria, Albert was also a Jew from Poland, who had survived the Holocaust in Hanover disguised as a Polish Catholic foreign worker. In Berlin, Brauner was reunited with several family members and married Maria, whose brother-in-law Joseph Einstein was a well-known black marketeer. While Brauner later asserted that "it was not right for Jews to take up residence in Germany again" after the Holocaust, he immediately became involved in film production in postwar Berlin and he ended up adopting the city as his home.[10] Brauner went on to become not only the most successful German producer of the 1950s, but the most successful independent film producer in all of postwar Europe, with revenue of over 30 million German Marks per year.[11] Indeed, his career, which spans six decades, presents one of the most unique and successful film careers in the postwar period altogether. At the same time, as Tim Bergfelder points out, "Brauner's status simultaneously as the 'Jewish conscience' within the West German film industry and as an unashamedly capitalist entrepreneur … has made him a disquieting and controversial figure in German cultural life, irritating to both sides of the political spectrum."[12]

Brauner came to filmmaking with little knowledge or experience of the industry, but he had two important qualities to contribute. He was one of the very few figures on the postwar film scene who had not begun his career in the studios of the Third Reich. More importantly, he had plenty of cash to bring to the impoverished postwar industry—cash that was most likely acquired in part through his family connections to the black market. Brauner's first film production was the very first postwar film made in the Western zones, Helmut Weiss's *Sag die Wahrheit* (Tell the Truth, 1946), a so-called *Überläufer-Film*, 75 percent of which had been finished during the Nazi period.[13] A commercial hit despite its poor reception among critics, *Tell the Truth* paved the way for Brauner's lifelong formula for success. Over the decades, he made numerous blockbuster films that appealed to audience demands for entertainment, and these box office smashes allowed Brauner to pursue less commercially viable projects that reflected his own interests, many of which became critically successful films that addressed the Nazi past and the Holocaust.[14]

On September 16, 1946, Brauner founded his own production company, Central Cinema Corp.-Film Gesellschaft, in Berlin. Brauner's first production for CCC, *Herzkönig* (King of Hearts, 1947), followed the model of *Tell the Truth*: an entertaining genre film, it was also directed by Helmut Weiss, and it also became a popular hit. Brauner followed *King of Hearts* with an early film about the Holocaust, *Morituri* (1948), which became his first critical success. Based in part on Brauner's own life story, *Morituri*, directed by Eugen York, was the first postwar film to show a concentration camp.[15] Already in this 1948 film, Brauner began a pattern that he would repeat many more times in future films about the Holocaust—*Morituri* focused mainly on the victims, while the perpetrators remained generally nameless and faceless, and the causes for the Holocaust went unexplored. In part due to the aesthetic inconsistencies that plagued so many postwar films and in part no doubt due to its subject matter, *Morituri* was a total commercial flop, causing Brauner to comment: "I never regretted that I made this film. I did learn, however—sadly and unfortunately—that the cinema is supposed to be first and foremost a site for entertainment and not for *Vergangenheitsbewältigung* <coming to terms with the past>."[16]

After the popular failure of *Morituri*, Brauner embraced entertainment, and his CCC quickly recovered, producing three highly successful films in 1949. Much of Brauner's success can be credited to his canniness about genre cinema, and many early CCC productions like *Epilogue* tested the limits of traditional film genres in the postwar period. As Bergfelder has noted, Brauner loved popular Weimar genre cinema as a child, and "most of CCC's output in the 1950s and into the 1960s can be seen as a consistent attempt to continue where the popular German film culture of the 1920s and early 1930s had been interrupted."[17] Not only did CCC seek to establish a postwar tradition of detective films and war films, genres that had been thoroughly delegitimated after National Socialism and World War II, but Brauner also sought to reinvent the *Zeitfilm* through the conventions of genre, inserting current and historical events into the compelling and suspenseful structures of genre cinema. For example, the successful and critically acclaimed *Sündige Grenze* (The Sinful Border, 1951), directed by R.A. Stemmle, tackles the problem of coffee smuggling from the Benelux countries into Germany, a huge controversy of the post-currency reform Federal Republic. *Die Spur führt nach Berlin* (All Clues Lead to Berlin, 1952), directed by Franz Cap, focuses on a group of illegal counterfeiters with allegiances to the Nazi Party. Like *Epilogue*, both films address contemporary social and political problems through the generic characteristics of the suspense thriller. Notably, the ideas for all three films came from Brauner himself, who was often inspired to make a film by stories he read in the press.

Epilogue, which was inspired by a small notice in a regional newspaper, held a personal interest for Brauner as a Holocaust survivor.

According to Claudia Dillmann-Kühn, "From the story of the sinking of a yacht, <Brauner> was fascinated by the idea of how each individual person in a group would react to the certainty of imminent death. Brauner was very interested in films with disastrous endings because of their representation of human behavior in the face of mortal fear."[18] Brauner passed his idea on to Helmut Käutner and R.A. Stemmle, who co-authored the screenplay for *Epilogue*.

Ever since *Morituri*, Brauner's production company had encountered problems caused by the poor working conditions in postwar Berlin, where there was only one functioning film studio in the Western zones, the former Ufa studio in Berlin-Tempelhof. These difficulties strengthened Brauner's resolve to build his own studio, and in October 1949 he began to renovate an abandoned chemical factory in Berlin-Spandau, which would become the new home for the CCC studios.

Emblematic of the often grotesque situations in which Brauner found himself as a Jew working in postwar Germany, the factory he was renovating had been used for experiments with poison gas, and the outbuildings had housed forced laborers whom the Nazis exploited to work in the chemical factory. During the shooting of CCC's early productions beginning in 1950, actors routinely complained of headaches, nausea, and burning eyes caused by the remnants of poison gas that had seeped into the walls of the studio buildings.[19]

Epilogue was one of the first productions shot under these conditions in the new CCC studios, and in many ways the film bears traces of the disturbing conditions of its production. This is evident not only in the material circumstances surrounding the shoot—which took place over only twenty-seven days in June and July of 1950 and which led to all sorts of conflicts among the ensemble cast of Nazi stars and remigrant Jewish actors as well as between director Helmut Käutner and producer Brauner—but also in a more immaterial sense, in some of the gaps, inconsistencies, and paradoxes that characterize this film.[20]

II

On the surface, *Epilogue* appears to be a classic suspense thriller, the kind of genre film that audiences demanded after the currency reform. One 1950 reviewer described the film's plot this way:

> This is the tale: A dark and unscrupulous racketeer married his lover off to a venal and compliant marionette and set off with the bridal couple, his wife, guests, and friends on a wedding trip on his yacht. The point of this macabre celebration is in actuality his rendezvous on the high seas with an even darker dealer in death and crime. An anticapitalist terrorist group has smuggled a time bomb on board; at the same time, an agent of the American secret service is on the ship to keep the organizer of this strange journey

under surveillance. However, the various dark secrets of the passengers come to light prematurely, as the party is seized by panic during their precisely foretold final hour. The bomb goes off <*sic*>; the ship sinks; the guests drown; all except for the Malaysian girl, who, having gone mute out of fright, later reports to the journalist who is so eagerly pursuing the mysteries of the *Orplid* about the strange events of this sad wedding night by painting and drawing.[21]

However, this account only hints at the fact that the film consistently frustrates audience expectations of closure, instead embedding mystery after mystery in a plot that rejects any clear-cut resolution. Like other postwar films, *Epilogue* presents a complicated structure involving a frame story, several layers of narrative time, and a discursive mode that places the veracity of the narrated events in question.

Epilogue lacks a credit sequence; instead the film opens with several frames of text that introduce the plot in a documentary style:

Recently the radio and press have repeatedly reported stories about unexplained plane crashes, explosions, and sunken ships. Often the underlying causes are political. It is dangerous to solve these crimes. The fate of the *Orplid* is among these mysterious cases. For that reason, *many things are only hinted at here, others are left open*. An officer of the secret service is on the trail of an international arms dealer. Independently of the secret agent, a member of an extreme political organization attempts to assassinate the arms dealer and his unscrupulous client. The journalist Peter Zabel has coincidentally discovered the background to these events. He offers his report to the editor of a tabloid newspaper. <my emphasis>

What is remarkable about this introduction is that it essentially gives the story of *Epilogue* away, revealing the plot behind the sinking of the *Orplid* in the first few seconds of the film, while also admitting straightaway that the film will not offer a detailed resolution of the mystery. While we learn more details over the course of the film about exactly how the ship sank, we never learn more about the political background of the various conspirators or the reasons for their actions, particulars that are indeed "left open."

After this introduction, a file titled "Epilogue" is opened, and the film proper begins with a frame story that recounts the "facts" about the ship uncovered by Zabel (Horst Caspar) in his research. The entire opening sequence of *Epilogue* strives to present the film as a *Tatsachenbericht*, or factual report: in addition to the documentary-style text at the beginning, we also see a rapid montage of pictures, newspaper clippings, and flashbacks to key moments in Zabel's investigation, all of which are meant to authenticate the story and lay claim to the truth. At the same time, however, *Epilogue* undermines its own truth claims together with Zabel's authority by presenting this information at such a breathtaking pace that, rather than clarifying the facts, this sequence further obscures the film's back story. Not only is the plot so convoluted as to be difficult to piece together, but it also contains glaring holes that will never be clarified, holes to which the film calls attention from the very beginning.

Thus *Epilogue* places in question not only the truth value of media and documentary reporting, but also the status of postwar cinema after the demise of the *Zeitfilm*, suggesting that both repress politics, thereby failing to uncover the truth. Just as the opening title sequence warns against exposing the "underlying political causes" of crimes, various characters throughout the film warn Zabel to stay away from politics, both in his investigation of the *Orplid* and in his written account of it. Responding to Zabel's inquiry about the sinking of the *Orplid*, one woman tells him, "You should leave politics alone." In voiceover, Zabel ruminates on her answer: "Politics—here the word was uttered for the first time. So it wasn't a crime. But there are political crimes too ... I followed up on every possibility." If Zabel's investigation hints at numerous continuities between the Nazi past and the present-day Federal Republic, it also ultimately forecloses on the possibility that a solution to the mystery of the *Orplid* may be located in ongoing conflicts that originate with the Third Reich. Instead, the film repeatedly suggests that exposing political truths is dangerous, not least because they are truths contemporary Germans would rather forget. *Epilogue* thus narrativizes the dilemmas of postwar filmmaking at a moment when audiences had rejected any attempt to tackle social problems and their political causes head on.

While Käutner's film highlights the corruption and repression upon which postwar society—and by extension postwar cinema—is based, *Epilogue* holds out hope for the project of renewed cinematic legitimacy by demanding productive spectatorship. The audience must take an active role in decoding and piecing together the information that is presented, a point that the film underscores not only by placing the "facts" in question, but also by constantly calling attention to its own construction through an exemplary display of form and an array of metacinematic devices. The opening montage sequence, for example, presents a tour de force of editing, a strong achievement by the editor Johanna Meisel, with dissolves, fades, graphic match shots, jump cuts, superimpositions, and montage-style edits, formal devices that disrupt identification both by contributing to the obscurity of the narrative and by making spectators aware of the film's formal construction.[22]

The second section of the film, the main narrative, consists of Zabel's reconstructed version of what happened on board the ship, an imagined version of events based largely on drawings by the ship's sole survivor, the mute Malaysian woman Leata (Bettina Moissi). This portion of the film introduces the plot we have seen outlined at the beginning of the film. An FBI agent (Peter van Eyck) has come on board the ship in order to monitor the activities of the arms dealer Mr. Hoopman (Fritz Kortner); at the same time a radical political organization has planted a bomb on the ship in order to assassinate Hoopman and his client, Mr. Hill (Arno Paulsen). Through a series of misunderstandings and coincidences, the passengers on the ship learn about the bomb and attempt to discover its location on board. The existence of the bomb is revealed seventy-two minutes before it is scheduled to explode; in one of the film's metacinematic devices, this suspenseful seventy-two minutes corresponds exactly to the length of *Epilogue* itself.

Zabel narrates the first two sections of the film in a diegetic voiceover; his diegetic audience is the editor of the tabloid newspaper to whom he hopes to sell his reportage account (entitled "Epilogue") together with Leata's drawings. Though it is Zabel's voice that sutures together the diverse information presented in the first section, and his voice that also narrates the confusing and sensational events of the second section, we never see Zabel's face during the first two-thirds of the film. We do, however, repeatedly see his hands, as well as the outlines of his reflection in the many windows present in the frame story. While *Epilogue* plays with a subjective point of view here, the camera does not consistently represent Zabel's perspective. Rather, it reflects a constantly shifting point of view that distances the viewer from Zabel as narrator, calling into question his narrative authority while also provoking reflection on the formal construction of the film's photography.

At the most suspenseful moment of the framed narrative, when only a short time remains before the bomb is scheduled to explode, the loud noise of a telephone ringing disrupts our immersion in the story and wrenches us back into the frame story, where we see the faces of all the characters in the editorial office of the tabloid, including Zabel, for the first time. As Zabel comes to the climax of his story, with Leata sitting at his side, the telephone rings loudly and incessantly. A stand-in for the spectator, the tabloid editor Beckmann (Hans Leibelt), who is thoroughly absorbed in the story, finally picks up the receiver and lays it on the table; while Zabel continues to narrate his story about the end of the *Orplid*, the caller on the other end of the line repeats into the phone, "Hello? Hello?" Eventually Beckmann picks up the phone, and a cutaway—the only instance of cross-cutting between two simultaneous events in the frame story—reveals that the caller is none other than Aldo Siano (Carl Raddatz), one of the men involved in sabotaging the *Orplid*. The phone call gives credence to Zabel's fear that he is being followed, escalating the suspense of the frame story. The very noticeable use of cross-cutting at this moment of the film, which makes only the audience privy to the identity of the caller, further engages viewers in the mysteries of the film and calls on them to produce their own explanations and resolutions.

As in several earlier instances in the film when Zabel has reported being followed, the knowledge that he is in danger only fuels his desire to solve the mystery of the *Orplid*. In particular, he proclaims again and again his intention to reveal the "truth" behind the political underpinnings of the plot against the *Orplid*, bringing to light the radical politics of his pursuers at the same time. However, the owner of the tabloid, Mannheim (O.E. Hasse), tells Zabel, "Nothing about politics in my newspaper! Politics is always black and white, and that makes gray. I have a *colorful* newspaper." Alluding to the largely female readership of the tabloid, Mannheim explains that simply reporting changing skirt lengths causes him to lose subscribers. "I wasn't thinking about subscribers," replies Zabel, "I'm interested in the truth." In a metacinematic moment similar to the cabaret scene in *Love '47, Epilogue* comments here again on the repression of politics in postwar Germany, in this case highlighting the incompatibility of commerce with uncomfortable political truths, a problem for both the media and the cinema. Yet far from granting credence to Zabel as the spokesperson of a truth that should be believed, the film portrays Zabel as a political naïf—after all, he is trying to sell his story to the tabloid, and thus his motivations are not entirely pure either—while also continuing to place the "truth" of Zabel's narrative in question.

A dissolve from one of Leata's drawings to a graphic match shot of the characters on board the *Orplid* initiates the final sequence of the main narrative, which itself delivers an allegorical message about politics by depicting the self-destruction of the characters on board when faced with the imminent threat of death. Notably, the film reveals in this sequence that the disillusioned *Heimkehrer* <former soldier recently returned home from battle> Martin Jarzombeck (Hans-Christian Blech) is essentially violent and evil, portraying the two gruesome murders he commits in a last-ditch effort to save himself. There are also two suicides on board. The dancer Ermanno (Arno Assmann) kills himself, as does the arms dealer Hoopman, in a misguided attempt to take responsibility for his own crimes at the last minute. Underscoring the film's point about self-destruction in the face of mortal fear, the bomb, discovered by the dying FBI agent, finally rolls off the side of the ship, but the arms dealer Hill sinks the *Orplid* anyway by opening its floodgates in his desperate search for the bomb he thinks is still on board.

When Zabel finishes narrating these events and we return to the frame story, Mannheim holds up one of Leata's drawings, remarking, "She's really very talented, the young lady—these are very imaginative!" Mannheim's comment highlights Leata's role in authorizing—indeed, in authoring—Zabel's account, casting doubt on the story's "truth" by suggesting that its origins lie in Leata's imagination. When Zabel refuses Mannheim's suggestion to expunge politics from his account for the sake of the tabloid's readership, Mannheim again comments on Leata's role, suggesting that Zabel take his account to a different newspaper: "Maybe elsewhere they'll believe his so-called documents and their *exotic garnish*." This penultimate scene of the film calls attention to Leata's position as a woman and racial other, questioning the status of the images she has produced, the truth value of the account that is predicated on those images, and thereby the epistemology of the film's entire narrative thus far.

The film's remarkable final sequence forms a kind of "epilogue" to the plot. Shot in Berlin's Shell Haus, that archetype of Weimar modernist architecture, the sequence recalls the visual language of late Weimar cinema. Leaving the tabloid office, Zabel and Leata board an open paternoster elevator. As the elevator travels downward, Siano jumps on board, stabs Zabel to death, steals the file with his report and Leata's drawings, and jumps off again. Leata grabs a gun from Zabel's pocket, and the camera cuts to a lengthy point-of-view shot that conveys her perspective for the first time in the film. From Leata's point of view, we hear Siano's footsteps descending the stairs, and we see the screen go completely black as the elevator crosses the space between two floors. When the elevator reaches the ground floor, we watch along with Leata as Siano crosses the lobby, and then we see Siano fall to the ground: Leata, revealed at the very end of the film to be a femme fatale, has shot him dead. In this penultimate scene, Leata takes control of the film's formal codes—conveyed through her long point-of-view shot—"shooting back," and thus demonstrating agency on the level of the narrative as well. In the film's final scene, the camera returns to a third-person point of view. We see the elevator as it reaches the bottom floor and begins to travel upwards again, bearing Leata who holds Zabel's dead body in the pose of a Madonna, a shot that comments ironically on the widespread use of this iconic image of woman in postwar visual culture.[23]

III

Like *Film Without A Title*, which Helmut Käutner also had a hand in, *Epilogue* makes the gaps and inconsistencies that marked so many postwar films into a conscious narrative strategy, albeit in very different terms from the earlier film. Joglekar has analyzed *Epilogue* as the first West German cinematic example of "anti-detection," demonstrating that the film systematically undermines the conventions of the detective or suspense genre, ultimately "revealing the unreliability of truth."[24] Indeed, the mystery that the film sets up, the sinking of the *Orplid*, is never completely solved by Peter Zabel; in the final sequence of the film, Zabel's attempt to solve this mystery leads to two new crimes that present their own mystery: the murders of both Zabel and Siano. Moreover, although *Epilogue* embeds multiple mysteries in its plot, none of which is ever completely solved, these mysteries all point back to another mystery at the center of the film: the mystery of Leata. Like many other postwar films, *Epilogue* demonstrates the imbrication of the postwar gender crisis with the postwar representational crisis, in this case through the character of Leata.

A woman with a mysterious past like other postwar heroines, Leata is the sole survivor of the sunken ship *Orplid*, but it is unclear just how she survived. In the main narrative imagined by Zabel, we see Leata on board the ship, which has been stripped of all rescue devices, just moments before it sinks. Yet there she is in the editorial offices of the tabloid, an eyewitness who ostensibly serves to substantiate Zabel's account. According to this account, Leata was on board the *Orplid* as a servant to the artiste Conchita (Irene von Meyendorff). Conchita, the mistress of the arms dealer Hoopman, has just married the former soldier Martin Jarzombeck. Their wedding, designed to give cover to the relationship between Conchita and Hoopman, provides the occasion for the yacht voyage, a cover story in turn designed to disguise the real purpose of the trip, an illegal arms deal between Hoopman and Hill. However, Leata is not merely Conchita's maid; she is also involved in a relationship with the shady Aldo Siano, who masquerades as the ship's piano player, but whose real purpose on board is to execute the plot to sink the ship. While the plot never makes clear the status of the relationship between Leata and Siano, that relationship is clearly implicated not only in the crime that led to the sinking of the *Orplid*, but also in the murders that take place at the end of the film.

Indeed, Leata plays a role in all of the film's most mysterious episodes, and it is only through unlocking her secrets that these mysteries might be solved. Amy Lawrence has noted that, "when there is a crisis in the representation of women, it often manifests itself as a crisis in the representation of women's *voices*."[25] In the classic Hollywood suspense thrillers Lawrence analyzes, "Women either talk too much or not at all … Those who are silent must be made to speak and those who talk too much must be silenced."[26] In many ways a classic film noir character—a woman without a past who is mute—Leata is, however, never made to speak in the film, and her secrets are never revealed. We are left only with her drawings, drawings that determine not only a substantial portion of the film's plot, but much of its visual language as well. In a film where nothing is as it seems and each character and plot twist conceals a double meaning, Leata is the ultimate unreadable text: not only is she female and mute, but she is racially other, as well, a point that the film and its publicity documents constantly highlight.

Mary Ann Doane has written of the femme fatale:

> The femme fatale is the figure of a certain discursive unease, a potential epistemological trauma. For her most striking characteristic, perhaps, is the fact that she never really is what she seems to be. She harbors a threat which is not entirely legible, predictable, or manageable. In thus transforming the threat of woman into a secret, something which must be aggressively revealed, unmasked, discovered, the figure is fully compatible with the epistemological drive of narrative, the hermeneutic structuration of the classical text. The imbrication of knowledge and sexuality, of epistemophilia and scopophilia, has crucial implications for the representation of sexual difference. … Both cinematic and theoretical claims

to truth about women rely to a striking extent on judgments about vision and its stability or instability.[27]

As Doane suggests, in classical Hollywood cinema, the femme fatale presents a site of condensation for issues of sexual difference, knowledge, and visual representation; by revealing the secret of the threatening or deadly woman, classical narratives strive for discursive mastery over "what can and cannot be known" and the limits of cinema's ability to represent "truth." However, as Doane's work makes clear, the femme fatale can never be fully contained, and the supplement or excess she leaves behind possesses "disruptive connotations" that point to precisely the instability and limitations of cinematic representation.

As a cipher for the formal and narrative gaps and inconsistencies of *Epilogue*, Leata certainly figures the "discursive unease and epistemological trauma" associated with the femme fatale; and like the femme fatale of classical Hollywood cinema, Leata is also illegible and unpredictable. Yet, as we have seen, Leata is, contrary to expectations, never transformed into the mystery that structures the film, and indeed, her mysteries are never solved. What is more, unlike the classic femme fatale, who is typically punished, often by death, Leata is the last character standing in *Epilogue*, which kills off all its *other* characters, villains and detectives alike.

We first see Leata in *Epilogue* as spectacle, as an image within the image, in a photograph of Conchita's wedding passed by Zabel's hands to the hands of the tabloid editor at the outset of the film. As Zabel names the various members of the wedding party, a hand moves a magnifying lens across the photograph from face to face, finally settling on Leata—the only person in the photograph whom Zabel does not name. Underscoring her mysterious nature, the camera and its diegetic stand-in, the magnifying lens, amplify the male gaze lingering on Leata's face as Zabel declares, "Back then I didn't know their names, but I looked at their faces over and over again. I sensed that something special, something uncanny <*unheimlich*> must have happened to these people."

A few minutes later, we see Leata's drawings for the first time, drawings which, as Zabel explains, "play a decisive role in uncovering the secret of the *Orplid*." The editor's hands examine a number of glossy photographic reproductions of the drawings, and then take hold of a series of Leata's works executed in a long narrow strip that resembles nothing so much as a film strip, highlighting from the beginning her role as producer of visual, even protocinematic representation.

Zabel explains his discovery of Leata's drawings during a trip to London as an exchange journalist: "At first I thought they were Chinese, but then I saw the European faces. ... They looked like book illustrations for a tale of the sea or a detective novel." As Zabel's comment suggests, Leata's drawings are at once foreign and familiar, they recall exotic forms of

Figure 4.1 The mysterious Leata as image maker and spectacle in *Epilogue*.
Source: Deutsche Kinemathek.

representation like Asian art as well as conventional illustrations for pulp
fiction. Noting that the faces in the drawings seem recognizable, Zabel
looks more closely and finds the word "Orplid" written on the illustration
of a ship. When he tracks down the artist who is exhibiting the drawings,
Phil Urban (Harry Tenbrook), at his studio, Zabel is amazed to see Leata
answer the door, since he immediately recognizes her as a survivor of the
ship. Zabel quickly realizes that the drawings are not Urban's at all, and
that the drunken artist has stolen them from Leata and signed them with his
own name. "He seemed to be exploiting her in other ways too," Zabel
declares, referring to the numerous nude paintings of Leata that cover the
walls of Urban's studio. This pivotal scene illustrates the slippages in the
representation of Leata as both image maker and spectacle that emerge in
the film's allegory of image production (see figure 4.1).

Zabel accuses Urban of forgery, causing a scandal, as we see from a
series of newspaper clippings about Urban that Zabel shows the tabloid
editors ("Urban's neo-primitivism—a hoax?"). Alluding to postwar
debates about abstraction and realism in painting, this montage sequence
references the interconnection of gender and race with styles of visual
representation, an issue that, as we shall see, became increasingly central
in the quest for legitimation pursued by West German films of the 1950s.
When Urban subsequently disappears without a trace, abandoning Leata,
Zabel brings her back to Hamburg. He hopes that Leata will help him
solve the mystery of the ship, but the only clues she provides come from
the drawings she produces compulsively—in Zabel's words, "as if to free
herself from a horrible experience." In a shot that again condenses many

of the film's themes, Leata's drawings are superimposed over her face and body, conflating Leata as spectacle and image maker once more and underscoring the unreadability of both the images and the artist herself. Repeatedly, men in *Epilogue* appropriate Leata's image and her images, while failing to decode them.

The femme fatale described by Doane is noteworthy for the sense in which she "overrepresents the body" and "produces nothing in a society that fetishizes production."[28] By contrast, there is a slippage in the representation of Leata between woman's conventional role as object of the male gaze and woman's potential role as author of images. This slippage is yet another example of the dilemmas encountered by the postwar film in its attempt to relegitimate German cinema and appeal to female audiences by turning to female experience as a strategy of representation. Like other postwar films that seek to represent female experience or grant women an unusual degree of narrative authority, *Epilogue* collides with the conventions of dominant cinema.

In the surprising ending of *Epilogue*, Leata commits an unexpected and unexplained act of violence, which we witness through her point of view, represented for the first time in the film. Not only does Leata finally seize complete control of the film's narrative and visual language in a move that resists the appropriation of her image and her images by men throughout the film, but she also does violence to the film text itself, rupturing our expectations of a conventional closure. In this sense, Leata may be read as a kind of femme fatale in reverse, the character who disrupts the epistemological drive and figures the impossibility of classical narrative structures in postwar German cinema, while also pointing to the instability of both cinematic representation and categories of gender in the aftermath of the Third Reich and World War II. Leata's status as the film's racial other is clearly at stake in the disruptive role she plays here.

IV

There is one scene in *Epilogue* that does provide some clues to Leata's mystery, albeit only to underscore further her unreadability in the film's elaborate allegorical language. After Zabel and Leata return from London to Hamburg, they visit the *pension* where Conchita used to live in an attempt to track down more information about the events that led to the sinking of the *Orplid*. This scene brings together a number of diegetic and extradiegetic elements in order to create an ostensible parody of postwar German racism and xenophobia, and its disturbing effects point to the limitations of popular cinema when it comes to representing race and ethnicity.

Though the landlady at the *pension* is pleased to see Leata again, she is astonished to learn that this "little bird," as she calls Leata, is now mute (see figure 4.2). The landlady tells Zabel that she "doesn't think much of

Figure 4.2 Spectral Others: Peter Zabel (Horst Caspar) and Leata (Bettina Moissi) visit the landlady (Camilla Spira). Source: Deutsche Kinemathek.

foreign languages, especially after the war," so she could never communicate with Leata, who only spoke French. According to the landlady, Leata was the star of a troupe of acrobats, who played for eight years in Hamburg, and who were "all yellow," a reference to their race. When the troupe was forced to leave Germany after the outbreak of the war, Leata could not travel with them because of a sudden illness, so Conchita kept her as a maid.

Escalating the racist discourse presented in the sequence, which is played for comic effect, the landlady repeatedly says that Leata is "not at all like a human being." And indeed, this "inhuman" quality—which is both exoticized and ghostly or *unheimlich*—is echoed in the film by the fact that Leata twice survives attacks that kill everyone around her. Thus, Leata is the spectral other who haunts the film—and indeed the German consciousness. There is a sense in which the figure of the absent Jew, as author of and audience for German cinema, is displaced onto the exoticized figure of the mute and traumatized Leata. At the same time, *Epilogue* conflates the threatening qualities of the Jew and the Asian in its representation of Leata as femme fatale. As an Asian, Leata represents the threat from the East, a threat tied strongly to anti-communism that originated with the depiction of Soviet soldiers in Nazi propaganda, grew stronger with the rapes and pillages committed by Red Army soldiers at the end of World War II, and began to escalate dramatically in the public imagination with the onset of the Cold War and the beginning of the Korean War in the late 1940s.[29]

Yet there is another dimension to the representation of race and racism in this strange scene, which relies in part on the extradiegetic resonance of the actress who plays the landlady, Camilla Spira. A star of Weimar cinema, Spira fled to Holland in 1933, where she was later arrested by the Nazis and interned in the concentration camp Westerbork. She survived the Holocaust only because of a sworn declaration by her mother that the Jewish actor Fritz Spira was not her real father. Camilla Spira was one of the few remigrants to re-establish a successful career as an actor in postwar Germany. Her role in *Epilogue* as the film's most virulent racist calls attention to the paradoxical situation of Jewish remigrants in postwar Germany, as the film disturbingly projects the persistent problem of postwar racism onto the Jew in a blame-the-victim strategy.

Spira is not the only remigrant actor whom *Epilogue* treats in troubling racist terms. The arms dealer Hoopman, played by the Jewish remigrant actor Fritz Kortner, is a mysterious character whom *Epilogue* variously portrays as a Nazi and through a series of Jewish stereotypes. The landlady mentions that Hoopman "looked very handsome in a uniform" and one of Zabel's informants about Hoopman discusses him in the context of denazification. Yet the film also presents him as a cosmopolitan magnate involved in shady financial transactions, an opportunist taking advantage of the fact that "armaments is the only business that's always booming." Marking him as other through his foreign name and the fact that he speaks several foreign languages fluently, the film also states that Hoopman "has his hands in all the conflicts of the Middle East."

Hoopman was only the second role for Fritz Kortner, a huge star of stage and screen in the 1920s, after his return to postwar Germany from Hollywood exile. His first role was the semi-autobiographical Professor Mauthner in *Der Ruf* (The Last Illusion, 1949), directed by Josef von Baky from a script by Kortner himself.[30] It is telling that in both of these postwar German films, Kortner, the remigrant Jewish actor, embodies a series of stereotypes of Jewishness, and then ultimately dies, unable to be integrated into the body politic of the Federal Republic. Furthermore, in *Epilogue*, which conflates perpetrator and victim in the figure of Kortner, Hoopman dies by his own hand, a gesture of self-punishment for his criminal deeds and outsider status. Expunging with Hoopman both "Nazi" and "Jew" from its framework, *Epilogue* presents an ambivalent message about political responsibility for the crimes of the German past and their relevance to the present.

Robert Shandley has written of the problems encountered by postwar filmmakers, including Jewish filmmakers such as Kortner, in representing

Jews, that "the film language they had at their disposal was precarious, given its recent misuse during the Third Reich. These filmmakers faced the aesthetic problem of creating a new image of 'the Jew' that would signify Jewishness in the wake of the vulgar filmic language of Nazi cinema."[31] As Shandley points out, the anti-Semitic stereotypes of notorious propaganda films such as Veit Harlan's *Jud Süss* (Jew Süss, 1940) created a representational language for identifying "the Jew," which "made it difficult for subsequent German filmmakers to portray a character as recognizably Jewish without resorting to ugly stereotypes."[32]

Epilogue hardly tackles the racist and anti-Semitic legacy of the Third Reich, nor does it constitute an attempt to resolve the representational dilemma of finding a new cinematic language to depict Jewishness. Yet to the extent that *Epilogue* is engaged in the quest to relegitimate postwar cinema in general—a project it undertakes through its interventions into genre and its allegorical treatment of the status of visual representation— it can hardly avoid questions of race and ethnicity, which return in trace form to haunt the text. E. Ann Kaplan has analyzed the way that the repressed issue of race (in this case primarily the relation between whites and African Americans) returns in American film noir, through a connection to issues of gender. Similar to films analyzed by Kaplan, *Epilogue*, which appropriates many elements of Hollywood noir films, is "concerned with the dark continent of the female psyche as this concern slips into unconscious fears of racial darkness."[33] This overlap between issues of race and gender is evident not only in the diegetic representation of Leata within *Epilogue* itself, but also in the publicity documents and accounts of the film published in the German press.

V

Leata bears some resemblance to other female characters in postwar cinema: like Susanne Wallner in *The Murderers Are Among Us*, for example, she is a woman without a history and an artist who uses her art to work through the traumas of the past. As the author of *Epilogue*'s images, Leata also possesses a unique degree of authority in structuring the film's narrative. Yet in sharp contrast to other postwar heroines, Leata's racial difference marks her as other—even inhuman—and prevents her from becoming a figure of identification for German audiences. This is made particularly clear in the publicity documents that accompanied the film.

As we have seen, the publicity documents for other postwar films such as *The Murderers Are Among Us* or *Love '47* actively sought to appeal to female audiences by highlighting the roles of their female protagonists. By contrast, the publicity documents for *Epilogue* do not appear to target female spectators, nor do they support a reading of the film as women's cinema. Rather, the press book for *Epilogue* underscores the film's presentation of Leata as mysterious and unreadable. Titled "A Woman Full of Riddles," the press book's article about the actress Bettina Moissi stresses her exotic heritage as the daughter of the Romanian-born stage actor and Nazi opponent Alexander Moissi, as well as the fact that she grew up in a panoply of different European countries. This incipiently racist profile of Moissi concludes that she "is not a mask, but a human being, and yet, through the exceptional gift of true dramatic talent, she remains the eternal female riddle."[34]

The film program for *Epilogue* published by the *Illustrierte Film-Bühne* echoed this exotic and mysterious characterization of Moissi/Leata.[35] Programs for other postwar films such as *Love '47* consistently emphasize the perspective of female characters, often neglecting to mention male characters at all. By contrast, the program's explanation of *Epilogue* does precisely the opposite, excising Leata almost entirely from the film's plot. In particular, the plot summary fails to mention that she survives the shipwreck of the *Orplid*, that she is the author of the drawings, or that she is a major character in the frame story. Notably, however, and consistent with Leata's status as spectacle in the film, she is strongly represented in the program's images. She occupies the prominent upper left-hand spot on the program's cover, and of the eight stylized figures drawn on the cover, she is the only one to gaze directly at the reader, while she in turn is the object of the male gaze of Aldo Siano. She is also pictured twice inside the program, and the only image on its back cover depicts her once more, standing over Zabel's dead body, again the object of Siano's gaze.

Like the film program, the pictorial retelling of *Epilogue* in the illustrated magazine *Film und Frau* also cuts Leata from the story almost completely.[36] While other pictorial features in *Film und Frau* often tried to steer the attention of the female reader/spectator to female characters and aspects of the plot that treated issues of interest to women, this one focuses only on the main narrative and the story of Conchita. Leata is present in only one of twenty still photographs from the film, a photo that shows only the back of her head. Although she is also shown in one of her drawings from the film that is reproduced here, the caption does not mention Leata as either the author or the subject of the drawing. These press documents all conspire to hold Moissi/Leata at a remove, contributing to her exoticization and specularization and/or preferring to elide her role in the film altogether. As the documents confirm, Leata's otherness marks her as taboo, and prohibits audience identification with her.

Publicity documents for other postwar films often shed light on the spectatorial appeal of the films, even inscribing or attempting to guide spectators' responses to certain characters and plotlines. In the case of *Epilogue*, this kind of publicity campaign did not take place. *Epilogue* was made at a moment when, on the one hand, race and racism were gaining new significance with the American occupation and the emergence of the Cold War, and, on the other hand, anti-Semitism and the Holocaust were quickly receding into the background, repressed as ancient history in the new Federal Republic.

As Heide Fehrenbach has argued, these two facts were demonstrably interconnected in postwar discourse, "when the issue of race and its peculiarly postwar meanings were explicitly addressed and performed by and for West Germans … by shifting the location of race from Jewishness to blackness in order to distance it from the Holocaust and Germans' crimes against humanity."[37] Moreover, as Fehrenbach demonstrates, discourses of race and gender were mutually constitutive: through a focus on interracial sex and so-called *Mischlingskinder*, "postwar German notions of race were formulated through sustained reference to German women's social roles and sexual behavior."[38] While racial otherness in the form of blackness was strongly implicated in postwar German identity formation (including gender roles), the Asian other also figured prominently in the construction of West German identities. Anti-communist discourse often figured the threatening aspects of the communist other by personifying him as Asian and emphasizing communism's Asiatic roots. Here again, race and gender were strongly interconnected, both through tropes of interracial sex (particularly the rape of the German woman by the "red threat") and through a focus on the family as a bulwark against such threats, discourses that again referenced women's social roles and sexual behavior.[39] Certainly, these associations with the threatening Asian were intensified at the moment of German division and the dawn of the Cold War.

It was at this moment that *Epilogue* allegorically located the origins of postwar film images with the figure of the traumatized artist, the racially other woman Leata. While in other postwar films, the turn to female experience constituted an effective strategy for finding a new cinematic language and appealing to largely female audiences, *Epilogue* demonstrates the limits of the "woman's film" as a strategy for relegitimating postwar filmmaking when it came to issues of race and ethnicity.

Despite its many limitations, *Epilogue* is notable for refusing closure on all fronts. Not only does the film frustrate audience expectations by killing off the figure of the detective rather than allowing him to solve the mystery, but it also refuses the typical solution offered by most other postwar films to date: the suggestion that the traumas and guilt of the Nazi past can be overcome by resolving the disturbed gender relations and sexual problems of the present. In contrast to other films in which female agency is ultimately instrumentalized to heal damaged masculinity, *Epilogue* concludes with Leata taking up arms and killing the man who steals her drawings, ending the film with the introduction of a race and gender problem that remains unresolved. As with the rest of its mysteries, gaps, and inconsistencies, *Epilogue* leaves it up to viewers to find their own solutions to this problem.

Perhaps better than most other films of the era, Brauner's and Käutner's *Epilogue* displays the persistent contradictions of popular filmmaking in postwar Germany. On the one hand, Käutner continued his attempt to make films that would force viewers to relinquish their passive stance and participate in the filmic process. By dismantling conventional genres, Käutner promoted productive spectatorship and also furthered the quest to relegitimate postwar cinema by working through the problems posed by dominant codes and forms. On the other hand, the end product of these efforts is marked by the return of a repressed racism, which bears traces not only of the difficulty of tackling the subject of race in postwar Germany, but also of the disturbing and paradoxical situation encountered by Jews who returned to work in the German cinema. As such, *Epilogue* is a testament to the ongoing difficulties of Käutner's professed goal of "dismantling the dream factory."

Notes

1. The Berlin Blockade represented a last-ditch attempt by the Soviets to stop the division of Berlin and Germany. The division had been made virtually inevitable by the currency reform, since it was not feasible for two competing currencies and two different economic systems to coexist within one state. Of course, the Soviet strategy backfired, and in the end the blockade further polarized East and West, becoming a decisive moment in the early Cold War.
2. See Hans Helmut Prinzler, *Chronik des deutschen Films 1895–1994* (Stuttgart, 1995), 182; and Elizabeth Prommer, *Kinobesuch im Lebenslauf. Eine historische und medienbiographische Studie* (Konstanz, 1999), 350–52.
3. "Überholte Filme," *Die Wirtschaftszeitung*, July 16, 1949.
4. Joseph Garncarz, "Hollywood in Germany. Die Rolle des amerikanischen Films in Deutschland: 1925–1990," in *Der deutsche Film. Aspekte seiner Geschichte von den Anfängen bis zur Gegenwart*, ed. Uli Jung (Trier, 1993), 200.
5. Heide Fehrenbach argues that *Heimatfilme* provide a cathartic space for audiences to come to terms with the traumas of the Third Reich and World War II (among them the common loss of *Heimat*), while also stressing the promises of modernity and the necessity of regeneration. See Fehrenbach, *Cinema in Democratizing Germany: Reconstructing National Identity after Hitler* (Chapel Hill, 1995). Johannes von Moltke analyzes the *Heimatfilm* as a "compromise formation" that helped to introduce and naturalize certain types of social and technological modernization for socially conservative West German audiences. See von Moltke, "Evergreens: The *Heimat* Genre," in *The German Cinema Book*, ed. Tim Bergfelder et al. (London, 2002), 18–28. See also his *No Place Like Home: Locations of Heimat in German Cinema* (Berkeley, 2005). For more on the *Heimatfilm*, see my chapter 6.
6. On the film's box office success, see Robert Scheuer, "*Epilog—Das Geheimnis der Orplid*," *Filmblätter* 42 (1950). See also Ernst Erich Strassl, rev. of *Epilog—Das Geheimnis der Orplid*, *Der neue Film* 41 (October 9, 1950).
7. Yogini Joglekar, "Who Cares Whodunit? Anti-detection in West German Cinema," Ph.D. diss. (Ohio State University, 2002), 59. See also her "Helmut Käutner's *Epilog: Das Geheimnis der Orplid* and the West German Detective Film of the 1950s," in *Framing the Fifties: Cinema in a Divided Germany*, ed. John Davidson and Sabine Hake (New York, 2007), 59–73.
8. My analysis of *Epilogue* is indebted to the discussion of the film at the German Film Institute, "After the War, Before the Wall: German Cinema 1945–1960," led by Anton

Kaes and Eric Rentschler at Dartmouth College in 2002.

9. Brauner has been notoriously reticent about the circumstances of his life during wartime and his survival, as evidenced by his autobiography *Mich gibt's nur einmal: Rückblende eines Lebens* (Munich, 1976). For a biography of Brauner that tries to fill in some of these gaps, see Claudia Dillmann-Kühn, *Artur Brauner und die CCC: Filmgeschäft, Produktionsalltag, Studiogeschichte 1946–1990* (Frankfurt am Main, 1990), 8–17.

10. Brauner, "Es war nicht richtig, daß Juden wieder in Deutschland seßhaft geworden sind," in *Fremd im eigenen Land: Juden in der Bundesrepublik Deutschland*, ed. Henryk M. Broder and Michael R. Lang (Frankfurt am Main, 1979), 76, qtd. in Dillmann-Kühn, *Artur Brauner und die CCC*, 18.

11. Dillmann-Kühn, *Artur Brauner und die CCC*, 12.

12. Tim Bergfelder, *International Adventures: German Popular Cinema and European Co-Productions in the 1960s* (New York, 2005), 106.

13. The ambiguous term *Überläufer* <"spillover" or "turncoat"> refers to films that were begun in the Third Reich, shelved or interrupted by the end of the war, and then completed and released in the postwar period.

14. Some of Brauner's most well-known films to treat the Holocaust and the Third Reich include Falk Harnack's *Der 20. Juli* (The Plot to Assassinate Hitler, 1955); Vittorio de Sica's *Il Giardino dei Finzi-Contini* (The Garden of the Finzi-Continis, 1970); Michael Verhoeven's *Die weisse Rose* (The White Rose, 1982); Istvan Szabo's *Hanussen* (1988); and Agnieszka Holland's films *Bittere Ernte* (Bitter Harvest, 1985) and *Hitlerjunge Salomon* (Europa, Europa, 1990).

15. Robert Shandley, *Rubble Films: German Cinema in the Shadow of the Third Reich* (Philadelphia, 2001), 90.

16. Qtd. in Dillmann-Kühn, *Artur Brauner und die CCC*, 38.

17. Bergfelder, *International Adventures*, 108.

18. Dillmann-Kühn, *Artur Brauner und die CCC*, 76.

19. Dillmann-Kühn, *Artur Brauner und die CCC*, 63.

20. On conflicts during the filming of *Epilogue*, see "Große Stars zu kleinen Preisen," *Der Spiegel* 34 (August 24, 1950): 34–35. The article presents Brauner in an anti-Semitic stereotype as a penny-pinching miser interested only in making money and not at all in the quality of his film productions, while it defends Kaütner as a misunderstood artist. A similar story is told by Curt Riess, *Das gibt's nur einmal: Das Buch des deutschen Films nach 1945* (Hamburg, 1958), 259–60.

21. "Der Kahn der Verdammten: ein 'Epilog,'" rev. of *Epilog—Der Geheimnis der Orplid*, *Der Kurier*, October 17, 1950. Given the incredibly confusing nature of the film's plot, it is not surprising that this reviewer got some details wrong: in fact, the bomb does not cause the ship to sink, as this review implies.

22. Editing has long been one part of the filmmaking process where women could leave their mark, since editing has often been seen as a craft appropriate to women's nimble fingers and aptitude for seeing and designing patterns. Johanna Meisel, who began her career in the Third Reich, was one of a number of successful female editors in the postwar period. Meisel worked for both DEFA and studios in the Western zones, and she edited many Artur Brauner productions in the late 1940s and early 1950s.

23. See Mariatte Denman, "Visualizing the Nation: Madonnas and Mourning Mothers in Postwar Germany," in *Gender and Germanness: Cultural Productions of Nation*, ed. Patricia Herminghouse and Magda Mueller (Providence, RI, 1997), 189–201; see also Erica Carter, "Sweeping up the Past: Gender and History in the Post-war German 'Rubble Film,'" in *Heroines without Heroes: Reconstructing Female and National Identities in European Cinema, 1945–51*, ed. Ulrike Sieglohr (London, 2000), 91–112, esp. 104.

24. Joglekar, "Helmut Käutner's *Epilog*," 71.

25. Amy Lawrence, *Echo and Narcissus: Women's Voices in Classical Hollywood Cinema* (Berkeley, 1991), 5.

26. Lawrence, *Echo and Narcissus*, 5–6.

27. Mary Ann Doane, *Femmes Fatales: Feminism, Film Theory, Psychoanalysis* (New York, 1991), 1.

28. Doane, *Femmes Fatales*, 2.

29. See Elizabeth Heineman, "The Hour of the Woman: Memories of Germany's 'Crisis Years' and West German National Identity," *American Historical Review* 101.2 (1996): 370ff.; and Eric Weitz, "The Ever-Present Other: Communism in the Making of West Germany," in *The Miracle Years: A Cultural History of West Germany, 1949–1968*, ed. Hanna Schissler (Princeton, 2001), 219–32.

30. On Kortner's postwar stardom, especially in *The Last Illusion*, see also Jaimey Fisher, *Disciplining Germany: Youth, Reeducation, and Reconstruction after the Second World War* (Detroit, 2007), 244–57.

31. Shandley, *Rubble Films*, 78.

32. Shandley, *Rubble Films*, 79. On the representation of Jews in postwar German cinema, see also Frank Stern, "Film in the 1950s: Passing Images of Guilt and Responsibility," in Schissler, *The Miracle Years*, 266–80.

33. E. Ann Kaplan, "'The Dark Continent of Film Noir': Race, Displacement and Metaphor in Tourneur's *Cat People* (1942) and Welles' *The Lady from Shanghai* (1948)," in *Women in Film Noir*, rev. ed., ed. E. Ann Kaplan (London, 1998), 186.

34. "Eine Frau voller Rätsel: Begegnung mit Bettina Moissi in dem Film 'Epilog,'" press booklet (Frankfurt am Main, 1950), in file on *Epilog: Das Geheimnis der Orplid*, Schriftgutarchiv, Stiftung Deutsche Kinemathek, Berlin.

35. "Epilog: Das Geheimnis der Orplid," *Illustrierte Film-Bühne* 905 (1950).

36. "Epilog," *Film und Frau* 2.23 (1950): 24–25.

37. Heide Fehrenbach, *Race after Hitler: Black Occupation Children in Postwar Germany and America* (Princeton, 2005), 14.

38. Fehrenbach, *Race after Hitler*, 14. On the imbrication of race and gender discourse in postwar German identity formation see also Maria Höhn, *GIs and Fräuleins: The German–American Encounter in 1950s West Germany* (Chapel Hill, 2002).

39. See Weitz, "The Ever-Present Other," and Robert Moeller, *Protecting Motherhood: Women and the Family in the Politics of Postwar West Germany* (Berkeley, 1993).

Part II

ART ON FILM: REPRESENTING GENDER AND SEXUALITY IN POPULAR CINEMA

Chapter 5

"THROUGH HER EYES": REGENDERING REPRESENTATION IN WILLI FORST'S *THE SINNER* (1951)

The turn to genre film paved the way for cinema's increasing popularity in the new Federal Republic. Audiences flocked to the cinemas: with 555 million tickets sold, each German citizen averaged twelve visits to the movies in 1951.[1] Notably, these viewers preferred German films to foreign imports, and the majority of the top ten most popular films of the year were German films.[2] Domestic film production held steady in 1951, with seventy-six new feature films released, including a range of popular *Heimatfilme*, suspense thrillers, comedies, and melodramas.

No doubt contributing to film's overall popularity, the German cinema also witnessed its first major scandal of the postwar period in 1951.[3] Willi Forst's melodrama *Die Sünderin* premiered at the Turm-Palast in Frankfurt am Main on January 18, 1951, causing an immediate outcry over the film's controversial subject matter. The sinner of the title, the prostitute Marina (Hildegard Knef), decides to quit her profession to devote herself to the man she has fallen in love with, the painter Alexander (Gustav Fröhlich). However, she soon learns that Alexander has a degenerative brain disorder that impedes his ability to see clearly, causing him to paint modern, abstract pictures. In order to pay for the operation that will cure his disturbed vision, Marina returns to prostitution. The painter is cured, and for a brief time he can see and paint again. Turning to a representational mode he calls "ultrarealism," he becomes famous with his paintings, which include risqué nudes of his girlfriend as well as abstract drip paintings. Before long, however, the painter falls fatally ill once more, and Marina, fulfilling an earlier promise to Alexander, kills him and then herself with an overdose of Veronal sleeping pills administered in a glass of champagne.

Although the newly formed self-censorship organization (*die Freiwillige Selbstkontrolle der Filmwirtschaft*, or FSK) had demanded that Forst cut numerous scenes from the controversial film, he refused, arguing that these cuts would result in the mutilation of his art. Despite grave reservations about the film, the Main Committee of the FSK ultimately approved the release of a largely uncut version of *The Sinner* for audiences over sixteen years of age.[4] Church leaders were outraged by the film's narrative, which they accused of damaging public morality by glorifying prostitution, extramarital sex, euthanasia, and suicide. They were particularly incensed by the film's notorious inclusion of postwar cinema's first nude scene. In protest over the FSK's decision, church representatives withdrew from the organization (though they soon rejoined it).

Over the course of the year, the scandal over *The Sinner* escalated into a full-blown debate about morality, freedom of speech, censorship, and, most importantly, the role of film and the limits of cinematic representation in postwar German society. Politicians throughout Germany debated banning the film, and in the state of Rheinland-Pfalz the issue of the film was even taken up in parliament.[5] Eventually, political debates about *The Sinner* led to reforms of the federal film credit program, which had helped finance the production of Forst's film. As Kirsten Burghardt explains, "A script submitted to the subsidy committee was no longer to be judged on the basis of its potential profitability, but rather cultural and artistic standards were to be incorporated in an altogether more objective assessment."[6] Meanwhile, despite the fact that it had been banned in many principalities, *The Sinner* went on to become one of the two most popular films of the year[7] (see figure 5.1). By the time

Figure 5.1 Long lines of spectators waiting in the stairwell of the Film-Bühne Wien cinema in Berlin to purchase advance tickets to *The Sinner*. Source: Deutsche Kinemathek.

it finally left cinemas in February 1953, two full years after its debut, *The Sinner* had become the top-grossing film of the entire postwar period to date in Western Germany.[8]

In her autobiography *The Gift Horse*, lead actress Hildegard Knef, who returned to Germany to make *The Sinner* after several years in the United States, recalled the remarkable scandal surrounding the film:

> I had lost my name, was now referred to exclusively as "The Sinner," threatening letters, detailed and illustrated proposals from countless sex maniacs, made up the bulk of my morning mail. The film was attacked from the pulpit, rent asunder by the clergy, shown amid clouds of tear gas and stink bombs, protest marches and processions, and had nevertheless or therefore been seen by two million Germans in its first three weeks of release. … I realized pretty quickly that I was being held mainly responsible for *The Sinner* nuisance. Having missed the formative years of moral renaissance, Wirtschaftswunder, and a society striving to reinstate virtue and moral order, I completely failed to grasp that stable currency, regular nourishment, and heated bedrooms had returned hand in hand with a prudery of the most insipid and nauseating sort, ignoring and disclaiming recent history. The reaction to a naked girl shown for a few seconds on the screen led me to believe that a lobotomy must have been performed on the majority of the demonstrators, relieving them of the memory of a diabolical past.[9]

As Knef's memoir suggests, general public outrage over the film was spurred on mainly by the churches, especially the Catholic Church. Church leaders called for a boycott of the film, telling parishioners that the act of watching the film could itself be construed as a sin. When audiences continued to flock to the film anyway, bishops in several principalities authorized more violent tactics, and their minions proceeded to drive customers out of the theaters by releasing tear gas and stink bombs in cinemas and even, on at least one occasion, by setting loose armies of mice on cinema floors.[10]

Protesters in many towns and cities also hung posters like this one, decrying the film: "ATTENTION! MURDER BY POISON! The film 'THE SINNER' glorifies the life of a prostitute! It is a slap in the face of every upstanding German woman! Whoring and suicide—should these be the ideals of our people? Poison for our people! Poison for our youth!"[11] As this poster emphasizes, the film's representation of gender and particularly female sexual promiscuity figured strongly in its negative reception. Gender also became a central issue in the many court challenges that followed after local police banned *The Sinner* or prevented its screening in municipalities throughout West Germany. For example, in August 1951 a cinema owner named Gertrud Heskamp filed a joint lawsuit with the distribution company Herzog Film against a ban placed on the film in the town of Lingen. Heskamp argued that the ban had caused her to lose money, and that it constituted a violation of the

Federal Republic's constitutional prohibition of censorship. As part of her case, Heskamp's lawyers submitted evidence that 384 of 536 reviews of *The Sinner* in the press had evaluated the film positively. Nonetheless, Heskamp's claim was rejected, and the provincial court ruled in favor of the police, pointing out that it was the duty of the police to protect the safety of the public, a duty they had exercised by banning the film. According to the case ruling:

> The council of the city of Lingen saw endangerment not only in the fact that the film directly injured spectators' conceptions of propriety and decency, but also in that it exercised a harmful influence on their morals. Thousands of German women and girls, war widows and refugees have lived in similar conditions as Marina, and have protected themselves from prostitution and led a proper, pure life, despite hard work, want, and privation, despite sexual degradation through the violent acts of enemy soldiers. The life of Marina must work like a mockery of their decency. Thousands of German men, blinded and injured by war, who bravely bear their burdens and do not steal away from this life through suicide, must listen to the film's message that the Christian conception of the commandment against suicide is false and that it would have been more natural to choose suicide.[12]

As this ruling makes clear, legal objections to the film centered on its representation of gender and, above all, its potential effects on spectators.

Willi Forst's first postwar film had been eagerly anticipated by audiences and critics alike. A native Austrian, Forst was considered a virtuoso filmmaker who might play a role in the rehabilitation of film culture in the Federal Republic. Through his stature as a filmmaker, Forst was able to lure two prominent actors to return to acting in West Germany for his project: Hildegard Knef, who had been pursuing a career in Hollywood, and Gustav Fröhlich, most famous for his role as Freder in Fritz Lang's *Metropolis* (1927), who had recently quit acting to pursue writing and directing. Forst himself had been a beloved director and actor of Third Reich cinema, known for his urbane musical comedies, including the immensely popular Vienna films, made for the production company Wien-Film. Though he was a central figure in the Nazi filmmaking apparatus, Forst maintained that his films were "unpolitical" and even examples of subversive resistance. As Sabine Hake notes, "For Forst himself, the 'Vienna' of Wien-Film provided a place of refuge and, through the metonymic slippage between capital and country, a locus of (imagined or imaginary) Austrian resistance."[13] In 1940, Forst had successfully managed to avoid being cast as the lead in Veit Harlan's notorious propaganda film *Jew Süss*, a fact he used to exculpate himself in the postwar years. Forst returned to Austria after the war ended, and he hoped to resume making films there. But the reconstruction of the film industry proceeded at a slower pace in Austria than in Germany, and it took Forst four years to arrange for the cinematic release of his *Überläufer* film *Wiener Mädeln* (Viennese Girls, 1945–49), shot in large part during the final months of the war.[14]

Hoping for better production conditions and the opportunity to make a different sort of film, Forst decided to return to the Federal Republic. During shooting of *The Sinner*, he insisted on complete secrecy, saying only that the film was "not a music film, not a Vienna waltz romp, but a film about a girl who sins."[15] Forst himself saw *The Sinner* as an opportunity not only to move away from the kind of films he had made during the Nazi period, but also to assist in the creation of a new postwar cinema.[16] In interviews after the release of the film, Forst repeatedly insisted that his Third Reich films had been escapist fare, but in the postwar period he intended to turn to "the problems of the day" in order to "save the German film from its own demise."[17] A dark domestic melodrama addressing contemporary social problems in view of the Nazi past, *The Sinner* contrasted sharply with the light musicals that had made Forst so popular with German audiences. As his biographer suggests, "The reason why there was such an unbelievable storm of indignation about Forst's 'The Sinner' at the beginning of the 1950s lies perhaps in the fact that people were so accustomed to Forst in a tuxedo or in the uniform of the Masters of the Teutonic Order that they simply could not bear a woman without clothing in connection with his personage."[18]

Perhaps because of the remarkable intensity of public debates about the film, critics have tended to read the film through the prism of the scandal it caused. While extensive documentation of the controversy now exists in important contributions by Kirsten Burghardt and Heide Fehrenbach, such historical material, while obviously pertinent to any analysis of *The Sinner*, emphasizes an examination of the film from the outside in, highlighting extradiegetic factors. As a counterpoint to these contributions, my reading of *The Sinner* proceeds from an analysis of the film's diegetic attention to questions of representation and perception, achieved through the metacinematic introduction of visual art and the modern, abstract painter into the filmic narrative. Further, I address the film's concern with questions of gender, sexuality, and difference, questions that are articulated in *The Sinner* through the binary pairs real/abstract and natural/artificial. As in other postwar German films, questions of gender and representation are articulated together in *The Sinner*. This articulation takes on a new form in Forst's film, which responds to new debates about visual representation that were gaining currency in West Germany in the 1950s, emerging from both the Cold War climate and the atmosphere of restoration that characterized the beginning of the *Wirtschaftswunder*.

I

Abstract art enjoyed a widespread popularity in West Germany in the 1950s, both in its elite form in galleries and painting exhibitions and in its mass form in home decoration, fabric patterns, and industrial design. Lauded by some as a regenerated form of high modernism and disparaged by others as primitive scribbling, abstract art was hotly debated in elite art journals and in the mass media, and articles about how to view an abstract painting appeared in magazines as diverse as *Die Kunst und das schöne Heim*, targeted at upper-middle-class art collectors, and *Film und Frau*, aimed at mainstream female film viewers.[19] Many of these texts constructed the activity of viewing abstract art in highly gendered terms as resistance to the lure of (feminized) mass culture, as abstention from certain types of (female) pleasures, and as participation in the condition of (masculine) modernity. More specifically, they tied abstract art to the process of democratization, using abstraction as the ground upon which to retrain the gaze and reconsider the role that visual representation ought to play in the emergent Federal Republic.[20]

Abstract art had already been introduced to the public in the first few years after the war by art journals such as *Das Kunstwerk* and exhibitions such as "Extreme Painting," held in Stuttgart in 1947.[21] Claiming to help German audiences "make up for lost time"[22] by exposing them to international trends vilified in the Third Reich, these educational efforts worked hard to explain abstraction as a (positive) response to the breakdown of rational, humanistic society in Europe, and to counter the Nazi epithet of "degeneracy."[23] At the same time, the West German discourse on abstraction also reacted against Soviet (and eventually East German) aesthetic doctrines, which trumpeted "socialist realism" and viewed abstraction as decadent individualism.

Writing in 1958, the art historian Will Grohmann noted that most German artists had broken with the past by turning almost immediately to abstract styles in the postwar period. "Only in the Russian occupation zone," notes Grohmann, "was there no new beginning, because the measures dictated by the Russian occupation were, in the realm of art, the same as those of the Third Reich. Almost all artists of rank moved to the West in the course of the years."[24] Grohmann's analysis of realism and abstraction was subsequently echoed by many Western art critics throughout the Cold War era: these critics vilify realism as the preferred stylistic mode of all "totalitarian regimes," including the Third Reich and the German Democratic Republic, while they endorse abstraction as a form that breaks with totalitarianism in a move of "distantiation from the optical reality" that has become unstable after fascism. As Grohmann and other postwar art historians suggest, in order to represent adequately the existential crisis brought about by the "end of history," the Holocaust, and the ascent of nuclear science, it is necessary for the visual artist to go beyond the "merely optical," to push images out of the realm of realist representation.[25] Portraying abstract art as pure individual expression or pure experiment with painterly form, postwar commentators and artists alike were (paradoxically) at pains to push forward their ideological agenda for abstraction by emphasizing its aggressively "apolitical" qualities.[26] Similarly, viewers were advised to shed any intellectual or theoretical assumptions about abstract art, in favor of both a studied examination of its artists and styles and an instinctual response to its visual forms.[27]

In her reading of the discourse on subjectivity surrounding the production and reception of abstract painting in West Germany in the early postwar years, Yule Heibel argues that the "twelve-year Hitlerian assault on the 'image of man'" and on prevailing notions of individuality and subjectivity led to a crisis of belief in the Cold War era that abstract painting thematized. Though postwar artists were very much concerned with looking back to art banned by the Nazis, Heibel points out, it is striking that they did not try to resuscitate styles associated with German Expressionism. Instead, in the quest to figure a non-fascistic form of subjectivity, West German abstraction purged not only the realistic portrayal of objects from its formal canon, but also affect and expression of any kind:

> The climate of reconstruction in the immediate postwar period stigmatized previous expressive modes—such affective phenomena as Romanticism and Expressionism, as well as the tradition of philosophical inquiry initiated by Nietzsche. These now became associated with social ruination and the cultural bankruptcy brought about by Nazism, but more insistently with the dangers posed by "Eastern"-style totalitarianism, that is, Soviet and East German communism. The combination of these two overriding factors—a desire to secure the subject on a stable ground and the willingness to project onto "the East" the dangerous qualities one is seeking to escape—set the terms for art's reception in the postwar period. These factors also helped determine what art would be produced, what would be viable.[28]

As Heibel argues, expression in visual art generally revolves around questions of authenticity and affect, and involves both self-expression and the expression of national and cultural identity. In the aftermath of Nazism and genocide, both of these modalities of expression had become suspect: "<E>xpression, Expressionism, and the body … were associated with 'dirty,' dangerous, unsavory things that could only threaten the closed contour of a stable image of man."[29] Thus abstraction became not only the sole adequate means of representing—indeed of reconstructing—the (male) subject in postwar West Germany, but it also became ideologically inseparable from the democratization of the emergent Federal Republic.

Heibel shows how expressionism, like mimetic representational styles in general, was explicitly linked in postwar Western discourses to the threats of Nazism and Eastern totalitarianism; it was perceived as being both too "political" and too "German" in an era when both these terms were suspect: "Expressionism was dangerous because it bore affinities to forbidden aspects of the recent past as well as to what generally came to be described as 'the Eastern': 'the barbaric,' 'the inhuman,' and the 'anti-individual.'"[30] Yet while she is clearly critical of what she terms the "essentialist and masculine ontology" of abstract painting at this time, Heibel never explicitly makes the link between the anxieties connecting expressionism with the East and the third term in this equation, Woman.

Postwar abstract painting intent on positing a new image of man sought to purge itself and its image of male subjectivity of all vestiges of the "feminine," including the feminized traits of affect and expression. While commentators repeatedly linked abstract art to science and music, they insistently dismissed any connections to the natural world, emphasizing abstraction's turn away from realism as its "renunciation of nature." As the lead article of a 1946–47 special issue of *Das Kunstwerk* on the subject of abstraction put it:

> <O>ne can claim of art of the twentieth century that it is characterized by a pronounced antinaturalistic tendency; all modern orientations, all -isms, however differentiated they may appear from one another, possess in the renunciation of nature a common denominator … Among the abstract artists, this "formal" tendency has been intensified: they have absolutized and "musicalized" the uses of form and color insofar as they, in extreme cases, completely detached them from the natural object. This signifies a radical break with the tradition of Western art, in which the use of form has always been connected to natural objects.[31]

While male artists were lauded for rejecting nature, female artists of the 1950s were often forcefully linked to the natural world, one reason for their virtual absence among prominent abstract painters of the period.[32] This idea undoubtedly had links to social and political commentaries on the family in the early 1950s that strongly asserted the "natural" role of woman as mother and nurturer, arguing that women should give up careers established during wartime in order to return to the home.

Abstraction sought to purge nature, the body, and all things female—including female artists—from its arsenal. At the same time, abstraction set out to delineate a revised and cleansed image of modern Western man that stood in stark contrast to the fascist man of Nazi Germany; the wounded, emasculated and ineffective man of the early postwar period; and the robotic, de-individualized automaton of the Eastern bloc. Indeed, abstract painting was situated at the interstices of a complex set of discourses that sought to encode a rational, Western male subject at the forefront of democratic modernity, who stood in opposition to and could help stave off the many threatening Others impinging on West Germany in the late 1940s and 1950s. Thus, abstraction was a highly politicized cultural form that was mobilized in the formulation of West German gender identities and national identities in light of both the struggle to "overcome" the Nazi past and the emergent Cold War. Paradoxically, however, in order for abstraction to succeed at this project, it was necessary that it appear to be completely apolitical.

Heibel suggests that to achieve this aim, abstraction was linked to a reified conception of autonomous art, whereby autonomy became a kind of fetish rather than a critical concept. For postwar artists, art's autonomy kept it separated from any kind of potentially totalitarian agenda, but also from the mandates of mass culture. In the discourse surrounding abstraction, abstract painting came to be seen as almost transcendentally autonomous, as absolutely separate from social life, political life, or the dictates of economics. The formal qualities of abstraction—the fact that it did not "express" any particular meaning or represent any particular objects—were integral to its status as autonomous.

Writing about the first "documenta" exhibition, which took place in Kassel in 1955, Walter Grasskamp argues that the conception of autonomous art papered over the failure of postwar artists and museums to respond to Nazism's attack on modern art.[33] Grasskamp suggests that one reason for the ascent of abstract art in the postwar period was its lack of connection to Expressionist styles influenced by primitive art, children's art, and the art of the insane, sources of inspiration for modern art that were the main object of Nazi attacks. Rather than historicizing modern art's use of these inspirations in order to diffuse Nazi critiques, postwar art discourse neglected them entirely. As Grasskamp explains, "The first documenta transformed a modern art that had come into being through difficult conflicts and disruptions into a timelessly valid contemporary art ... <The organizers of the exhibition> relied on the autonomy of the works of art, as though they could legitimate and justify themselves all by themselves."[34] Clearly, the purging of modern art of its links to the insane, the primitive, and the childlike—all coded feminine—was also necessary to the establishment of a rational, Western "image of man."

Autonomy was not only a myth that served to disguise abstract art's political goals. It also legitimized the high culture aspirations of an art form that played an increasingly dominant role in mass culture over the course of the 1950s.[35] Painters like Willi Baumeister were not only key advocates of autonomous abstract art in West Germany, but their designs for textiles and home furnishings were also immensely popular.[36] Abstract painting styles were swiftly commodified in a vast array of consumer products such as curtains, furniture, toasters, vacuum cleaners, and women's dresses. Industrial design from the late 1940s on took most of its cues from the trend towards abstraction in the other visual arts, and fashion designers were increasingly drawn to the styles of abstraction as well. Indeed, the ideal home, which by the end of the 1950s had become the entitlement of every middle-class West German under the sign of the Wirtschaftswunder, was a home burgeoning with products whose shape, line, and color were taken from the canon of abstraction. This ideal home was not simply a sign of emergent bourgeois affluence in the wake of decades of war, poverty, and reconstruction, but it was stylistically coded in popular culture as the emblem of its occupants' modern mentality.

Increasingly, the home was to be purged of "affective," pathetic kitsch, of the reigning Biedermeier and petit-bourgeois ornaments in favor of a new, Western, cosmopolitan elegance signified by the kidney-shaped coffee table and the abstract painting on the wall.[37] Thus, not only was the art itself to be purged of affect and confused emotions, but increasingly its role within first public and then domestic spaces contributed to the dulling of emotion and affect in these spaces as well. The trend in this new direction of decoration began first in the new white-collar public spaces of the postwar period (banks, corporate offices, government buildings) before encroaching on the homes of those heads of industry and government who had begun by hanging abstract paintings on their office walls. From here it was simply a matter of time before abstraction began to trickle down as a predominant mode of representation not only within the art world, but within the realm of everyday life as well.[38]

The increasing predominance of abstraction in public spaces and in home decoration during the 1950s had significant implications for the discursive construction of the public and private spheres in postwar West Germany. If abstraction was constituted as excluding emotion, affect, and pathos of all kinds, it came to symbolize the difficulty encountered by postwar Germans in finding visual representations of any kind that thematized complex emotional responses to the radical upheaval of their lives and their social and political systems during the first half of the twentieth century. Abstract art undeniably offered viewers possibilities for visual, intellectual, and corporeal pleasure, and art critics were at pains to inculcate in viewers the perceptual faculties necessary to understand and respond to these possibilities. But abstract art did not create possibilities for identification with the work of art, nor did it explicitly work through social and political issues confronting its viewers. As the art historian Martin Damus has observed,

> National Socialism, war, and their consequences hardly found a place in West German art. Inasmuch as the modern view of art and art history has taken art for art's sake as its object, subject and content have receded into the background. Pronouncedly representational, content-based painting was no longer modern. But only such art could take a concrete stance, could bring the times into the picture.[39]

In many ways, it was the cinema that continued to fulfill this function in West Germany in the 1950s. As numerous critics have disparagingly determined, the West German cinema of the period was marked by sentimentality, kitsch, melodrama, pathos, and emotion—in short, an overabundance of excessive affect. This provincial cinema had no chance of competing on the world market, but it was a uniquely *West German* cinema, which provided a kind of liminal space—not entirely public, not entirely private—in which individual viewers could engage, within collective audiences, with emotional and affective representations that had been purged from other types of visual culture.[40]

The rise of abstraction over the course of the 1950s as the exclusive Western, democratic, modern mode of visual representation in the Federal Republic had a strong impact on the ways in which critics and spectators alike perceived postwar visual culture. If I have dwelled at length on the postwar debates over abstraction in West Germany, it is because the discourse surrounding abstract art contributed particularly to the negative evaluation of film in several specific ways. In contrast to the clean break with the past accomplished by abstract painting, West German film from the early postwar period was seen as having failed to break with the aesthetic heritage of the Weimar and Nazi periods in any way. Unlike abstraction, which sought to create a new, cleansed image of man through purging art of suspect forms associated with expression, objectivity, and realism (and by extension, fascism and totalitarianism), film, it was argued, perpetuated images of problematic male subjectivity through its resuscitation of tropes and aesthetic styles linked precisely to these suspect forms. Furthermore, the film industry was seen to be driven exclusively by economic imperatives in the 1950s and made no attempt to dissociate itself from the feminized sphere of mass culture. Film returned to residual German cultural formations coded as retrograde during this period, rather than striving for new styles associated with democratic modernity. The fetishization of autonomous art, understood as art cleansed of problematic links to politics, social life, and economic dictates, led to a demand for a new autonomous art cinema during this era. This demand was articulated in film criticism again and again during the 1950s, and reached its apotheosis in the "Oberhausen Manifesto" of 1962, which proclaimed the birth of the New German Cinema. Understanding film as a failed mode of visual representation within the wider continuum of visual culture in the 1950s, many critics condemned the West German cinema of this era. Nonetheless, the films of the period were immensely popular with vast audiences in the Federal Republic—the same audiences who were consuming abstract art on a wide scale at the time. Moreover, many of these films paid conscious attention to contemporary debates about visual representation and to the status of cinema in the 1950s through metacinematic narratives that featured abstract painting and visual artists.

II

The melodramatic story of a painter who must be cured of his tendency to paint abstract pictures, *The Sinner* entered into debates about postwar visual representation at the levels of both form and content. The film's plot stages a narrative conflict between realism and abstraction that turns the tables on the conventional equation of abstraction with restored, democratic masculinity by both pathologizing and satirizing abstract painting. However, *The Sinner* is not merely a retrograde film that resorts to Nazi-era clichés about "degenerate art." Rather, the film's attention to gendered discourses of realism and abstraction complicates the way these binaries were invoked in public discourse, revealing some of the unresolved contradictions at stake in the social and representational problems facing postwar Germans. At the same time, the film's metacinematic focus on visual art represents another step in the ongoing quest to relegitimate cinematic representation in the postwar period.

A self-proclaimed experiment with a new formal language for postwar filmmaking, Forst's film was tagged as an "art film" for its innovative use of sound and image.[41] Ironically, while *The Sinner* was almost universally praised by critics for this artistry of cinematic form, many of these same critics disparaged the film for the moral turpitude of its melodramatic narrative content. Writing in the film journal of the Protestant Church, *Evangelischer Film-Beobachter*, Werner Heß articulated a representative view of the film, criticizing what he believed to be the film's torrid and tired clichés of plot and expressing moral outrage at its representation of prostitution, euthanasia, and suicide, but also emphasizing respect for its brilliance of form:

> The girl Marina is the child of a rotten, decayed world. Her mother's second marriage has broken up because of her stepfather's economic misfortunes and her mother's love of life. However, it was her stepbrother from whom she learned that love has nothing to do with the heart and everything to do with earning money. <We see> images of a "night club" filled with young people and images of nightlife at a typical bar, until she experiences her first real love with a debauched and drunken painter. This story of the prostitute who is transformed by true love has been portrayed often over the last century. The same goes for the story of the painter, who has the inevitable movie brain tumor in his skull and turns to drinking out of fear of going blind. One could write an entire cultural critique of the tumor in recent film production. Where, then, do we find the progress that Willi Forst has proclaimed to achieve for the German film industry with this film?
>
> What this film ventures in the realm of direction, photography, and editing succeeds without a doubt. This life story is told by the pensive voice of the beautiful sinner herself, while the camera captures the individual scenes optically. But she does not narrate events chronologically; rather, proceeding from thought associations, the different episodes are represented at different temporal intervals. The sight of a lighter or the image of a wine bottle triggers particular flashbacks, which slowly come together, until by the end of the film an entire life's fate has emerged. Without a doubt this is an unusual path, which only allows the actors to converse directly with one another in a very few scenes, something which lends their words a particular forcefulness, while large portions of the film, commented on almost

undramatically by the voice of Hildegard Knef, are animated by the contrast between image and word. We set particular value on emphasizing so clearly the positive cinematic achievements of Willi Forst, because we must say an equally decisive "No" to the content of his film.[42]

Heß's account highlights the film's formal innovation, chiefly its complex flashback structure and its constant juxtaposition of sound and image, accomplished in particular by the film's astonishing use of female voiceover, which virtually precludes dialogue in *The Sinner*. Like other critics of the film, however, Heß argues that this artistry of form ultimately elevates the film's most dangerous qualities, allowing Forst to pass off a poisonous message in the guise of a masterful art film.[43] This accusation, which finds expression repeatedly in reviews of *The Sinner*, is explicitly linked to another common critical concern: the film's negative representation of German men and women and its potential effects on audiences, especially young and female viewers.

Critics of *The Sinner* consistently point to the fact that in Germany there are "countless men, blinded by war, who didn't commit suicide" and "thousands, maybe even millions of women who experienced worse things than the sinner" without turning to prostitution.[44] Not only does the film abase these "real heroes," men who learned to live with injuries and women who worked hard at legitimate professions to overcome adversity, but it insinuates troubling messages to a suffering population: "After the beautiful death scene <at the end of the film>, who wouldn't want to reach for the Veronal pills?"[45] As Heß puts it, "This film is an artwork, but that is no excuse—rather it elevates the film's danger, for it will inject its poison into our people with the ability of a master. This film review is not really a film review but the scream of an oppressed heart: Who will help to prevent this spiritual murder of our young people and our sorely afflicted women and physically broken men?"[46]

By linking the "dangerous" artistry of *The Sinner* directly to its troubling portrayal of gender issues and its appeal to gendered spectators, reviewers explicitly acknowledged the extent to which the film, like many of its precursors, articulated the problem of delegitimated cinematic representation together with postwar social problems, particularly the ongoing public debate about women's sexual behavior, but also issues of emasculation, damaged masculinity, and strained relations between the sexes. Like *The Murderers Are Among Us* and *Love '47*, *The Sinner* thematizes the incommensurability of male and female perspectives, figured literally through the male and female protagonists' different ways of seeing in the film. In contrast to the blind Alexander, Marina exhibits a clear, realistic mode of vision that is figured by her control of the gaze throughout the film. Indeed, Marina not only possesses an active gaze, but she in fact controls the aural and visual codes of the film at large. Indeed, her remarkable voiceover dominates the film so much that other characters virtually never speak. In this sense, *The*

Sinner goes further than perhaps any other postwar film in granting its female protagonist formal and narrative authority.

The Sinner begins with a cryptic scene: the camera pulls back from a close-up showing a nude woman in a painting to reveal the woman herself, Marina, lifting a champagne glass to toast her lover, the painter Alexander. They sit in front of a fire, over which the painting hangs. The woman gets up and walks around the house, touching familiar objects, as her actions are narrated in a voiceover that we subsequently learn is her own. Then Marina speaks diegetically: "It's finally happened … It's finally happened … I've killed you." Already in this opening sequence, the film addresses questions of representation and perception that will recur throughout the narrative: the first shot highlights the image of woman through its focus on the painting and then on the painting's "real-life" subject, while the voiceover marks the woman's subjective but authoritative perspective on the events we see. This doubling of Marina's image on the canvas and on film recurs as a motif throughout the film, calling attention to gendered questions of spectacle and spectatorship, a point I will return to below.

The voiceover now initiates a dissolve that leads to a series of densely layered and elliptically structured flashbacks that piece together the events leading up to this opening scene. The first flashback takes place in Italy, where we see the painter Alexander throw an unexplained violent tantrum. The tantrum appears to relate to a particular failed work of art that was supposed to represent fishing boats and cliffs over the sea, but which looks rather more like an "abstract," modern painting. Proclaiming

Figure 5.2 Problems of sexuality and representation: A Naples art dealer purchases Alexander's failed painting in exchange for sex with Marina (Hildegard Knef). Source: Deutsche Kinemathek.

that "even the craziest pictures have been sold at times," Marina tries unsuccessfully to sell the painting at a series of art galleries in Naples. Eventually, she agrees to sleep with an art dealer who will buy the painting in exchange for sex (see figure 5.2).

Emblematic of the complex flashback structure of *The Sinner*, which resembles a series of nesting boxes, Marina's sexual encounter with the art dealer triggers a second embedded flashback that narrates the events leading up to Alexander's tantrum, events that appear oblique because no explanation is offered for them. Again, we see Alexander's violent outburst in an exact repetition of the first scene of the first flashback. At the end of this sequence, the narrative returns to the Naples art gallery. After Marina leaves the gallery, the film's third flashback recalls her first encounter with Alexander, which took place in a bar in Munich where she worked as a high-class prostitute. Here both Marina's controlling and appraising gaze and her status as spectacle are foregrounded, as we see her using a cleverly installed mirror to survey the men in the crowd behind her as she sits on display at the bar.

The film's subsequent flashbacks return to earlier times, extending as far back as Marina's childhood in order to slowly explain these elliptical opening scenes. In particular, Alexander's "abstract" painting forms the mystery at the heart of the film, a mystery that Marina's extensive flashbacks work to explain. The plot of the film thus revolves around the cause behind this painting's "disturbed" mode of representation, linked to both Alexander's tantrum, which we see repeated twice in the first minutes of the film, and to Marina's decision to exchange sex for money. From the outset of the film, then, this painting presents a site of condensation for male violence, female sexuality, and the gender trouble that is at the heart of *The Sinner*.

Eventually, Marina quits working as a prostitute in order to live happily together with Alexander, who has moved in with her, transforming her apartment into an art studio. One day, Marina finds a package of Veronal tablets in Alexander's pants pocket. Confronting him about the pills, she finally learns the truth about the malignant brain tumor that will eventually kill him. Determined to make his final months count, Marina decides to take Alexander to Italy, where he paints happily until the day when he begins to lose his eyesight, which is also the day he loses his temper, the event we witnessed in the very first flashback.

Only now does the film reveal that Marina was unable to sell Alexander's painting in Naples because it was "deformed" as a result of his damaged vision, and that she turned to prostitution with the Naples art dealer in order to earn enough money to bring Alexander back to Munich for an operation she hoped would restore his health. On the surface, the explanation for the disturbed vision represented by Alexander's painting lies in the fact that he has a brain tumor that is slowly causing him to go blind. However, in the film's symbolic economy, the brain tumor serves as a stand-in for problematic male subjectivity in general. Indeed, Alexander represents yet another incarnation of the conspicuously passive and lacking male protagonist of postwar German cinema, as emblematized by the symbolic castration of his blindness.

Reviewers of *The Sinner* noted that the scandal surrounding the film was caused in part by the clear metonymy between Alexander and Marina and their real-life counterparts: the war injured, in particular men who had sustained eye injuries and gone blind, and women who had experienced adultery, prostitution, or sexual victimization in the war and early postwar years. The metonymy between Alexander and the war injured is underscored by this key sequence of the film, when we finally learn that Alexander is going blind. As Marina searches through his papers, hoping to find information about the doctor who has diagnosed his illness, she comes upon a picture of Alexander dressed in a Wehrmacht uniform. This is the single clue about Alexander's past offered by the film, a clue that links Alexander's disturbed vision with his service as a German soldier and his status as a *Heimkehrer*.

Equipped only with a cartoon drawing of the doctor made by Alexander, Marina sets out to find the man who can save her lover's life, deciding once again to return to prostitution to earn money for the operation. Coincidentally, Marina finds Alexander's doctor in the very bar where she once worked. In the melodramatic world of *The Sinner*, the doctor propositions her immediately, and the two rent a room at a shabby hotel, the aptly named Hotel Terminus. While undressing, Marina drops the drawing of the doctor, who, remembering Alexander, immediately promises to perform the operation for free. The doctor does not sleep with Marina, but instead successfully operates on Alexander, restoring his vision.

After the operation, Alexander and Marina move to Vienna, where Alexander begins to paint again. Explaining that he has to "learn to see again with new eyes," he paints only nudes of Marina. Alexander becomes a successful artist once again, practicing a new style of painting that he refers to satirically as "ultrarealism," a term that celebrates his ability to reject abstract styles. However, this happy period is short-lived, and when Alexander suddenly goes blind, Marina does as promised: she gives Alexander a glass of champagne loaded with twenty Veronal tablets.

We have now returned to the opening scene of the film. Only when Alexander can no longer hear her speak—when he is no longer cognizant of her actions—does Marina administer the remainder of the Veronal to herself, following Alexander into death. The film closes with a zoom in on the nude painting of Marina with which the film began, a painting that Alexander has titled *The Sinner*. At first, the painting is barely visible in the dimness of the room, but then it is illuminated by bright bars of light that seem to spill down on it from above, signaling not only the redemption of Marina and Alexander but also the redemption of realist art—and by extension cinematic representation as well.

In her analysis of *The Sinner* as "an allegory of postwar gender relations," Heide Fehrenbach attributes great significance to this ending, suggesting that the closure offered by the film reinstates traditional values along with conventional sex and gender roles. Thus, in Fehrenbach's view, while the film presents a threatening narrative about a world in which traditional ideologies have been turned upside down, *The Sinner* ultimately reinforces a conservative agenda emblematic of the climate of restoration pervading the Adenauer Era. Reading the film primarily as a narrative about the crisis of male subjectivity, Fehrenbach stresses the story of Alexander, the painter who ultimately loses his "aesthetic and sexual control" when he goes blind. For Fehrenbach, the "aesthetic death scene at the end" of the film in which Marina kills Alexander and then herself, "serves to 'right' the skewed world of male impotence and gender inversion."[47]

Attributing heightened significance to the film's closure, Fehrenbach's analysis overlooks the gendered dynamics of the film's formal composition, which suggest some alternative conclusions about both the meaning of the plot and the stance on ideologies of gender articulated by the film. Furthermore, Fehrenbach's very convincing analysis of the film's reception by church and government leaders leaves open several questions about its wider popular reception. First, if the film served a conservative agenda, what accounts for the extremity of the outcry against it? Fehrenbach clearly outlines the reasons why the film struck a chord with conservatives who protested so vehemently against it. However, she also contends that the film's ending charted an ideological transformation that nullified any cause for controversy: "Remarkably, critics of the film disregarded this transformation and attacked Marina's role as prostitute and murderess."[48] Given the tensions involved in the film's reception, however, this conclusion seems rather surprising.

Second, what accounts for the immense popularity of the film with German audiences? Despite the best attempts of church and government leaders to keep audiences from seeing the film, viewers flocked to *The Sinner*, eventually making it the top-grossing film of the postwar period to date. Fehrenbach is right to point to the film's implication in larger discourses surrounding gender identity in the emergent Federal Republic. However, she contends that the film revolves around the question, "Who killed the German man?," implicating women in the production of problematic male subjectivity. Yet the film's formal codes combined with the story told by Marina about the experiences leading up to her suicide suggest that its focus is rather the opposite: the question of responsibility for the death of the German *woman*.

Like the postwar Hollywood films analyzed by Kaja Silverman and the rubble films discussed by Jaimey Fisher, *The Sinner* compensates for male lack by dispersing narrative authority and access to formal cinematic codes onto the film's female protagonist, thereby staging a conspicuous gender reversal.[49] However, this gender reversal does not occur by default, but rather was developed by director Willi Forst as a self-conscious strategy for investigating the Nazi past and addressing the social and representational problems of the postwar present. As in precursor films such as *Love '47*, then, the turn to female experience emerges once more as a key facet in the quest to find a new film language and relegitimate cinema in postwar Germany.

Like *The Murderers Are Among Us* as well as *Love '47*, *The Sinner* addresses the legacy of the Nazi past through the key issues of male violence and female sexuality. If those earlier films offered provisional solutions to the social problems they thematized, however, *The Sinner* ends with a more pessimistic message. Writing about the transition from the rubble film to the cinema of the Adenauer Era, Thomas Brandlmeier focuses on the social conflicts—in particular "the conflict between the traumatized man and the strong woman"—that 1950s films slowly erase from view.[50] As Brandlmeier suggests, "Around 1950 there was a passing period in which these unresolved conflicts escalated violently, before the hangover of the 1940s finally gave way to the hectic, breathless conformity of the 1950s."[51] For Brandlmeier, the death of Marina in *The Sinner* is a prime example of this violent escalation of unresolved gender conflicts. Far from successfully righting the gender inversions it stages, then, *The Sinner* suggests precisely the impossibility of such a successful resolution to the gender trouble of postwar Germany, as reflected by its highly ambivalent ending.

Stepping into the fray of public debates over realism and abstraction in visual art and the role of cinema in the Federal Republic, *The Sinner* stages not only a battle of the sexes, but also a virtual battle between dichotomous modes of representation. Both a bawdy melodrama and an accomplished "art film," *The Sinner* became a public scandal and a popular success by encompassing postwar cinema's most contradictory possibilities within one filmic text. If politicians and church leaders excoriated the film for its lascivious content and critics disparaged its melodramatic plot, the film achieved popularity with the still largely female audiences of the early 1950s through a combination of melodramatic structures and formal artistry that satisfied spectatorial desires both for the possibility of affective identification and for a new postwar cinematic language.

Again, Forst accomplished both goals by turning to the strategy of women's cinema, addressing female experience and granting women a unique degree of agency in both the narrative and the formal codes of his film. On a narrative level, *The Sinner* delves deeply into women's experiences of wartime and the postwar period encapsulated in Marina's (auto)biography. On a formal level, the film is transparently structured according to Marina's perspective, utilizing flashback, voiceover, and control of the gaze as signifiers of her authority. Like *The Murderers Are Among Us* and *Love '47*, *The Sinner* conspicuously exhibits the decentering of the male protagonist and the concomitant gendered inversion of cinematic codes, dispersing narrative authority and identificatory structures onto the female protagonist. Those earlier films aimed toward a closure that would restore male authority and reinstate traditional gender roles, through the symbolic restoration of the gaze to the male protagonists Mertens and Beckmann. In *The Sinner*, by contrast, this aim toward closure never takes place: Alexander dies blind, while Marina retains mastery of the gaze and the voiceover until the (albeit highly ambivalent) end of the film.

III

In a reading of postwar West German melodrama, Erica Carter suggests that the genre dealt explicitly with transformations in feminine identity during a period when women's identities were in flux. In a decade when the reconstruction of the family was the focus of public discourse and of new social, political, and economic policies, melodrama, traditionally a genre that affirms the bourgeois family, was strongly implicated in the national project of promoting traditional "family values." Carter focuses in particular on the ways in which melodrama narrativized the transition of the female protagonist "from luxury consumer to bourgeois housewife" (a transition that can be seen in Forst's film), and women's contradictory relations to this transition.[52]

On the one hand, the narrative trajectory of *The Sinner*, which virtually picks up where *Love '47* left off, charts Marina's transformation from a sexually promiscuous woman into a housewifely caregiver in a normative heterosexual relationship. In this sense, Marina's self-sacrificing suicide at the end of the film suggests, as Fehrenbach puts it, that "female martyrdom brings gender redemption and the containment of once-threatening female sexuality."[53] On the other hand, *The Sinner*, like most of its postwar precursors, actually fails to affirm the vaunted domestic idyll of the bourgeois family, brutally suggesting that a "happy ending" can occur only in death. Far from simply reining in out-of-control female sexuality or promoting traditional family values, the plot of Forst's film in fact demonstrates Marina's ambivalent reaction to such values given her experiences in the Third Reich.

After Marina has administered the fatal dose of pills to Alexander and before she ingests the pills herself, she remembers her life with the clear insight of someone who is about to die. Reconstructing the sequence of specific events that brought her to the present moment is a powerful act of remembrance for Marina, through which she is able to bestow meaning, order, and causality on her life story. As Marina reconstructs her past, she provides an explanation for her transgressions that elucidates her turn to prostitution. While her story narrates her fall from grace and redemption through love, it is significant that each fall was occasioned by an act of violence directed against her by a man. In each instance, this explanation is grounded in public and private history.

As Marina—and the film—suggest, her "moral decline" was precipitated by militarism and Nazism, which were responsible for both the disintegration of her family and for male violence in both the public and private spheres. Far from allowing herself to be victimized by male violence, however, Marina repeatedly sought to establish her own agency to overcome it. That she did this primarily through "immoral" acts is attributed to the social and economic strictures to which she was subjected in wartime and the postwar period. For female viewers who might have engaged in similar acts, which were strongly demonized in public discourse in the early 1950s, the film thus presented one paradigm for remembering and working through these experiences, a paradigm that was articulated at both narrative and formal levels.

In her analysis of gendered myths of German responsibility in the postwar period, Elizabeth Heineman cites *The Sinner* as "one of the most well-known expressions of female responsibility for a postwar decline <in moral values>."[54] Heineman suggests that the film fit in to a larger public discourse that situated the sexually promiscuous woman as a symbol of moral collapse, allowing Germans to "avoid thinking about much more troubling characters" like Nazi soldiers who had committed crimes against humanity.[55] As Heineman explains, women's fraternization was reserved for the most extreme criticism:

> The Yanks' Sweetheart (*Ami-liebchen*)—the "fraternizer" in the zone where fraternization was probably most common—came to be as deeply associated with these years as the Woman of the Rubble. Like her, the Yanks' Sweetheart eventually represented something much larger than herself. Unlike the Woman of the Rubble, however, the Yanks' Sweetheart was no heroine. She became the symbol of Germany's moral decline—and, as such, implied that the decline occurred with the collapse of, rather than during, Nazi rule.[56]

However, far from suggesting that Germany's deterioration occurred with the end of the Third Reich, *The Sinner* departs markedly from Heineman's paradigm by repeatedly grounding women's "moral decline" in their experiences *during* the Nazi period. In one key sequence, for example, we see Marina working as a prostitute in a Munich bar with Nazi soldiers; through a dissolve, the Nazi soldiers are replaced by Allied soldiers. Marina's voiceover explains that as a prostitute she experienced a strong continuity between the Third Reich and the postwar period: only the uniforms of the soldiers were different. Here, *The Sinner* suggests that fraternization was an extension of actions learned during the Nazi period, actions necessary for women's survival.

In a similar fashion, Marina's flashbacks are constructed to establish causal links between the Third Reich and the social problems of postwar

Germany. Notably, issues of representation figured by Alexander's abstract painting provide the occasion to excavate these social problems and explore their causal links. If Marina cannot fit comfortably into the ideal female role she so desperately wishes to occupy because of her past as a prostitute, Alexander's abstract painting is pathologized as the signifier of his inability to occupy the ideal male role. The plot of *The Sinner* suggests that if Marina can only restore Alexander's eyesight and heal his troubling tendency to paint perverse, even pathological pictures, then the two will be able to establish a normative heterosexual relationship based on their "natural" gender roles.

Marina's very first flashback memory recalls a scene in which Alexander loses his temper, destroys a painting, and throws things around the room. Not only the first flashback, this is also a scene we see repeated twice in the film, a repetition that emphasizes the episode's significance for Marina's subsequent actions, including her brief return to prostitution and her eventual decision to euthanize Alexander. Her recollection of this return to prostitution, occasioned by a scene of male violence, triggers Marina's memory of a chain of events in her life in which male violence was a constitutive force. Notably, this scene originally showed Alexander assaulting Marina, brutally throttling her and demanding that she hand over his Veronal pills. While the suggestion of this assault still remains in the violent scene, the production company found the actual assault too violent, and demanded that it be cut.[57]

In this sequence, Marina first remembers the evening she met Alexander. Responding to the brutality of a nightclub bouncer, a man in uniform, who violently threw Alexander into the street, Marina was moved to rescue him literally from the gutter. Next, she recalls the events of her childhood and her initial turn to prostitution. Here, a causal link is established between the Gestapo's arrest of her stepfather and Marina's first sexual experience, when she agreed to sleep with her stepbrother for money. The film suggests in no uncertain terms that National Socialism was responsible for the destruction of Marina's family and for her own moral decline.

Marina's next childhood memory posits a further connection between militarism, male violence, and sex. When her stepfather is released from prison, he is welcomed home with a family dinner. In the middle of the dinner, a car outside honks, and Marina's mother abruptly gets up to leave for one of her "dates." While Marina's stepfather has always mutely and passively accepted his wife's transgressions, her departure on his first night out of prison pushes him over the edge. He follows her and slaps her, screaming, "Whore! Whore!" When she leaves anyway, the stepfather removes from a closet a package containing his officer's uniform from World War I. Unwrapping the uniform, he rips off his decorations and medals, including an Iron Cross. Through this gesture, he professes his complete emasculation: he has been betrayed by both his wife and the state.

Marina's stepfather storms out of the house, and her stepbrother immediately begins to fondle her. She consents to sex when he offers her all the money in his wallet. Her stepfather returns home, finding Marina and Eduard in bed. In a return of his repressed, lost authority and militant masculinity, he beats Eduard, who is subsequently carried out of the apartment unconscious or perhaps even dead. Marina lands on the streets, eventually turning to prostitution to survive.

Significantly, the one time Marina's attempt to prostitute herself is not precipitated by an act of violence is the only time in the film when she does not go through with it. Walking down a darkened Munich street, Marina decides to return to the club where she once worked to earn money for Alexander's operation. In order to get to the club, she must climb over a large pile of rubble, a literal spatial metaphor for Marina's return to the sexual promiscuity of the past. But Marina does not ultimately sleep with the doctor. Instead, her transformation from sexual promiscuity to devoted monogamy is confirmed by this sequence, when the doctor concludes that Marina must be Alexander's wife.

In Marina's own retelling and in the film's larger narrative, the only possibility for salvation and personal redemption appears to be romantic love and heterosexual union. As such, *The Sinner* is certainly implicated in the larger project of reconstructing the family, the mutual goal of both melodrama and the postwar West German nation. However, even Marina's experience of domesticity and romantic union is marred by the violence of Alexander's tantrum, a point that is driven home by this event's repetition in multiple scenes of the film. In this sense, the death of the couple at the end of *The Sinner* suggests, in the tradition of melodrama, precisely the impossibility of fully reintroducing the characters and plot elements into the dominant order. As such, this ending is not only part and parcel of the hegemonic attempt to rehabilitate the family in the early 1950s, but it also reveals the tensions and contradictions inherent in that precarious project.

IV

In constructing the film's appeal to female viewers, the melodramatic content of *The Sinner* is complemented by its artistry of form, in particular its use of sound and image. If the film investigates women's experiences of the Third Reich and the postwar period, then it does so by granting Marina a unique degree of agency in telling her own story through a montage of images tied together by a remarkable voiceover. Because it virtually excludes dialogue altogether, Forst had originally titled his film *Monologue*, but the title was changed just before the film's release to capitalize on the emergent scandal over its representation of the sins of prostitution, adultery, suicide, and euthanasia.[58] This "film that thinks out loud," as Forst termed his project, sought to reconstruct the inner thoughts of one (notably female) character as a means of formal and narrative experimentation.[59]

Forst attempted this experimentation through the structure of Marina's flashbacks, which excavate layers of memory that interlace and double back on themselves. *The Sinner* invokes a wide array of editing devices to accomplish this excavation: the flashbacks are set off by dissolves, fades, iris shots, and graphic match shots that bridge time and space by cutting from one object to its historical or future parallel object, shot from Marina's perspective. These visual effects and editing techniques foreground the continuities and breaks in Marina's story: a fade to black generally indicates a break; graphic match shots and dissolves establish continuity; and iris shots focus the viewer's attention on a specific visual signifier.

What consistently ties these disparate flashbacks and visual effects together is Marina's voiceover, which represents one of the most extended uses of female voiceover in postwar film. This unusual and striking use of voiceover is diegetically grounded at the outset of the film: the first scene mixes images of Marina speaking into the camera with shots in which we see Marina moving in front of the camera but hear her speaking in voiceover. As Marina's flashbacks begin, the voiceover continues, signifying her memory. Throughout the film, Marina's voiceover often addresses Alexander in the second person. *The Sinner* thus circumscribes the potentially threatening or subversive aspects of this female voiceover through the use of particular devices such as linking the voice inextricably to the female body and using it to address a male character.[60] Nevertheless, through the voiceover, Marina seeks to reconstruct her story, her own subjectivity, and to grant meaning to her "identity transformations," which are emblematic of common female experiences of wartime and the postwar period.

The Sinner's formal address to the female spectator and its engagement of postwar social and representational problems condense around one key sequence, which takes place after Alexander's eyesight has been successfully restored by surgery. Heide Fehrenbach reads this sequence as the penultimate moment of the film's conservative message, in that it functions to affirm Alexander's dominant masculinity and to achieve Marina's absolute redomestication. For Fehrenbach, it is significant that Alexander paints only Marina, in particular highly specularized images of Marina nude. Yet Fehrenbach's reading focuses only on the narrative content of the sequence, failing to note that Marina, far from being simply the passive object of the gaze here, is in fact its primary subject and enunciator in this sequence. The formal structure of the sequence introduces us to Alexander's sketches through Marina's gaze, complicating conventional structures in which men look and women are looked at. In the discourse on spectatorship developed by this sequence and the general focus on painting in *The Sinner*, Marina's view of

Figure 5.3 The privileged female gaze: Marina looks at one of Alexander's paintings. Source: Deutsche Kinemathek.

Alexander's artwork is privileged—indeed, she is virtually the only character in the film to actually look at the paintings[61] (see figure 5.3).

The sequence begins with a simple cut from the internal space of Marina's Munich apartment to an external shot of the city of Vienna, where Alexander and Marina have just moved. This simple cut marks the sequence from the outset, contrasting strongly with all the other flashbacks in the film, which are uniformly initiated by dissolves, graphic match shots, or fades to black. In the sequence, Marina narrates Alexander's rise to success as a painter in the Viennese art world. As her voiceover explains these events, Marina pictures herself lying under an umbrella in the garden, posing for Alexander. She gazes up at the umbrella, and projects a striking montage of Alexander, his paintings, scenes of gallery openings, and newspaper articles about his success. This montage is enclosed in a box—reminiscent of nothing so much as a movie screen—that is superimposed on Marina's umbrella, the outline of which frames the entire sequence. Multiple filmic effects are invoked here to indicate Marina's narrative, aural, and visual authority. Not only does her voiceover initiate the sequence, but within the flashback Marina also controls the gaze. The continued presence of the umbrella reminds us throughout the sequence that we are literally seeing through Marina's eyes.

This lengthy montage is one of the most visually dense sequences in the film, presenting layers of superimposed images of paintings, words, and people in glamorous clothing. Granting respite from the dark and melodramatic tenor of the rest of the film, this comic sequence, presented through Marina's eyes, emphasizes visual pleasure in the *mise en scène* of the artistic milieu. We see two kinds of images here: a series of amusing parodies of contemporary abstract paintings and a number of realist paintings featuring Marina's bare breasts. Notably, while the remainder of the film consistently works to code abstract painting as "perverse" and realist painting as "natural," in this sequence both modalities are subject to parody and both are implicated in the pleasurable fantasy space of art viewing. Marina explains in voiceover that Alexander has become so successful that collectors will buy anything he has painted, including the "abstract" works he made in Italy when his vision was impaired. Amazed at this turn of events, Alexander makes fun of people who will buy this art by creating a series of Jackson Pollock-like works, crafted by throwing paint at the canvas and even by sitting on a freshly painted canvas and smearing it with his rear end.

These parodies of abstract painting are contrasted with Alexander's preferred style of "ultrarealism," itself a parody of realist genres since it includes only nude paintings of Marina. The contrast between realism and abstraction in this sequence highlights questions of artistic representation, dismantling received polarities and emphasizing visual pleasure. More importantly, however, this sequence also engages issues of filmic representation, in particular the display of the female body on screen. Poking fun at the cinematic codes that eventually made *The Sinner* into the scandal of the decade, this sequence demonstrates the charged nature of cinematic realism and the double standard that allows high art to portray highly realistic painted images of nudity and bare breasts—even on screen—while showing a "real" naked body is proscribed.

This point is reiterated after Marina's montage sequence ends, in a scene that again foregrounds the female gaze. We see Alexander painting another nude picture of Marina while she reclines on the lawn under the umbrella, which she has set up to shield herself from the looks of other men who might pass by, and, by extension, from viewers in the audience, whose view of Marina nude is minimized because her naked body is shown only in long shot. As Marina explains in voiceover, Alexander finds the umbrella superfluous, since their garden is enclosed by a wall and shady trees. However, in this scene, Marina peers through a hole in the umbrella to gaze at two men who have climbed up on the wall to catch a glimpse of her. Strikingly, their gaze is obscured by the umbrella, while Marina's gaze penetrates it in order to look at *them*. She sees them climbing over the wall and covers herself up in time to hinder their look once again. They are left only with Alexander's painted representation of Marina's nude body, which they are able to view before Alexander throws them out of the garden.

In her well-known analysis of the way conventional structures of narrative cinema encode "sexual imbalance," Laura Mulvey notes,

> Mainstream film neatly combines spectacle and narrative ... The presence
> of woman is an indispensable element of spectacle in normal narrative film
> ... Traditionally, the woman displayed has functioned on two levels: as
> erotic object for the characters within the screen story, and as erotic object
> for the spectator within the auditorium, with a shifting tension between the
> looks on either side of the screen.[62]

The distinction between woman's role as spectacle, as object "to be looked
at," and man's role as activator of the narrative and subject of the gaze is
central to Mulvey's analysis of the gendered structure of the gaze "on
either side of the screen," both within dominant cinema and as it is
mirrored by spectators in the movie theater.

The Sinner complicates this structure in a number of ways. While
Marina literally embodies the role of spectacle in the sequence described
above, she also activates the narrative and the gaze, both here and
throughout the film, confounding conventional structures of
spectatorship and encouraging contemplation of gendered issues of
representation and perception implicated in visual culture in the 1950s.
Parodying conventions of the film industry that limit what can be shown
realistically on screen, the film problematizes its own "realistic"
representation of women. At the same time, it parodies abstract art, which
is portrayed as a representational style that arises from damaged
perceptive faculties, and which only obscures objects of representation.

Not coincidentally, the thematization of both "realist" filmmaking and
"abstract" painting in this sequence is achieved through the multivalent
figure of the screen. Like *The Murderers Are Among Us*, in which screen
surfaces crystallize problems of gender and representation, screens are
omnipresent in *The Sinner*, from Alexander's canvasses that both
spotlight postwar disturbances of vision and question the appropriate
visual representation of woman, to Marina's montage, projected onto a
stand-in cinema screen, which foregrounds issues of spectacle and
spectatorship as they are linked to sexual difference.

In a critique of feminist film studies in general and Laura Mulvey's
theories in particular, Judith Mayne argues that "an exclusive focus on
spectacle defined ... as a relation between male subject and female object
obscures other functions of cinematic spectacle which do not lend
themselves to such easy dichotomies."[63] Mayne invokes the ambivalent
figure of the screen, which functions as both boundary and threshold, as
a metaphor for "the complex ways in which cinema functions *both* to
legitimatize the patriarchal status quo *and*, if not necessarily to challenge
it, then at the very least to suggest its weak links, its own losses of
mastery, within which may be found possibilities or hypotheses of
alternative positions."[64] In the classical Hollywood films Mayne analyzes,
the screen figures the intersection of spectacle and narrative and "marks
the possibility of a desire where the boundaries between identification
and objectification are no longer clear."[65] And in the feminist films she

discusses, the screen emerges as a signifier for "a preoccupation with the difficulty and complexity of the relationship between women and cinematic representation."[66]

The Sinner virtually literalizes this function of the screen as boundary and threshold, as Marina first projects a narrative about her own specularization onto the screen surface of the umbrella that shields her naked body from the intrusive male gaze of passersby and then penetrates that same screen surface to look at these men from a hole in the umbrella, reversing the structure of the gaze and complicating conventional notions of spectacle.

V

In his quest to invent a new language for postwar filmmaking, Willi Forst endowed the character of Marina with an unusual degree of agency in structuring the narrative of *The Sinner* and the formal codes of the film. In so doing, Forst followed a strategy that had been used to a greater or lesser degree by many other filmmakers seeking to relegitimate cinematic representation in the postwar period. However, Forst was much more explicit about this strategy than other postwar filmmakers had been, expressly stating that his film sought to address both social problems and representational problems by developing new techniques to give voice to female experience. This point is even underscored in the press booklet that accompanied *The Sinner*:

> A new technique of making thoughts visible and audible finds expression as a stylistic device in the new Willi Forst film "The Sinner," with Hildegard Knef in the title role. Marina, a young girl of our times, a cast away, narrates her life story, her downfall into the abyss, which she climbs out of only later through a selfless, devoted love. The continuity of this narrative is interrupted through flashbacks. Marina does not always depict the different stations of her love chronologically, but rather in the order that the thoughts come to her. In her memory, the episodes of her past scroll by, and she comments on them in *her* show <emphasis in the original>. The image does not always serve to illustrate the word, but rather often shows something completely different from that to which the spoken words attest. In this way, the viewer experiences through the eyes of this unique woman the harrowing story of a young girl, who has been tormented and hounded by life, with such strong forcefulness and intensity that, as eyewitnesses to her account, we no longer condemn this "sinner," but love her. The partner of this unusual love affair beyond good and evil is Gustav Fröhlich.[67]

This promotional text seeks to guide critical responses to the film by elaborating on the film's aesthetic construction as well as its social interventions, and the goal of both is to give audiences insight into women's experiences of the Nazi period, wartime, and postwar Germany in order to promote audience understanding and empathy with the choices women were forced to make. Emphasizing that *The Sinner* is Marina's "show," which movie goers experience "through her eyes," this advertising copy focuses on the film's melodramatic qualities and its appeal through conventional structures of identification as well as new techniques of sound, image, and flashback. Consistent with its exclusive focus on Marina's story, this text barely mentions the character of Alexander.

Drawing from the promotional materials for *The Sinner*, the film program published by *Illustrierte Film-Bühne* also foregrounds the story of a "girl of our times," emphasizing identification with Marina and promoting the film's message, "Do not judge other people too quickly."[68] Like the press booklet, the film program also stresses Marina's redemption through selfless, devoted love to a man: "From this moment <when she meets Alexander> onward, a great transformation and clarification takes place inside her: yesterday still a calculating prostitute, she raises herself up out of the depths of her vagrant life into the heights of pure and true love, ready to make sacrifices and in selfless devotion to a needy person."[69]

As these publicity documents suggest, *The Sinner* offered a highly ambivalent set of solutions to the gender trouble of the postwar period. Seeking to promote understanding of female experiences that were the subject of much negative scrutiny in the conservative climate of restoration that marked the birth of the Federal Republic, Forst's film also promoted the conservative agenda of redomesticating women, proposing self-sacrifice and devotion to the heterosexual family unit both as the appropriate tasks for women and as an imagined solution for the social problems of postwar Germany. Yet in foregoing a conventional happy ending to portray Marina's euthanasia of Alexander and her self-sacrificing suicide as devotional acts, *The Sinner* took the idea of redomestication to a logical extreme that displayed the cracks in this solution, causing an outcry among the leading conservatives of the day.

The popularity of the film with mass audiences attests to Forst's success in combining easily digestible platitudes about true love with a story that explores some of the darker corners of recent German history, in particular the still contentious issues of adultery, prostitution, and fraternization, which, as we have seen, continued to function as ciphers for social problems of all kinds in the postwar period. However, the success of *The Sinner* also certainly reflected Forst's creative solutions to the representational problems of postwar cinema, including both his artful combination of melodramatic genre conventions with an unusual use of sound, image, and narrative structure as well as his insertion of a metacommentary on postwar visual representation through a parody of both abstract painting and film's own circumscribed codes.

By focusing on female experience and telling Marina's story "through her eyes," *The Sinner* suggests that, despite the limitations of postwar cinema, film still provides a forum for affective identification, especially among female viewers, that is lacking in the highly vaunted forms of modern painting. In its foregrounding of the female gaze, and its use of the female voiceover to create further identificatory possibilities for female spectators, *The Sinner* provided a model of formal innovation within the confines of dominant cinema during the 1950s. Marina's memories, constructed in flashbacks to which she gives voice and sight, present a causal version of her personal history, linked to larger structures of public history. As the film narrates Marina's transformation from sexually promiscuous woman to bourgeois housewife, it repeatedly provides points of identification through which female spectators are encouraged to contemplate their own histories.

Thus, *The Sinner* opens up viewing positions that encourage reflection not only on visuality, but also on historical experience and its imbrication with dominant forms of representation. These viewing positions seek to legitimate film as a realistic art form in *The Sinner* at a moment when filmic realism was facing not only the representational problems posed by contending with cinema history in the wake of the Nazi past, but also new challenges to cinematic legitimacy raised by the ascendance of new modern visual forms like abstract painting. Beginning with *The Murderers Are Among Us*, postwar films often represented an active female gaze linked to realist art forms in an attempt to engage the female spectator. This "realist" female gaze was often contrasted with an "abstract" male gaze figured as disturbed, sick, even perverse. While this evocation of realism and abstraction was one element in the film industry's appeal to the predominantly female viewing public, it served another function as well. By inverting the dominant discourse that linked abstraction to democracy and realism to totalitarian regimes, filmmakers sought to rehabilitate filmic realism and endow it with a new legitimacy.

Notes

1. See Hans Helmut Prinzler, *Chronik des deutschen Films 1895–1994* (Stuttgart, 1995), 186; and Elizabeth Prommer, *Kinobesuch im Lebenslauf. Eine historische und medienbiographische Studie* (Konstanz, 1999), 350–52.
2. According to Joseph Garncarz, in the 1950/51 season, seven of the top ten films were German, while in the 1951/52 season, nine of the top ten films were German. Garncarz, "Hollywood in Germany. Die Rolle des amerikanischen Films in Deutschland: 1925–1990," in *Der deutsche Film. Aspekte seiner Geschichte von den Anfängen bis zur Gegenwart*, ed. Uli Jung (Trier, 1993), 200.
3. Proportional to the popularity of cinema in postwar Germany, repeated scandals surrounding various films came to permeate public discourse, leading to lengthy bouts of self-examination about censorship, the limits of free speech, and the (self-)image of the Federal Republic. Other films that generated scandals include Helmut Käutner's *Der Apfel ist ab!* (The Apple Is Off!, 1948); Veit Harlan's *Anders als du und ich* (Different From You and Me, 1957); and Rolf Thiele's *Das Mädchen Rosemarie* (The Girl Rosemarie, 1958). For an exhaustive consideration of the scandal over *The Sinner*, see Kirsten

Burghardt, *Werk, Skandal, Exempel. Tabudurchbrechung durch fiktionale Modelle: Willi Forsts* Die Sünderin (Munich, 1996). For an account of the scandal in English, see Heide Fehrenbach, *Cinema in Democratizing Germany: Reconstructing National Identity After Hitler* (Chapel Hill, 1995), 92–117, 129–47.

4. For more details about the FSK's decision, see Burghardt, *Werk, Skandal, Exempel*, 16–18 and 261–64; and Fehrenbach, *Cinema in Democratizing Germany*, 129–31.

5. Burghardt, *Werk, Skandal, Exempel*, 39–42.

6. Burghardt, *Werk, Skandal, Exempel*, 43–44.

7. According to Garncarz, *The Sinner* was the second most popular film of the 1950/51 season; the number one film was Hans Deppe's *Schwarzwaldmädel* (Black Forest Girl). See Garncarz in Jung, *Der deutsche Film*, 200.

8. Burghardt, *Werk, Skandal, Exempel*, 51.

9. Hildegard Knef, *The Gift Horse: Report on a Life*, trans. David Anthony Palastanga (New York, 1971), 243–44. As Knef suggests here, the scandal over *The Sinner* was in part based on the extradiegetic resonances that she brought to the part of Marina. Through her friendship with Erich Pommer, the famous Weimar producer, émigré to Hollywood, and later lead film officer of the American occupation army in postwar Germany, Knef made contacts that led both to a Hollywood contract with David O. Selznick and to her marriage to Kurt Hirsch, a Jewish American film officer under Pommer. Knef left Germany for Hollywood in 1948, and was soon portrayed in the German press as an international diva. Thus, when she returned to Germany to star in *The Sinner*, Knef's star sign had very different associations from those of her rubble film days in movies like *The Murderers Are Among Us* and *Film Without a Title*. No longer the socialist heroine or ingénue of those earlier films, Knef's performance in *The Sinner* relied on her projection of a more glamorous—but also more promiscuous, in terms of both sexuality and national identity— model of femininity that linked her to beloved but contested figures like Marlene Dietrich.

10. Incidents involving tear gas and/or stink bombs were recorded in Aschaffenburg, Frankfurt, Düsseldorf-Oberkassel, and Villingen. Mice were released in Duisburg. Protests that succeeded through other means in preventing the film from being shown occurred in Regensburg (where the protests got so out of hand that police turned fire hoses on the protesters), Werne an der Lippe, and Berlin. See *"Die Sünderin": Zwölf Monate später* (Düsseldorf, 1952), 8–10. Some of the protestors and organizers were arrested and prosecuted, such as the pastor Dr. Karl Klinkhammer, who organized stink bombings in Düsseldorf-Oberkassel. See "'Sünderin' stirbt nicht," *Die Abendzeitung*, September 4, 1952.

11. Poster in file on *Die Sünderin*, Schriftgutarchiv, Stiftung Deutsche Kinemathek, Berlin.

12. Decision of the Landesverwaltungsgericht in Niedersachsen (Kammer Osnabrück), January 31, 1952, file on *Die Sünderin*, Schriftgutarchiv, Stiftung Deutsche Kinemathek, Berlin. This decision was eventually overturned on November 4, 1952, by the Oberverwaltungsgericht in Lüneburg.

13. Sabine Hake, *Popular Cinema of the Third Reich* (Austin, 2001), 158.

14. On Forst's *Viennese Girls*, see Hake, *Popular Cinema*, 162–68.

15. *Der Taggesspiegel*, January 21, 1951, qtd. in Burghardt, *Werk, Skandal, Exempel*, 15.

16. See for example "Von Leinwand und Lautsprecher. Neues über Film und Funk: Willi Forst über seine Sünderin," *Westfälische Rundschau*, January 12, 1951, rpt. in Ursula Bessen, *Trümmer und Träume. Nachkriegszeit und fünfziger Jahre auf Zelluloid* (Bochum, 1989), 196–97.

17. Burghardt, *Werk, Skandal, Exempel*, 15.

18. Robert Dachs, *Willi Forst: Eine Biographie* (Vienna, 1986), 166.

19. See Juliane Roh, "Wie betrachtet man ein gegenstandsloses Bild?," *Die Kunst und das schöne Heim* 49.9 (1951): 320–21; and "Die moderne Malerei—oder 'Toleranz' der Männer," *Film und Frau* 11 (1949): 23.

20. On the politicization of abstract art in West Germany see Walter Grasskamp, *Die unbewältigte Moderne. Kunst und Öffentlichkeit* (Munich, 1989); see also Jost Hermand,

"Modernism Restored: West German Painting in the 1950s," trans. Biddy Martin, *New German Critique* 32 (1984): 23–41. The most well-known advocate of abstract art in the 1940s and 1950s was of course the American art critic Clement Greenberg, who published several highly influential articles that were crucial to the ascent of American Abstract Expressionism to artistic hegemony in the early postwar period. Greenberg was one of the earliest critics to articulate the idea that abstract art was the best means for contemporary artists to capture the spirit of the times and communicate content in the modern world. His advocacy of young American abstract artists (in particular Jackson Pollock) catapulted many of them into the public eye, and helped to create a cult of personality that situated these (male) artists as the representatives of a victorious American ideology of individualism and democratic values. See Greenberg, "Avant-Garde and Kitsch" (1939) and "Towards a Newer Laocoön" (1940), *Clement Greenberg: The Collected Essays and Criticism*, v. 1, ed. John O'Brian (Chicago, 1986). On the American politicization of Abstract Expressionism, see also Serge Guilbaut, *How New York Stole the Idea of Modern Art: Abstract Expressionism, Freedom, and the Cold War* (Chicago, 1983).

21. See for example *Das Kunstwerk* 1.8–9 (1946–47), spec. issue on abstract art.
22. Walter Grasskamp suggests that the idea of "making up for lost time," which became a catchphrase in postwar exhibition politics, is in fact misleading, since "there could hardly have been a people in the world in the 1930s who were so widely informed about modern and even avant-garde art as the Germans were. The traveling exhibition 'Degenerate Art' apparently had over two million visitors at its first stop in Munich alone. … As a result it was less making up for lost time than repeating a grade, giving a new meaning and value to the modern art that had previously been so demonstratively defamed, which were tasks of the postwar period." Grasskamp, *Die unbewältigte Moderne*, 120.
23. One of the most prominent dissenting voices in the debate about abstraction, the conservative critic Hans Sedlmayr also viewed abstraction as a reflection of the breakdown of European society. However, in his 1948 attack on abstract art, Sedlmayr pathologized art history as the history of a sick society and situated abstraction as a culprit in the confusion of the modern world. He suggested that figural art could help the "godless society" that he believed emerged with the French Revolution return to its Renaissance origins. See Sedlmayr, *Der Verlust der Mitte: Die bildende Kunst des 19. und 20. Jahrhunderts als Symptom und Symbol der Zeit* (Salzburg, 1948).
24. Will Grohmann, "Deutschland, Österreich, Schweiz," *Neue Kunst nach 1945*, ed. Will Grohmann (Cologne, 1958), 151.
25. Grohmann, *Neue Kunst nach 1945*, 159. Somewhat paradoxically, postwar commentators often sought to explain abstraction as a new kind of representationalism, while at the same time lauding its nonrepresentational qualities: they presented abstraction as a medium concerned with expressing in visual terms the advances in modern science, in particular modern nuclear science and other insights of the atomic age. They also often used an analogy to music in order to explain abstraction's interest in color, rhythm, and form.
26. See Roh, "Wie betrachtet man ein gegenstandloses Bild?," 321. The artist Willi Baumeister, the most famous German abstract painter of the 1950s, portrayed his work in similar terms, as a spiritual, metaphysical form of representation in a distinctly modern vein. See Willi Baumeister, "Warum ich gegenstandslos male," *Die Kunst und das schöne Heim* 48.9 (1950): 325–26.
27. See Baumeister, "Warum ich gegenstandslos male," 326.
28. Yule F. Heibel, *Reconstructing the Subject: Modernist Painting in Western Germany 1945–1950* (Princeton, 1995), 2–3.
29. Heibel, *Reconstructing the Subject*, 69.
30. Heibel, *Reconstructing the Subject*, 104.
31. Leopold Zahn, "Abkehr von der Natur," *Das Kunstwerk* 1.8–9 (1946–47): 3–4.
32. The "Kleines Lexikon abstrakter Maler," published in *Das Kunstwerk* 1.8–9 (1946–47): 60, lists only one woman, Jeanne Mammen, among the sixty-two artists mentioned.

Gisela Breitling suggests that female artists in the 1950s tended to work in modes that "did not fit the aesthetic conception of the fifties" (such as politically engaged art; objective, realist art; art that explored the human body; and affective or expressionist art). See Breitling, "Kunst und Künstlerinnen in den 50er Jahren," in *Perlonzeit: Wie die Frauen ihr Wirtschaftswunder erlebten*, ed. Angela Delille and Andrea Grohn (Berlin, 1985), 62–71.

33. A comprehensive exhibition of modern and contemporary art, "documenta" premiered in Kassel in 1955. Now considered one of the most important art exhibitions in the world, "documenta" continues to be held in Kassel every five years.

34. Grasskamp, *Die unbewältigte Moderne*, 82.

35. For a much more differentiated account of design in the Federal Republic than I am able to offer here, see Paul Betts, *The Authority of Everyday Objects: A Cultural History of West German Industrial Design* (Berkeley, 2004).

36. See for example "Neue Dekorationsstoffe nach Entwürfen von Professor Willi Baumeister," *Die Kunst und das schöne Heim* 55.4 (1956): 145.

37. This trend is captured in Rolf Thiele's 1958 film *The Girl Rosemarie*. The dashing Frenchman Fribert (Peter van Eyck) has promised to transform the small-time prostitute Rosemarie Nitribitt (Nadja Tiller) into a high-class call girl in exchange for her spying on her clientele for him. The first step in her transformation is the removal of kitschy statues of deer and faux-gilt framed landscape paintings from her walls; they are replaced with abstract paintings. At the same time that her visual surroundings are transformed, Rosemarie must purge herself of a sentimental attachment to her former lover Hartog and metamorphose into a ruthless and cold-hearted exploiter. For more on *The Girl Rosemarie*, see chapter 9.

38. According to one account, by the late 1950s art galleries were so perplexed about the widespread popularity of abstraction that they commissioned an empirical study in order to attempt to understand the demographics of their buyers: "The result was that modern paintings of a moderate type were being bought (as they had been for decades) by bank directors, lawyers, architects and intellectuals. What was surprising was that totally new classes of buyers were appearing to snap up the avant-garde paintings of tachism and post-tachism (i.e. for the works referred to at that time as 'active abstraction'): chemists, heads of factories, insurance agents, and electrical engineers." Martin Warnke, "Von der Gegenständlichkeit und der Ausbreitung der Abstrakten," in *Die fünfziger Jahre. Beiträge zur Politik und Kultur*, ed. Dieter Bänsch (Tübingen, 1985), 214.

39. Martin Damus, *Kunst in der BRD, 1945–1990* (Reinbek bei Hamburg, 1995), 49.

40. On the affective quality of 1950s German cinema, see for example Gerhard Bliersbach, *So grün war die Heide ... Die gar nicht so heile Welt im Nachkriegsfilm*, abridged ed. (Weinheim and Basel, 1989), esp. 33–63; and Ingrid Schmidt-Harzbach, "Rock 'n' Roll in Hanau," in Delille and Grohn, *Perlonzeit*, 38.

41. See Werner Heß, rev. of *Die Sünderin*, *Evangelischer Film-Beobachter* 3 (February 1, 1951): 26–27; K.B., rev. of *Die Sünderin*, *Katholischer Filmdienst* 5 (February 2, 1951): n.p.; M.J., "'Weder neu noch originell': Gedanken zum Forstfilm 'Die Sünderin,'" rev. of *Die Sünderin*, *Westfälische Rundschau*, February 2, 1951, rpt. in Bessen, *Trümmer und Träume*, 198–99; Gunter Groll, "Die vielumstrittenen 'Sünderin' oder Sekt mit Veronal," rev. of *Die Sünderin*, *Süddeutsche Zeitung*, February 15, 1951, rpt. in *Zwischen Gestern und Morgen. Westdeutscher Nachkriegsfilm 1946–1962*, ed. Hilmar Hoffmann and Walter Schobert (Frankfurt am Main, 1989), 354–56. *Film und Frau* focused on the artistry of Forst's directorial skills in "Forst führt Regie," *Film und Frau* 2.28 (1950): 15–16.

42. Heß, *Evangelischer Film-Beobachter*, 26.

43. The claim that Forst's film was smut disguised as an art film was echoed by one of the principal antagonists in the debate over the film, the archbishop of Cologne, Cardinal Frings. On March 4, 1951, Frings issued an exhortation, which was read from all the pulpits in his diocese: "It pains me very much to announce that, despite all the protests

of the responsible departments, the infamous film 'The Sinner' is now playing in Cologne, the metropolis of our archdiocese ... I expect that our Catholic men and women and especially our healthy Catholic youth will stay away from the cinemas in justifiable indignation and in Christian unanimity, <for these cinemas>, misusing the name art, are presenting a spectacle that amounts to a corruption of the moral notions of our Christian people." Qtd. in Bessen, *Trümmer und Träume*, 184.

44. Groll, "Die vielumstrittenen 'Sünderin'," 354. Heß makes the same point in strikingly similar language. Heß, *Evangelischer Film-Beobachter*, 26.

45. Heß, *Evangelischer Film-Beobachter*, 27. The aptness of Heß's question is substantiated by one of the most bizarre moments in the history of *The Sinner*, and, indeed, in the history of product placement. In a letter dated January 24, 1951, the Veronal corporation thanked the production company Junge Film-Union for its use of Veronal in *The Sinner*: "In your latest film 'The Sinner' the effectiveness of our product Veronal is demonstrated in an outstanding fashion. We are receiving enthusiastic letters from audiences about the downright transformative qualities of our sleeping pills. In the future, we will have you to thank for a large increase in sales. In order to present you with a small thank you, we are sending you 100 bulk packages <of Veronal> at no cost." The letter goes on to request permission to use the film's final image of Hildegard Knef and Gustav Fröhlich in a Veronal advertising campaign. Veronal A.G., letter to Junge Film-Union, January 24, 1951, Niedersächsisches Landesverwaltungsamt Hannover, rpt. in Burghardt, *Werk, Skandal, Exempel*, 362.

46. Heß, *Evangelischer Film-Beobachter*, 27. Gunter Groll also asserts that the film is particularly dangerous because of its masterful artistic qualities. Groll, "Die vielumstrittenen 'Sünderin'," 354.

47. Fehrenbach, *Cinema in Democratizing Germany*, 110.

48. Fehrenbach, *Cinema in Democratizing Germany*, 110.

49. See Kaja Silverman, *Male Subjectivity at the Margins* (New York, 1992); Jaimey Fisher, *Disciplining Germany: Youth, Reeducation, and Reconstruction after the Second World War* (Detroit, 2007); Fisher, "Deleuze in a Ruinous Context: German Rubble-Film and Italian Neorealism," *iris* 23 (1997): 53–74; and Fisher, "On the Ruins of Masculinity: The Figure of the Child in Italian Neorealism and the German Rubble Film," in *Italian Neorealism and Global Cinema*, ed. Laura E. Ruberto and Kristi M. Wilson (Detroit, 2007), 25–53.

50. Thomas Brandlmeier, "Und wieder Caligari ... Deutsche Nachkriegsfilme 1946–1951," in Jung, *Der deutsche Film*, 158.

51. Brandlmeier in Jung, *Der deutsche Film*, 162.

52. Erica Carter, "Deviant Pleasures? Women, Melodrama, and Consumer Nationalism in West Germany," in *The Sex of Things: Gender and Consumption in Historical Perspective*, ed. Victoria de Grazia and Ellen Furlough (Berkeley, 1996), 361.

53. Fehrenbach, *Cinema in Democratizing Germany*, 110.

54. Elizabeth Heineman, "The Hour of the Woman: Memories of Germany's 'Crisis Years' and West German National Identity," *American Historical Review* 101.2 (1996): 382, n. 73.

55. Heineman, "The Hour of the Woman," 382.

56. Heineman, "The Hour of the Woman," 380–81.

57. See "Sünderin: Achtzig Meter lang gestorben," *Spiegel*, January 17, 1951, rpt. in Bessen, *Trümmer und Träume*, 199–201.

58. See "Sünderin: Achtzig Meter lang gestorben," 200.

59. See "Sünderin: Achtzig Meter lang gestorben," 200.

60. See Kaja Silverman, "Dis-Embodying the Female Voice," in *Re-Vision: Essays in Feminist Film Criticism*, ed. Mary Ann Doane et al. (Los Angeles, 1984), 131–49.

61. For an analysis of the way painting thematizes spectatorship in narrative cinema, see Judith Mayne's reading of Albert Lewin's *The Picture of Dorian Gray* (1945) in *Cinema and Spectatorship* (London and New York, 1993), 105–22.

62. Laura Mulvey, "Visual Pleasure and Narrative Cinema," in *Visual and Other Pleasures* (Bloomington, 1989), 19.

63. Judith Mayne, *The Woman at the Keyhole: Feminism and Women's Cinema* (Bloomington, 1990), 13–14.

64. Mayne, *The Woman at the Keyhole*, 25.

65. Mayne, *The Woman at the Keyhole*, 32.

66. Mayne, *The Woman at the Keyhole*, 50.

67. "Kann man Gedanken photographieren?," press booklet (Munich, 1951), in file on *Die Sünderin*, Schriftgutarchiv, Stiftung Deutsche Kinemathek, Berlin.

68. "Die Sünderin," *Illustrierte Film-Bühne* 1030 (1951).

69. "Die Sünderin," *Illustrierte Film-Bühne*.

Chapter 6

LOOKING AT HEIMAT: VISUAL PLEASURE AND CINEMATIC REALISM IN ALFONS STUMMER'S *THE FORESTER OF THE SILVER WOOD* (1955)

As the pace of reconstruction hastened and the *Wirtschaftswunder* began to take shape, film culture benefited immensely from new economic developments. Not only did the film industry continue to expand during the first half of the 1950s, but this period also saw a proliferation of film-related institutions and a growing interest in all forms of cinema. Film festivals began to spring up in many cities, among them the Berlin Film Festival, started in 1951 in West Berlin. New forums for the promotion and reception of documentary and short films emerged, including the *Filmwochen* in Mannheim (1952) and the *Filmtage* in Oberhausen (1954). The annual international film conference of the Association of German Film Clubs, which took place each year in October, took on increasing importance not only as a central meeting place for film enthusiasts but also as a conduit to foreign films, contemporary and historical. In 1952, the Bundesarchiv was established in Koblenz with a mission that included collecting newsreels, documentary films, and government-produced movies.

At the same time, the popularity of mainstream movies increased dramatically. An average of 365 new movie theaters was built every year in the early 1950s, and by 1955 the Federal Republic boasted 6,239 cinemas in all. Ticket sales increased by leaps and bounds during this period: 766 million tickets were sold in 1955—an average of 15.4 visits to the movies for each West German—over 200 million more tickets than were sold only four years before. Film production also multiplied, from seventy-six West German movies in 1951 to 122 features in 1955.[1] As these statistics show, the West German film industry experienced a boom during the early 1950s, and German and Austrian film productions continued to predominate among top-grossing movies.[2] In particular, the *Heimatfilm* and its cousins, the *Revuefilm* and the *Schlagerfilm*, became the top box office draws during the heyday of West German cinema in the Adenauer Era.

One of the top two most popular films of the year in West Germany, Alfons Stummer's Austrian production *Der Förster vom Silberwald* profited from both the increased enthusiasm for documentary films among West German audiences and from the *Heimatfilm* wave of the early 1950s[3] (see figure 6.1). In an exception to dominant trends, Stummer's film tells the story of a *female* artist, Liesl (Anita Gutwell), whose turn from abstraction to more representational forms parallels her return from Vienna to her native village in rural Austria. Embracing the natural landscapes and traditional culture of Styria, Liesl turns away from the modern urban lifestyle embodied by her Viennese boyfriend Max Freiberg (Erik Frey) and begins an affair with the local forest ranger, Hubert Gerold (Rudolf Lenz). A paradigmatic exemplar of the genre, *The Forester of the Silver Wood* foregrounds emblematic tropes of the *Heimatfilm*, including the conflict between city and country; tensions between tradition and modernization; expulsion and migration; and threats to the rural landscape posed by deforestation and poaching. At the same time, *The Forester of the Silver*

Figure 6.1 The 100,000th ticket is sold to a female viewer of *The Forester of the Silver Wood*. Source: Deutsche Kinemathek.

Wood participates in dominant discourses about visual representation and perception that were a hallmark of postwar cinema across genres.

The Forester of the Silver Wood celebrates the beauty of the pan-German landscape—which is listed as one of the film's main stars in the opening credit sequence—through lengthy "documentary" shots that interrupt the narrative to focus on the spectacle of nature.[4] The Austrian director Stummer was known primarily for his *Kulturfilme*, documentary films about nature or cultural themes that were often shown before the main feature in cinemas during the 1950s. *The Forester of the Silver Wood*, Stummer's first feature, was marketed as a mixture of narrative film and documentary film that drew on Stummer's cinematic virtuosity in shooting artistic, documentary-style footage of natural landscapes. According to the credits, the film was "produced according to an idea by, and on commission for, the State Hunter of Styria Franz Mayr-Meinhof." The film was shot on location in the Austrian state of Styria over three seasons, and the actors, who learned to hunt and hike for their roles in the film, were both tanned and frostbitten during extensive scenes in the sun and snow. As the publicity documents for the film emphasize, everything about *The Forester of the Silver Wood* was "real," including the shots of nature and especially the footage of animals—eagles, foxes, badgers, and deer. According to the press book,

> The popular folk-oriented plot of this Agfacolor film, which was shot with an exceptional expenditure of effort, time, and money, is interlaced with such singularly unique shots of the wondrous world of our mountain forests that no one who has maintained a place in his heart for unadulterated nature should be allowed to miss this film. This Union film proves once and for all that European film is capable of producing magnificent achievements even in those areas in which the achievements of America had appeared unsurpassable until now.[5]

Produced and released in Austria as *Echo der Berge* (Echo of the Mountains) in 1954, *The Forester of the Silver Wood* premiered in the Federal Republic at the Theater am Karlstor in Munich on February 8, 1955. The film had a slow start, but positive reviews and word of mouth created increasing interest among audiences. By June 1956, ten million viewers had seen the film, and by the end of 1958 it had booked 22 million viewers, becoming the most popular *Heimatfilm* of the decade, and spawning several sequels and spin-offs.[6] Reviewers praised the film for its beautiful camerawork, its amazing documentary footage of animals, and the general realism of its photography. Taking a page from the press book, reviewers often compared *The Forester of the Silver Wood* to the popular nature films of Walt Disney, which were criticized as highly artificial and over-technologized, with their symbolic, artistic editing style and shots that highlighted the presence of the camera in nature.[7] By contrast, reviewers lauded the authenticity of *The Forester of the Silver Wood*, arguing that the filmic process could not be detected in Stummer's film: the camera was simply set up and recorded whatever unfolded before it.

While critics praised the film's realistic, documentary qualities, they generally saw the plotline as extraneous, tacked on for good measure to justify the film's feature-length status. As one reviewer put it, "The simple and somewhat wooden plot, which runs parallel <to the documentary sequences> and deals with a forester and a girl from the city, is of only subordinate significance and could easily have been left out. The shots of animals and nature—as a high point, the fight between a golden eagle and a fox—offer much more genuine drama than any sugar-sweet love story."[8] In his groundbreaking study of the *Heimatfilm*, Johannes von Moltke notes that contemporary reviewers often called attention in this way to the "preponderance of image over action and of showing over telling," thus emphasizing that the *Heimatfilme* constituted a "peculiar, generically specific, and qualitatively new kind of spectacle."[9] Indeed, *The Forester of the Silver Wood*, with its spectacular, lengthy nature sequences, presents a paradigmatic example of this new "cinema of attractions" analyzed by von Moltke. At the same time, however, and contrary to the view of some contemporary critics, Stummer's film is notable among *Heimatfilme* precisely for its successful integration of plot and spectacle: not only is the interplay of narrative and "documentary" footage accomplished seamlessly in the film, but the narrative frames and shapes the nature scenes in significant ways.

Characters in the film survey the landscape, and the documentary nature shots are almost always triggered by their looks. These looks are often filtered through visual tools like binoculars that emphasize the mechanical reproduction of nature by the cinematic apparatus, contrary to critics' claims that the presence of the camera was undetectable in the film. Through the introduction of prosthetic visual devices into the plot and the formal play with subjective camera, the gaze of the viewer in the audience is structured by the gaze of the character on screen (see figure 6.2). Documentary footage is routinely sutured into the film as follows: establishing shot of a character looking (often lifting binoculars to his or her eyes); long shot of panoramic naturescape; reaction shot of character. The film thus utilizes modern filmic conventions to highlight structures of looking, and nature is filmically bracketed and circumscribed by the characters' gazes. While reviews of *The Forester of the Silver Wood* suggest that the bulk of the film consists of dynamic documentary footage, in fact images of nature represent only a small portion of the total film, and they consist primarily of static tableaux.

Explaining the immense popularity of Stummer's film with 1950s viewers, Claudius Seidl focuses on the formal intersection between plot and documentary footage:

> A mere retelling of the plot cannot explain why this film in particular was such a great success. Without a doubt, an important reason lay in the

Figure 6.2 Prosthetic visual devices structure the gaze and emphasize the mechanical reproduction of nature: The forester Hubert Gerold (Rudolf Lenz). Source: Deutsche Kinemathek.

> function of looking. *The Forester of the Silver Wood* is full of scenes in which people remain passive and do nothing but admire the great landscape. The spectator looks at the forest, the animals, and the mountains from the same angle as Hubert and Liesl, and is allowed to imagine that he <*sic*> is therefore taking part in their happiness. Again and again, the camera lets the spectator look through Hubert Gerold's binoculars: pleasure in looking is strongly fueled by *The Forester of the Silver Wood*. We are all tourists, the film seems to call out to its audience.[10]

Seidl's analysis suggests that the film promoted a voyeuristic pleasure in looking akin to (virtual) tourism. Indeed, for viewers of *Heimatfilme*, many of whom lived in still rubble-strewn cities and towns, the sweeping vistas, ice-capped peaks, and sun-drenched landscapes clearly exerted the appeal of an exotic, vacation-like escape from everyday life. However, it was not only the mountain landscapes that promoted pleasure in looking in *The Forester of the Silver Wood* and other *Heimatfilme*. Their representation of cosmopolitan city life similarly sought to engage the voyeuristic gaze in ways that contrasted sharply with the visual pleasures offered by nature. This is often achieved through the introduction of modern consumer goods, including automobiles and fashionable clothing, as well as through a focus on visual art, including modern abstract painting and sculpture.[11] As in other film genres, artists are common characters in *Heimatfilme*, providing metacinematic insight into postwar representational problems as well as diegetic models for spectatorship. In *The Forester of the Silver Wood* and other *Heimatfilme*, the gaze is insistently foregrounded not only in relation to the natural landscapes around which the films are constructed, but also through the figure of the artist.

Beginning in the 1960s, many critics have seen *Heimatfilme* as affirmative representations of German nationhood, which exemplify the continuities between Nazi cinema and West German filmmaking.[12] Other critics have re-evaluated *Heimatfilme* such as *The Forester of the Silver Wood*, suggesting that they encode a series of conflicts—especially conflicts between tradition and modernity—in order to work through changes in the fundamental structures of society brought about by National Socialism, war, and defeat.[13] As these critics point out, *Heimatfilme* were particularly implicated in the reconstruction of national identities and gender identities in democratizing Germany.

However, as Johannes von Moltke has noted, the project of re-evaluating the ideological status of *Heimatfilme* carried out by these critics in recent years has generally been limited to narrative content and has not included a concomitant focus on film form.[14] To the extent that they have overlooked crucial formal issues, critics have neglected the fact that the social problems and narrative conflicts thematized by *Heimatfilme* are mirrored by a focus on visuality, representation, and perception. Indeed, the tensions and contradictions at stake in *Heimatfilme* bring together social and representational problems that crystallize around gender and sexuality. However, while it is now a critical commonplace to suggest that *Heimatfilme* appealed in particular to female viewers,[15] critics have also overlooked the gendering of form in general and gaze in particular in these films.

Through its thematization of voyeurism and scopophilia, together with its combination of spectacular documentary-style footage and conventional narrative, *The Forester of the Silver Wood* participated in the ongoing project of redefining cinematic representation for the postwar period. At the same time, *The Forester of the Silver Wood*, like *The Sinner* before it, made the case for a relegitimated cinema by invoking film's possibilities as a realist art form promoting affective identification and by contrasting these possibilities with the decadent tendencies of modern abstract art.

I

As postwar commentators continued to laud abstract art as *the* new democratic form of visual representation, discussions of film aesthetics circled around the function of filmic realism, in particular as it pertained to the process of apprehending, perceiving, and consuming film on the part of the audience. Film spectatorship was the subject of much public discussion and controversy in the 1950s. In diverse publications, critics expressed concern about the impact of film viewing on individual groups of spectators and on society at large. Sociologists carried out empirical studies to quantify the demographics of film audiences in an attempt to gauge the effects of movies on spectators.[16] Church leaders worried about the role of movie going in the declining church attendance of their congregations and in the ostensible moral deterioration of the nation.[17] Other commentators unequivocally defended film, arguing that cinema played a pivotal function in society by expanding viewers' experience and knowledge of the world.[18] Film critics wrote about the prehistory of cinema, seeking to locate the development of film in the larger contexts of visual culture and early forms of protocinematic entertainment.[19] Their new theories of film sought to legitimate film viewing as one of the primary aesthetic experiences available in modern society. These theories also attempted to vindicate entertainment film as a necessary outlet from the pressures of the modern world by offering analyses of the emergent postwar conception of leisure.[20]

Across the political spectrum, these critics were preoccupied with the question of whether film could be considered an art form on a par with literature, painting, or theater. Popular writers on cinema and academically trained film critics alike investigated film form, seeking to invest cinema with an aesthetic genealogy and arguing for improvements to contemporary filmmaking practices that would allow movies to adhere better to the "innate" aesthetic qualities of film. The question of film aesthetics led these writers to contemplate the phenomenological and empirical aspects of film spectatorship as well: How did film spectatorship differ from the process of apprehending other arts? How did the process of film viewing influence or contribute to individual experience? Did film stimulate or impede imagination and fantasy? In discussing all of these tricky questions, critics returned again and again to the issue of realism.

Most early West German film critics proposed a notion of cinematic realism akin to the theories of film advocated by such well-known critics as Andre Bazin and Siegfried Kracauer.[21] Andrew Tudor sums up the contributions of Bazin and Kracauer to debates about realism: "<T>he effective kernal <sic> of the argument is that the essence of film is photography, photography's principle characteristic is that it impassively reveals the world, and so film will *fulfill its true nature* by doing likewise."[22] In the words of Kracauer, film, as a photographic medium, is uniquely suited to reveal and "redeem" the often ephemeral and fleeting essence of physical reality. Likewise, West German critics defended filmic realism on the basis of film's innate mimetic function, seeking to specify the significance of realist cinematic practices for the reconstruction of cinema in postwar Germany, with particular reference to their impact on postwar spectators.

In a critique of postwar German cinema published in 1950, the author Wolfdietrich Schnurre defined film as an art form whose central purpose is "to be true. True, in this sense, means: corresponding to life, to reality—namely, at the level of art. And that means at the level of aesthetics as well as on a human level, whereby the human level must be the crucial factor."[23] For Schnurre, the essential function of film is to clarify or elucidate the human situation: "However, that consistently requires from film the unconditional incorporation of reality and the commitment to artistic veracity."[24] Schnurre sought to defend film as an art form while also investigating the reasons for what he saw as the poor quality of much contemporary filmmaking, and his diagnosis of the latter focuses on the deficit of realism in postwar German films. To the extent that reality is present here, it is the "wishful reality of the little man, the pipe dream fantasy of the pottering washerwoman and the streetcar conductor. … For even our supposedly so 'realistic' rubble and homecoming films do not get by without such illusions."[25] Thus for Schnurre, cinema continues to incorporate the twin possibilities of dream factory entertainment and realist exposé; he argues that to improve the quality of German cinema, filmmakers must discard the former in favor of the latter. Schnurre pays lip service to the notion that the poor quality of German filmmaking is *not* in fact the fault of the audience, arguing that "the audience is not guilty, for it can be educated."[26] Nonetheless, he returns again and again to the fantasies of young women and the petit bourgeoisie as the propellers of cinematic illusionism.[27]

Like other early West German film critics, Schnurre draws on longstanding debates in film theory to differentiate between modes of cinematic realism.[28] He indicts the seamless realism of contemporary filmmaking, which disguises its illusionism and ultimately naturalizes social realities, and he calls for a new type of aesthetically motivated realism, which would strive to unmask the naturalizing and illusionary qualities of cinema, while shedding light on social problems.

Working with similar categories as Schnurre but drawing somewhat different conclusions in his book *Film Between Fantasy and Reality*, critic Karl Klär seeks to defend film and its audience from attacks by detractors who characterize film as kitsch and its spectators as tasteless, uncritical, passive, and sentimental. By contrast, Klär argues that film occupies a liminal aesthetic space between high art and entertainment that allows it to appeal to a diverse, sophisticated audience:

> Only the greater or lesser degree of masterful use of the means of expression specific to film, and the extent to which it is true and genuine to life, determines the value of an individual work. Any classification made according to other criterion disregards the inner laws of film, because it derives from ignorance of filmic means and intentions. In addition, it should not be forgotten that film is the first art form that holds spellbound in the same way the vast masses of millions of people of all levels, classes,

and generations. Whether we are dealing with a serious film, a popular piece, a farce, a musical, or a thriller, all of these address the same mass audience, which is so diverse in its interests and preferences.[29]

Klär argues that the realism of film form must be understood in order to grasp both the aesthetic nature of film and the impact of film viewing on the lives of spectators: he argues that film's innate realism provides viewers with access to realms of life and the world that they would never have been able to enter otherwise. As he observes, perhaps "the most decisive reason for the mass appeal of film" is that "it is a great, inexhaustible source of experience for people who are overstressed by the demands of life in our time."[30] Klär's defense of film dovetailed with two other predominant explanations for the popularity of cinema in the postwar period: the *Nachholbedürfnis* (need to catch up) of Germans after the prohibitions of the Nazi period, and the promotion of leisure in the new consumer society of the Federal Republic.

For Klär and other 1950s commentators, the expansion of experience offered by movie going constituted the aesthetic potential, indeed the aesthetic promise of film. For example, the sociologist Hans von Eckardt argued that film could provide the masses with social insight by showing them, and encouraging them to identify with, segments of experience thoroughly outside their purview. Eckardt, who claims that "we live in a century in which film creates life,"[31] explains the impact of film not only on structures of perception, but also on the critical faculties of audiences:

> Now everyone can contemplate things psychologically, without having studied psychology and its insights. It is as though a curtain had been pulled back. In dim light or in the brightest light, we see people as they are, which forces us to be tolerant and makes us empathetic, even if we were fully indifferent before. We can now compare ourselves with others to a completely different extent than we could before. We are amazed to see how connected we are with others … Film helps us in this regard. It ties together social divisions to a certain extent. It accomplishes a humane enterprise. And this enterprise bears decidedly social traits. Contemporary sociology teaches us that social grievances and discrepancies will never really be dealt with from the top down, or from the bottom up, through laws and social policies. To deal with these we need other possibilities of action. And film, on the long path of a laborious development, has begun to create these.[32]

Commentators like Klär and Eckardt thus located film within the auspices of a rational-humanist democratic sociopolitical project. Their defense of filmic realism as a central element in the "democratization" of postwar West Germany had high stakes at a time when realism in visual art was vilified as "totalitarian," while rational-humanist qualities were often considered to be the domain of modern, abstract art. As Eckardt himself put it, "While … painting and sculpture have developed into the realm of the abstract and are no longer inclined to be so naturalistic, … film has distanced itself neither from the human being nor from realism, but has rather become phantasmagoric realism or realist fantasy through the medium of the spirit *<Geist>* and the configurations of intuition."[33]

While critics across the political spectrum agreed about the productive function of filmic realism, the question of fantasy was much disputed. Even conservative commentators affiliated with the churches advocated for film on the basis that it could expand viewers' experience of reality and even promote Christian moral values. Writing in a series of popular missionary tracts published by the Protestant Church, Waldemar Wilken defended film against those pious readers who might consider the cinema merely dangerous and immoral:

> Who will blame people if they occasionally want to laugh or cry a little? The whole world opens up before them. The cinema leads them into lands that they would hardly be able to see personally. It satisfies intellectual curiosity and desire. It shows us the great tragedies of world history and human lives. People experience the infinite greatness of this world and the infinite smallness of this earth. We look into people's hearts and recognize ourselves as characters of the performance. We look for answers to many questions in our lives and find them there in some of the films that are shown to us.[34]

Like other commentators on film in the 1950s, Wilken emphasized the mimetic qualities of the filmic medium. However, his conservative conception of film spectatorship saw viewers as passive vessels who identified fully with the camera eye and the events unfolding on screen: "In film, not only is the light turned out, but so is my fantasy. The eye of the camera becomes my eye … Film forces me to see the action on screen as reality. It is not my own life that is genuine, but the life that is *acted out* in the cinema."[35] According to Wilken, this subsumption of fantasy into an "acted out" reality differentiated film from other art forms that forced viewers to participate more fully in the process of apprehension by exercising their own fantasies and critical faculties. Herein lay both the merit and the danger of the cinema for Wilken, for while the mimetic qualities of film and the identification they produced had the potential to influence viewers positively, individual films could nevertheless convey immoral ideas.

By contrast, Karl Klär argued that it was precisely film's role in stimulating individual fantasy that allowed the cinema to expand viewers' realm of experience. By invoking all the senses in a wide-ranging representation of reality, film promoted productive fantasy in viewers:

> Different functions play a role in <the reception of film by individual viewers>: in addition to the eye and the ear, fantasy, active thought, feelings, and impulses of volition all take part. Through the common effects of all these functions, the experience emerges. The idea that no fantasy is

necessary in order to experience a film is just as false as the even more extreme assertion that film completely inhibits the development of fantasy by the precision of its mode of representation, by the rigid leading of spectators through image and sound.[36]

According to Klär, film provided viewers with new visual memories, thus expanding their capacity for fantasy. Furthermore, film could even correct the errant or extravagant fantasy by enforcing an integral connection to reality.

For all of these commentators, film was defensible on the grounds that it provided an aesthetic experience that expanded the social, intellectual, emotional, and even spiritual horizons of its viewers. While film entertained spectators, giving them respite from the frenetic pace of an increasingly fragmented and stratified modern world, it therefore also fulfilled the relevant functions of art in a bourgeois, democratic society. Indeed, through its integral realism, its innate mimetic qualities, film was, according to these commentators, the consummate contemporary art form, providing audiences with both an escape from and an intensified access to reality.

II

The Forester of the Silver Wood appealed to audiences on both of these counts, offering the escapist pleasures of the *Heimatfilm* in combination with highly lauded documentary-style footage of authentic naturescapes. Publicity materials for the film emphasized documentary-style realism as a bridge between the film's aspiration to appeal to a wide popular audience and its ambition to be considered legitimate art: "The longing for a lost paradise is awakened in us by the Agfacolor Union-Film 'The Forester of the Silver Wood' … A film, which can be regarded as a calling card for both popular <*volkstümliches*> and artistic filmmaking."[37] While Stummer's film certainly did not emulate the sort of filmic realism that writers like Wolfdietrich Schnurre advocated, the film's achievements in combining narrative strategies with realist, documentary-style cinematography were in keeping with the general promotion of film's mimetic qualities among critics in the 1950s, and reviewers of *The Forester of the Silver Wood* seized on this aspect of the film. Writing in the trade journal *Filmblätter*, the critic Ponkie described the visual mastery displayed by the film:

The forester showcased in the film's title is only the (inevitable) human ink spot on this magnificent Agfacolor painting of the untouched timber forest. For this is predominantly a documentary film <*Kulturfilm*>; indeed, it is a documentary film of very high quality: a singular eavesdropping of the camera on the forest and the meadows, the cliffs and the fields, in the quiet and deserted world of the mountains, where the shy animals live according to age-old rules. In the process, nature is not arranged in an artistically symbolic fashion as with Disney, but rather simply and quietly captured on film without any technical refinement—whereby the rhythm of life in this imposing mountain world of Carinthia and Tyrol becomes a sensational event when, for example, the eagle attacks the fox and the creatures fight their eternal struggle for existence. A hunting ground of noble natural beauty not only for the hunter bearing game, but also a feast for the eyes for any animal or nature lover. Given the illuminating power of this milieu in and of itself, the loud accompanying music, standard for the timber forest, and the poacher/love story that is woven in hardly increase the business value of the film. However, as a feature-length sportsmanlike mountain hike the film has so much quality that if it is exhibited properly, it will find a strong resonance with audiences.[38]

Notably, Ponkie compares the documentary realism of *The Forester of the Silver Wood* to a painting in this review, further blurring received distinctions between film and other forms of visual art. She also echoes the critical commonplace that the plot adds little value to this film, presumably because, like the nondiegetic music that is also the subject of her critique, it appears to undercut the authenticity of the film's worthy contribution to documenting nature.

From its very outset, however, *The Forester of the Silver Wood* inextricably links narrative and documentary footage in ways that almost certainly contributed to the film's remarkable popularity with German audiences. What is more, the film's plot about several abstract artists from the city, in combination with its realist images of the rural landscape, presents a metacinematic consideration of issues of vision and visuality, spectatorship and perception that link Stummer's film to the ongoing postwar attempt to relegitimate cinema.

The Forester of the Silver Wood begins with a sequence that clearly establishes the male gaze.[39] After the white on black credit sequence that lists the Austrian landscape as a player in the film, the camera pans down from an image of blue sky framing mountains to close in on two men putting up bales of hay to feed the wild animals. Documentary shots of deer loping through the forest are followed by a close-up of a man, clearly identified as the eponymous forester by his clothing, who lifts a set of binoculars to his eyes. This establishing shot marks the following sequence as originating from the forester's perspective. With him, we as spectators look at deer grazing peacefully; suddenly they start and bound away. The forester speaks: "What's wrong?!" This exclamation sets the plot of the movie in motion, suggesting that, in contrast to reviewers' claims that the film portrays a placid, pastoral landscape, in fact all is not well in the Silver Wood. The forester looks again at the mountain landscape and sees a huge pine tree falling to the ground. "They're cutting down the Silver Wood! Unbelievable!," he yells.

This initial sequence serves an identificatory function, aligning the gaze of the spectator with that of the forester. Utilizing the visual apparatus of the binoculars, the forester surveys the forest: what is captured in his sight lines is not a tranquil naturescape, but a threatening incursion on nature. Again and again throughout the film, the forester will discover such threats to his domain through the use of prosthetic visual devices such as binoculars and a telescope.

Subsequently, the forester, Hubert Gerold, learns that townspeople from the village of Hochmoos are responsible for cutting down the trees. When he expresses concern that deforestation will scare away the animals living in the woods, Hubert is reminded by the villagers of his status as an expellee, a refugee from the East who has lost his home as a result of the war, and he is told in no uncertain terms to "butt out": "If I were an outsider like you, I wouldn't concern myself with other people's business." Nonetheless, he confronts his employer, the privy counselor Leonhard. Learning that the town has decided to sell its trees as lumber to cope with financial difficulties, Leonhard, together with the mayor, convinces the town council that the forest is Hochmoos's primary asset and that deforestation should be stopped.

Meanwhile, in Vienna, the privy counselor's granddaughter Liesl Leonhard, a sculptor, is preparing to leave for a trip to Hochmoos, where she plans to attend the annual Hunters' Ball, staying with her grandfather in the country while her city boyfriend Max takes a trip to Paris to sell some of his art. While in Hochmoos, Liesl learns to love rural life and wonders whether she should ever return to Vienna. Her infatuation with Hochmoos comes about when she meets the forester and embarks on a series of forest hikes with him.

In several lengthy nature sequences, Liesl and Hubert observe together the beauty of the local flora and fauna, employing prosthetic devices such as binoculars that emphasize the function of looking. Notably, while Gerold is alone in the forest, he repeatedly uses binoculars and telescopes to view threatening incursions on nature such as deforestation and poaching. It is only when he is accompanied by Liesl that these tools allow him to unlock the wonders of the forest—the illuminating footage praised by critics—opening up a space of visual pleasure and a *mise en scène* of desire that is connected to the female gaze. Like so many other postwar films, *The Forester of the Silver Wood* thus opposes the gendered gazes of its male and female protagonists, suggesting that men and women literally *see* differently. As in those other films, too, men here are linked to a disturbed mode of vision, while women evidence a more productive way of seeing. Consistent with postwar cinema's strategy to overcome the crisis of representation linked to problematic male experience by turning to women's stories and formal strategies that appealed to female spectators, *The Forester of the Silver Wood* thus endows its female protagonist with an active gaze invested with constructive powers, powers that emerge from Liesl's artistic vision of the real(ist) landscapes of Styria. Another "woman who looks," Liesl's role as an artist and her mastery of the gaze not only complicate conventional cinematic codes, but also point to her narrative authority and her key role as producer of meaning—rather than as mere object or spectacle—in the film.

One day, Max arrives in Hochmoos in his shiny red convertible, hoping to bring Liesl back to the city. At the suggestion of the locals, he decides to go hunting, borrowing a gun from the innkeeper. Max shoots the prize young stag in the forest and is caught red-handed by the forester, who plans to file criminal charges against him. However, when Hubert notices that Max is in possession of a gun monogrammed with the privy counselor Leonhard's initials, he refuses to divulge the identity of the poacher in order to protect Liesl, who he believes borrowed the gun. Max leaves Hochmoos in the middle of the night without saying goodbye. Assuming that Hubert is at fault, Leonhard fires him. When Hubert catches Liesl's dog killing a deer in the forest and shoots him, Liesl assumes that Hubert has taken out his vengeance on the dog, a present from Max, and Liesl, too, decides to return to the city.

Months later, Liesl and Max throw a party in Vienna. The dance music coming from the radio abruptly ends, and a Bach organ concerto begins. The music sends Liesl into a reverie as she thinks back to the day when she discovered Hubert playing the same Bach piece on the church organ in Hochmoos. As Max and Liesl argue about the music, Max reveals the truth about his poaching in Hochmoos. Stunned, Liesl sets out to find Hubert, but through a series of miscommunications she is led to believe that he has a new love interest, and their relationship is not re-established.

In the film's final sequence, Liesl accompanies her grandfather to a local chapel for the celebration of Hubertustag ("Hubert Day"), the feast of the hunter, where the priest blesses a procession of hunters. Liesl learns that, through her intervention, her grandfather has decided to give Hubert his old job back, and Liesl and Hubert exchange meaningful glances. The film ends with a long shot of a mountain, framed by the church arch. While this ending hints at an eventual relationship between Liesl and Hubert, significantly this closure is accomplished without a word, only through the exchange of gazes. Like many other postwar films, this one also fails to attain the consummation of a relationship between its protagonists. However, closure is achieved nonetheless through the integration of both Liesl, the modern woman from the city, and Hubert, the outsider expellee, into the rural community of Hochmoos. The assimilation of these two characters, who both represent threats to traditional order, emblematizes the successful negotiation of contemporary conflicts that is a major subtext of the film.

III

When Liesl first arrives in Hochmoos, she dresses up for the Hunters' Ball in a daringly cut fashionable modern evening dress, which her grandfather compels her to take off immediately. "But I think it fits me perfectly!," objects Liesl. "Yes, it fits you, but not us," replies Leonhard.

Because Hochmoos is Liesl's ancestral *Heimat*, she is automatically accepted there, but the film's narrative follows the attempts of her grandfather and the locals to train her in the culture and customs of the community. Presumably orphaned as a result of the war, Liesl gravitates toward the familial connections represented by Hochmoos, but she maintains allegiances to her background in the city culture of abstract art and high fashion as well. Referring to the difficulties posed by her boyfriend, "that abstract sculptor," Liesl's grandfather tells her, "I promised your father to maintain a home for you here, but you aren't making it easy for me." By contrast, Hubert intuitively understands local traditions, but as a recently arrived expellee, he is treated with suspicion and classified as an outsider. When Hubert acts honorably to protect Liesl, he is assumed to be in the wrong, summarily dismissed from his job, and cast out of the community once again.

Significantly, Hubert plays a central role in facilitating Liesl's integration into the community and vice versa: while Hubert introduces Liesl to the natural landscape of Styria and the traditional codes of the forest, Liesl helps Hubert to uncover the aesthetic qualities of the landscape and, ultimately, to overcome the many conflicts that plague both the forest and his relationship to the community. During Liesl's first visit to Hochmoos, Hubert catches her skiing through the nature preserve. Outraged at the threat to nature presented by her incursion, he points her to the posted signs that ban skiing, signs that she has overlooked. "You city folk never see what you are supposed to see," fumes Hubert. "We 'city folk' need to be trained to see," replies Liesl, giving voice to the film's mission to retrain the gaze and reorient the priorities of "city folk," including the extradiegetic viewers of *The Forester of the Silver Wood* itself.

In subsequent scenes, Hubert and Liesl make repeated expeditions into the forest together, where they watch birds, badgers, and baby deer through binoculars. "Sometimes I begin to doubt my life in the city," Liesl remarks after one of these trips. Through both contrastive editing and narrative devices, the film routinely counterposes the natural beauty of the Hochmoos flora and fauna with the artifice of city life embodied by Max and Liesl's Vienna art studio. Just as Liesl is set to return to Vienna, Hubert shows up and invites her on a hike up in the mountains, to view the aerie of a group of golden eagles, a trip that the local men have deemed too dangerous for Liesl up until now. When Liesl postpones her departure for the city in order to accompany Hubert on the hike, her grandfather remarks, "Even an abstract artist can't compete with a real eagle."

The climax of the film, Liesl and Hubert's hike to the eagle's nest, includes a lengthy documentary sequence of a fight between an eagle and a fox that was extensively praised in reviews. Moreover, the sequence presents the pinnacle of the budding romance between Liesl and Hubert, who engage in a lengthy kiss after witnessing the stimulus of the eagle and the fox. Notably, the tension of this sequence is heightened through constant cross-cutting between the many documentary shots of eagles, bracketed by the gazes of Liesl and Hubert, and images of Max's red convertible racing along rural roads on its way to Hochmoos. Not only does this cross-cutting escalate the conflict between Max and Hubert as Liesl's diametrically opposed suitors, but it also heightens the contrast between the traditional beauty of nature and the glamour of modern accoutrements like Max's car.

While *The Forester of the Silver Wood* sets up a series of dichotomies between modernity and tradition, abstraction and realism, it is noteworthy that both poles are mobilized by the "cinema of attractions" offered by this *Heimatfilm*. The publicity documents for the film sought to stress both the appeal of nature and the attractions of the city art world. The press book included advertising images of both the Styrian landscape and Max and Liesl's Vienna art studio; one prominent image of the studio carries the caption: "The idiosyncratic artist Max Freiberg doesn't understand why his colleague Liesl feels so attracted to the authenticity of nature."[40] Similarly, the film program posts numerous photos of the Vienna art studio—replete with visually appealing shots of abstract sculpture and modern fashions—along with the requisite images of Liesl and Hubert surrounded by nature that predominate on the front and back covers.[41]

Indeed, within the diegesis of *The Forester of the Silver Wood*, not only do the documentary naturescapes appeal to audiences, but modern consumer goods and abstract art linked to the city attract the eye of the spectator. When Max travels to Hochmoos, lengthy tracking shots encourage viewers to feast their eyes on his sporty convertible; when he arrives in town, a flock of children shows up to gawk at the car. The final Vienna sequence, Liesl and Max's party, is shot in color, but virtually all the costumes and objects in the room are black and white. Patterns and shapes seem to dance along with the jazzy soundtrack. Liesl's dress, printed with an op-art pattern, is so visually enticing that it distracts attention from her conversation with Max.

The visual and aural pleasures promoted by this sequence are disrupted only by the soundtrack, when the swing on the radio is abruptly interrupted by Bach's organ music. A significant moment in the film, this switch to Bach is the catalyst for Liesl's decision to take off her modern, op-art dress and leave the city behind. As in other films from the 1950s, "modern" music—whether popular or avant-garde—is aligned with abstract art in an aggregate modern form that is coded urban and perverse. Classical church music, by contrast, is sacred art that can harmonize with a natural landscape.

In *The Forester of the Silver Wood*, Bach's music is immortal and timeless; at the same time, it is linked to regional identity. Hubert Gerold explains to Liesl that he learned to play this music "on our estate in my lost *Heimat*." Liesl's discovery that the refugee Hubert can play Bach organ concertos by heart, that high culture exists in the mountains, represents the moment in the film when she begins to contemplate staying in Hochmoos for good. This moment coincides with another scene that condenses the film's thematization of artistic representation. When Liesl hears Gerold's Bach performance emanating from the church, she is in the midst of transporting a birthday present for her grandfather, a sixteenth-century sculpture of a Madonna that she found in an old barn and painstakingly restored. Her grandfather, deeply touched by the gift, proclaims, "Made with so much love and so much talent! ... Now I really don't understand what you see in that newfangled stuff—a natural and healthy girl like you!" As in *The Sinner*, the conservative narrative trajectory of *The Forester of the Silver Wood* codes modern, abstract art as perverse in contrast to the natural, healthy qualities of religious statuary and the sacred music of Bach. Furthermore, the trappings of modernity— including modern art, sports cars, and high fashion—are marginalized as antithetical to the prevailing heteronormativity of the rural region, with its natural landscapes and heritage culture.

Notably, however, Liesl's accommodation to the "natural, healthy" economy of Hochmoos is not simply a matter of acceptance of rural norms. Rather, Liesl actively negotiates the rifts between tradition and modernity, while also negotiating her own independence as an artist and a woman. As Johannes von Moltke puts it, "Maintaining their professional commitment, <women in *Heimatfilme*> therefore also bear the second, larger burden of functioning as agents of modernization charged with bringing the traditional values and norms of a rural community up to speed with the changing reality in the urban centers."[42] As an artist, Liesl controls representation and perception, and she is invested with the ability to revive traditional culture in Hochmoos, injecting it with a shot of modernity. In one of the most well-known sequences of *Film Without a Title*, Christine, the Hildegard Knef character, mistakenly scrubs away the patina from an antique Madonna, a gesture that signifies the destruction of aesthetic value and the problematic relation of form and content in the postwar period. By contrast, in *The Forester of the Silver Wood*, Liesl restores the Hochmoos Madonna to a new splendor, using modern means to recalibrate its antique form, thereby preserving its aura and thus its traditional aesthetic value. Similarly, when Liesl accompanies Hubert into the woods, the two do not encounter poachers or lumberjacks bent on destroying the landscape, but rather golden eagles, bears, and fields of daffodils, rendered in splendid Agfacolor. By introducing Liesl to the forest, the forester himself learns to see the natural landscape in new ways. While the film marginalizes modern forms of abstract representation, its foregrounding of technologies of vision and its virtuoso realism legitimate film as a modern art form that can assist in retraining the gaze and revitalizing traditional culture.

IV

As we have seen in other postwar films, the problem of visual representation is inextricably tied to gender issues in *The Forester of the Silver Wood*. Just as Liesl serves as a mediator between tradition and modernity in Hochmoos, she also navigates postwar gender roles, presented here through the convention of the love triangle that develops between Liesl, Max, and Hubert. Liesl must choose between two men who are linked both to different aspects of recent history and to different forms of modern representation.

Liesl's city boyfriend Max, the abstract sculptor, is the film's representative of decadent, perverse, and troubling masculinity. A domineering man who does not wish to let Liesl out of his sight, Max is an unsympathetic character from the outset of the film. Indeed, Max is the only character in the film who is directly linked to the Wehrmacht, the war, and, by extension, to Nazism, a link that is made explicit when the hostess at Hochmoos's guesthouse encourages him to go hunting. "You can shoot, can't you?," she asks. "Of course I can," he replies, "We all had to learn how back then." When Max proceeds to use his shooting skills for the purposes of illicit poaching, his transgressive, violent qualities are confirmed.

Hubert Gerold, by contrast, represents a more respectable masculinity bound to tradition and honor, emblematized by his position as forester. Linked to nature, Hubert is associated with the realism of the film's highly praised documentary footage, which he views, along with the spectator, through binoculars and telescopes. However, Hubert, like Max, is unable to negotiate successfully the terrain of postwar Hochmoos. From his silence about Max's poaching to his decision to shoot Liesl's dog, Hubert consistently makes poor decisions that lead him to lose both his job and the girl. Unlike the aggressive Max, Hubert is positioned as a victim in *The Forester of the Silver Wood*, a position consistent with his status as an expellee who has lost his true *Heimat* as a result of the war. As Johannes von Moltke has shown, however, *Heimatfilme*—along with the larger public discourse on expulsion in the 1950s, including a number of influential sociological studies—saw the refugee not only as a victim, but also "as a figure for new departures, explicitly ascribing to this figure some crucial modernizing impulses."[43] As we have seen, the closure of Stummer's film is predicated on the successful integration of both Liesl and Hubert into the community of Hochmoos, and this integration also figures the incorporation of modernizing tendencies into Hochmoos's traditional culture.

Writing about the double burden of women in *Heimatfilme*, Georg Seeßlen argues that, with the exception of the 1950s secretary film, "no other genre describes the role of the woman in the economic miracle with the same precision, demanding two faces of her, both radiant: one gazing in confirmation on the Fascist man, who wants to remain Fascist, and the other turning an eye on the money, on modernization, corruption, industrialization."[44] For Seeßlen, "The ideal woman of the *Heimatfilm* emancipates herself in a reactionary role, she keeps the books on progress and mops away all contradictions."[45] While Liesl is certainly charged with the double burden that Seeßlen describes, his schematic formulation is not quite accurate when it comes to *The Forester of the Silver Wood*. For the film opposes two kinds of masculinity in the figures of Max and Hubert, deciding in favor of Hubert, a decision that is reflected by Liesl's choice at the end of the film. In rejecting Max, Liesl foregoes city life, presumably embracing the traditional, even reactionary, female role offered by life in rural Hochmoos. In so doing, however, she also emancipates herself from a relationship with the kind of "Fascist man who wants to remain Fascist" described by Seeßlen.

In rejecting Max, Liesl also implicitly rejects abstract art, embracing nature, and by extension, in the discursive world of *The Forester of the Silver Wood*, realism. Yet the film complicates such clear dichotomies. Like the female protagonists of *Heimatfilme* discussed by von Moltke, Liesl is an independent, professional woman, who sacrifices some of her independence when she falls for the forester. However, she also continues to develop as an artist in Hochmoos. When Max first arrives in Hochmoos, hoping to take Liesl back to Vienna, she explains to him the

Figure 6.3 The artist Liesl Leonhard (Anita Gutwell) learns to see with her own eyes. Source: Deutsche Kinemathek.

allure of the rural countryside: "It's just that I see things differently from here. I have become uncertain …, because I was used to seeing everything with your eyes and not having my own opinion any more." The narrative of the film literally follows Liesl as she learns to see with her own eyes. At a key moment in the film, when she learns that Hubert has killed her dog, an event that precedes her return to the city, we see Liesl painting a watercolor (see figure 6.3). Her painting is a representationalist—though not realist—image of a herd of deer, rendered in a quasi-Expressionist style, a visual synthesis of Liesl's training in abstract styles and her newfound vision of nature.

By outlining the development of a female artist, *The Forester of the Silver Wood* reflects the imbrication of problems of representation with problems of gender and sexuality. The closure of the film solves both sets of problems on a narrative level by suggesting a synthesis of abstract and realist visual forms as well as a synthesis of tradition and modernity through the assimilation of Liesl and Hubert into the rural community of Hochmoos. At the level of form, too, Stummer's film seeks to resolve the problems faced by postwar filmmakers in finding a new film language. If its diegetic narrative sought to synthesize the competing visual styles of abstraction and realism, however, on a formal level the film offers a resounding defense of cinematic realism.

Indeed, *The Forester of the Silver Wood* seeks to legitimate postwar filmmaking by foregrounding the visual pleasure that cinema can offer through revealing the world as it is. Relying on the spectacle offered by its "cinema of attractions," the film presents the conventional escapist pleasures associated with the *Heimatfilm* genre. At the same time, through its metacinematic narrative about spectatorship and visual representation and its formal combination of narrative and documentary footage, the film also promotes fantasy and active engagement with the filmic image. In line with prominent 1950s theories of cinematic realism, Stummer's film thus defends realist cinema on the grounds that it provides viewers with both an escape from and an intensified access to reality. Notably, this defense of realism is once again built on the ground of female spectatorship, as *The Forester of the Silver Wood* sought to appeal to female viewers by mobilizing a female gaze that controls artistic representation and unlocks the visual pleasures of nature, modeled through the character of Liesl Leonhard.

Notes

1. See Hans Helmut Prinzler, *Chronik des deutschen Films 1895–1994* (Stuttgart, 1995), 186–204; and Elizabeth Prommer, *Kinobesuch im Lebenslauf. Eine historische und medienbiografische Studie* (Konstanz, 1999), 350.
2. According to Joseph Garncarz, of the fifty films that were most popular with West German audiences from 1950/51 to 1954/55, thirty-five were West German and six were Austrian (including one Austrian–Yugoslavian co-production). The remaining nine most

popular movies included six Hollywood films, one British film, one Swedish film, and one French–Italian co-production. Garncarz, "Hollywood in Germany. Die Rolle des amerikanischen Films in Deutschland: 1925–1990," in *Der deutsche Film. Aspekte seiner Geschichte von den Anfängen bis zur Gegenwart*, ed. Uli Jung (Trier, 1993), 200–201.

3. *The Forester of the Silver Wood* won a Bambi prize as the financially most successful foreign film in the West German market in 1955. See Garncarz for its ranking as the second most popular film among West German audiences in the 1954/55 season. Garncarz in Jung, *Der deutsche Film*, 201.

4. According to Manfred Barthel, an Austrian production company showed the film to the head of the West German distributor Union-Film, Rosemarie Kraemer, who agreed to distribute it on the stipulation that a full 60 percent of the final feature consist of documentary footage of animals. Barthel, *So war es wirklich: Der deutsche Nachkriegsfilm* (Munich and Berlin, 1986), 101. However, without having undertaken a statistical study of the film, I would estimate that the amount of documentary footage included in the final cut is closer to 30 percent.

5. See "Presse-Information: *Der Förster vom Silberwald (Echo der Berge),*" ed. Karlfriedrich Scherer (Munich, 1954), 14, in file on *Der Förster vom Silberwald*, Schriftgutarchiv, Stiftung Deutsche Kinemathek, Berlin.

6. For an early assessment of the film's success, see "Zehn Millionen sahen den 'Förster vom Silberwald,'" *Abendzeitung* (Munich), August 21, 1956. Sequel and spin-off films seeking to capitalize on the success of *The Forester of the Silver Wood* included the Austrian film *Die Sennerin von St. Kathrein* (The Milkmaid of St. Kathrein, 1955) and the West German film *Der Wilderer vom Silberwald* (The Poacher of the Silver Wood, 1957).

7. For reviews that echoed the language of the press book, see rev. of *Der Förster vom Silberwald/ Echo der Berge*, *Katholischer Filmdienst* 8.4 (1955); rev. of *Echo der Berge*, *Evangelischer Film-Beobachter* 6 (1954): 613; and Ponkie, rev. of *Der Förster vom Silberwald*, *Filmblätter* 7 (1955).

8. Rev. of *Der Förster vom Silberwald/ Echo der Berge*, *Katholischer Filmdienst*.

9. Johannes von Moltke, *No Place Like Home: Locations of Heimat in German Cinema* (Berkeley, 2005), 83.

10. Claudius Seidl, *Der deutsche Film der fünfziger Jahre* (Munich, 1987), 84–85.

11. On the introduction of fashionable clothing and modern consumer goods into the *Heimatfilm*, see also von Moltke, *No Place Like Home*, 85, 114–34.

12. See for example Walther Schmieding, *Kunst oder Kasse: Der Ärger mit dem deutschen Film* (Hamburg, 1961); Seidl, *Der deutsche Film der fünfziger Jahre*; Bärbel Westermann, *Nationale Identität im Spielfilm der fünfziger Jahre* (Frankfurt am Main, 1990); Barbara Bongartz, *Von Caligari zu Hitler—von Hitler zu Dr. Mabuse? Eine "psychologische" Geschichte des deutschen Films von 1946 bis 1960* (Münster, 1992); Marc Silberman, *German Cinema: Texts in Context* (Detroit, 1995), 114–27; and Ingeborg Majer-O'Sickey, "Framing the *Unheimlich: Heimatfilm* and Bambi," in *Gender and Germanness: Cultural Productions of Nation*, ed. Patricia Herminghouse and Magda Mueller (Providence, RI, 1997), 202–16.

13. See for example Gerhard Bliersbach, *So grün war die Heide … Die gar nicht so heile Welt im Nachkriegsfilm*, abridged ed. (Weinheim and Basel, 1989); Georg Seeßlen, "Durch die Heimat und so weiter: Heimatfilme, Schlagerfilme und Ferienfilme der fünfziger Jahre," in *Zwischen Gestern und Morgen. Westdeutscher Nachkriegsfilm 1946–1962*, ed. Hilmar Hoffmann and Walter Schobert (Frankfurt am Main, 1989), 136–63; and Heide Fehrenbach, *Cinema in Democratizing Germany: Reconstructing National Identity After Hitler* (Chapel Hill, 1995).

14. Von Moltke, *No Place Like Home*, 83.

15. See for example Fehrenbach, *Cinema in Democratizing Germany*, 164.

16. See Walter Hanke, "Die Bedeutung des Filmbesuchs für die deutsche Jugend: Untersuchung der Filmbegeisterung nach ihren Ursachen und Wirkungen," typescript 1955, Bibliothek der Deutschen Film- und Fernsehakademie Berlin; Kurt Gustmann, "Zusammensetzung und Verhalten des Filmtheaterpublikums in der Großstadt," *Filmstudien: Beiträge des*

Filmseminars im Institut für Publizistik der Westf. Wilhelms-Universität Münster 3, ed. Walter Hagemann (Emsdetten, 1957); Helga Haftendorn, "Zusammensetzung und Verhalten des Filmtheaterpublikums in der Mittelstadt," *Filmstudien* 3: 27–44.

17. See Waldemar Wilken, *Und Abends ins Kino*, Volksmissionarische Schriftreihe Heft 69 (Gladbeck, 1959). For an extensive analysis of the relationship of the churches to postwar cinema, see also Fehrenbach, *Cinema in Democratizing Germany*.

18. See Karl Klär, *Film zwischen Wunsch und Wirklichkeit: Gespräche mit den Freunden des Films und seinen Gegnern* (Wiesbaden-Biebrich, 1957). The argument that film viewing expands experience is also made forcefully by Wilken, *Und Abends ins Kino*.

19. See Hans von Eckardt, "Von der Wirklichkeitsnähe des Films," *Der Film als Beeinflussungsmittel: Vorträge und Berichte der 2. Jahrestagung der Deutschen Gesellschaft für Filmwissenschaft*, ed. Erich Feldmann and Walter Hagemann (Emsdetten, 1955), 67–76.

20. See Klär, *Film zwischen Wunsch und Wirklichkeit*; Eckardt, "Von der Wirklichkeitsnähe"; Wilken, *Und Abends ins Kino*; the essays collected in *Filmstudien* 3; and especially Kurt Wortig, *Ihre Hoheit Lieschen Müller: Hof- und Hinterhofgespräche um Film und Fernsehen* (Munich, 1961).

21. See Andre Bazin, "The Ontology of the Photographic Image" <1945>, rpt. in *What Is Cinema?*, vol. 1, trans. Hugh Gray (Berkeley, 1967), 9–16; and Siegfried Kracauer, *Theory of Film: The Redemption of Physical Reality* (Oxford, 1960).

22. Andrew Tudor, "The Many Mythologies of Realism," *Screen* 13.1 (1972): 29.

23. Wolfdietrich Schnurre, *Rettung des deutschen Films: Eine Streitschrift* (Stuttgart, 1950), 14. With this pamphlet Schnurre, who was a founding member of the influential literary "Group 47," contributed to a growing cineastic movement among postwar film commentators that Johannes von Moltke has termed "high-minded film criticism" (*No Place Like Home*, 97). In addition to Schnurre, von Moltke refers specifically to Gunter Groll and Arthur Maria Rabenalt, as well as to the younger critics Joe Hembus and Walther Schmieding. This cineastic movement, which was consolidated with the founding of the critical journal *Filmkritik* in 1957, laid the groundwork for the "Oberhausen Manifesto" and the birth of the New German Cinema in the 1960s.

24. Schnurre, *Rettung des deutschen Films*, 14.

25. Schnurre, *Rettung des deutschen Films*, 37.

26. See Schnurre, *Rettung des deutschen Films*, table of contents and 44.

27. See esp. Schnurre, *Rettung des deutschen Films*, 28–29.

28. For a useful summary of these debates see Christopher Williams, ed., *Realism and the Cinema: A Reader* (London, 1980).

29. Klär, *Film zwischen Wunsch und Wirklichkeit*, 68.

30. Klär, *Film zwischen Wunsch und Wirklichkeit*, 31.

31. Eckardt, "Von der Wirklichkeitsnähe," 70.

32. Eckardt, "Von der Wirklichkeitsnähe," 73–75.

33. Eckardt, "Von der Wirklichkeitsnähe," 71.

34. Wilken, *Und Abends ins Kino*, 10.

35. Wilken, *Und Abends ins Kino*, 15.

36. Klär, *Film zwischen Wunsch und Wirklichkeit*, 33–34.

37. Press book in file on *Echo der Berge* <*Der Förster vom Silberwald*>, Schriftgutarchiv, Stiftung Deutsche Kinemathek, Berlin, 14.

38. Ponkie, rev. of *Der Förster vom Silberwald*, *Filmblätter*, February 7, 1955.

39. See also Westermann, *Nationale Identität*, 157.

40. Press book, 14.

41. "Der Förster vom Silberwald," *Illustrierte Film-Bühne*, 2677 (1955).

42. Von Moltke, *No Place Like Home*, 126.

43. Von Moltke, *No Place Like Home*, 139.

44. Georg Seeßlen, "Der Heimatfilm. Zur Mythologie eines Genres," in *Sprung im Spiegel: Filmisches Wahrnehmen zwischen Fiktion und Wirklichkeit*, ed. Christa Blümlinger (Vienna, 1990), 343–62, qtd. in von Moltke, *No Place Like Home*, 126.

45. Seeßlen, "Der Heimatfilm," 350.

Chapter 7

DEGENERATE ART?:
PROBLEMS OF GENDER AND SEXUALITY IN VEIT HARLAN'S *DIFFERENT FROM YOU AND ME (§175)* (1957)

The year 1956 marked the height of cinema's popularity in West Germany. A remarkable 817 million tickets were sold, 120 feature films were made, and the top seven most popular films were German or Austrian.[1] Beginning in 1957, however, West Germany witnessed a precipitous decline in the fortunes of its domestic film industry.[2] Brought about in part by changes in the structure of the industry, the decline in ticket sales for German films was fueled by increased competition from abroad, the rise of television, and the rapid economic development of the *Wirtschaftswunder*, which led to new leisure-time activities such as shopping and tourism.

During this period, the film industry adopted a number of strategies in an attempt to attract new spectators and to win back its old audiences. Studios could no longer expect blockbuster profits from the *Heimatfilm*, which had been the most popular genre of the first half of the decade. While *Heimatfilme* thematized the concerns of the reconstruction-era Federal Republic, with plots about refugees and fragmented families, by 1955 these plots no longer addressed the realities of West German life. Instead, the relative stability and growing prosperity of the *Wohlstandsgesellschaft* (affluent society) produced new concerns about the rebellious younger generation, changing class and gender roles, and the ethical dilemmas and moral values of a newly self-confident nation powered by material wealth. Filmmakers addressed these topics in a variety of genres designed to cater to changing audience tastes and demographics.

To appeal to younger viewers, youth-oriented genres such as the *Halbstarkenfilm* (rebel film) and the *Schlagerfilm* (pop-music film) were introduced, and younger filmmakers such as the dynamic team of Georg Tressler and Will Tremper were given the opportunity to try their hand at making movies.[3] At the other end of the spectrum, production companies such as Filmaufbau Göttingen found success by turning to literary adaptations in order to appeal to the highbrow tastes of the ascendant middle classes.[4]

At the same time, filmmakers tried to draw old and new audiences into the cinemas with sensationalist films that drew on tried and true themes of sex and violence. From thinly disguised skin films such as Edouard von Borsody's *Liane, Das Mädchen aus dem Urwald* (Liane, Jungle Goddess, 1956) to Robert Siodmak's *Nachts, wenn der Teufel kam* (The Devil Strikes at Night, 1957), a film noir about a psychopathic mass murderer set in the Third Reich, many of these films met with great success among increasingly fastidious West German audiences.

In part due to an atmosphere of increased competition, the established genre of the *Problemfilm* or social problem film also saw a comeback during these years. Like the skin film or noir thriller, the *Problemfilm* often titillated audiences with scenes of sex and violence, here cloaked in the legitimate guise of didactic narratives about contemporary social issues such as juvenile delinquency, prostitution, race, or homosexuality. Similar to other popular genres of the 1950s such as the domestic melodrama and the *Heimatfilm*, the *Problemfilm* was fueled by ongoing postwar anxieties about gender, sexuality, and family relations. Essentially realist in style, the *Problemfilm* also grappled with questions of representation and form at stake in postwar cinema's ongoing quest for legitimacy.

Veit Harlan's *Problemfilm Anders als du und ich (§175)* attests to postwar concerns with gender, sexuality, and representation both within its diegesis and in the extradiegetic debates that informed the context of its reception. The film tells the story of a seventeen-year-old Gymnasium student, Klaus Teichmann (Christian Wolff), a talented abstract painter, whom his parents fear is "homosexually endangered." Klaus shows no interest in girls, and instead spends most of his time with the effeminate Manfred Glatz (Günter Theil), a classmate and aspiring writer. For Klaus's parents, Christa (Paula Wessely) and Werner (Paul Dahlke), their son's situation takes a turn for the worse when Manfred introduces Klaus to Dr. Boris Winkler (Friedrich Joloff), an antiques dealer and art collector. Boris, who is homosexual, hosts salons at his house where groups of young men discuss modern painting and poetry, listen to electronic music, and hold Greco-Roman wrestling matches. Seeking to rescue their son from the double threat of modernist culture and homosexuality, the Teichmanns consult encyclopedias to learn about the "Third Sex" and visit several doctors to ask about a potential "cure" for Klaus's nascent homosexuality. The doctors agree that the best cure for Klaus would be "the love of a woman"—one doctor even refers to heterosexual sex as a "homeopathic cure."

Following up on this advice, Christa Teichmann persuades her maid Gerda Böttcher (Ingrid Stenn) to seduce Klaus. While Christa and Werner are away traveling for a week, Gerda not only initiates Klaus into heterosexual sex, but also inspires him to produce realist art, thereby bringing him onto the "right path" both sexually and aesthetically.

However, this erstwhile solution only leads to a new set of problems, exchanging the threat posed by homosexuality for the dilemma of family relations gone awry. Over the course of the film's narrative, the story of Gerda, a young expellee from Pomerania whom the Teichmanns have taken in as a kind of foster daughter, ultimately displaces the story of Klaus. This displacement is achieved most dramatically through the frame story that brackets the narrative of this *Problemfilm*, in which Christa Teichmann is prosecuted for pandering. Here, the problem revealed to be at stake is not that of male homosexuality and disturbed paternal relations, but rather female sexuality and troubled maternity.

Different From You and Me premiered in Vienna on August 29, 1957, under its original title *Das dritte Geschlecht* (The Third Sex). On October 31, a much-altered version of the film premiered in the Federal Republic, after final approval by the censorship board, the FSK (*Freiwillige Selbstkontrolle der Filmwirtschaft*). Concerned about the film's purportedly positive representation of homosexuality, the FSK had demanded substantial alterations. The title was changed from the ambiguous *Das Dritte Geschlecht* to the more normative and legalistic *Anders als du und ich (§175)*. The FSK also demanded the arrest of Dr. Boris Winkler at the end of the film, as well as the addition of several scenes portraying homosexual characters in a negative light. To accommodate the FSK's demands, some scenes were cut from the film, some were reshot, and some were merely redubbed, all of which doubtless contributed to the film's formal and narrative incongruity.

Indeed, Harlan's film presents a paradigmatic case study of the contradictory and ambivalent qualities of 1950s cinema, and not only as a result of the censorship process. One of only a handful of commercial films to explicitly address homosexuality to date, *Different From You and Me* provides an ostensibly sympathetic view of the problems faced by gay men in light of the criminalization of homosexuality under Paragraph 175 of the German penal code. With performances by homosexual actors Friedrich Joloff, Otto Graf, and Günter Theil, and several scenes shot in actual Berlin gay bars, the film also lays claim to some degree of authenticity in its representation of homosexuality in the Adenauer Era. Moreover, the film paints a quite unsympathetic portrait of Christa and Werner Teichmann and their efforts to "cure" their son. Nonetheless, *Different From You and Me* ultimately suggests that homosexuals can and should be "rehabilitated" and successfully integrated into the normalized heterosexual family unit, thus revealing the film's essentially homophobic bent.

The often-contradictory messages about homosexuality presented by *Different From You and Me* are mirrored by the ambivalence of the film's form. Like *The Forester of the Silver Wood*, Harlan's film deploys a series of dichotomies (modernity and tradition, abstraction and realism), coding the former as perverse and the latter as "normal" and "healthy." Yet like Stummer's film too, *Different From You and Me* relies as much on the audiovisual attractions of modern abstract painting and electronic music for its appeal to spectators as it does on conventional elements such as the heterosexual love story that is supposed to produce its "happy ending." To be sure, Harlan's film trafficks in the sensationalism that fueled the *Problemfilm*'s popularity, titillating mainstream spectators with a lurid view into the homosexual subculture that ultimately affirms their own comfortable place within the status quo. At the same time, however, *Different From You and Me* also presents that status quo—the patriarchal family unit—as a space of anxiety and conflict, complicating the film's message.

Critical discussion of *Different From You and Me* has long focused on the authorship of Veit Harlan, perhaps the most notorious director of Nazi cinema and the only major Nazi filmmaker to stand trial for his role in creating propaganda for the Third Reich, in particular the anti-Semitic film *Jud Süss* (Jew Süss, 1940).[5] Writing in the journal *Filmkritik* in 1957, Enno Patalas emphasized the ideological mainstays of Harlan's *oeuvre*: "Veit Harlan's opus is closed and indivisible. A direct line leads from the early adaptation of the Halbe story *Youth* through *Jew Süss* and *The Great King* to *Hanna Amon* and *Different From You and Me*: the line of protofascistic anti-intellectualism."[6]

Ever the opportunist, Harlan himself tried to present *Different From You and Me* as proof of his liberal, even anti-Nazi tendencies.[7] He claimed to have agreed to direct the project in the hopes of helping the public to understand the "problem" of homosexuality by casting homosexuals in a sympathetic light.[8] Upon the release of the film in the Federal Republic, Harlan even attempted to have his name withheld from the censored version of *Different From You and Me* as a gesture of protest against the FSK, and he circulated a nine-page letter in the media that explained what had happened in the censorship process. This letter generated little sympathy, however, as most critics believed that, coming from Harlan, it was too little, too late.

Any discussion of Harlan's work must take into account the particular dilemmas posed by his Nazi past. Yet the critical preoccupation with the continuities in his *oeuvre* has sometimes led to an exclusive focus on Harlan's authorship at the expense of other dimensions of the films.[9] The case of *Different From You and Me* presents an analytical challenge, in that the film addresses issues of sexuality and representation that bore a particular political charge in the aftermath of Nazism and in the postwar period. Conditioned no doubt in part by Harlan's ideological and aesthetic framework, the film also exhibits many traits common to the other postwar films I have discussed in previous chapters. Thus, as my analysis will demonstrate, the context of postwar filmmaking is as central to understanding *Different From You and Me* as is the stamp of Harlan's authorship.

This is particularly so when considering the film's critical reception in the 1950s, which focused to a remarkable degree *not* on the controversial topic of homosexuality, but rather on the film's depiction of abstract art and electronic music. Across the political spectrum, critics strongly objected to Harlan's conflation of homosexuality and modern art, which was seen as a sign of the director's unrepentant Nazism.[10] As Frank Noack has noted, these objections were by no means fueled by sympathy for the plight of gay men, for mainstream critics were "more upset about the defamation of modern art than of homosexuals."[11] As we have seen, films such as *The Sinner* and *The Forester of the Silver Wood* had incorporated postwar debates about realism and abstraction into their narratives as a way of thematizing social and representational problems in the postwar period, and they had done so in ways not altogether different from Harlan's film. In objecting to Harlan's depiction of modern art, critics were clearly responding to the director's Nazi past. Yet the critical outcry against *Different From You and Me* also attests to the changing status of debates about both visual art and cinematic representation in the second half of the decade.

Responses to *Different From You and Me* in the gay press during the 1950s also tended to note Harlan's authorship as a seal of doom. Gay spectators were highly critical of the film's homosexual stereotypes and of the pseudoscientific discourse on homosexuality espoused by the "experts" and encyclopedias in the film. However, the gay press also reported extensively on various aspects of the film's diegesis, including a scene in a gay bar that was purportedly one of the first ever depictions in dominant cinema of a space belonging to the homosexual subculture. The number of articles that addressed extradiegetic issues, such as the film's censorship hearings and its reception in the mainstream press, demonstrated the gay community's interest—despite the director's Nazi past—in a film that was one of the very few dominant cultural productions to address the subject of homosexuality during the postwar period.[12]

In her excellent discussion of the film, Alison Guenther-Pal convincingly argues that *Different From You and Me* displays both continuities and breaks with Nazi ideology. Thus the film presents a homophobic conception of homosexuality, while also advocating a critical view of Werner Teichmann's fascist masculinity. Departing from Guenther-Pal's analysis of the film's selective use of Nazi tropes in its construction of postwar masculinity, this chapter turns to an examination of the film's demonstrative concern with postwar femininity and the nature of its appeal to female spectators. On the surface *Different From You and Me* appeared to employ many of the same strategies that made other films from the era popular with female viewers. However, the ambiguity of the film's narrative regarding issues of gender and sexuality is matched on a formal level by Harlan's bewildering use of cross-cutting, and the combination of these elements creates a confusing experience for the (female) spectator.

Nevertheless, Harlan's film proved moderately successful with audiences.[13] Certainly, bombastic accounts by critics along with the public controversies surrounding the film's censorship fueled ticket sales among curious viewers. At the same time, the film's success was driven by its voyeuristic sensationalism in combination with a return to familiar themes, including visual representation and female experience. If viewers flocked to the cinemas expecting the moral resolution associated with the *Problemfilm*, however, they were likely disappointed. Though it strives for objective clarity through its pseudodocumentary style, *Different From You and Me* actually communicates a series of fundamentally ambivalent messages about social and representational anxieties that were of great public concern in postwar West Germany.

I

In the ongoing postwar debate about cinema, the conflict between fantasy and reality—between the cinematic illusionism of the "dream factory" and the realist mandate of a new German cinema—remained at center stage. In the second half of the 1950s in particular, the *Problemfilm* provided the film industry with one popular solution to this conflict. Relying on a cinematic template dating back to the 1920s, successful postwar *Problemfilme* such as Georg Tressler's *Die Halbstarken* (The Rebels, 1956), Frank Wisbar's *Nasser Asphalt* (Wet Asphalt, 1958), and Rolf Thiele's *Das Mädchen Rosemarie* (The Girl Rosemarie, 1958) united the conventions of mainstream genre film with narratives that addressed contemporary social issues. On a formal level, these films generally employed a realist visual language drawing on documentary motifs, and they often also exhibited some degree of formal experimentation.

Thomas Elsaesser and Michael Wedel define the conventional *Problemfilm* as a film "where the individual confronts social contradictions (class difference, moral conventions, poverty) beyond his/her control and/or comprehension."[14] According to Elsaesser and Wedel, the *Problemfilm* took on a particular incarnation in postwar West Germany, where it emphasized "emotional misery and moral isolation in the increasingly materialist world of opportunism during the 'economic miracle.'"[15] As Alison Guenther-Pal rightly points out, the social problem film of the Adenauer Era did little by way of promoting social change or reforms; instead "it ultimately tended to present viewers with a vision of society that solidly affirmed the status quo."[16] However, within the realm of filmmaking, the *Problemfilm* did represent a further step in the ongoing quest to redefine cinema for the postwar era, once again addressing social problems in tandem with representational problems, both of which most often revolved around issues of gender and sexuality.

Ostensibly, the central problem presented by *Different From You and Me* is homosexuality and its contested status in the Federal Republic. Homosexuality was criminalized by the West German constitution in Paragraph 175, which was adopted from the Nazi legal code.[17] While multiple lawsuits were brought against Paragraph 175 over the course of the 1950s, West German courts refused to overturn the law. In 1957, the year in which *Different From You and Me* was released, one such challenge made it as far as the German Federal Constitutional Court. Two men who had been jailed for homosexuality in the early 1950s appealed their convictions, arguing that they had been convicted under a Nazi law, that this law violated the constitution's guarantee of personal freedom, and that the law was unconstitutionally discriminatory because it targeted homosexual men but not lesbians.[18] The court rejected their appeal on all counts.

Homosexual men, already persecuted during the Third Reich, continued to suffer arrest and detention throughout the postwar period; convictions on the charge of homosexuality reached their peak in 1959.[19] Paragraph 175 was not amended until 1969, and it was repealed only in 1994. Nonetheless, the paragraph remained in dispute throughout the 1950s, as evidenced by the wide range of sentences passed down by courts throughout West Germany for violations of the law: "It was apparent to all parties involved that court behavior varied by region, and by individual judges, and that the administration of the paragraph was in a state of limbo."[20]

In the late 1950s, the general public increasingly perceived homosexuality as a threat to social stability. The preoccupation with juvenile delinquency and youth criminality that developed in connection with the *Halbstarken* movement—a youth subculture of (mainly) boys who wore jeans, rode motorcycles, and listened to rock music—fueled public fears. So-called "criminal" homosexuals, considered seducers of young men, were thought to be endangering Germany's male youth.[21] As Dagmar Herzog has argued, these concerns stemmed directly from Nazi conceptions of homosexuality, which regarded male sexuality as fluid, and therefore in need of protection: "The persistence of homophobia into the postwar era has been well documented. What has been less frequently acknowledged is that, to a remarkable degree, the notion that men had a potentially bisexual disposition and that young men in particular were vulnerable to conversion via seduction, was explicitly named as *the* reason for retaining Paragraph 175."[22]

Drawing on public worries about homosexuality for its appeal to audiences, *Different From You and Me* sought to legitimate itself as a film that would promote thoughtful discussion and thus serve a didactic function. According to the publicity brochure for the film:

> Certainly, cinema as "dream factory" has its place and its justification. But cinema also has a right to hold up to the public a mirror of the present and of contemporary problems. Precisely because of cinema's clarity and broad appeal, this right can even become a duty. There is a particularly conclusive example of this. For years, a debate has been raging in Germany, largely unnoticed by the masses, about the pros and cons of Paragraph 175. Most people do not have a sense of what this debate is really about. They only know the problem of homosexuality from hearsay.[23]

Comparing *Different From You and Me* to such controversial but highly successful films as *From Here to Eternity* (Fred Zinneman, 1953), *On the Waterfront* (Elia Kazan, 1954), and *La Strada* (Federico Fellini, 1954), the press booklet suggests that Harlan's film performs a valuable public service by addressing a "theme about which one does not like to speak in public."[24] At the same time, the publicity materials hint at the film's strategy for box office success: luring audiences to the cinema with the voyeuristic appeal of a glimpse behind closed doors, at what the masses know only "from hearsay."

Harlan's highly ambivalent film approaches the "problem" of homosexuality from several different angles. On the one hand, *Different From You and Me* sanctions the notion that young men such as Klaus may be "endangered" by homosexuality. From this perspective, the film casts Dr. Boris Winkler in the role of the pederastic seducer who threatens the patriarchal family that the film endorses as the central productive unit of postwar West German society. On the other hand, the film complicates this equation by contrasting a largely sympathetic portrayal of Boris as Klaus's mentor with an unsympathetic and at times satirical representation of Klaus's tyrannical, even fascistic, father Werner. Whereas Boris encourages Klaus's forays into aspects of high culture that were central to the democratic identity of the postwar Federal Republic, Werner views Klaus's abstract paintings and his interest in poetry and concrete music as "abnormal." From this angle, the conflict represented by this *Problemfilm* suggests the "emotional misery and moral isolation" of individuals such as Boris and Klaus in the atmosphere of petit-bourgeois conformity perpetuated by the patriarchs of the *Wirtschaftswunder*, not least the successful banker Werner Teichmann.

The fact that Harlan's film thus equivocates on the subject of homosexuality should come as no surprise. For the real problem at stake in *Different From You and Me* is less homosexuality after all than the status of the patriarchal family in postwar Germany. Claudius Seidl has noted of postwar cinema that any specific issues tackled by the *Problemfilm* could always be traced back to the question of the family and its restoration.[25] As Alison Guenther-Pal argues, in the case of Harlan's film, "Homosexuality is merely utilized as a means to stage the public anxieties surrounding gender and the status of the family that were intimately tied to the postwar reconstruction of a national identity that was neither emasculated nor corrupted by the pathological authoritarianism of fascism."[26]

For Guenther-Pal, *Different From You and Me* employs the homosexual "as an organizational locus for the production of a specifically non-German category of otherness against which the 'new German man' is constituted."[27] In this analysis Harlan's film reaches its resolution by presenting Klaus as "cured" of homosexuality and fixed in a heterosexual relationship. Guenther-Pal's convincing reading foregrounds the reconstruction of masculinity achieved in Harlan's film. Less central to her discussion, though, is the representation of the female characters, who also suffer from the social contradictions portrayed in this ambivalent *Problemfilm*. Inasmuch as *Different From You and Me* employs homosexuality as a cipher for postwar anxieties about gender, sexuality, and the family, the film's female characters are strongly implicated both in the production of these anxieties and in their potential resolution. Indeed, by the end of the film, the problem of homosexuality has been subsumed into a new set of problems concerned with the reconstruction of postwar femininity.

In an era when the so-called surplus of women continued to be a source of anxiety, homosexuality threatened not only to take young men away from their parents, but also to remove eligible young bachelors from the small pool of men available for marriage and reproduction. Structured around the story of a mother who goes so far as to criminalize herself in her quest to keep her son within the fold, *Different From You and Me* taps into general public anxieties about homosexuality and specifically women's anxieties about the troubled family structure in the postwar period. Notably, Christa's quest to cure Klaus implicates her housemaid and erstwhile foster daughter Gerda, who, as a twenty-year-old unmarried refugee from the East, is a prime example of the "surplus of women."

Different From You and Me opens and closes with a frame story that takes place in a courtroom, where Christa Teichmann is on trial. Contrary to the expectations raised by the film's subtitle, the trial does not concern Paragraph 175. Instead, because Christa bribed Gerda to seduce her son Klaus, she is accused of violating Paragraph 181, which outlaws *Kuppelei*, or sexual procurement. By shifting the emphasis away from the problem of homosexuality in favor of problems surrounding heterosexual sex and female sexuality, the frame story suggests that Christa Teichmann, rather than Klaus, is the film's central protagonist. Indeed, the film opens by framing Christa in long shot and then tracking in to a close-up of her face, thus formally establishing her narrative significance.

In the opening sequence of the frame story, we are introduced to the film's cast of characters as they are called one by one to appear before the court. The first order of business in Christa's trial is a motion from the prosecutor asking the judge to exclude the public from observing the trial for fear of "moral endangerment." The judge approves the motion and clears the court of spectators. In a gesture that confirms to the film's viewers that they are literally about to be granted a glimpse of what goes on behind closed doors, the camera closes in on a sign on the courthouse door that reads "The public is excluded." Thus, the frame story creates the expectation that viewers will subsequently be treated to the voyeuristic pleasures of watching something unknown and taboo, an expectation that is met by the film's representation of the homosexual subculture as a site of aural and visual pleasure.

As the trial begins, the judge asks Christa Teichmann to recall the sequence of events that led up to her arrest. Christa's response initiates a flashback that provides the narrative of the film. Notably, like other films from the period, *Different From You and Me* is thus structured through the perspective of a female character, and the first and last scenes of the film frame the narrative as a story about Christa. This framing device was designed to appeal to female viewers, encouraging them to identify with Christa and her plight. Curiously, however, this identification is blocked for most of the film. In contrast to *The Sinner*, where the entire narrative of the film is reconstructed through Marina's perspective, *Different From You and Me* constantly switches back and forth among different narrative perspectives, approaching the problems of its plotline from different vantage points. In the process, the viewers' allegiances constantly shift among various characters. The film's choppy editing style, which relies almost excessively on cross-cutting, exacerbates this identificatory uncertainty. In both form and content, then, *Different From You and Me* establishes an atmosphere of piqued anxiety about gender and sexuality, which further intensifies the film's essential ambivalence toward the social and representational problems it addresses.

II

In Harlan's film, "curing" Klaus of homosexuality is an enterprise inseparable from teaching him to perceive (and represent) the world in normative terms. Thus *Different From You and Me* conflates social and representational problems, offering a common resolution to both. Similar to other films of the era, Harlan's film ultimately reifies the status quo by reinstating the essential validity of a dichotomous worldview that pits the "normal, natural, and healthy" against the "abnormal, perverse, and deviant," but only after a lengthy narrative in which these dichotomies are blurred.

Social and representational problems are bound together from the outset of *Different From You and Me*. Consider the following sequence, which establishes the film's central thematic tension between normalcy and deviance alongside the generational and familial conflicts that drive the narrative. It is Christa Teichmann's birthday, and Klaus is expected for a celebratory dinner, but he does not come home. Instead, through cross-cutting, we see Klaus at Manfred's house, where the two friends are engaged in their own celebration of Manfred's first published poem. While Klaus and Manfred discuss modern poetry and Klaus's paintings, the Teichmann family examines several of Klaus's abstract works on display in their living room. Contemplating a cubist-inspired work titled "Airplane," Klaus's uncle Max jokes that he wouldn't want to fly in Klaus's plane: "That thing will certainly crash!" While Christa protests that people in fact consider Klaus very talented, Werner grumbles, "Talented, indeed! I wish he were a bit more normal." Meanwhile, Klaus and Manfred listen to a recording of electronic music, which, Klaus exclaims, "sounds just like my pictures!" Werner complains to Max that he believes Klaus is homosexual, while Klaus complains to Manfred in turn about his tyrannical father.

Through Werner's commentary, this sequence suggests that Klaus (and Manfred) are "abnormal," linking their interest in modern forms of representation with their supposed homosexuality in an amalgam of perceived deviance. What is "normal" in this sequence is ostensibly the patriarchal family, embodied by Christa and Werner Teichmann and their middle-class home and petit-bourgeois values. However, this sequence complicates the conflict between normalcy and deviance by introducing a second set of conflicts, between the generations and between Klaus and his family. This particular blend of tensions does nothing to clarify the ideological message served up by Harlan's film. First, Klaus and Manfred are presented as avatars of modern culture, while the bumbling response of the middle-aged Max and Werner to abstract painting—by 1957 a central facet of contemporary West German life and a marker of modern, democratic values—satirizes their outdated tastes. Second, this sequence depicts the patriarchal family as a space of anxiety and discord, demonstrated here most clearly by the conflict between father and son, which further generates sympathy for the likeable Klaus rather than his obnoxious father.

Starting with this initial sequence, within the film's diegesis it is primarily the unsympathetic Werner Teichmann who labels Klaus "abnormal" and who associates his son's interests in abstract art, poetry, and other intellectual pursuits with deviance. Werner is a typical *Wirtschaftswunder* parvenu, who values money above all and has little understanding of his son's artistic proclivities—or of high culture in general. The film constantly makes light of Werner's ineffectual floundering, cultural ignorance, and social naivety, portraying him as a would-be tyrant, a throwback to Nazism who cannot negotiate the new democratic order of the postwar world. Werner's attempts to bully and dominate others fail in both the public and private spheres. For example, when Werner cannot persuade Boris to terminate contact with his son, he goes to the police, hoping to have Boris prosecuted under Paragraph 175. This plan not only fails—the police find no evidence against Boris and do not prosecute him[28]—but it also backfires, pushing Boris to file the pandering complaint against the Teichmanns that eventually leads to Christa's trial. At home, despite his attempts to dominate his wife and son, Werner fails to produce the regimented patriarchal family he so desires. As he himself puts it, "My wife screams at me, my brother-in-law ridicules me, and my son runs away—a fine family!" If the film were truly invested in defending normalcy against deviance, it might have employed a less dubious mouthpiece for uprightness and decency than the ridiculous Werner.

Somewhat surprisingly, Boris actually features in *Different From You and Me* as a kind of alternate father figure for Klaus. After all, Klaus rejects the heteronormative family unit that Werner so desperately seeks to uphold in favor of a new "family" that better suits his ostensibly deviant affinities, both sexual and, above all, cultural. In contrast to Werner, Boris is a highly educated cultural connoisseur who fosters Klaus's talents and expands his horizons. When Boris first welcomes Klaus into his home, he lectures him on the history of concrete music, quotes Plato, and encourages Klaus's painting. At one point in their discussions, Boris asks Klaus where he sees what he paints: "In your fantasy—your inner eye?" When Klaus replies that he was influenced by Picasso and Kandinsky, Boris suggests that he should explore and paint from his own imagination—only then will his painting be truly original. In contrast to the Teichmann family, whose response to Klaus's paintings demonstrates a literal and unimaginative, even ignorant, spectatorial relation to visual representation, Boris suggests a more productive and fantasy-driven approach.

These opposing spectatorial responses are mirrored by the film's *mise en scène*. At Boris's home, the assembled group of young men listens to a performance of modern music played on a special synthesizer, the Elektron[29] (see figure 7.1). Boris's home is absolutely filled with music, art, and exotic antique furniture, presenting a feast for the senses that is

Figure 7.1 The cinema of attractions in *Different From You and Me (§175)*: A performance of modern music on the Elektron at the home of Dr. Boris Winkler (Friedrich Joloff, center). Source: Deutsche Kinemathek.

heightened by the filmmakers' use of chiaroscuro lighting and canted angles when shooting the scenes that take place there. In contrast to the Biedermeier world of the Teichmann home, this milieu, much like the artist's studio in *The Forester of the Silver Wood*, is packed with visual and aural stimulants that appeal strongly to viewers of the film, deploying elements of a cinema of attractions. To be sure, the exaggerated mélange of signifiers for homosexuality in this sequence also played into many viewers' stereotypical conceptions of youth endangerment and homosexual decadence. As Gary Schmidt has argued, "In Harlan's film, these motifs <youth, asocial conduct, and the aesthetic avant-garde> tend to mobilize social anxieties about homosexuality."[30]

Notably, however, the cross-cutting deployed here mitigates to some extent the reinforcement of such stereotypes because it highlights the contrast between Klaus's disparate father figures, once again satirizing the patriarchal authority that Werner seeks to exert. The scene at Boris's house is juxtaposed with Werner's search for his son, which he carries out with help from his brother-in-law Max. When Boris's servant refuses to let them enter the house to look for Klaus, Max decides to educate Werner about homosexuality by bringing him to a gay bar in the neighborhood where a drag show is taking place. The naive Werner is flabbergasted that the drag queen is actually a man, and he is unable to pick out other men in drag from the crowd. When he realizes that none of the "women" in the audience are women, he becomes increasingly agitated. Max encourages Werner to have a sense of humor and enjoy the drag show. But when Max tries to stop Werner from making disparaging homophobic comments, Werner storms out of the bar.

The contrast between Boris and Werner achieved by cross-cutting in this sequence suggests that while Boris understands and controls artistic representation and perception, Werner is unable to navigate cultural representations or performances of any kind—he can neither understand the play of signifiers in a drag show nor can he properly perceive abstract art. Furthermore, while Werner is the primary representative of dominant, heteronormative culture and the mouthpiece of homophobic ideology in the film, he himself is unable to distinguish between the "natural" and the "artificial," the "normal" and the "abnormal," elements that confirm the film's depiction of him as an unsympathetic character.

III

The ambivalence of the film escalates as it moves towards an ostensible resolution: the attempt to "cure" Klaus of his nascent homosexuality. In parallel scenes, Werner and Christa Teichmann pursue two different strategies towards this end. While Werner hopes to help Klaus by removing the "threat" posed by Boris, which leads to his fruitless efforts to have Boris arrested, Christa plans to heal Klaus by arranging his initiation into heterosexual sex. Acting on the advice of a psychiatrist and the family doctor, Christa convinces Gerda to seduce Klaus. As we have seen, Werner's denunciation of Boris is portrayed in unsympathetic terms in this sequence, which suggests his inability to navigate the new postwar legal system. And while Christa's attempts on behalf of Klaus are represented as those of a well-meaning mother, the film makes it clear that they come at the price of manipulating Gerda.

Finally, Klaus's turn to heterosexuality and to a realist style of artistic representation is itself portrayed in a highly ambivalent fashion in *Different From You and Me*, a point that again complicates the film's normative ideology. The Teichmanns have departed on a fabricated business trip, leaving Gerda and Klaus alone. Klaus draws a self-portrait rendered in an abstract style, which Gerda ridicules, telling Klaus that it doesn't look like him at all. When Klaus attempts to explain to Gerda that his style of drawing is about capturing the inner essence, rather than verisimilitude, she replies, "I wouldn't want you to draw me—something horrible would certainly come out of it if you did." Gerda's comment foreshadows the subsequent scene, in which Klaus's attempt to draw her portrait leads to what from Gerda's perspective does turn out to be "something horrible," extramarital sex between people of unequal social status, which ends up casting doubt on her virtue.

Klaus tells Gerda that if he were to draw her, he would focus on her eyes—"Your whole face is all eyes"—a comment that highlights Gerda's gaze, which has emerged in this scene not only through her examination of Klaus's artwork, but also through her desiring look at Klaus himself. Yet in contrast to other films of the period, where the female gaze is foregrounded in order to thematize female experience and appeal to female spectators, *Different From You and Me* offers only a brief glimpse into Gerda's point of view before shifting perspectives once again.

While Gerda and Klaus are discussing his artwork, Manfred arrives at the Teichmann residence with a suitcase, planning to spend the duration of the Teichmanns' absence together with Klaus, painting and writing. However, when Gerda turns Manfred away, Klaus does not intervene, succumbing instead to Gerda's seduction. In the remarkable sequence that follows, Klaus enters Gerda's room in order to draw her portrait. She poses for him in an open bathrobe, exposing her naked breast. Though at first Klaus pretends not to notice it, finally Gerda's breast provides the trigger for the violent transformation Klaus performs in this scene, where artistic representation and sexuality are again strongly imbricated. Seeking first to prove his artistic talent, Klaus draws a realistic likeness of Gerda (see figure 7.2). Then, moving menacingly across the room towards her, Klaus speaks in a gruff and accusatory tone: "You all say that I'm not a man." As Klaus threatens Gerda physically, she escapes out the window of her room. Screaming and thrashing, Gerda tries to run away, but Klaus

Figure 7.2 Klaus Teichmann (Christian Wolff) proves himself as an artist and as a man by drawing a realist portrait of Gerda Böttcher (Ingrid Stenn). Source: Deutsche Kinemathek.

overpowers her. Though the censors demanded that a shot in which Klaus tears off Gerda's dress be edited out, the elliptical representation of the sex scene that follows suggests violence, even rape. Shot in dark tones, the melodramatic expressiveness of this scene contrasts sharply with the classical realist style that characterizes the bulk of the film. Far from representing the consummation of heterosexual desire according to the conventions of classical cinema, this scene hints at the potential violence at stake in heterosexual sex and in Klaus's forced "cure," once more pointing to the conflicted status of the patriarchal family.

In the aftermath of this seduction scene, we see images of Klaus and Gerda as a happy couple, riding on Klaus's moped and picnicking together. Meanwhile, the jilted Manfred investigates the absence of his friend, sneaking into the Teichmann's lawn and peering through the window of the house. Foregrounding once more the intertwined strands of Klaus's sexual and aesthetic cure, the film shows us through Manfred's eyes Klaus's realist drawing of Gerda, propped up against a messy bed whose twisted sheets are highly suggestive of the acts that have likely taken place there.

IV

Shifting the plotline away from the fiction of Klaus's "endangerment," the penultimate sequence of the film's main narrative displaces the problem of male homosexuality by focusing instead on female sexuality and women's experience. If Gerda had been led by Christa Teichmann to believe that, by seducing Klaus and thus helping to "cure" him, she might find a permanent place in the Teichmann family through an eventual marriage to Klaus, her hopes are shattered in the aftermath of the seduction. Instead of welcoming her into the family, Christa offers Gerda a bracelet she has admired, wordlessly placing it on the table within Gerda's reach in a silent gesture that confirms Gerda's status as a social inferior, indeed as someone who must be paid for her services. Underscoring Gerda's victim status, a subsequent scene portrays her brutal interrogation by the police, who dwell on the bracelet, forcing Gerda to confess that she has slept with Klaus and that Christa Teichmann has bribed her to do so.

An expellee from Pomerania, Gerda, like Hubert Gerold in *The Forester of the Silver Wood*, is consistently treated as the outsider she is. As in the earlier film, however, the refugee is portrayed not only as a victim, but also as a symbol of change, something that is reflected both formally and thematically. In the conclusion of *Different From You and Me*, Gerda becomes both the focal point of the narrative and a stand-in for all that is wrong with bourgeois German society. As the prosecutor tells Christa and Werner, "After all, Gerda Böttcher is also a human being. It is really a question of human dignity, whether one should be allowed to use a young girl for these purposes."

In the end, the narrative of Klaus's possible homosexuality is subsumed by another story, that of Christa's failure as a mother, both in relation to Klaus and in relation to her "foster daughter" Gerda. If the film's closure effects Klaus's reintegration into the patriarchal family unit, it also dramatizes the ambivalent significance of Christa's wrong-headed self-sacrifice. In trying to do right by her son, Christa has contributed to Gerda's victimization. While Christa assures Klaus in the film's last shot that "everything is all right again," it is far from clear that this is so.

Notably, the decision to prosecute Christa Teichmann for endangering Gerda Böttcher suggests that, in the world of Harlan's film, the German state is concerned less with postwar masculinity than with postwar femininity, a telling commentary on postwar German society. By displacing the problem of homosexuality with the twin problems of female sexuality and unruly mother–child relations, Harlan's film returned to the postwar representational mandate of focusing on women's experience as an allegory for national identity. *Different From You and Me* demonstrates that, twelve years into the postwar period, the common female experiences of victimization, rebuilding, and sexual promiscuity continued to possess important cultural currency and symbolic value in mainstream cinema. To return once more to Elizabeth Heineman's argument, these specifically female experiences were generalized in public discourse to describe the nation after 1945, due to the focus on and centrality of women in the immediate postwar period and as a means of filling the "representational vacuum" left by problematic male experience in light of Germany's total defeat.[31] In Harlan's film, resolution is not achieved by prosecuting Boris under Paragraph 175, and the "problem" of homosexuality ultimately proves peripheral to the film's project of restoring order to the patriarchal family. Furthermore, the problem of rebuilding the family can only be resolved by focusing on the film's female characters.

However, in contrast to other postwar films that turned to female experience as a means of relegitimating cinema, Harlan's film does not feature a strong female protagonist who is invested with narrative authority. Far from displaying the kind of agency that leads to the production of meaning in the film, both Christa and Gerda contribute to the film's resolution largely by negative example. Their punishment produces the ambivalent closure of *Different From You and Me*. Gerda is castigated for her sexual promiscuity first by Klaus's violent sexual response to her seduction and later by Christa's bribery and the harsh interrogation of the cruel police detective. Regarding Christa, she is sentenced to serve jail time after her trial. What is more, she is also scolded repeatedly, by her lawyer and then by the judge at her trial, for her treatment of Gerda.

Not only do the women in Harlan's film lack narrative authority, but they also lack access to the film's formal language. Although *Different From You and Me* was marketed to a female audience, female viewers remained puzzled by its ambiguous message. While the film encouraged (female) viewers to sympathize with Christa, the ending, consistent with the general tenor of the film, did not provide spaces for affective engagement, clear structures of identification, or resolution of the emotions aroused by the film. *The Sinner* and *The Forester of the Silver Wood* thematized representation and perception in complex ways, foregrounding female voiceover and the female gaze. By contrast,

Different From You and Me barely strayed from dominant cinematic conventions. The film's editing style is a notable exception, but this exaggerated use of cross-cutting contributes on a formal level to the film's marked ideological ambivalence. The film effectively impedes identification with its female characters at the level of narrative by subjecting them to punishment and rebuke. But it does so even more thoroughly on a formal level by constantly blocking access to their narrative perspective through editing.

Virtually every sequence of *Different From You and Me* is marked by an extensive and dramatic use of cross-cutting. A staple convention of classical filmmaking, cross-cutting is employed not only as a way of escalating dramatic tension and producing suspense in the viewer, but also to demonstrate the relationship between two different elements, scenes, or events. Cross-cutting thus suggests that "there will be a resolution in one space and time of these two sets of action."[32]

In the case of *Different From You and Me*, cross-cutting does highlight the contrasts between two different spaces, perspectives, and ideologies. By constantly disrupting any unified narrative perspective, however, it ultimately sabotages the possibility of identification. Moreover, while cross-cutting traditionally creates the expectation of a resolution between contrasting sets of action, in Harlan's film the viewer is frustrated by delayed or even non-existent resolution. By shifting from one cross-cut sequence to the next, the film produces layer upon layer of conflict, but resolves very little. This structure of delayed or denied gratification is reproduced once again by the frame story, which displaces many of the central conflicts of the film into a new set of problems. No doubt more by accident and as a by-product of the censorship process than by design, cross-cutting in Harlan's film thus produces ambivalence and contradiction rather than the clear resolution viewers might expect, especially from a *Problemfilm*.

The ambivalent narrative and formal structure of *Different From You and Me* was replicated by the publicity materials created to promote the film. Information sent to cinema owners urging them to book the film suggested that its bankability was guaranteed by the popular stars who played Christa and Werner, Paula Wessely and Paul Dahlke, who were certain to appeal to an older generation of female viewers who had followed these actors since their careers during the Third Reich. Yet the poster for the film that accompanied these materials did not feature images of either star, instead showing a silhouette of Boris touching Klaus's chin above a picture of Gerda and Klaus reclining together.[33] Similarly, the film program sold in cinemas retells the story of the film largely from the perspective of Christa Teichmann, suggesting the film's focus on the problem of the family. But the accompanying images, which prominently feature Gerda and Klaus, imply that the film is primarily a love story.[34] Just as the film itself repeatedly shifts narrative perspective, these promotional documents signal an attempt to attract a variety of different viewers by emphasizing different storylines and points of view. In contrast to other films of the era, then, the publicity documents for *Different From You and Me*, like the movie itself, fail to reflect a clear appeal to the largely female audiences of postwar cinema.[35]

V

While other films of the period experimented with a new filmic language by appealing to women, *Different From You and Me* produced a narrative that addressed female experience without breaking with cinematic conventions. Nonetheless, the film did share much in common with other postwar films. As in the case of *The Sinner* and *The Forester of the Silver Wood*, the introduction of visual art into *Different From You and Me* set in motion a plot that explicitly addressed questions of representation, perception, and difference. Like those other films, *Different From You and Me* assumes that the disturbed vision of the abstract artist must be cured, and the artist's turn to a realist mode of representation is linked to his successful integration into heteronormative culture. For Harlan, abstract art continued to provide a metacinematic foil through which to thematize issues of cinematic language in the postwar period.

It is notable, then, that the reception of *Different From You and Me* was remarkably uniform in its indictment of the film's intertwined depiction of social and representational problems. As Enno Patalas put it in his 1957 review of the film:

> For Harlan, <homosexuality> is invoked only as an excuse for a very characteristic simplification: the interpretation of life as a conflict between the "normal" and the "abnormal." For him, "abnormal" is represented not only by sexual deviance, but he associates this with modern painting, electronic music, and intellectual things in general. "Normal," on the other hand, is conduct that is fed purely by instinct. ... "Normal" is primitive, unreflected and unsublimated emotion, above all the <heterosexual> sex act, which not only brings the homosexually endangered Klaus onto the right path sexually, but also cures him of his artistic "perversions": from this point on, he no longer paints abstractly, but rather "properly," and the background music—electronic in the "homo" scenes—pays homage to temperately romantic Chopin imitators.[36]

The retrograde linkage of homosexuality with abstract art and heterosexuality with realist art in *Different From You and Me* actually brought critics on the left, such as Patalas, into the same camp as their conservative counterparts. Together, these critics viewed Harlan's association of abstraction with perversion, so reminiscent of Nazi conceptions of "degenerate art," as one legacy of the director's residual fascism at a time in the late 1950s when abstraction had come to signify democracy, virile masculinity, and indeed, heteronormativity. As the Catholic film journal *Film-Dienst* put it,

> The representation of <the> endangerment <of youth through homosexual seduction> is also primitive: not every group of friends who sit around all night and passionately discuss abstract art constitutes a danger, and it is strange to see that the endangered Klaus at first paints abstractly, only to begin drawing "properly" during his erotic encounter with the girl. Critics of Veit Harlan have rightly protested against the all-inclusive insinuations against modern art, which are wholly in the style of the "Third Reich."[37]

Progressive and conservative critics alike displayed no strong objections to Harlan's homophobic representation of homosexuality. Rather, they disputed Harlan's linkage of modern art with perversion in order to distance themselves—as advocates of modern art—from any association with homosexuality. In one of the more bizarre outgrowths of the debates surrounding *Different From You and Me*, a coalition of abstract artists, jazz enthusiasts, and other advocates of modern representational forms signed a petition effectively declaring the group's own heterosexuality and demanding that the film be banned because of its damaging representation of abstract art. According to one newspaper account of the protest, "They object above all to the fact that the film couples modern art with homosexuality in a slanderous fashion."[38] Nonetheless, these protests against *Different From You and Me* were telling in their critical response to what was perceived as Harlan's Nazi aesthetics.

As the reaction of these postwar critics and artists demonstrates, by 1957 abstract art had been co-opted fully by the dominant culture in West Germany. No longer the focus of vital debates about the politics of representation after fascism, the abstract/realist split appeared to be an outmoded means of addressing the quest for cinematic legitimacy in the postwar period. Instead, dominant cinema sought alternative strategies for resolving the conflict between fantasy and reality, increasingly distancing itself from its own conventionalism. Far from helping Veit Harlan to relegitimate his career as a filmmaker, his incorporation of gendered dichotomies of abstraction and realism in *Different From You and Me* now appeared redolent of Nazi ideology, and the rejection of the film by many critics and viewers spelled the end of Harlan's career as a director.[39] More importantly, the tepid response to Harlan's film signaled a fundamental shift in the postwar film industry, as audiences and filmmakers alike looked to a more aesthetically and politically critical cinematic practice. As the demands placed on cinema began to shift and filmmaking entered a new transitional period, issues of gender remained central to the ongoing quest for a new German cinematic language.

Notes

1. See Hans Helmut Prinzler, *Chronik des deutschen Films 1895–1994* (Stuttgart, 1995), 208; Elizabeth Prommer, *Kinobesuch im Lebenslauf. Eine historische und medienbiografische Studie* (Konstanz, 1999), 350; and Joseph Garncarz, "Hollywood in Germany. Die Rolle des amerikanischen Films in Deutschland: 1925–1990," in *Der deutsche Film. Aspekte seiner Geschichte von den Anfängen bis zur Gegenwart*, ed. Uli Jung (Trier, 1993), 202.

2. The last federal film subsidies (*Bundesbürgschaften*) expired in 1955, and the last films produced under the subsidy program were released in 1956. Though they were designed in part to strengthen the native film industry (as well as seeking to promote certain types of filmmaking), the subsidies ended up having the opposite effect. Because of the way the subsidy program was structured, production companies were weakened while distributors gained strength. Around 1957, large studios began to merge in order to fortify their position in the marketplace. On the film subsidy system see Heide Fehrenbach, *Cinema in Democratizing Germany: Reconstructing National Identity After Hitler* (Chapel Hill, 1995), 145–46; and Jürgen Berger, "Bürgen heißt zahlen—und manchmal auch zensieren: Die Filmbürgschaften des Bundes 1950–55," *Zwischen Gestern und Morgen. Westdeutscher Nachkriegsfilm 1946–1962*, ed. Hilmar Hoffmann and Walter Schobert (Frankfurt am Main, 1989), 80–99. On film subsidies and mergers between studios, see Walther Schmieding, *Kunst oder Kasse: Der Ärger mit dem deutschen Film* (Hamburg, 1961), 139–41.

3. Tressler's first feature film, *Die Halbstarken* (The Rebels, 1956), which was co-written with the journalist Tremper, introduced to the German film landscape a new documentary-style realism as well as a new concern with youth-oriented topics, strongly influenced by Hollywood rebel films like Nicholas Ray's 1955 *Rebel Without a Cause*.

4. The 1957 Filmaufbau production *Die Bekenntnisse des Hochstapler Felix Krull* (Confessions of Felix Krull), directed by Kurt Hoffmann, was one of many Thomas Mann adaptations that brought great success to the company.

5. Harlan was accused of crimes against humanity for his role in the Nazi filmmaking apparatus. His two trials (1949 and 1950), which ended in Harlan's acquittal, were lengthy and controversial. Numerous film directors and industry figures wrote letters for or against Harlan, and several testified at the trial for the prosecution (Erich Engel) or the defense (Wolfgang Liebeneiner). The court apparently believed Harlan's claim that he was forced by Goebbels to make films during the Third Reich, and that he had nonetheless managed to sabotage the production of several propaganda films. The trials focused especially on the case of the notorious *Jew Süss*. Harlan claimed that the material had been forced on him, but that he had tried to avoid any explicit propaganda and make "a good film" out of it. The court ultimately agreed with Harlan that, because of its historical setting, *Jew Süss* could not be accused of slandering Jews in the 1940s. Though the film was (paradoxically) deemed by the court to be anti-Semitic, they found that it did not explicitly contribute to the Nazi genocide of European Jews. The fact that Harlan was never a member of the Nazi Party, and that his first wife was Jewish, were strong factors in his defense. For in-depth accounts of the legal proceedings against Harlan, see Siegfried Zielinski, *Veit Harlan: Analysen und Materialien zur Auseinandersetzung mit einem Film-Regisseur des deutschen Faschismus* (Frankfurt, 1981) and Frank Noack, *Veit Harlan. "Des Teufels Regisseur"* (Munich, 2000), 300–25.

6. Enno Patalas, rev. of *Anders als du und ich, Filmkritik* 12 (1957). Forty years later, Eric Rentschler echoed Patalas's diagnosis, calling *Different From You and Me* "an antihomosexual tirade, whose gay seducer assumed <Jew> Süss's position as tempter and undoer." Eric Rentschler, *The Ministry of Illusion: Nazi Cinema and Its Afterlife* (Cambridge, 1996), 166. For a similar, though much more detailed, reading of the film, see Fehrenbach, *Cinema in Democratizing Germany*, 195–204.

7. Despite his acquittal at trial, Harlan remained largely a persona non grata in the Federal Republic. While this led to many difficulties in securing funding to make films, Harlan

nevertheless managed to direct nine feature productions over the course of the 1950s and to collaborate on several more productions before his death in 1962. Because of his personal history, these films were generally controversial, often occasioning public protests, but several did garner critical and popular acclaim. Harlan sought to cast himself as an apolitical artist, and he hoped to restore his damaged reputation by making new films that would cleanse his image of fascistic traces. Primary among these was *Different From You and Me*.

8. Describing the controversy surrounding the film in a passage that ends his posthumously published biography, Harlan wrote: "The version of this film that I made was ... forbidden by the FSK. They claimed that it made a statement against Paragraph 175, and that it could only be permitted to be shown if decisive changes were made. Not only did the homosexual have to be arrested at the end, which did not happen in the first version, but also all scenes had to be cut in which homosexuals were likeable and acted justly. ... The consequence of the changes was that I was characterized by many newspapers as a man who had hounded Jews in the Nazi period and was now hounding homosexuals." Veit Harlan, *Im Schatten meiner Filme*, ed. H.C. Opfermann (Gütersloh, 1966), 244.

9. One exception is the recent monograph on Harlan by Frank Noack, who seeks to draw out "the ideological contradictions in Harlan's work," distinguishing himself and his scholarship from the bulk of secondary literature, which he sees as either "condemning <Harlan> ruthlessly" or "excusing everything." While Noack brings a fresh eye to the films, at times he comes too close to serving as an apologist for Harlan. This is particularly the case in his discussion of *Different From You and Me*. See Noack, *Veit Harlan*.

10. On Harlan's conflation of modern art and deviant sexuality, see also Robert Kiss, "Queer Traditions in German Cinema," in *The German Cinema Book*, ed. Tim Bergfelder et al. (London, 2002), 53–54; and Alison Guenther-Pal, "Sexual Reorientations: Homosexuality versus the Postwar German Man in Veit Harlan's *Different From You and Me (§175)* (1957)," in *Light Motives: German Popular Film in Perspective*, ed. Randall Halle and Margaret McCarthy (Detroit, 2003), 148–70.

11. Noack, *Veit Harlan*, 362.

12. See, for example, Rolf, "Wovon man in Deutschland spricht: 'Anders als du und ich'," *Der Kreis* 26.1 (1958): 7–8; "Film eines films, oder: wie kam es zu 'anders als du und ich'," *der neue ring* 2 (1958): 10–11; and several pieces, including a satirical poem, in *Der Weg* 7.12 (1957).

13. According to Frank Noack, the film generated strong ticket sales in the first week after its West German premiere, and it continued to prove bankable for its distributor as late as January 1959. Noack, *Veit Harlan*, 363.

14. Thomas Elsaesser and Michael Wedel, "*Problemfilme*," *The BFI Companion to German Cinema*, ed. Elsaesser with Michael Wedel (London, 1999), 120.

15. Elsaesser and Wedel, "*Problemfilme*," 120. The *Problemfilm* is often linked to or distinguished from other similar genres, including the *Zeitfilm* (a social-critical genre addressing contemporary reality) and the *Gesellschaftsfilm* (bourgeois melodrama). In the case of postwar West Germany, Elsaesser and Wedel suggest the latter term to designate the predominance of movies about alienation and class conflicts during the *Wirstchaftswunder*. However, for the purposes of this chapter, I will retain the umbrella term *Problemfilm*. While the issue of class is certainly central to *Different From You and Me*, the "problems" that drive the film's narrative are (homo)sexuality and the deterioration of the patriarchal family.

16. Guenther-Pal, "Sexual Reorientations," 151.

17. While Paragraph 175 had been part of the German legal code before the Nazi period, it was revised by the Nazis in 1935. The new constitution of the Federal Republic, known as the Basic Law, adopted this Nazi version of the paragraph wholesale. Paragraph 175 was amended for the first time in 1969 (several later amendments followed), and only then did the process of decriminalizing homosexuality begin. On the history of

Paragraph 175 in the postwar period, see Christian Schulz, *Paragraph 175. (abgewickelt): Homosexualität und Strafrecht im Nachkriegsdeutschland—Rechtsprechung, juristische Diskussionen und Reformen seit 1945* (Hamburg, 1994).

18. For a comprehensive account of this court challenge, and an analysis of the discourses of sexuality at stake in it, see Robert G. Moeller, "'The Homosexual Man is a "Man," the Homosexual Woman is a "Woman"': Sex, Society, and Law in Postwar Germany," *Journal of the History of Sexuality* 4.3 (1994): 395–429.

19. For general historical accounts of the politics of homosexuality in West Germany during the 1950s, see Martin Dannecker, "Der unstillbare Wunsch nach Anerkennung: Homosexuellenpolitik in den fünfziger und sechziger Jahren," in *Was heißt hier schwul?: Politik und Identitäten im Wandel*, ed. Detlef Grumbach (Hamburg, 1997), 27–44; and Hans-Georg Stümke, *Homosexuelle in Deutschland: Eine politische Geschichte* (Munich, 1989), esp. 132–66.

20. Dagmar Herzog, *Sex After Fascism* (Princeton, 2005), 90.

21. On the *Halbstarken* phenomenon, see Uta Poiger, *Jazz, Rock, and Rebels: Cold War Politics and American Culture in a Divided Germany* (Berkeley, 2000).

22. Herzog, *Sex After Fascism*, 94.

23. "Der Zeitfilm—eine Notwendigkeit. Themen, die in der Luft liegen," press booklet (Constantin-Film) 8, in file on *Anders als du und ich (§175)*, Schriftgutarchiv, Stiftung deutsche Kinemathek, Berlin.

24. "Heißes Eisen im Film. Themen, von denen man in der Öffentlichkeit nicht gerne spricht," press booklet 10.

25. Claudius Seidl, *Der deutsche Film der fünfziger Jahre* (Munich, 1987), 182.

26. Guenther-Pal, "Sexual Reorientations," 148–49.

27. Guenther-Pal, "Sexual Reorientations," 150.

28. In one of the changes demanded by the censors, the prosecutor assures Werner that the police will find some evidence against Boris one day; at the end of the censored version of the film released in the Federal Republic, Boris is indeed detained by the police, though we aren't explicitly told why.

29. The Elektron was based on a real instrument, the Trautonium, invented by Friedrich Trautwein in 1929. Oskar Sala, a student of Paul Hindemith and a master Trautonium player, perfected the instrument, for which Hindemith, Paul Dessau, and Carl Orff composed music. Sala himself composed and played many film scores on the instrument, including scores for *Different From You and Me* and Alfred Hitchcock's *The Birds* (1963).

30. Gary Schmidt, *Koeppen—Andersch—Böll: Homosexualität und Faschismus in der deutschen Nachkriegsliteratur* (Hamburg, 2001), 80.

31. Elizabeth Heineman, "The Hour of the Woman: Memories of Germany's 'Crisis Years' and West German National Identity," *American Historical Review* 101.2 (1996): 354–95.

32. Susan Hayward, *Key Concepts in Cinema Studies* (New York, 1996), 78.

33. "Wir stellen zur Diskussion: *Anders als du und ich (§175)*" (Constantin-Film), press booklet in file on *Anders als du und ich (§175)*, Schriftgutarchiv, Stiftung deutsche Kinematek, Berlin.

34. "Anders als du und ich (§175)," *Illustrierte Film-Bühne* 3847 (1957).

35. This is perhaps one reason why the women's magazine *Film und Frau* chose not to print a feature on Harlan's film.

36. Patalas, *Filmkritik*.

37. Rev. of *Anders als du und ich*, *Katholischer Film-Dienst* 44 (1957): 453. For a similar critique, see rev. of *Anders als du und ich*, *Deutsche Woche*, December 4, 1957.

38. "Künstler protestieren gegen Harlan-Film," *Stuttgarter Zeitung*, December 6, 1957.

39. Harlan went on to direct only two more films, both released in 1958.

Part III

TOWARDS THE NEW WAVE: GENDER AND THE CRITIQUE OF POPULAR CINEMA

Chapter 8

PLEASURABLE NEGOTIATIONS: SPECTATORSHIP AND GENRE IN HELMUT KÄUTNER'S "ANTI-TEARJERKER" *ENGAGEMENT IN ZURICH* (1957)

The year 1957 marked the beginning of a steady decline in both film production and ticket sales in the Federal Republic. With 111 feature films made and 801 million tickets sold (fourteen visits to the movies per person), West German cinema remained immensely popular among audiences.[1] But the phenomenal success the film industry enjoyed during the first half of the 1950s had begun to wane, and it would never be regained. An increasingly sophisticated West German public was growing weary of the provincial quality of West German films. The appeal of foreign films and especially of television ushered in a new period of transition for the film industry.[2] Indeed, more than half a million television licenses were granted in 1957, up from only one thousand licenses in 1953. By 1958, the number of television licenses surpassed one million.[3]

As we have seen, the film industry sought new strategies to engage audiences in light of competition from novel forms of entertainment and because of social changes resulting from the booming *Wirtschaftswunder*. Employing different genres and new stars, filmmakers in the late 1950s turned to innovation as one means of preserving the appeal of domestic movies. At the same time, the always self-conscious West German cinema quickly began to thematize the transformations in both society and the film industry in the late 1950s, incorporating the shifting socioeconomic landscape and changing demands on cinematic representation into the narratives of the films themselves.

Postwar German films had long made use of metacinematic narratives as a means of working through social and representational problems in the aftermath of the Third Reich. As the popular entertainment cinema that had characterized the first postwar decade was subjected to increasing scrutiny in the late 1950s, metacinema once again offered filmmakers and audiences alike the possibility of contemplating the status of image making and spectatorship in postwar Germany. Early postwar filmmakers had employed metacinema as a way of acknowledging the problems they faced in developing legitimate forms of cinematic representation. By the latter half of the decade, however, filmmakers combined metacinema with satire in narratives that tested the limits of the mainstream film language that had emerged as the dominant, if never wholly legitimate, idiom of postwar cinematic representation. Indeed, some of the most popular films of this period achieved success with audiences by implicitly acknowledging the bankruptcy of dominant cinema while still making use of many of its conventions. Films such as Rolf Thiele's *Das Mädchen Rosemarie* (The Girl Rosemarie, 1958) and Kurt Hoffmann's *Wir Wunderkinder* (Aren't We Wonderful?, 1958) were critical of political and socioeconomic developments in the Federal Republic and of mainstream representational styles. As these films demonstrate, the process of solving social and representational problems continued to be inextricably intertwined in the late 1950s, as the desire to create social and political alternatives to the hegemonic status quo of the Adenauer Era placed increased pressure on filmmakers to imagine a new kind of cinema.

Tackling issues of cinematic representation, gender, sexuality, and national identity germane to this transitional period, Helmut Käutner's *Die Zürcher Verlobung* is both the swan song of 1950s popular cinema and a lampoon of the postwar German film industry, a combination at once paradoxical and consistent with the ambivalent nature of this era's movies. Reprising the successful strategy of *Film Without a Title*, *Engagement in Zurich* narrates the production of a film within a film in order to interrogate once more questions implicated in cinema debates throughout the decade, including the tensions between escapist fantasy and social reality, "dream factory" entertainment and *Autorenfilm*. The film's self-conscious parody of West German filmmaking also takes a satirical look at female-oriented genres and at competing images of screen femininity at play in the 1950s.

Engagement in Zurich premiered on April 16, 1957, at the Weltspiele Film Theater in Hanover. Based on a bestselling novel by Barbara Noack, Käutner's film tells the story of the creation and production of a woman's film called *Love in Switzerland*. The film within the film is written by an aspiring screenwriter, Juliane Thomas (Liselotte Pulver), who bases her script on her own experiences and fantasies. Her thinly veiled narrative of the crush she develops on a Swiss man, Jean Berner, kicks off a comedy of errors when she sells a treatment of her proposed screenplay to a film director who happens to be Jean's best friend. Featuring star cameos and a satirical appearance by Helmut Käutner himself, the film presents a running commentary on the transitional state of West German filmmaking. Through the character of Juliane, the film also reflects on the relationship of the female spectatorial imagination to the conventional genre cinema of the day. The plot of the film is fueled by the interplay of events in Juliane's life, the fantasies that she develops about these events, and the film script into which she pours both her experiences and her desires. Ultimately, her quest to write a good film narrative begins to shape what happens to Juliane in real life. Another film that articulates social and representational problems together, *Engagement in Zurich* pokes fun at changing moral standards regarding women's sexuality and the failure of mainstream film to reflect social realities, like sex outside of marriage. The problem of "eroticism" in Juliane's screenplay becomes an emblem in the film for the archaic and provincial qualities of West German cinema as well as the limitations of dominant cinema when it comes to portraying female desire.

In many amusing sequences, the film parodies the struggles of the team of producer, director, and writer to create *Love in Switzerland*, the film within the film. The producer wants the film to be touching and successful with audiences; the director doesn't want it to be sentimental kitsch; and the writer, Juliane, wants the film to reflect accurately her everyday experiences as a woman in 1950s Germany. The narrative of the film satirizes the impossibility of meeting all these goals at once and so clearly encapsulates the issues faced by the German film industry at the time. Yet, judging by the popularity of the film with audiences, *Engagement in Zurich* did manage, to some extent, to meet all three goals, precisely through its metacinematic thematization of the tensions these diverse and contradictory aims produced within commercial cinema.

Käutner's film envisions filmic representation and perception as female-coded processes, situating film spectatorship within the wider context of women's experience and imagining mainstream film, in particular the *Schnulze*, or tearjerker, as a product of female fantasy. However, the film's interrogation of cinematic representation and perception is marked by ambivalence, both about the limits of dominant cinema to convey female desire and about the role of generic conventionalism in the decline of the West German film industry.

It is no coincidence that Käutner's send-up of the German film industry returns to the terrain of women's cinema. Certainly, female experience and issues of gender and sexuality continued to play a central role in the transitional films of the late 1950s, providing fertile allegorical ground for narratives addressing the changing social problems of the period. At the same time, as women's experiences and the concomitant demands that female viewers placed on cinema began to change mid-decade, the film industry responded. Seeking to maintain cinema's appeal to female audiences, filmmakers pursued new genres and incorporated new images of women on screen, as demonstrated by female stars such as *Engagement in Zurich*'s Liselotte Pulver who became popular at this time.

However, Käutner returned to women's cinema for another reason as well. By the late 1950s, the association of dominant cinema with women's genres and female viewers had become commonplace. The escalating critique of German movies articulated by a growing chorus of mostly young, male voices pointed explicitly to the predominantly female audience of postwar cinema as one reason for its failure. Issues of gender were highly implicated in the transition away from the popular cinema of the 1950s and toward the new, more critical and experimental cinema that would characterize the 1960s. A participant in the debates surrounding this transition, Helmut Käutner invoked them in his film. Indeed, *Engagement in Zurich* both parodies and utilizes conventions of dominant cinema (structures of identification, the happy ending, and so on) in order to address a key question that occupied critics and filmmakers alike in the late 1950s: who is to blame for the stagnation of the cinema—the conventional German film industry itself, or the audience, the female viewers who fueled the production of generic films by flocking to them in great numbers and identifying with their narratives and characters? As we shall see, *Engagement in Zurich* tried to have it both ways, engaging female spectators with all the elements of a woman's film, while lampooning those elements at the same time—a strategy that proved surprisingly successful at this transitional moment.

I

As a consensus formed in the late 1950s about the mediocrity of the domestic film industry, commentators increasingly debated the role of the audience in perpetuating the poor quality of West German cinema. One woman took center stage in these debates: the allegorical Lieschen Müller. Fabricated by the film industry and the mainstream press, Lieschen Müller embodied the average spectator and representative consumer of commercial entertainment culture in Germany. Though she was not invented during the 1950s, Lieschen Müller definitely gained prominence in public discourse during the decade, when, as we have seen, women were understood to be the primary consumers of film, television, and the popular press. Based in part on a statistical understanding of the composition of West German audiences at the time, the construction of Lieschen Müller also drew on the longstanding discursive tendency to gender the masses as female.[4]

In his book, *Her Highness Lieschen Müller* (1961), the film publicist Kurt Wortig described this fictional figure and her significance:

> Lieschen Müller is a commercial, normative, collective term for the mass public, for the broad audience of consumers of entertainment. … This concept of Lieschen Müller distinguishes the "broad masses," and among experts it has become virtually a synonym for the average consumer of mass entertainment productions. In the expression "broad masses" there is—justified or not—the indication of something derogatory. At the same time, however, Lieschen Müller is—in general and not in a discriminatory way—the term for "the people," "the audience," the customers of mass

media. … The fact that one speaks of Lieschen Müller and not, say, Fritz Schulze, can be explained by this percentage: 70 percent of all moviegoers are women.[5]

As Wortig's book suggests, the commercially driven film industry defined Lieschen Müller in positive terms, conceiving of her as its ideal spectator in the quest to formulate entertainment products that would appeal to largely female audiences. At the same time, however, the figure of Lieschen Müller evoked a derogatory association with the passive consumer of mainstream entertainment who was not interested in being challenged by art, but merely wanted to escape from the demands of everyday life by spending, in the words of the West German film industry's advertising motto, "a few nice hours at the movies." As the film publicist Karl Klär put it, "<Lieschen Müller> is that imaginary person who is cited again and again in discussions about film and its effects on the masses … Across all national borders it is said to be precisely those masses of Lieschen Müllers and their male escorts who are impressed by kitsch and only by kitsch. It is purportedly these passive, uncreative masses who descend to the lowest and most trivial level of emotional states."[6]

The kitsch consumed by spectators like Lieschen Müller was encapsulated by the emblematic product of the postwar West German film industry: the *Schnulze*. Usually translated as "tearjerker," the word *Schnulze* has been described by the popular film director Arthur Maria Rabenalt as an "acoustic word montage," in which "concepts like *Schmacht* <appetite>, *Schmalz*, *Schluchzer* <sob>, *Schnuller* <pacifier>, … and reminiscent ideas ring together."[7] The *Schnulze* was defined not only by its melodramatic appeal to female spectators, but also by its "flight from reality"[8] in favor of harmless entertainment. Focusing on these elements, critics centered their diagnosis of commercial cinema's crisis on the *Schnulze* and its audience of Lieschen Müllers.

Once again, the mandate to reflect social reality rather than promote escapist fantasies emerged as the central issue for these critics of 1950s cinema. The call for films to better reflect social reality was a hallmark of reviews in the journal *Filmkritik*, founded in 1957 by a group of young cinephiles. Again and again, they criticized mainstream films for their trivial qualities and their failure to present authentic images of German society and history.[9] In his 1961 book *Art or Commerce: The Trouble with the German Film*, the critic Walther Schmieding summed up this growing dissatisfaction with postwar cinema: "The weaknesses of German films surrounding war and National Socialism, the vague attempts at social critique, and the problematics of artless or artful entertainment all can be traced back to the same causes: the lack of honest attempts or the sheer inability to recognize—and reproduce—reality."[10]

For Schmieding, the audience can hardly be blamed for consuming the entertainment it is spoon-fed; he blames the predominance of the

Schnulze on both the artlessness of the film industry and the acritical, undemocratic sensibility of German society. Others continued to blame the poor taste of "Lieschen Müller" for driving the production of escapist entertainment. Despite his status as one of the most popular directors of mainstream cinema in the postwar period, Helmut Käutner himself was highly critical of the role played by the audience in determining the (poor) quality of postwar films. Käutner had already stressed the negative role of the audience in his 1947 essay "Dismantling the Dream Factory." A decade later, Käutner reiterated the equation between audience demand and bad films in the short-lived 1956 magazine *Film—Monatshefte für Film und Fernsehen* that he edited together with Gunter Groll and Walter Talmon-Gros. In the magazine's inaugural editorial, "Every Audience, as Everybody Knows, Has the Films It Deserves," the three editors invoked Lieschen Müller as the embodiment of the poor taste their magazine worked against:

> Every audience, in the long run, also has the magazines it deserves ...
> <Lieschen Müller>, for example, the allegorical <Lieschen>, has her films
> by the lot, and she also has her magazines. Things are going well for them,
> the <Lieschen> magazines, and we, for our part, wish them no harm
> whatsoever. They should not be the only ones, though. The friend of good
> film unfortunately did not have what <Lieschen> had, at least not in
> Germany. He came away once again empty-handed—quite empty-handed
> in the movie theater and absolutely empty-handed at the magazine stand.[11]

In contrast to Lieschen Müller, the ideal reader of *Film* was "not at all a so-called fan," but a "regular attendee of art film theaters," someone who reads film reviews rather than gossip rags, seeks out foreign films rather than beauty queens, and likely belongs to a film club.[12] The magazine's editors ("three people who attempt to work for good film in three different areas and through various means"[13]) addressed this ideal reader with gratitude:

> We owe much to you. Your mere existence results in the fact that movie
> theaters do not show exclusively tearjerkers <*Schnulzen*>; that anti-
> tearjerker directors are not boycotted, at least not always; that critics have
> not been silenced by advertising bans, at least not all; that the art film
> theaters are far from bankrupt, but, quite to the contrary, are finding more
> and more followers (namely, you and your friends) ...[14]

The *Film* editorial posits two sorts of spectators, who are notably gendered: Lieschen Müller, who drives the production of the female-oriented *Schnulze*, and the presumably male cinephile addressed by this alternative magazine, who is responsible for the existence of "good film" in postwar Germany. Written just one year before the release of *Engagement in Zurich*, this editorial already outlined the debate that characterized not only public discourse about the decline of West German cinema in the late 1950s, but also Käutner's own representation of questions of spectatorship and genre in his lampoon of the film industry. Like many of Käutner's previous films, however, *Engagement in Zurich* provided a more complex and equivocal exploration of the issues at stake than the director's extradiegetic commentary on Lieschen Müller and the *Schnulze* would suggest.

II

As in the earlier Käutner production *Film Without a Title*, the metacinematic narrative of *Engagement in Zurich* highlights the compromises at stake in popular filmmaking, demonstrating the interplay of authorship, genre, spectatorship, and stardom in the production of a successful movie. The highly self-conscious satire of *Engagement in Zurich* addresses each of these integral aspects through the character of Juliane, who is at once a film author experimenting with genre, a stand-in for the female spectator, and, through the actress who plays her, Liselotte Pulver, one of the most significant new stars of the late 1950s.

The film begins when Juliane, frustrated by the infidelities of her businessman boyfriend Jürgen (Wolfgang Lukschy), leaves Hamburg to visit her uncle Julius (Werner Finck), a dentist, in Berlin. Seeing the opportunity to write an exposé for a women's magazine on the experiences of a dental hygienist, Juliane agrees to help her uncle when his assistant unexpectedly gets pregnant. Soon the dashing Swiss Jean Berner (Paul Hubschmid) arrives at the dentist's office with his friend Büffel (Bernhard Wicki), who is suffering from a toothache. Juliane begins to fantasize about Jean, fabricating a story about her imminent engagement to the Swiss man, which she uses to stave off the attempts of the remorseful Jürgen to win her back. Juliane's fantasies about Jean become so creative that she decides to forego the magazine exposé, instead choosing to write a screenplay. Her screenplay tells the story of a dental assistant who falls in love with her patient, a famous Swiss conductor. While the conductor seeks to escape from his oppressive life in the limelight through his relationship with this unknown woman, his friend and agent Büffel constantly tries to break the couple apart.

Juliane sends a treatment of her screenplay to a producer at Famosa Film who has agreed to meet with her, but when she arrives there, she finds that the producer is absent and one of the company's directors has read her treatment in his stead: the very same "Büffel"[15] Juliane met in the dentist's office, whom she has portrayed unfavorably in her film story. Despite the mutual embarrassment that ensues, the director, Paul Frank (nicknamed Büffel), agrees on behalf of Famosa Film to finance the film and work together with Juliane on the project. Over the course of their collaboration, Büffel and Juliane travel back and forth between Switzerland, Hamburg, and Berlin, and along the way Juliane collects experiences that she uses in her screenplay. Despite the attempts of Büffel's young son Pips to engineer a relationship between Juliane and his father, Juliane remains beholden to the handsome Jean. However, her work on the script initiates a series of transformations in Juliane's fantasies and desires that culminate, predictably, in a happy ending. Juliane rejects Jean, who turns out to be boring, strait-laced, and uptight, in favor of the chaotic, creative, and trying Büffel. While the film's conclusion suggests the formation of a new family unit in which Juliane will replace Pips's dead mother, the film ends not with a wedding—or even with the engagement promised by its title—but rather with the successful premiere of *Love in Switzerland*, featuring Juliane as author and spectator.

While satirizing the West German film industry and its indebtedness to female audiences, *Engagement in Zurich* also employs structures of identification, star prowess, and other generic conventions of popular cinema to appeal to precisely those audiences. Viewers are meant to identify with the protagonist Juliane and gain insight from her privileged access to the film industry. As a first-time screenwriter, Juliane experiments with authorship, and she is granted the possibility of seeing her own fantasies realized as film spectacle. But Juliane also functions within the film as a kind of diegetic model spectator, mediating reality, fantasy, and filmic image.

An early sequence sets up the metacinematic interrogation of cinematic representation and perception in *Engagement in Zurich*, condensing Käutner's satire. This sequence presents competing versions of the film within a film, *Love in Switzerland*, which showcase contrasting male and female conceptions of how that film should look. Employing the device of a screen within a screen, the sequence literally visualizes the fantasies of the screenwriter Juliane and the producer Krämer. This emblematic sequence comments not only on questions of authorship, spectatorship, stardom, and genre, but also on the construction of both femininity and national identity in popular cinema.

Juliane is invited to a cocktail party at the home of Krämer, the head of Famosa Film, to celebrate the acceptance of her screenplay. In a cameo appearance, the popular star Sonja Ziemann plays the actress who has been cast in the principal role in Juliane's film. The party guests gather in a circle in the living room, and Ziemann asks Juliane to explain the plot of the film to her. As Juliane dramatically narrates the plot, a miniature version of the film she imagines is projected on the screen. We see Juliane's head in color close-up at the bottom left of the screen, while the events she describes appear in black and white behind her. In this sequence, Juliane's fantasy is literally transmuted into an ironic film spectacle before our very eyes, as she imagines herself, played by Sonja Ziemann, in a romantic tryst with her real-life love interest Jean.

According to Juliane's narrative, the famous conductor Bernhard (played by Paul Hubschmid, the same actor who plays Jean) meets up with the dental assistant Eva Maria after a concert to which he has invited her. Wishing to escape to a place where no one will recognize him, Bernhard accompanies Eva Maria to her studio apartment (which looks very much like Juliane's own residence). Juliane explains that the apartment is located in a tower high above the city, where Bernhard feels at home because it reminds him of the Swiss Alps.

In a shot that is representative of the many layers of doubling that occur during this sequence, we see Juliane's characters through a window. Torrential rain falls outside, coating the windowpanes and partially obstructing our view of the actors inside. Not only does this shot emphasize the presence of the screen, thereby foregrounding cinematic representation and spectatorship, but, as the first sequence of the nascent film *Love in Switzerland* that we see, it doubles the first shot of *Engagement in Zurich*, itself an external traveling shot of Juliane's apartment building in the rain that tracks in to a close-up of her window. Juliane's projection is interrupted for a moment, and the screen behind her head fades to white before the camera cuts away.

When the party reconvenes, the guests debate whether the characters in the film will be able to spend the night together. One of the running gags in *Engagement in Zurich* is a constant concern about where people will sleep and whether it is possible for men and women to sleep together—whether chastely or sexually. As the film makes clear, the self-censorship code of the film industry (FSK) circumscribes what may be shown on screen, impeding the ability of films to reflect common social practices such as sexual relationships between consenting adults. However, the film plays with these circumscriptions by repeatedly showing Juliane spending the night with different men (albeit without ever really casting doubt on her virtue). Regarding Juliane's screenplay for *Love in Switzerland*, the question of whether Jean and Eva Maria consummate their relationship becomes a central plot element of *Engagement in Zurich*, driving the film's satirical take on the interplay of fantasy and social reality in popular cinema, as well as the limitations of mainstream cinema when it comes to conveying female desire.

Sonja Ziemann exclaims, "Of course the conductor will spend the night with Eva Maria!" But the director Paul Frank counters that, though such things may happen in real life, they certainly can't be shown on screen—it would be considered immoral. Ziemann suggests that the couple might be able to spend the night together if they were caught in a storm and they happened upon a hay stall, noting dryly that she has played several such scenes herself. The group decides that it would be possible for Bernhard and Eva Maria to sleep together if they were stranded by inclement weather in a mountain hut. By highlighting the limitations imposed by censorship, *Engagement in Zurich* reflexively demonstrates the way in which filmmakers employ the generic conventions of popular cinema to encode contemporary issues, while also indicting the outdatedness of such limitations.

In considering the question of generic conventionalism, the sequence pits the imagination of the female author/spectator against the mind of the male producer, Krämer, who now narrates a scene that stands in sharp contrast to Juliane's film fantasy. In a mirror image of the previous sequence, Krämer's head appears in close-up at the bottom right of the screen, and the film scenes he narrates are again pictured as a black and white projection. Here, we see the characters in traditional Swiss costumes against the backdrop of a typical mountain landscape. In contrast to Juliane's dramatic rendering of her film plot, Krämer's narrative is highly sentimental—he even wipes away a tear as he describes one romantic sequence—and despite its location in a mountain hut, it is notably unerotic.

Juliane's sequence is glamorous, urban, and noirish, and the actors are shown in close-up, acting in a melodramatic style. Relying on predictably romantic female fantasies, Juliane nonetheless envisions a film that conforms closely to the new genres of the late 1950s. By contrast, Krämer's sequence shows a long shot of the characters posed in traditional costume in a standard mountain landscape, clearly recalling the conventional *Heimatfilm*. His scene is a caricature, but he is convinced that it will appeal to audiences, that it is "full of emotion." While Juliane's sequence is as generically conventional as Krämer's, its relationship to her experiences and desires—which the film has already let us in on—creates a dynamism lacking in Krämer's static tableau. Both Juliane and Krämer narrate plot-driven sequences, but Juliane's scene tells a dramatic story in miniature, a story where the characters' emotions are in fact at stake, while Krämer's scene relies exclusively on genre expectations for its emotional appeal. It is hard to imagine these two scenes appearing in the same film, so different are the visions they represent.

Like other postwar films, *Engagement in Zurich* thus foregrounds differences in male and female vision, emphasizing the vitality of the latter in contrast to the hackneyed clichés of the former, while gently parodying both. The film scene imagined by Juliane differs strikingly from the scene of her film that Krämer narrates. Invested not only with the power of the gaze, but also with the authority to visualize whole film sequences, Juliane exhibits control of the formal codes of the film here. Moreover, the film suggests vital connections between Juliane's melodramatic vision and her real-life experiences. By contrast, Krämer's vision is spoofed as trite and passé.

When Krämer's narrative is complete, his wife exclaims, "Isn't it *very* original?!" In a moment of self-parody that relies on audience knowledge of her own long career in *Heimatfilm*, Ziemann, rolling her eyes, responds, "Yes, I do think people like to see scenes like this over and over again." Krämer blithely replies, "But we've had so many conductors in the cinema lately. Shouldn't we make the Swiss man a forester?" "*The Forester of Berner Lake!*," says Paul Frank, and the collective group laughs knowingly at his double entendre, which evokes both the immensely popular *The Forester of the Silver Wood*, and the last name of his friend and Juliane's crush, Jean Berner.

Juliane's ex-boyfriend Jürgen interrupts the conversation to announce that Juliane is planning to get engaged. Embarrassed at this revelation of her lie about Jean in the company of his friend Paul Frank, Juliane spontaneously weaves an elaborate tale about a fiancé named Uri and an upcoming trip to celebrate her engagement in Zurich. The group toasts Juliane, and Krämer exclaims, "To the engagement in Zurich—a good title, by the way. Tasteful, but appealing to the audience." "Yes," replies Ziemann, "To love in Switzerland." "That's a good title too," responds Krämer.

The dense layering of commentary on filmmaking in the late 1950s is achieved here diegetically at the levels of both form and content. The sequence employs the formal device of a screen within a screen in order to project contrasting gendered visions that chart the changing appeal of popular stars and genres, and the comic dialogue in the sequence pokes fun at both the preferences of German audiences and the conventionalism of the film industry. As we shall see, Käutner's satirical message about popular genres and stars also depends on extradiegetic associations. Through its metacinematic discourse on the shifting popularity of particular stars and on the decline of the *Heimatfilm*, the film's satire also targets changing conceptions of gender and Germanness in dominant cinema.

III

As we have seen in the case of Hildegard Knef in particular, female stars played an important role as sites for the resolution of social conflicts in the postwar period, presenting spaces for the negotiation of new notions of femininity and national identity. At the same time, female stars figured largely in the cinema's own quest for relevance and legitimacy in postwar Germany. Commenting on all of these functions of female stars, *Engagement in Zurich* featured two of the most prominent and popular stars of the 1950s, Sonja Ziemann and Liselotte Pulver[16] (see figure 8.1). Representing very different models of femininity and national identity, Ziemann and Pulver shared in common a markedly desexualized and unerotic womanhood that is crucial to the representation of gender and sexuality in Käutner's film.

Replacing Hildegard Knef as both the iconic screen woman and the most beloved actress of the period, Sonja Ziemann became the emblematic star of the first half of the decade. She was almost synonymous with the genre of the *Heimatfilm*, which she helped to

Figure 8.1 *Engagement in Zurich's* metacinematic discourse on stardom: Sonja Ziemann with director Paul Frank (Bernhard Wicki) on the set of *Love in Switzerland*. Source: Deutsche Kinemathek.

popularize with starring roles in the immensely successful *Schwarzwaldmädel* (Black Forest Girl, 1950) and *Grün ist die Heide* (Green is the Heath, 1951). Together with Rudolf Prack, her co-star in both of these films and many that followed, Ziemann formed a screen partnership ("Zieprack") that virtually guaranteed the success of any film production during the first half of the decade. In her roles in both *Heimatfilme* and melodramas, Ziemann embodied a cheerful and proper yet efficient and strong-willed femininity. Her characters ultimately functioned to ground the disrupted family unit, investing it with a new stability. Comfortable in a dirndl or a ball gown, Ziemann was fresh-faced and glamorous in turn, but, in keeping with her status as a star of *Heimatfilme*, she embodied a kind of domestic, homespun beauty that was accessible to viewers. This also made her an extremely popular advertising model and spokeswoman for cosmetics.[17]

Focusing on her accessibility and domestic charm, the women's magazine *Film und Frau* featured Sonja Ziemann in articles and fashion spreads throughout the early postwar period. In 1949, the first year of its publication, the magazine ran a feature on Ziemann at home in her Berlin apartment along with two portraits of the star. One image portraying Ziemann smiling is captioned "Optimistic," while the other, in which she wears a headscarf, is titled "Rustic."[18] These two aspects of Ziemann's star persona perfectly capture the version of femininity that she came to define for cinema audiences: a woman who traversed the divide between traditionalism and modernity, rooted in the past, but looking to the future. *Film und Frau* consistently represented Ziemann as the model woman of the early 1950s, both on screen and in real life. Like the female film viewers who idolized her, Ziemann was depicted as working hard in both the public and private spheres: she had a successful career, but she continued to fulfill her domestic obligations cheerfully, all the while appearing to be the epitome of innocence and charm.

At a time when female sexual promiscuity was a predominant concern in public discourse, Ziemann projected a decidedly unerotic, desexualized and even childlike star persona, an image that was reinforced by her screen alliance with Prack, who was almost old enough to be her father. A 1952 feature on Ziemann in *Film und Frau* described her appeal as follows: "She looks like a teenage girl: charming, fresh, and natural. In all her film roles ... she comes across as pleasantly uncomplicated and free of any enigmatic eroticism. Her softly rounded face, with the gray-green eyes and full, gracefully shaped mouth, appears childlike and cheerfully naïve. And despite—or perhaps because of—this, Sonja Ziemann received the 'Bambi' in 1950, the prize for the most beloved German film actress."[19] By 1959, when *Film und Frau* published a retrospective article on Ziemann's career, the magazine took a slightly more ironic stance on the construction of her screen femininity: "After the box-office smash <*Black Forest Girl*> ... Sonja Ziemann was defined as the sweet, dear, tender, and complaisant girl: she was supposed to be charming, nice, and graceful—but nothing more! ... Critics repeatedly reiterated to Sonja Ziemann that the secret of her success in the *Heimatfilme* rested on the fact that she did not have to play the nice, sweet, pretty little girl—she *was* that girl."[20]

Ziemann's heyday was over by the mid-1950s, when the career of Liselotte Pulver began to take off. In contrast to Ziemann, the image of woman embodied by Pulver was characterized by her tomboy qualities, her clumsiness, and her trademark disruptive laugh.[21] Pulver was well known for her "trouser roles," which *Engagement in Zurich* made light of in several episodes featuring jokes about ski pants (see figure 8.2). Though Ziemann and Pulver had little in common, it is noteworthy that star profiles in *Film und Frau* repeatedly emphasized that both stars were immune to public scandals. While they embodied two distinct, almost diametrically opposed ideals of femininity, both actresses were nonetheless "good girls," whose desexualized star personae were mirrored by their "clean" lifestyles off screen.

Figure 8.2 Liselotte Pulver as Juliane Thomas in a send-up of the star's famous trouser roles. Source: Deutsche Kinemathek.

The fact that she was Swiss was pivotal to the construction of Pulver's star persona. Not only did her Swiss nationality highlight the constructedness of Pulver's "German" identity, something that is especially crucial to her role in *Engagement in Zurich*, but more importantly, only a non-German like Pulver could be so innocent and laugh so heartily. Unlike native German actresses such as Sonja Ziemann, whose sober femininity was constructed as a response to the psychic burden and the physical damages of the recent German past, Pulver represented a femininity unfettered by the social and political obligations of reconstruction. Pulver's breakthrough role came in Kurt Hoffmann's *Ich denke oft an Piroschka* (I Often Think of Piroschka, 1955), which was described by *Film und Frau* as "the playful story of a loveable Hungarian girl in a forgotten village, taking place sometime more than thirty years ago, when the world did not yet suspect anything of the horrible events that would one day divide it."[22] Only a non-German actress like Pulver could convincingly represent such an innocent, happy world.

Like Sonja Ziemann, Liselotte Pulver was an accessible star. She was not renowned for her glamour or beauty, but rather for her talent as a comic actress and for the simple cheer she exuded. In 1957, *Film und Frau* ran several spreads of Pulver modeling clothes made from its own fashionable line of simple dresses that were easy for readers to sew from patterns the magazine sold for a small fee. Pulver was quoted as saying that one of the patterns was so easy she might even dare to attempt sewing the dress herself.[23] In contrast to Ziemann, whom *Film und Frau* had consistently represented as a woman who excelled at domestic tasks, Pulver thus embodied a new image of woman for whom domesticity was anathema. The *Film und Frau* spreads featuring Pulver as a model were an exception. Most profiles of Pulver focused on her talent and individuality rather than her looks, and unlike other actresses of the era she rarely served as a spokeswoman for advertising. Thus a 1958 feature on Pulver in *Film und Frau* emphasized the fact that she avoided parties, public appearances, and the glamorous world of film in favor of developing her own individuality through autodidactic pursuits.[24] In life and on film, Pulver was represented as an independent, unattached woman, who earned her own living, pursued her own interests, and kept a sense of humor about it all. Even when she married, Pulver continued to pursue her own career, often leaving her husband behind to run the household and take care of the children.

Like her independence and occasional assumption of masculine traits, critics considered Pulver's comic persona a departure from traditional femininity, which differentiated her from other German screen actresses. As *Film und Frau* put it, "German film has not been able to maintain many funny actresses … This may be due to the fact that genuine humor does not always seem convincing in women."[25] With strong comic turns in films such as Kurt Hoffmann's Thomas Mann adaptation *Die*

Bekenntnisse des Hochstaplers Felix Krull (The Confessions of Felix Krull, 1957) and his *Das Wirtshaus im Spessart* (The Inn in the Spessart, 1958), Pulver helped to effect the generic transition of popular German cinema away from the *Heimatfilm* in the second half of the 1950s.

Temby Caprio describes Pulver as one of the most "semiotically complicated" stars of the postwar period: "Pulver's star persona and her roles foreground the construction of Germanness and femininity. Her normalcy combined with her discursively constructed 'Germanness,' her uproarious laughter, and her famous trouser roles suggest a moment of bourgeois femininity in crisis, a femininity aesthetically and ideologically grounded in *Papas Kino* and yet thematically anticipating the radical gender politics of feminist film culture a decade later."[26] Indeed, *Engagement in Zurich* relied on the transitional quality of Pulver's star sign for its satirical thematization of changing conceptions of gender, sexuality, and national identity, as well as the changing status of cinematic representation in the late 1950s.

In Käutner's film, the down-to-earth femininity embodied by Pulver's star sign is rendered on screen by Ziemann's more proper femininity, and the star personae of both actresses are lampooned in the process. The "real" Ziemann is portrayed as a bored and cynical diva, wholly different from the wholesome girl she routinely embodied in her *Heimatfilm* roles. Not only is Pulver's mode of femininity contrasted sharply with Ziemann's, but the tension between Pulver's Swiss nationality and the innocent Germanness she came to embody as a popular star is also parodied. The mountain hut scene in Juliane's film script is filled with kitschy stereotypes about Switzerland; when she fabricates a story about marrying a Swiss man, she can only think to name him Uri, after the paradigmatic Swiss canton. And when Jürgen comments on how unlikely it is that Juliane would fall in love with two separate Swiss men in such short order, Pulver's character smirks, "But after all, there are many interesting people from Switzerland."

IV

Through its caricatures of Swiss people and particularly of the Swiss German accent, *Engagement in Zurich* posits strong differences between Switzerland and the Federal Republic. The film represents Switzerland as alien, a country with different customs, other landscapes, and even an indecipherable "foreign" language. By highlighting these contrasts, the film parodies the timeless, ahistorical, transnational Germanic landscapes of *Heimatfilme* like the one produced in the narrative of *Engagement in Zurich*. Popular *Heimatfilme* like *The Forester of the Silver Wood* elided salient national differences and skirted the tricky issue of nationalism by presenting the possibility of an affirmative patriotic alliance with the local traditions of a regional *Heimat*. Whether a *Heimatfilm* took place in Austria, Germany, or Switzerland was not crucial to its narrative: although traditional regional dress and dialect might provide local color, these factors rarely affected the plots of the films, which took up similar issues regardless of their settings. By contrast, *Engagement in Zurich* satirizes this diversionary tactic through its reinforcement of the distinctions between Switzerland and West Germany.

A romantic comedy about the creation of a *Heimatfilm*, *Engagement in Zurich* also thematizes the generic transition taking place in the film industry in the second half of the 1950s. Immensely successful during the first half of the decade, the *Heimatfilm* suffered a precipitous decline in popularity that caught the film industry by surprise. As one 1956 article described it:

> Now even some film firms are becoming afraid that they have stuck their necks out too far for the *Heimatfilm*. The fear that the glut of *Heimatfilme* means that certain accounts will not balance out has led to the first renamings. Thus "Three Birches on the Heath" became the sleek "Young Blood," and the kitschy "In the Forest and on the Heath" was transformed into "Red Poppies." And what the swallow was supposed to sing to us ("What the Swallow Sang") we will instead see in our local cinema as "Undying Love." But not even that was enough: several products of the worst tearjerker sort are being taken out of commission and hung out to dry.[27]

Forcing the film industry to retool, the waning popularity of the *Heimatfilm* was caused both by the socioeconomic changes taking place in the Federal Republic and by the German public's increasing rejection of the sentimental conventionalism of mainstream genre cinema. In the late 1950s, the *Heimatfilm* no longer appeared to be the most suitable vehicle for addressing the social and representational problems of the postwar period. If *Film Without a Title* predicted already in 1948 the eventual rise of the *Heimatfilm*, *Engagement in Zurich* charted that genre's decline, parodying not only the conventions and stars that had made the genre so successful, but pointing also to the reasons for its demise.

V

By rejecting the *Heimatfilm*, film audiences in the latter half of the 1950s influenced the course of film production in Germany. Similarly, *Engagement in Zurich* imagines cinematic representation and spectatorship as a dialogic process, in which film is influenced and even transformed by the experiences and fantasies of (female) viewers. In the sequence discussed above, Juliane encodes her real-life experiences and her fantasies in a narrative that is projected immediately into visual imagery, as a film within a film. Here and throughout the movie, the metacinematic plotline explores the impact of Juliane's personal experiences and desires as well as production requirements and audience demands on the creation of *Love in Switzerland*. Käutner's film ultimately suggests that popular cinema achieves success precisely by combining aspects of social reality with elements of fantasy and imagination, a formula that the film criticizes, but also reproduces.

In pitting Juliane's vision against Krämer's and Frank's, *Engagement in Zurich* thus lampoons the film industry's patented strategy for renewing the legitimacy of cinematic language in the postwar period: the incorporation of *female* experience and fantasy at the levels of both form and content. Parodying both the naivety and predictability of women's fantasies and the stale shape such fantasies took when appropriated by male filmmakers, Käutner's film lays blame for the decline of popular cinema on both sides of the equation. At the same time, however, much of the appeal of the film derives from its comic take on the interplay between fantasy and reality in the female spectatorial imagination. Somewhat despite itself, then, the film demonstrates the vital and pleasurable qualities of popular genre cinema.

In her important contribution to debates about female spectatorship within feminist film theory, Christine Gledhill has proposed the concept of "pleasurable negotiation" as a way of understanding the relationships among film text, ideology, and viewer. As Gledhill describes it, "<T>he term 'negotiation' implies the holding together of opposite sides in an ongoing process of give-and-take. As a model of meaning production, negotiation conceives cultural exchange as the intersection of processes of production and reception, in which overlapping but non-matching determinations operate. Meaning is neither imposed, nor passively imbibed, but arises out of a struggle or negotiation between competing frames of reference, motivation and experience."[28] In Gledhill's framework, the process of negotiation affects cultural production at the level of institutions, texts, and audiences. Thus, the negotiation of contradictory or conflicting elements characterizes the institutional and aesthetic production as well as the extratextual reception of any given film. For Gledhill, the process of negotiation also contributes substantially toward the pleasures of popular culture for the (female) viewer.

In its depiction of both the collaborative process of popular filmmaking and female spectatorship, *Engagement in Zurich* strongly reflects Gledhill's model of pleasurable negotiation. Institutional and aesthetic negotiations about *Love in Switzerland* drive the film's narrative, including a longstanding dispute between Juliane and Büffel about the realism of the film's closure and an ongoing conflict between Juliane and Krämer about the film's generic traits. Notably, gender differences characterize both these sets of negotiations. Juliane's writing process also emphasizes her negotiation of real-life experience and fantasy: while she is pressured by Büffel to make her script conform to the dictates of reality, Juliane wishes that her life would imitate a woman's film.

Paradigmatic of the model of negotiation presented by *Engagement in Zurich*, the scene of *Love in Switzerland* that takes place at the mountain hut becomes the central event that drives the film's interrogation of social and representational problems. The metacinematic debates about this scene focus on the impossibility of representing female desire in popular cinema, both due to the aesthetic and industrial interventions of (male) directors and producers and because of West German censorship codes. Already at the outset of the film, Juliane has planned to include in her screenplay a scene taking place at a mountain hut in the Alps, but she has not yet decided what will take place there. When she travels to Switzerland hoping to meet up with her love interest Jean, Juliane discovers that he actually owns a mountain hut, and she wangles an invitation to accompany him there.

Before the two depart, Juliane sits down with Büffel to work on the screenplay. Shooting is set to begin soon, and the director hopes to nail down the climax of the film. "Now, what is actually supposed to happen at this mountain hut?," he asks, "Profound conversations, holding hands, admiring the view, or what? I mean, does *it* happen or doesn't it?" Exasperated, Juliane replies, "Of course it happens—only tenderly, on a higher plane." After cracking a few jokes about her unrealistic representation of a love affair between adults, Büffel proclaims, "I've been trying to make it clear to you for days now that this whole relationship between Eva Maria and the conductor simply doesn't work—either on a personal level or on an erotic level. Eva isn't a teenager anymore. This whole infatuation is pure melodrama. It simply doesn't exist in reality." Considering her own infatuation, which has thus far produced no reciprocal feelings from Jean, Juliane responds, "So, you don't believe that it happens in real life that a woman in her mid-twenties—despite being somewhat experienced—might really fall in love for the very first time!" Dismissing her script as "sky blue or hot pink soda pop swill," Büffel provokes Juliane to storm off angry, hoping to prove him wrong on her date with Jean.

Juliane sets off for the tryst at Jean's remote mountain abode, planning for a romantic encounter with the handsome doctor. If she equivocates about the mountain scene in her screenplay, it is only because she doesn't want to give away a climax that, as it were, she has not yet experienced for herself. However, her trip to the mountain hut leads only to disappointment. Jean appears more interested in building a fire and making tea than in retiring to the hay stall with Juliane, and when Büffel shows up at the hut despite a thick fog, his presence ensures that the evening does not turn romantic.

Now that her real experience at the mountain hut has failed to satisfy her romantic fantasies, Juliane's screenplay reflects her disillusionment with the generic conventions of women's cinema. Back in Hamburg, Krämer visits Juliane to discuss the script with her, and the conversation that ensues epitomizes Käutner's lampoon of the film industry:

Krämer:	One thing that really doesn't work for me anymore is the whole scenario at the mountain cabin. I imagined that very differently.
Juliane:	So did I.
Krämer:	Originally that was a strong erotic situation, but now nothing decisive happened there.
Juliane:	Unfortunately.
Krämer:	But you're the author! You were holding all the strings in your hand!
Juliane:	That's true, but it just didn't happen.
Krämer:	It's the damned influence of Büffel. He always changes everything.
Juliane:	But he's right. What I had written before was extravagant and romantic. It doesn't happen that way in real life.
Krämer:	But people are romantic. They don't want to see on screen what they can have every day at home.
Juliane:	But Büffel says the audience is much more sensible than we all think.
Krämer:	… I don't like producing sentimental tearjerkers <*Schnulzen*> either. Oh well, at the end it's all right again, when the two finally get together in Zurich. But in the middle, at the mountain cabin, there's something missing. If it could at least have been a forest cabin, with a tame deer …
Juliane:	A conductor with a tame deer?
Krämer:	I've always said he should be a forester!

While the rich double entendre of this sequence is played for high comic effect, it also raises questions about genre, spectatorship, and dream factory vs. social reality that were hotly debated during this transitional period. Krämer, clearly ignorant of the fact that Juliane's screenplay is based on the events of her real-life relationship with Jean, argues once again that the script should be brought into alignment with the generic conventions of the typical *Heimatfilm*. Juliane, whose experiences have caused her to reflect on the cleft between film fantasy and reality, argues for a more realistic approach to filmmaking that would more explicitly accommodate true female experience—her own. Nonetheless, as it has throughout the film, Juliane's fantasy will continue to play an indispensable role as she imagines a finale for her screenplay.

In considering the appeal of popular media to women, Christine Gledhill argues in particular that "a considerable source of textual negotiation lies in the use by many mainstream film and television genres of both melodramatic and realist modes. This dual constitution enables a text to work both on a symbolic, 'imaginary' level, internal to fictional production, and on a 'realist' level, referring to the socio-historical world outside the text."[29] While the West German cinema debates of the 1950s often emphasized the necessity of abolishing melodrama and fantastic elements in favor of a closer connection to social reality, Käutner's film both reflects and parodies the strategy of negotiation between both modes typical of the women's genres described by Gledhill.

The question of fantasy and reality figures once more in the final conversation between Juliane and Paul Frank about the film script, which Juliane has rewritten under the influence of Krämer's demands. "Büffel," long enamored of Juliane, has finally begun to try to win her over, albeit in his own bumbling, klutzy fashion. While Juliane is still infatuated with Jean, she has begun to tire of her pursuit of a man who will go no further than kissing her on the forehead, and she begins to open up to Büffel's flirtations. Unhappy with the unrealistic and sentimental aspects of Juliane's screenplay, Büffel comments, "The ending is still hot pink and sky blue. Your dangerous fantasy really did it again … Well, up until the whole scenario of the mountain cabin it is really quite viable. One senses that your own experiences are behind it." Juliane interjects, "Do you want to wait for the script until I have had the right experiences for the ending too?" "That's not a bad idea at all," replies Büffel, "In any case everything goes much too smoothly in your fantasy, without interesting complications. Eva Mariechen and her conductor run into one another through some stupid coincidence and they get together—the end. When does that ever happen?" Juliane responds that it might happen to her, since Jean has just invited her to visit him in Zurich. When Büffel begs her to stay with him instead, she coyly responds, "But then we'll have to rely on my fantasy."

Throughout its metacinematic narrative about Juliane's screenplay, *Engagement in Zurich* addresses the possibility of representing female desire and sexuality, comically highlighting the "pleasurable negotiations" involved in conveying female experience in mainstream cinema as well as the negotiations of fantasy, imagination, and social reality that inform Juliane's film authorship and spectatorship. Despite its self-reflexivity about these issues, however, Käutner's film, itself a product of dominant culture, quickly reaches its own limits in regard to representing female subjectivity and especially female sexuality. The film endows Juliane with both sexual and authorial agency and then proceeds to destabilize this agency. For example, Juliane fantasizes repeatedly about spending a romantic night with Jean. However, when she actually does spend the night with a man—something that happens several times over the course of the narrative—the film winks at the possibility of a sexual encounter without ever seriously placing into question Juliane's virginity and moral rectitude. Furthermore, when Juliane expresses her own sexual desire, she is accused of having a dangerous or licentious imagination and fantasy life.

Juliane's fantasies surrounding sex and love are explicitly linked to her creative imagination and her ability to write a successful film script. Her desires fuel both her real-life experiences and the ultimate shape her screenplay takes. Thus *Engagement in Zurich* implies, on the one hand, that Juliane's creative process is inseparable from her autobiography, echoing a typical stereotype of female authorship. On the other hand, through the figure of Juliane, the film excuses the conventionalism of the *Schnulze*, suggesting that only the pliability of genre allowed German cinema to accommodate investigations of female experience at a time when social problems could not be easily addressed in a less veiled context.

VI

At the end of *Engagement in Zurich*, Paul Frank brings Juliane to the studio's screening room to show her the final scene of his film. In the scene, the conductor, played by Frank himself, is united with Eva Maria at long last. As Juliane watches the scene, she smiles, but as soon as the cut comes, she frowns, telling Büffel that she doesn't like his vision at all: instead, the woman should have the last word. "She should say, 'I love you,'" says Juliane. Büffel tells her that no one says that anymore, before realizing that Juliane is in fact confessing her love for him. The highly sentimental ending that Büffel sought to avoid in his film thus happens in "real life," and Büffel and Juliane embrace. Juliane rejects Büffel's representation of the final scene of her film, refusing to identify with the scene she sees on screen. Not only does Juliane rewrite the filmic image with her own authorial vision once more, but she is also the one to take charge in real life, creating her very own happy ending.

The final scene of *Engagement in Zurich* takes place at the gala premiere of *Love in Switzerland*. The cast sits in a long row in the audience as the opening credits roll: "Sonja Ziemann in / Love in Switzerland / Screenplay by Juliane Thomas." In these credits, which attribute the creation of the film exclusively to women, the male role in the film's production is completely elided. A cut to the audience shows Büffel looking at Juliane, who in turn looks at his son Pips. The last word in the film, literally Juliane's name, grants final authorship to her, and the last look in the film belongs to her as well (although, consistent with the film's ambivalence about Juliane's sexual desire, it is a maternal, rather than erotic, gaze).

Thus the film ultimately portrays the West German cinema of the 1950s as women's cinema, both the product of a female authorial imagination and a creation that caters to the fantasies of the female spectator. Notably, the film's publicity campaign focused on precisely these aspects of *Engagement in Zurich* rather than on Käutner's lampoon of the film industry. Highlighting the appeal to female spectators, the film's publicity brochure began its plot summary of the film, which was reprinted in the film program, as follows:

Even as a modern, happy girl, one doesn't exactly have it easy
- when one is engaged to a man who doesn't exist,
- in love with another, who unfortunately doesn't realize it, and
- loved by a third, whom one wants to have absolutely nothing to do with.[30]

Emphasizing identification with the female character and plot elements such as the love triangle, this synopsis portrayed the film as a consummate *Schnulze*, something that was further underscored in the film program's visuals. The program featured an exaggerated montage of funny images of Juliane that shed little light on the plot, alongside several pictures of Helmut Käutner's poodle, who made his own cameo appearance in the film.[31]

In its pictorial retelling of *Engagement in Zurich*, the women's magazine *Film und Frau* emphasized an appeal to female spectators through a focus on Liselotte Pulver's comic talent and on Juliane's role as a screenwriter: "Liselotte Pulver … now plays, under the direction of Helmut Käutner in 'Engagement in Zurich,' a film author: intelligent in her profession, but, as is sometimes the case with clever women, a bit dumb in matters of love. She plays the role charmingly."[32] Representing Juliane as "a bit of a bluestocking," the *Film und Frau* synopsis stressed the role played by her fantasy in driving the film's plot. As these documents suggest, the distributor Europa Filmverleih banked on the straightforward appeal of Käutner's film as women's cinema, underplaying the film's critical and metacinematic elements in an attempt to attract a traditional audience of female viewers.

However, these elements were by no means neglected in the popular or critical reception of the film. A film club handbook presented the following suggestions for discussion of *Engagement in Zurich*: "Did Käutner only want to make an entertaining film? Is the critique of the film industry justified? What about ability of actors to transform themselves in different roles (Wicki)? Why does Julchen 'get' the director in the end?"[33] Emphasizing Käutner's satire of the film industry and of the conventional generic traits of the *Schnulze*, these questions suggest that viewers did catch on to the satire articulated by the film.

The question of Käutner's satirical message challenged critics, who were split in their response to the film. For those who were receptive to the film's humorous critique of the provincialism and sentimentality of the West German cinema, the parody articulated by the film was hard to reconcile with its embeddedness in precisely those genres that it set out to satirize.[34] By contrast, others found the film too "intellectual" or "artificial" for the romantic comedy it purported to be.[35]

Bridging this gap, Gunter Groll dubbed *Engagement in Zurich* an "anti-tearjerker" <*Anti-Schnulze*>, noting: "A German film that makes fun of the typical German film—that is as funny as it is atypical, and Käutner does it very artfully."[36] While Groll applauded Käutner's comedic ability, he also highlighted the paradox at stake in the film: "He wants to parody the effects of the so-called audience film, but at the same time make use of them as audience effects. Thus he does in the background precisely that which he makes fun of up front. He does so, admittedly, in a very funny way."[37]

Indeed, Käutner's film was so funny to contemporary audiences because it catered to the ongoing demand for genre cinema while also acknowledging the imminent demise of the *Schnulze*, or "audience film." Through the figure of Juliane, the film made the allegorical Lieschen Müller into a multidimensional character, giving form to debates about the role of female spectators in driving the production of conventional films. Like *Film Without a Title*, *Engagement in Zurich* thus achieved popularity with viewers by directly commenting on the ongoing crisis in postwar cinematic representation. However, while *Film Without a Title* speculated on the possibility of establishing a new film language in the postwar period, *Engagement in Zurich* parodies this possibility at the moment of postwar cinema's incipient decline. While the film demonstrates once again the imbrication of social and representational problems centering around gender and sexuality, its lampoon of the film industry represents a last gasp for the strategy of women's cinema as a means of relegitimating filmmaking.

Notes

1. See Hans Helmut Prinzler, *Chronik des deutschen Films 1895–1994* (Stuttgart, 1995), 213; and Elizabeth Prommer, *Kinobesuch im Lebenslauf. Eine historische und medienbiografische Studie* (Konstanz, 1999), 350.
2. According to Joseph Garncarz, foreign films comprised half of the top ten most popular films during the 1956/57 season. See Garncarz, "Hollywood in Germany. Die Rolle des amerikanischen Films in Deutschland: 1925–1990," in *Der deutsche Film. Aspekte seiner Geschichte von den Anfängen bis zur Gegenwart*, ed. Uli Jung (Trier, 1993), 202.
3. For statistics on television licensing see Prommer, *Kinobesuch im Lebenslauf*, 350. On the impact of television on the film industry, see Knut Hickethier, "Vom Ende des Kinos und vom Anfang des Fernsehens: Das Verhältnis von Film und Fernsehen in den fünfziger Jahren," in *Zwischen Gestern und Morgen. Westdeutscher Nachkriegsfilm 1946–1962*, ed. Hilmar Hoffmann and Walter Schobert (Frankfurt am Main, 1989), 282–315.
4. See Patrice Petro, "Mass Culture and the Feminine: The 'Place' of Television in Film Studies," *Cinema Journal* 25.3 (Spring 1986), rpt. in Petro, *Aftershocks of the New: Feminism and Film History* (New Brunswick, NJ, 2002), 13–30; and Andreas Huyssen, "Mass Culture as Woman: Modernism's Other," in *After the Great Divide: Modernism, Mass Culture, Postmodernism* (Bloomington, 1986), 44–62.
5. Kurt Wortig, *Ihre Hoheit Lieschen Müller: Hof- und Hinterhofgespräche um Film und Fernsehen* (Munich, 1961), 15.
6. Karl Klär, *Film zwischen Wunsch und Wirklichkeit: Gespräche mit den Freunden des Films und seinen Gegnern* (Wiesbaden-Biebrich, 1957), 19.
7. Arthur Maria Rabenalt, *Die Schnulze* (Munich, 1959), 9, qtd. in Walther Schmieding, *Kunst oder Kasse: Der Ärger mit dem deutschen Film* (Hamburg, 1961), 84.
8. Schmieding, *Kunst oder Kasse*, 85.
9. See for example rev. of *Die Zürcher Verlobung*, *Filmkritik* 6 (1957): 93.
10. Schmieding, *Kunst oder Kasse*, 88–89.
11. Gunter Groll, Helmut Käutner, and Walter Talmon-Gros, "Jedes Publikum, bekanntlich, hat die Filme, die es verdient," *Film—Monatshefte für Film und Fernsehen* (December

1956): 6–7, rpt. as "Every Audience, as Everybody Knows, Has the Films It Deserves," trans. Lance W. Garner, in *German Essays on Film*, ed. Richard W. McCormick and Alison Guenther-Pal (New York, 2004), 199. Garner's translation substitutes the name "Jane Doe" for Lieschen Müller.

12. Groll et al., "Every Audience," 200.
13. Groll et al., "Every Audience," 199. Groll was a film critic for the *Süddeutsche Zeitung* and Käutner, of course, was a director. Walter Talmon-Gros was a film historian who also directed the Mannheim Film Festival.
14. Groll et al., "Every Audience," 201.
15. The nickname translates literally as "buffalo" and carries the sense of a bullish or ox-like person.
16. Käutner's send-up of stars and stardom is achieved through both effective casting and the use of star cameos. To play the director of *Love in Switzerland*, Paul Frank ("Büffel"), Käutner cast Bernhard Wicki, who himself was not only a well-known leading actor but also an aspiring director. Wicki would go on to become one of the most promising new directors of the transitional West German cinema, scoring a popular and critical success with his anti-war film *Die Brücke* (The Bridge, 1959). The popular star couple of actress Anny Ondra and boxer Max Schmeling show up in cameo during the cocktail party at Krämer's house. And Käutner himself makes a rare appearance on screen to register his own ambivalent opinion of *Engagement in Zurich*, stopping by the set of *Love in Switzerland* to criticize Paul Frank for playing a role in his own film.
17. On the role of film and film stars in establishing feminine models of consumption in the Federal Republic in the 1950s, see Erica Carter, *How German Is She?: Postwar West German Reconstruction and the Consuming Woman* (Ann Arbor, 1997), 171–201. On Ziemann in particular, see 179–80 and 191–95.
18. "Sonja Ziemann," *Film und Frau* 14 (1949): 10–11.
19. "Sonja Ziemann: Triumph der Naivität," *Film und Frau* 22 (1952): 32–33.
20. Kurt Joachim Fischer, "Sonja Ziemann: Vom 'Schwarzwaldmädel' zum 'Achten Wochentag,'" *Film und Frau* 3 (1959): 44–47.
21. If Ziemann and Pulver represent two poles of postwar femininity, these poles were perhaps mediated by the other iconic star of 1950s cinema, Ruth Leuwerik. Leuwerik, whose career spanned the entire decade, was immensely popular with audiences throughout the 1950s. While she epitomized a sober, caring femininity similar to Ziemann's, hers was a mature, maternal, womanly femininity that contrasted with Ziemann's girlishness and Pulver's tomboy qualities. Leuwerik was also a more versatile actress than either Ziemann or Pulver, which enabled her to transition among domestic melodrama, classical roles, *Heimatfilm*, and romantic comedy. On Leuwerik, see *Die ideale Frau: Ruth Leuwerik und das Kino der fünfziger Jahre*, ed. Peter Mänz and Nils Warnecke (Berlin, 2004).
22. Kurt Joachim Fischer, "Liselotte Pulver: Karriere ohne Skandal," *Film und Frau* 8 (1958): 78.
23. See "Das Mädchen in Weiss," *Film und Frau* 9 (1957): 132; and "Aus dem Ferienkoffer eines Filmstars," *Film und Frau* 10 (1957): 106–7.
24. Fischer, "Liselotte Pulver."
25. Fischer, "Liselotte Pulver."
26. Temby Caprio, "Women's Film Culture in the Sixties: Stars and Anti-Stars from *Papas Kino* to the German New Wave," *Women in German Yearbook* 15 (2000): 206.
27. Hans R. Beierlein, "Angst vor der Heimatfilm-Courage," *Abendzeitung*, August 18–19, 1956.
28. Christine Gledhill, "Pleasurable Negotiations," in *Female Spectators: Looking at Film and Television*, ed. E. Deidre Pribram (London, 1988), 64–89; 67–68.
29. Gledhill, "Pleasurable Negotiations," 75.
30. Press booklet (Hamburg, 1957), in file on *Die Zürcher Verlobung*, Schriftgutarchiv, Stiftung deutsche Kinemathek, Berlin.
31. "Die Zürcher Verlobung," *Illustrierte Film-Bühne* 3689 (1957).

32. G.A., "Der liebe und der böse Nerv: Käutner dreht die 'Zürcher Verlobung,'" *Film und Frau* 9.4 (1957): 6.

33. *Handbuch für Filmclubarbeit* (Verband der deutschen Film-Clubs e.V., n.d.), in file on *Die Zürcher Verlobung*, Schriftgutarchiv, Stiftung deutsche Kinemathek, Berlin.

34. See for example rev. of *Die Zürcher Verlobung, Filmkritik* 6 (1957): 93; rev. of *Die Zürcher Verlobung, Der Tagesspiegel*, May 30, 1957; Georg Ramseger, "Das Spaßvergnügen fand nicht statt," *Die Welt*, April 20, 1957.

35. See for example rev. of *Die Zürcher Verlobung, Katholischer Filmdienst* (May 2, 1957): 145. This criticism was also articulated by the working committee of the self-censorship organ of the film industry (FSK) that evaluated the film to decide whether it was appropriate for young audiences. The committee agreed that the film was appropriate for all viewers over ten years of age, despite their contention that, "For a *Lustspiel* the film is, all in all, somewhat too intellectual and seems perhaps at times somewhat constructed." See "Jugendprotokoll" (April 3, 1957), photocopy in file on *Die Zürcher Verlobung*, Schriftgutarchiv, Stiftung deutsche Kinemathek, Berlin.

36. Gunter Groll, "Die Anti-Schnulze," *Süddeutsche Zeitung*, May 9, 1957, rpt. in *Käutner*, ed. Wolfgang Jacobsen and Hans Helmut Prinzler (Berlin, 1992), 234.

37. Groll, "Die Anti-Schnulze," 234.

Chapter 9

SOUND AND SPECTACLE IN THE *WIRTSCHAFTSWUNDER*: THE CRITICAL STRATEGIES OF ROLF THIELE'S *THE GIRL ROSEMARIE* (1958)

The West German cinema rallied in 1958.[1] Due in large part to the efforts of the film industry to respond to changing audience tastes, eight of the top ten films of the year were West German.[2] The popularity of these domestic movies brought to fruition the strategy of innovation pursued by filmmakers bent on appealing to new audiences while also winning back old viewers. In addition to introducing new stars and genres, several of the top films of 1958 found success by combining tried and true strategies of popular cinema with elements of formal experimentation. These films kicked off a new wave of critical filmmaking that not only contended with mainstream representational styles but also questioned the political and socioeconomic status quo in the Federal Republic.

Foremost among them was Rolf Thiele's *Das Mädchen Rosemarie*, a huge box office smash that was one of the most popular *and* most socially critical films of the decade.[3] An indictment of the collective amnesia and moral hypocrisy that characterized the Adenauer Era, Thiele's film underscores its critical appraisal of *Wirtschaftswunder* consensus culture by disrupting the conventional unity of sound and image characteristic of postwar genre cinema. In a decade when, as we have seen, visual representation was particularly burdened with political associations, music and sound constituted a less overdetermined aspect of cinematic language for German filmmakers. Accordingly, for transitional films like *The Girl Rosemarie* and Herbert Vesely's *Das Brot der frühen Jahre* (The Bread of Those Early Years, 1962), the aural track presented a uniquely important space for experimentation with form. By employing both popular music and ominous synthetic sounds as part of its formally innovative soundtrack, Thiele's film showcases sound as an essential component of spectatorial appeal.[4] At the same time, the film's experimentation with sound as a primary site for the articulation of its critical message about German rearmament and the power of industry bosses demonstrates the ongoing interconnection of social and representational problems in postwar filmmaking. Once more, both sets of problems crystallize around issues of gender in a film that returns to the charged terrain of female sexuality. More explicitly critical than its precursors, *The Girl Rosemarie* not only seeks to appeal to female spectators at the level of both content and form, but in fact offers an analysis of postwar gender relations along with formal innovations that depart from the conventions of dominant cinema.

Based on a true story, *The Girl Rosemarie* tells the tale of the unsolved murder of a high-class prostitute, Rosemarie Nitribitt, who was found dead in her Frankfurt apartment in November 1957. During a search of the premises, police found pictures of Nitribitt's clientele as well as a "little black book" listing their names. Many of these clients were instantly recognizable: they were influential politicians and industry bosses who played a vital role in shaping the *Wirtschaftswunder*.[5] From the beginning, the press covered the murder extensively, and police soon called for a media blackout. Since the 1950s, commentators have continued to speculate about the case, generally assuming that the investigation was intentionally sabotaged to protect the identities of Nitribitt's clients and to cover up the high-society intrigue surrounding her murder.[6]

Spurred on by this emergent scandal, the filmmaking team of screenwriter Erich Kuby, producer Luggi Waldleitner, and director Thiele immediately set about utilizing Nitribitt's story to create a social-critical film that would tackle the double moral standard of the *Wirtschaftswunder* as national mythos and lived reality.[7] *The Girl Rosemarie* also extrapolates from the few known facts of Rosemarie Nitribitt's life to posit an explicit connection between her murder and German rearmament—and by extension the escalating Cold War.

The film begins as Rosemarie (Nadja Tiller) is still a small-time streetwalker, living with two street musicians, her brother Horst (Mario Adorf) and his friend Walter (Jo Herbst), who double as her pimps. Rosemarie has high aspirations and makes frequent journeys to a Frankfurt luxury hotel, hoping to seduce rich men. One day she succeeds in capturing the attentions of an industry boss, Bruster (Gert Fröbe), who is a member of the mysterious *Isoliermattenkartell* (Insulation Matting Cartel), a cover for a top-secret armaments cooperative involving numerous captains of industry. This encounter turns out to be Rosemarie's big break, and she eventually becomes the mistress of the cartel member Hartog (Carl Raddatz). Hartog gives Rosemarie her own apartment and a wardrobe of nice clothes, but she wants more: she seeks to transcend class boundaries and hopes to participate in Hartog's life, or at least his lifestyle.

When Hartog refuses to introduce Rosemarie to his colleagues and relatives or to include her in his social life, she turns to his French colleague Fribert (Peter van Eyck), with whom she hopes to have an affair. Fribert, however, has something else in mind. As he tells her, "Here I am trying to explain to you the connection between your bed and the *Wirtschaftswunder*, and you're trying to unbutton my jacket." He then proposes a plan to Rosemarie: he will school her in true elegance and glamour, clothe her "like a suburban Paris housewife," and help her to become "a great coquette." In return, she will spy on her clients for him. Fribert gives Rosemarie a tiny spy camera and a reel-to-reel tape recorder that she hides in her boudoir. One by one, the men from the arms cartel enter Rosemarie's bedchamber and confess to her—and the tape recorder—secrets about their shady business dealings. It is significant that, though Rosemarie does photograph the contents of the men's calendars and address books with her spy camera, the film does not focus on the visual secrets that are thereby revealed. Instead, it is the aural revelations of the tapes that constitute Rosemarie's primary transgression.

Rosemarie prospers in her new role, but her ascent does not last long. When Fribert receives the first installment of information from Rosemarie, he leaks it to the French press, blowing her cover and exposing the secret activities of the German cartel. Realizing the source of the information, the cartel plots to get rid of Rosemarie. The men try to pay her off and send her out of the country, but she refuses, withholding the tapes and demanding that Hartog marry her. When he declines, Rosemarie's life spirals out of control. Returning home from a confrontation with her clients at a bar, Rosemarie is murdered by a dark figure lurking behind a curtain in her luxury apartment. While neither the murder nor the murderer is shown, the film clearly implicates the cartel in the crime. By suggesting that West Germany's most prosperous business leaders were not only philanderers and shady arms dealers but murderers as well, the film highlights continuities between the Third Reich and the Federal Republic. Moreover, by implying that these men will not only avoid punishment for their crime, but continue to consolidate their profits in its aftermath, the film indicts the double moral standard that still governs gender relations in the postwar period.

Already during production *The Girl Rosemarie* was the subject of numerous protests and lawsuits, primarily from businesses and individuals who feared their reputations would be damaged by their portrayal in the film.[8] After it was completed, the controversy took on international proportions. *The Girl Rosemarie* was set to premiere at the Venice Film Festival as the official West German contribution to the competition. However, shortly before the festival, an assistant reviewer on the cultural board of the Federal Republic's Foreign Office completed an evaluation of the film, demanding that it be pulled from the festival because it would "damage the reputation of West Germany abroad."[9] As a result, the Venice organizers issued an official invitation to the filmmakers to show their film outside the competition. When they accepted, the West German Foreign Office and the Export Union filed an unsuccessful protest with the festival, asking them not to show the film.

The Girl Rosemarie ultimately premiered in Venice on August 25, 1958, where it met with an enthusiastic audience reception. Due in large part to the controversy the film had generated, the Italian press displayed great interest in it, praising its self-critical depiction of Germany. German newspapers, in turn, reprinted the positive Italian reviews at great length, fueling interest in the film at home.[10] Before the film could be shown in West Germany, however, it was evaluated and rated by the film industry's censorship board (*Freiwillige Selbstkontrolle der Filmwirtschaft*, or FSK). The Central Committee of the FSK decided to endorse the film's release for adult audiences, but only over the objections of the censorship board's Working Committee. Echoing the conclusions of the Foreign Office, the Working Committee of the FSK argued that the vicious portrayal of the "deplorable state of affairs" among an entire social class of German men would be perceived as fact by international audiences and would thus damage the political reputation of West Germany. Furthermore, the Committee contended that the film presented a "primer" in prostitution that endorsed women's pursuit of fortune by immoral and exploitative means "under the sign of the *Wirtschaftswunder*."[11] Anxieties about gender roles, economics, and the unstable political identity of the emergent West German nation were conflated in the objections articulated by these censorship documents.

While the FSK endorsed the film's release despite these objections, it demanded two changes to *The Girl Rosemarie*. The filmmakers were asked to add a new "preface" to the film, a disclaimer of its accurate depiction of events despite the fact that it was based on a true story. More significant was the censorship of a montage sequence that accompanied one of the film's most critical songs, a point I will return to below. The lengthy censorship documents that were generated about the relationship between sound and image in this sequence suggest that contemporary spectators took notice of the film's formal innovations.

A duly altered version of *The Girl Rosemarie* premiered in the Federal Republic at Frankfurt's Europa Cinema on August 28, 1958. While reviewers expressed mixed opinions about the success of the film's critical satire, most agreed that the formal qualities of the film represented an achievement when compared with the majority of popular German films.[12] Writing in the *Süddeutsche Zeitung*, Friedrich Luft criticized what he saw as the film's ineffective satire, but he praised its artistic construction:

> In terms of form and content, there are impressive moments. The outstanding Klaus Rautenfeldt's camera, which uses symbols well, captures macabre points of view in order to make social contrasts visible. The tiresome wanderings of a certain new German class of busybodies are often displayed with nightmarish precision. The dialogues at times demonstrate an apercu-like double entendre that is remarkable. It is not often that one hears the like coming out of our cinema loud speakers. The director Thiele has prepared transitions that are optical delicacies harking back to the most

courageous epochs of German film. Expression is attempted <through> visual imagery. Visual effects evoke time lapses, creating optical pleasures again and again.[13]

Reviewers repeatedly compared *The Girl Rosemarie* to *The Threepenny Opera*, placing its use of songs to disrupt and comment on the narrative within a Brechtian tradition of alienation effects and also connecting this aspect of the film to the popular tradition of cabaret.[14] While Luft argues that the distantiation produced by these songs ultimately plays down the film's critical message, he does emphasize that the film's use of sound and music contributes to its success on a formal level. Indeed, Thiele and composer Norbert Schulze built on traditions of German film music as well as new elements borrowed from Hollywood in creating a soundtrack that would appeal to contemporary viewers. At the same time, they worked together with sound engineer Erwin Schänzle to create prominent and unusual sound effects that served as a hallmark of the film's attempt to break with convention and develop new formal innovations.

I

In his book *The Sounds of Commerce*, Jeff Smith describes the 1950s as a decade in which movie goers experienced a fundamental transformation of Hollywood scoring practice, in large part due to what Smith identifies as the rise of the pop soundtrack. While the scores of classic Hollywood cinema were dominated by classical-romantic background music that remained nearly inaudible to spectators, pop scores elevated the status of musical sounds so that they became virtually equal to visual elements within the cinematic experience.[15] A similar transition in film music had already occurred in Germany almost ten years earlier. While Nazi cinema had strongly adhered to its own inflection of the classical-romantic film score, the collapse of the Nazi filmmaking apparatus after 1945 brought an end to the hegemonic romantic soundtrack. Eager to catch up with the rest of the world, German consumers articulated a demand for diverse styles of popular music that had been banned or restricted during the Nazi period. Whereas visual representation was subject to intense public scrutiny after the iconophilia of fascism, as we have seen for example in the case of debates about abstract art, a wide range of musical styles shaped the acoustic landscape of postwar Germany.

In this environment, German filmmakers responded by integrating the performance of popular music into film narratives. In the rubble films, performances of jazz, swing, and cabaret songs are common, and the *Heimatfilme* of the early 1950s often feature diegetic performances by choral groups and wandering minstrels. Though *Heimatfilm* scores were often vehicles for the resurrection of German folk songs, they also typically included other types of popular music, including jazz and swing, contrasting the modernity of the latter's style with the traditionalism of the folk songs.

By the mid-1950s the presence of folk songs and light orchestral compositions began to give way to the musical model presented in recent Hollywood films like Richard Brooks's *The Blackboard Jungle* (1955), which used rock and roll and jazz music to attract young audiences and authenticate its gritty visual realism.[16] This move to adapt American popular musical styles and Hollywood compositional strategies to German film in the second half of the 1950s accompanied the larger transition in the film industry toward new genres, as the *Heimatfilm* was replaced by the vacation film, the crime film, the problem film, and the urban comedy, among others. In addition to staple jazz and swing numbers, these films frequently included compositions or standard hits by American musicians. The most sustained attempt to apply the Hollywood model to the domestic film market came in the uniquely German genre of the *Schlagerfilm*, an adaptation of the mainstream Hollywood "teenager film." *Schlagerfilme* like *Tutti Frutti* (1957) and *Wenn die Conny mit dem Peter ...* (When Conny and Peter ..., 1958)—like *The Girl Rosemarie*, one of the top ten films of 1958—were built around performances of rock and roll and exhibited the latest dance crazes.

As we have seen, West German films throughout the 1950s, like Hollywood films from the same era, evidenced a broad range of aural strategies that contributed to their spectatorial appeal. "Modern" music (from jazz to rock to early electronic music) shows up in many mainstream films, generally evoking that which is threatening, disruptive, or unconventional. In *The Forester of the Silver Wood* and *Different From You and Me*, swing and electronic music are clearly characterized as perverse, but they also provide aural and visual pleasure. In these films and others, sonic strategies open up multiple and sometimes contradictory spaces of reception. Though popular music often familiarizes the exotic and facilitates structures of identification, it also distorts habitual perceptions and suggests the uncanniness of familiar images to the spectator. In the case of *The Girl Rosemarie*, the filmmakers at times employ sound and music predictably, as a means of appealing to spectators used to diegetic performances of popular songs. At other times, they implement both unconventional sound effects and music in order to undermine mainstream cinematic language and highlight the film's critical message about the immorality and hypocrisy of the new affluent society. Thus the use of sound in *The Girl Rosemarie* is indicative of the film's transitional status at the moment of postwar popular cinema's imminent decline.

Like other mainstream films from the period, *The Girl Rosemarie* evidences traits typical of the 1950s Hollywood "pop soundtrack": it combines traditional musical components, popular songs built around hooks, diegetic musical performances, and modern stylistic elements taken from jazz and swing. The film's songs, which proved both catchy and controversial, were an essential tool in the marketing campaign for *The Girl Rosemarie*. Promotional stills showed Nadja Tiller together with Mario Adorf and Jo Herbst, posed with their musical instruments, and the press kit included a reprint of all the song lyrics. In contrast to the contemporary trend toward the inclusion of American-style film music, however, Thiele and composer Norbert Schultze instead resuscitated two German traditions for the score: cabaret-style music, associated with the rubble films as well as with the tradition of Weimar cinema, and the folksy idiom of roving musicians, typical of the *Heimatfilm*. The resounding success of *The Girl Rosemarie* can be attributed in part to the film's strategy of recycling musical conventions familiar from popular genres throughout the postwar period.

Written by Herbst and Rolf Ulrich, the film's cabaret-style songs put a modern spin on the dissonant tonal compositions associated with Weimar-era musical and theatrical traditions.[17] Like Kurt Weill's compositions for *The Threepenny Opera*, Herbst and Ulrich's songs incorporate various popular idioms taken from jazz, swing, ballads, military marches, dance hall music, and commercial folk songs. Compositionally diverse, the songs range from simple folk ballads for banjo, accordion, and trombone, to swing numbers performed by showgirls in the local gentleman's club, to more complex compositions that present a pastiche of disparate musical styles.

Several of Herbst and Ulrich's songs recall nothing so much as Friedrich Hollaender's compositions for Josef von Sternberg's *Der blaue Engel* (The Blue Angel, 1930), a film that *The Girl Rosemarie* clearly references both in individual scenes and in its larger narrative trajectory. Like *The Blue Angel*, *The Girl Rosemarie* narrates the construction of a female persona that both conforms to and threatens dominant male fantasies. Both films address issues of female sexuality in the context of class mobility and transgression. However, in *The Blue Angel*, narrative authority and audience sympathy for the most part lie with Professor Rath, who dies at the end of the film. By contrast, like other postwar films, *The Girl Rosemarie* is not structured around male narrative authority, but rather produces audience sympathy and identification with the prostitute Rosemarie.

Dressed in a bow tie and top hat like Lola Lola (Marlene Dietrich) in *The Blue Angel*, the showgirl Do (Karin Baal) in *The Girl Rosemarie* performs a racy Dietrich impersonation that ends in a strip show (see figure 9.1). In contrast to Dietrich's "Falling in Love Again," however, Do dances to a song sung by the bar's proprietress called "Boredom," a slow swing number whose musical style is sexy, but whose lyrics are far from seductive: "<Boredom> sits next to you in an evening dress / Mixes you a cocktail of uncertainty / Fills your glass with melancholy / Kisses you with lips so cold and pale … / Boredom has many eyes at night / But all

Figure 9.1 Problematizing the spectacle: Do (Karin Baal) performs a striptease to the song "Boredom" in *The Girl Rosemarie*. Source: Deutsche Kinemathek.

the eyes are dead and blind!"[18] Like "Boredom," the lyrics to songs throughout *The Girl Rosemarie* typically enunciate a critique of the visual spectacle taking shape on screen: the spectatorial relationship to Do's striptease, both within the diegetic space of the nightclub and for the audience in the cinema, is necessarily problematized by the song's accusation about "dead and blind" eyes. In the case of "Boredom," however, this critique stands in tension with the popular musical styles of the song. If "Boredom" articulates the perspective of a woman who is fed up with the sexual role she is compelled to play as the object of the voyeuristic gaze, this textual message is partially defused by the associations suggested by the song's slow, rhythmic sounds. Numbers such as this one, which combined a critical apprehension of gender relations with familiar elements of popular music, contributed strongly to the film's commercial viability and eventual success.

In addition to its accessible soundtrack, *The Girl Rosemarie* also used a second aural strategy to underscore its criticism of the immorality of the *Wirtschaftswunder*. Time and again, ominous, disorienting synthetic sounds accompany visual images that evoke wealth and power: a line of black Mercedes cars, the revolving doors of a luxury hotel, the elevator of Rosemarie's chic apartment complex. The diegetic noise made by each of these mechanisms is abstracted and musically embellished: rhythmic sets of processed sounds, produced with a tone generator or primitive synthesizer, replace the mechanical sounds of the engines, door, and elevator.[19] The taped, filtered, and electronically processed noises are aurally decoupled from their sources, but remain visually connected by the presence of the sources on screen. Like the song texts, the warped soundtrack functions as a distantiation effect, signifying the artifice of the spectacle on screen. These menacing tones further evoke the Cold War climate of surveillance that is the subtext of the film.

II

The opening sequence of *The Girl Rosemarie* establishes a series of aural and visual links that will recur throughout the film. Rosemarie enters the lobby of the luxury hotel through the revolving doors whose ominous whooshing implies that something is amiss. The diegetically motivated noise of the doors is a rhythmically modulated set of two electronically processed flat tones that resembles an inhalation and exhalation, or a decelerated, flanged radar blip. The first is a wheezy bass tone that steadily rises in pitch; it is followed by a muted blast of white noise, and then by a sliding, reverberating treble tone that falls in pitch. This set of tones is repeated in a rhythm that evokes the pneumatic turning of the doors, but the rhythm picks up and slows down independently of the doors' actual pace. The sound is clearly linked to the doors, but its abstraction of their noise verges on the musical. The aural space created by this distorted noise clashes with the naturalistic sound space that characterizes the rest of the film, an effect that immediately draws the spectator's attention to the soundtrack of *The Girl Rosemarie*. The intermittent moments of emphatically synthetic sound also stand in tension with the realist visual style of the film, thereby denaturalizing the film's images.

The concierge is shocked that Rosemarie has dared to penetrate the space of the hotel, and he scuttles over to throw her out. As she walks out of the hotel, the camera pans down Rosemarie's body to close in on her legs and high heels, and the title of the film appears on screen. As the credits continue, the soundtrack shifts to foreboding modern music, an atonal composition featuring haunting woodwinds. We see external shots of Frankfurt in the thrall of the *Wirtschaftswunder*: the facades of brand new buildings, neon signs, the sparkle and glow of life in the affluent late 1950s. The music's jazzy tempo matches the pace of the montage, but its sinister tones stand in tension with the upbeat images. Like the sound of the revolving doors, the music mediates the visual spectacle of the luxurious signifiers of reconstruction, underscoring their artifice. The soundtrack abruptly shifts to a popular, folksy instrumental arrangement featuring accordion and banjo, an aural cut away from modern music to a more traditional—and more conventionally German—sound. The camera focuses on a bombed-out building and slowly pans down its exterior, in a shot that parallels the previous pan down Rosemarie's body,

Figure 9.2 Rosemarie (Nadja Tiller) and the street musicians (Mario Adorf and Jo Herbst). Source: Deutsche Kinemathek.

thus establishing a link between the female figure and the rubble of the building: neither has been reconstructed, neither reflects the glamorous sheen of the *Wirtschaftswunder*.

Next, the camera tracks down from the bombed-out building to the music's diegetic source: the street musicians, whose song ends with the words, "Yes, the blossoms of our Miracle shine brightly in neon light. And if you fail to pluck them, you'll always remain a poor mite." The implication of the lyrics is clear as the film cuts away to a shot of Rosemarie, who hopes to profit from the *Wirtschaftswunder*, a point that is underscored by the soundtrack's return to jazzy modern music (see figure 9.2). Back in front of the hotel, a long line of black Mercedes cars race by, producing a warped, synthetic sound like that of the revolving doors in the hotel lobby. Again, though the noise is diegetically motivated by the cars, what we hear is a processed and synthetic abstraction of engine noise.

The soundtrack thus stands in tension with the film's realist visual style throughout the entire opening sequence of *The Girl Rosemarie*. While the image track focuses on material signifiers of wealth and power, manifesting the scopophilia of a socioeconomic order obsessed with turning rubble to riches, the soundtrack—whether diegetic music or nondiegetic sound effect—signifies that things are not always as they appear. Fragmenting conventional synchronization of sound and image, Thiele draws attention to the hollowness of the postwar spectacle as well as the bankruptcy of dominant cinematic language.

As the opening sequence makes clear, *The Girl Rosemarie* maps the rags-to-riches transformation of the Federal Republic in the 1950s onto the body of a prostitute. Along with other postwar narratives, Thiele's film thus turns to female experience as a means of addressing both social and representational problems. Like the women of the rubble films, Rosemarie wears a wrinkled trench coat at the outset of the film. As the narrative proceeds, her image is slowly reconstructed; in one of the film's final sequences, a party held by the industry bosses that Rosemarie crashes, we witness her wearing a remarkably expensive Dior dress. If the trench coat linked her to the street and the crumbling facades of the rubble, the Dior dress marks her arrival in the upper echelons of the nouveau riche, her move from the street into the private sphere, and the transformation of her body into a luxury commodity. This party is the pinnacle of Rosemarie's success, but at the same time it marks her imminent decline. Of course she has not really arrived—as a prostitute, she will never truly transcend class boundaries, and she is punished by death for her attempt to do so. In this sense, the Dior dress, with its layers of glistening and translucent fabric, serves as yet another marker for the false sheen of the *Wirtschaftswunder*.

The film utilizes acoustic devices to narrate Rosemarie's transformation as well. In the opening sequence, she sings with the street musicians, and she is thereby linked to the traditional music they perform. The synthetic, distorted sounds that accompany her attempt to enter the luxury hotel in this sequence highlight her transgression of class boundaries. As she moves up in the world, Rosemarie rejects the street musicians and their music. She becomes rich and truly glamorous only through her use of a modern sound apparatus, the tape recorder. She seeks to consolidate her entry into the upper class by taking control of the tapes and refusing to turn them over to the cartel. However, like the transition from trench coat to Dior dress, the move from cabaret music to modern sound apparatus indicates the superficiality of Rosemarie's transformation.

The tape recorder was a relatively new commodity on the German market in 1958. Though it was based on magnetic recording technology invented by German engineers in the early 1940s, the tape recorder was developed for the home market by an American company, the Brush Development Corporation, which released its first models in the United States in 1946. In creating its small, portable reel-to-reel recorders, Brush relied on technical information obtained by the American army from German industrial records after Germany's defeat.[20] As the market for durable goods opened up in West Germany in the mid-1950s, the tape recorder was sold next to televisions, radios, and stereo equipment. Like the television that Hartog gives Rosemarie to distract her from the boredom of living in isolation as his kept woman, the tape recorder manufactures only illusions for Rosemarie. When she is lonely late at night, she plays back the voices of her patrons, editing out their diatribes about business and listening only to the compliments they pay her. As the film suggests, the modern technical apparatuses that surround Rosemarie propel her illusory belief that she will be able to transcend her past and make it in the *Wirtschaftswunder*.

The representation of both fashion and consumer durables therefore functions as a central conduit in *The Girl Rosemarie* for demonstrating the critical connections among gender, modernization, denazification, and the Cold War in the Adenauer Era. The film displays the way in which the rapid modernization of everyday life in Europe during the 1950s (not least through the sudden influx of consumer goods) sought to create a privatized and depoliticized culture of consensus. As Kristin Ross has argued in her well-known analysis of postwar France, consumer modernity sought to create a broad middle stratum that would paper over distinctions of sex, class, race, and ethnicity. However, as Ross demonstrates, modernization was of course "a *means* of social, and particularly racial, differentiation" closely linked in France to the story of decolonization.[21] In the case of postwar West Germany, Erica Carter has documented how the consuming *woman* in particular figured significantly in the symbolic reconstruction of the Federal Republic.[22] Not only was the figure of the rational housewife mobilized to effect the economic rebuilding and cultural modernization of the nation, but the female consumer was also deployed ideologically in the project of creating a Western national identity differentiated from both Nazi Germany and the GDR. Drawing on these associations, *The Girl Rosemarie* portrays consumerism as a central political problem for the Federal Republic, whose immense prosperity can hardly mask the corruption and oppression at its core.

III

Sound in *The Girl Rosemarie* suggests events and associations that the film's realist visual style cannot fully represent. The film's soundtrack works in tension with its conventional images, a strategy that allowed the filmmakers to capitalize on the appeal of dominant cinema, while also distancing themselves from mainstream representational styles that were increasingly subject to censure in the late 1950s. In one of the film's most controversial sequences, visual images, sonic distortion, and cabaret music form a dense web of associations connected to consumerism that encapsulate the film's critical message.

Hartog has returned from his first night with Rosemarie to his sister Magda's hotel room. Magda pokes fun at Hartog for being "in love" and warns him about neglecting his professional responsibilities. One of Hartog's colleagues enters the room, wishing to discuss a business matter. The colleague tells him only that "it has to do with this French business." At this precise moment, Hartog's gaze crosses a reproduction of Manet's

Olympia that hangs over the bed in the hotel room. The camera follows his gaze, zooming in on the nude prostitute in the picture in a fast, zigzagging motion that is particularly striking in a film that is otherwise visually conventional. Hartog's colleague tells him that the business is worth "50 million dollars" and mentions the name Fribert in connection with spying. When their conversation is interrupted by Magda, Hartog's gaze returns to the nude Olympia, and a reverberating, synthetically processed ringing sound on the aural track draws the viewer's attention to the significance of this conversation. This scene establishes for the first time in the film connections among money, sex, power, and rearmament that will subsequently shape the rest of the narrative. Nondiegetic noise here highlights the continuity between Hartog's illicit patronage of a prostitute and his role in illicit business practices. At the same time, it implicates Rosemarie herself in the process and project of spying.

A dissolve from the Manet reproduction reveals Rosemarie in her apartment, posed on a divan in the same manner as Olympia. The time is five weeks later, and Horst and Walter are visiting Rosemarie for a pay-off. They threaten to blackmail her if she does not come through with more money. Throughout the film, the shady business dealings of legitimate captains of industry are echoed by the pimps' financial arrangements with Rosemarie, in an intersecting narrative that points to the economic opportunism that transcended class divides during the *Wirtschaftswunder*. Hartog drives up just as the two men are leaving Rosemarie's building. He offers them a tip to carry some things upstairs: a radio, a television, and a kitchen mixer. As they carry these emblematic consumer goods to Rosemarie's apartment, they sing the film's most viciously satirical song, "Kanal: voll!"[23] An indictment of excessive consumption during the *Wirtschaftswunder*, the song protests the remilitarization of the Federal Republic and its role in strengthening economic prosperity. The song begins when Walter turns on the radio he is carrying upstairs and tunes it to a station that is playing brass marching band music. Horst and Walter march upstairs in time to the music and sing the song, which begins:

We haven't nearly—we haven't nearly—
We haven't nearly had our fill!
We've achieved prosperity overnight,
We're playing in major and no longer in minor!
A radio appliance, a mixing appliance,
In every household a television appliance!
Gem on the hand, Picasso on the wall,
Too bad we burned *Mein Kampf*.

We love pomp and high finance,
Advertising, snobs and arrogance.

> And here a mink coat and there a mink coat,
> And the bells of freedom in our hearts!
>
> Out of social feelings and a sense of community,
> We quickly build an insurance agency.
> And here a bank and there a bank,
> And we manage ourselves till we're sick![24]

As they sing these lyrics, the musicians stop on the landing of the stairs and plug in the television. Images of banks and mink coats flash across the television screen. The two men then continue marching in step up the stairs, delivering the goods to Rosemarie. The tune of the song now shifts to a military march built around a citation from the "Badenweiler Marsch"—one of the most prominent pieces of military music during the Nazi period—and at this moment the film cuts to documentary footage of marching boots. Another cut reveals the helmeted heads of soldiers who now march past Horst and Walter as they sing the rest of the song. This citation of the "Badenweiler Marsch" makes not only a clear aural reference to Nazism, but a visual one as well: the documentary images of uniformed men marching immediately recall the penultimate sequence from Leni Riefenstahl's *Triumph des Willens* (Triumph of the Will, 1935), the procession to the strains of the "Badenweiler Marsch" of Hitler, other prominent Nazi party members, and the SS through the streets of Nuremberg towards the end of the Nazi Party rally.

The "Kanal: voll!" sequence of *The Girl Rosemarie*—through its montage of Nazi music and imagery as well as in its lyrics—foregrounds the extent to which the affluent society of the 1950s is predicated on the Nazi past. What is more, the critique articulated by this sequence suggests that excessive consumption and prosperity are ultimately as morally questionable as sex for sale. It should therefore come as no surprise that the FSK objected so fiercely to "Kanal: voll!" Demanding a number of cuts, including most prominently the removal of a scene showing marching soldiers from the newly reconstituted West German army (*Bundeswehr*), the FSK wrote:

> The working committee of the FSK ... held the removal of this scene necessary because the Federal Armed Forces, as a constitutional state establishment of the Federal Republic of Germany, is degraded by the popular song sung by street musicians in the named scene, and because, through the inclusion of the Federal Armed Forces, a generalization of the circumstances criticized by the film is shown and therefore an effect is called forth that is detrimental to the reputation of Germany.[25]

The tortured language of the document never explicitly names the "circumstances criticized by the film." Specifically, the censors refer to neither the song's musical citation of the "Badenweiler Marsch" nor the mention of Hitler in the song's lyrics—"too bad we burned *Mein Kampf*"—both explicit references to the Nazi past that are unusual in films from the period. The document suggests, however, that the censors objected primarily to the connections posited by the film between illicit sex, rearmament, and the *Wirtschaftswunder*, a constellation that is made clear throughout this sequence.

IV

In the "Kanal: voll!" sequence and throughout Thiele's film—as in many other postwar films—issues of gender and sexuality are allegorically linked to larger social and political problems. In particular, *The Girl Rosemarie* responded to the debate over rearmament and remilitarization that reached its pinnacle in 1958, the year of the film's release. From early on, the Adenauer government had been open to the idea of remilitarization within the framework of Western European military cooperation. With the advent of the Korean War and the escalation of the Cold War, the question of a new German army became more urgent, and in light of these events the Western Allies, who had originally opposed remilitarization, now changed their policies. From the outset, not only the Social Democratic Party but also the general public opposed remilitarization. Objections centered on the potential role of rearmament in preventing the hoped-for reunification of the two German states as well as on fears about atomic warfare.

Nonetheless, in 1955, Adenauer's Christian Democratic Union succeeded in securing a majority of votes in parliament for the Paris Accords, which included the entry of the Federal Republic into NATO. The Adenauer government subsequently provided for the re-establishment of the *Bundeswehr*; in 1956, it formed the first troops and implemented compulsory military service for all men. In April of 1957, Adenauer declared publicly that he was in favor of arming the *Bundeswehr* with atomic weapons, a declaration that led to mass protests in the Federal Republic. By the spring of 1958, when parliament endorsed the armament of the *Bundeswehr* with atomic weapons within the framework of NATO, organized protests against atomic warfare took place in all the major cities of West Germany. Not only did *The Girl Rosemarie* respond to (and profit from) this climate of outrage against German remilitarization among the wider public, but the film exposed the degree to which the successes of the *Wirtschaftswunder* were fueled precisely by rearmament, the escalating Cold War, and, in general, Germany's failure to learn the lessons of its Nazi past.

The film's critical exposé of rearmament as a central facet of the *Wirtschaftswunder* is underscored by one further sequence that reiterates the connections between illicit arms deals and illicit sex. Fribert and

Rosemarie visit the industry boss Bruster, who takes them on a tour of his factory. Fribert attempts to enter a door marked "No entry for unauthorized personnel." An employee prevents him from gaining access to the room, but Bruster promises to show him something much more interesting instead. Outside, in front of the factory, Bruster presents a missile that he has covered in gold leaf to memorialize the fact that the site of his factory was razed by Allied bombs in 1945. Fribert asks if the bomb was American, and Bruster replies, "But of course! It had the words 'Greetings from Morgenthau' emblazoned on it. But they were mistaken. Now we export to ninety-two countries!" Bruster refers, of course, to Henry Morgenthau, Franklin D. Roosevelt's Secretary of Treasury, whose plan would have demilitarized, politically decentralized, and economically disenfranchised Germany after World War II in the interest of preventing it from re-emerging as a world power. Bruster's gloating statement suggests not only the scope of his (and the Federal Republic's) renewed power, but also the potential danger inherent in that power. As Bruster utters these words, Fribert photographs Rosemarie together with the missile. "Two golden bombshells," Bruster comments, suggesting that those who traffic in arms traffic in women as well.

In addition to the problem of rearmament and remilitarization, female sexuality in *The Girl Rosemarie* is also linked to ongoing anxieties about gender roles and women's emancipation in the late 1950s. Like many films about prostitution, *The Girl Rosemarie* thematizes the conflicted issue of women's social and economic mobility. One central objection that certain censors posed concerned the film's ostensible suggestion that not only male industry bosses but also working women could benefit substantially from the climate of immoral profit-mongering fostered by the *Wirtschaftswunder*. As the censorship documents put it, "<T>he film shows a striking modern means of advancement for young women and girls. The career of Rosemarie Nitribitt could, precisely as a result of its matter-of-fact representation <in the film>, be seen by many labile characters as a tutorial in fornication for profit."[26] This was seen as a particularly dangerous message at a moment when women were increasingly rejecting the familial role the state envisioned for them in the 1950s, and at a time when constitutional equality for women was hotly debated in the Federal Republic.

In the late 1940s, many German women had quit working. Some voluntarily left to devote themselves to their families after the upheavals of wartime and others were forced out of jobs to make way for men returning from war and imprisonment. According to the historian Eva Kolinsky, in 1950 only 8.5 million women were employed in West Germany, the lowest number since World War I.[27] But as Klaus-Jörg Ruhl has documented, this number increased significantly beginning in the mid-1950s when the *Wirtschaftswunder* created a huge demand for workers, and women once again sought employment outside the home in large numbers. Contrary to dominant ideas about the period, in fact more women were employed by the end of the Adenauer Era (1963) than at any time in the postwar period, including the immediate postwar years.[28] Significantly, however, the state repeatedly attempted to lure women back into the private sphere, for example through social policies that provided incentives for reproduction.

The Girl Rosemarie presented a threatening image of a woman who climbs the social ladder through shrewd business dealings. Of course, Rosemarie is ultimately punished with death for her attempt to transgress the social and economic strictures of patriarchal culture. In contrast to earlier films of the decade, whose heroines virtually always prevail in the end, Thiele's film exposes the fact that Rosemarie's fate actually lies in the hands of men. Consistent with the film's social critical message, *The Girl Rosemarie* offers neither satisfactory closure on Rosemarie's story nor solutions to the social conflicts that shape it. Rather, Rosemarie ultimately serves as an example of the hypocrisy and double moral standard of a society that rewards men for profiting from immoral behavior, while punishing women for doing the same.

As we have seen, women in postwar German cinema were often granted a unique degree of narrative authority, including control of the gaze and mastery of visual and aural codes. As in *The Murderers Are Among Us* and *The Sinner*, postwar films often contrasted gendered modes of vision, with male characters manifesting a disturbed gaze and female characters demonstrating a marked visual acuity. The narrative of *The Girl Rosemarie* quite self-consciously revolves around Rosemarie's control of aural codes and visual codes, as demonstrated, for example, by her use of the tape recorder, as well as her manipulation of the spectacle of her own body for profit. However, in the film's penultimate sequence, Rosemarie's death is foreshadowed in a remarkable scene that grants her subjective point-of-view shots only to narrate her loss of control, thereby underscoring at the level of both form and content the film's analysis of gender inequities in the 1950s.

In this sequence, Rosemarie goes to the Rialto Bar to confront the members of the cartel, who have demanded that she turn over the tapes containing their industry secrets. In desperation, Rosemarie makes a last-ditch effort to blackmail Hartog into marrying her in exchange for the tapes. When she realizes that this plan has failed, Rosemarie gets drunk. Emphasizing both her drunkenness and the film's message about the circularity of history and the lack of progress in postwar Germany, the camera moves in swirling, circular figures throughout this sequence. Twirling the drunken Rosemarie around in circles to the music, Fribert asks her, "Are you getting drunk in order to see more clearly?" As Fribert's comment suggests, Rosemarie's drunken loss of control finally indicates her recognition that she does not have power over her own destiny, or even her own image. Instead, despite her best efforts, as a woman and a prostitute she remains a victim of patriarchal oppression.

In the same scene, Rosemarie rips the glasses off the face of the man who has accompanied her to the bar, a Jehovah's Witness whom she has befriended. This gesture suggests her recognition that, despite his piety, this man is no different from the others who objectify and exploit her. Dancing obscenely with him, Rosemarie begins to sing very loudly, explicitly making a spectacle of herself. The camera's excessive circular movement creates a dizzying effect, which is underscored by a lengthy point-of-view shot from Rosemarie's perspective showing the Jehovah's Witness in blurry triplicate. Contrasting Rosemarie's willful loss of visual mastery with the cold, objectifying gazes of the male characters who surround her, this sequence demonstrates Rosemarie's desperate rebellion against their exploitation. By making a spectacle of herself, Rosemarie calls attention to the commodification of her body in a grotesque parody of conventional gender relations on screen. Markedly inverting the gendered structure of the gaze that we have seen in other postwar films, *The Girl Rosemarie* invests its title character here with a drunken, disturbed mode of vision, while its male characters display a gaze both voyeuristic and calculating. Notably departing from the postwar commonplace of granting female characters the ability to see clearly, this sequence nonetheless uses the female gaze to critique both gender relations in the Federal Republic and the scopophilia of dominant cinema. Clearly foreshadowing Rosemarie's imminent death, this sequence also lays the groundwork for the film's unhappy ending and lack of resolution, elements that further distance *The Girl Rosemarie* from the popular genre cinema that preceded it.

The film's critical assessment of both postwar inertia and the commodification of the female body is echoed once again in an epilogue that brings the film full circle. In a repetition of the opening sequence, we see the aspiring prostitute Do, dressed in a trench coat and high heels, standing outside the Palast Hotel and singing with Horst and Walter. She enters the hotel through the whooshing revolving doors, and the concierge throws her out, using the same words with which he dismissed Rosemarie at the outset of the film. The camera pans down Do's legs, and the screen fades to black, suggesting that Rosemarie's tragic death has failed to effect progress in a corrupt and rotten society.

The Girl Rosemarie articulates a biting appraisal of the West German consensus culture of the *Wirtschaftswunder* years through an analysis of gender relations at the level of both cinematic representation and social problems. By repeatedly foregrounding the sense in which both cinema and society are built on the exploitation of the female body, *The Girl Rosemarie* articulates a critical message that is new for the transitional cinema of the late 1950s. While the focus on female experience—the story of a female character played by a popular new star—spoke to the film's attempt to appeal to female spectators, its analytical message and formal innovations constituted a new stage for postwar women's cinema that prefigured the feminist *Frauenfilm* of the late 1960s and 1970s.

Notes

1. An earlier version of this chapter was published as "Sound Money: Aural Strategies in Rolf Thiele's *The Girl Rosemarie,*" in *Sound Matters: Essays on the Acoustics of German Culture*, ed. Nora Alter and Lutz Koepnick (New York, 2004), 91–103.
2. See Joseph Garncarz, "Hollywood in Germany. Die Rolle des amerikanischen Films in Deutschland: 1925–1990," in *Der deutsche Film. Aspekte seiner Geschichte von den Anfängen bis zur Gegenwart*, ed. Uli Jung (Trier, 1993), 203. Two of the eight West German films were international co-productions. Ticket sales in 1958 did decline slightly, with 750 million sold (12.1 visits to the movies per person). However, feature film production held steady, with 109 features made. See Hans Helmut Prinzler, *Chronik des deutschen Films 1895–1994* (Stuttgart, 1995), 218; and Elizabeth Prommer, *Kinobesuch im Lebenslauf. Eine historische und medienbiografische Studie* (Konstanz, 1999), 350.
3. According to Garncarz, *Das Mädchen Rosemarie* was the second most popular film of the 1958/59 season. Garncarz in Jung, *Der deutsche Film*, 203. The film also won the "Kassenschimmel" award in 1958/59, granted to the movie that booked the most dates in cinemas in sixteen key West German cities. See "'Das Mädchen Rosemarie' erfolgreichster deutscher Film," *Der Tagesspiegel*, January 3, 1960. Upon its American release, *Time* magazine called *The Girl Rosemarie* "the second most popular picture made in Germany since the war." See rev. of *Rosemary*, *Time*, February 8, 1960.
4. Larson Powell also focuses on the soundtrack's mixing of musical styles in his reading of the film's modernist citations, "Allegories of Management: Norbert Schulze's Sound Track for *Das Mädchen Rosemarie,*" in *Framing the Fifties: Cinema in a Divided Germany*, ed. John Davidson and Sabine Hake (New York, 2007), 180–93.
5. According to Jost Hermand, during the 1950s 70 percent of production in West Germany was in the hands of just 1.7 percent of the population, and 0.01 percent of the population owned one-third of commercial land and three-fourths of forest land. Hermand, *Kultur im Wiederaufbau. Die Bundesrepublik Deutschland 1945–1965* (Munich, 1986), 227. Hermand cites a newspaper report that states: "Altogether there are 94 men who, in their combined function in boards of trustees and boards of directors, control the great part of the German economy and determine employee politics for several million personnel and business politics for a sum of sales and acquisitions in the double digits of billions. Last but not least, these men are decisive for their donations to the election funds of the parties, to institutes for influencing public opinion, and to special interest advocacy groups." *Christ und Welt*, September 6, 1964, qtd. in Hermand, 227–28. *The Girl Rosemarie* proffers a strong critique of the influence wielded by this small group of men, emphasizing not only their immense economic power, but also their profiteering through rearmament, which the film indicts as morally loathsome in light of Germany's Nazi past.
6. See Marli Feldvoß, "Wer hat Angst vor Rosemarie Nitribitt? Eine Chronik mit Mord, Sitte und Kunst aus den fünfziger Jahren," in *Zwischen Gestern und Morgen. Westdeutscher Nachkriegsfilm 1946–1962*, ed. Hilmar Hoffmann und Walter Schobert (Frankfurt am Main, 1989), 164–82; and Erich Kuby, *Rosemarie—des deutschen Wunders liebstes Kind* (Stuttgart, 1958).
7. This dream team of filmmakers was well situated to score a hit with *The Girl Rosemarie*. A co-founder of the famous postwar periodical *Der Ruf*, Erich Kuby became one of the most important journalists of the 1950s, when he was especially well known as an outspoken critic of German rearmament and atomic weaponry. Luggi Waldleitner, one of the most successful film producers of the postwar period, was a co-founder of the important production and distribution company Gloria-Filmverleih and a producer for Berolina-Film before founding his own production company, Roxy-Film in 1951. Waldleitner later went on to produce several of Fassbinder's films, which were clearly influenced by both the visual style and plotline of *The Girl Rosemarie*. Rolf Thiele was the co-founder of the production company Filmaufbau (see chapter 3) and a highly successful producer in his own right before he turned to directing in the mid-1950s. A

trained sociologist, Thiele brought a critical eye for social content to his films, but he was best known for his focus on erotic subjects, and he eventually found success in the 1960s and 1970s with a series of softcore porn films.

8. On the various lawsuits, protests, and scandals surrounding the film, see a series of articles in *Spiegel*: "Nitribitt. Des Wunders liebstes Kind," *Spiegel* 12.18 (April 30, 1958): 50–52; "Nitribitt. Glückauf," *Spiegel* 12.33 (August 13, 1958): 44–45; and "Nitribitt. Die notwendige Klarheit," *Spiegel* 12.38 (September 17, 1958): 58–59. Kuby presents his own account of the scandal in *Alles über Rosemarie: Vom AA in Bonn bis Zensur* (Munich, 1958). Manfred Barthel provides an historical overview of the scandal in *Als Opas Kino jung war: Der deutsche Nachkriegsfilm* (Frankfurt, 1991), 351–57. See also "Das Mädchen Rosemarie II. Teil: Ein Film, der nicht gedreht wurde," *Weltbild* 21 (October 1, 1958).

9. According to Kuby, the reviewer from the Foreign Office, Dr. Rowas, "said that this bird Rosemarie—not the prototype, who was murdered in Frankfurt, you understand, but the film—fouls the German nest." See Kuby, *Alles über Rosemarie*, 3. Kuby actually dedicates his book to Rowas and the Foreign Office for giving the film so much free publicity.

10. See "Beifall für Mädchen Rosemarie," *Frankfurter Rundschau*, August 27, 1958; "Beifall für den Nitribitt-Film," *Ruhr-Nachrichten*, August 27, 1958; "Rolf Thiele will Selbstkritik üben," *Badisches Tageblatt*, August 27, 1958; "Rosemarie mit Berliner Ballade verglichen," *Der Kurier*, August 27, 1958; and "Rosemarie gefiel in Venedig," *Telegraf*, August 27, 1958.

11. Qtd. in Kuby, *Alles über Rosemarie*, 8.

12. Many reviewers criticized the film for relying on caricature rather than delving into the specificity of the social reality it sought to satirize. See for example Karena Niehoff, "Satire im Niemandsland," rev. of *Das Mädchen Rosemarie*, *Der Tagesspiegel*, September 3, 1958, rpt. in Hoffmann and Schobert, *Zwischen Gestern und Morgen*, 402.

13. Friedrich Luft, rev. of *Das Mädchen Rosemarie*, *Süddeutsche Zeitung*, August 27, 1958.

14. A comparison to the *Threepenny Opera* was first made in the Italian press and was echoed by reviewers in both the *Katholischer Film-Dienst* and the *Evangelischer Film-Beobachter*, among others. See rev. of *Das Mädchen Rosemarie*, *Katholischer Film-Dienst*, September 4, 1958, 328–29; and rev. of *Das Mädchen Rosemarie*, *Evangelischer Film-Beobachter*, September 4, 1958, 425–26.

15. This breakthrough, as Smith argues, was a response to "a number of industrial, historical and sociological factors in the 1950s and early 1960s, including the trend toward diversification and conglomeration in film distribution, the emergence of studio-owned record labels, the establishment of radio and records as important ancillary markets, and changes in popular music tastes and consumption patterns." Jeff Smith, *The Sounds of Commerce: Marketing Popular Film Music* (New York, 1998), 2. See also Russell Lack, *Twenty Four Frames Under: A Buried History of Film Music* (London, 1997).

16. *Blackboard Jungle* was both immensely popular and controversial in Germany, as Uta Poiger has documented. See Poiger, *Jazz, Rock, and Rebels: Cold War Politics and American Culture in a Divided Germany* (Berkeley, 2000), 85–91.

17. Indeed, Herbst and Ulrich, who performed as part of the well-known Berlin cabaret *Die Stachelschweine*, were recruited by Kuby and Thiele expressly to lend to the film their expertise with cabaret.

18. "Die Langeweile," *Lieder und Songs aus dem Roxy/ NF-Film* Das Mädchen Rosemarie (Munich, 1958), 7.

19. According to Karlheinz Stockhausen, the first real synthesizer (he mentions one developed by RCA in the U.S. in the mid-1950s) had not yet been imported to West Germany by 1958. While electronic instruments such as the melochord and the Trautonium had been in use in Germany for decades, composers and sound engineers generally used equipment that had been designed for other purposes when experimenting with synthetic sound. Commonly used equipment included noise

generators, sine-wave generators, electroacoustical generators, electronic filters, and synchronic tape recorders. See Karlheinz Stockhausen, "Electronic and Instrumental Music <1958>," trans. Ruth Hein, in *Postwar German Culture*, ed. Charles E. McClelland and Steven P. Scher (New York, 1974), 355–70. I have been unable to locate any information on the equipment used in producing the soundtrack to *The Girl Rosemarie*.

20. For a history of sound recording technologies in the U.S. such as the tape recorder, see David Morton, *Off the Record: The Technology and Culture of Sound Recording in America* (New Brunswick, NJ, 2000).

21. Kristin Ross, *Fast Cars, Clean Bodies: Decolonization and the Reordering of French Culture* (Cambridge, MA, 1995), 11.

22. Erica Carter, *How German Is She?: Postwar West German Reconstruction and the Consuming Woman* (Ann Arbor, 1997).

23. Literally translated "Canal: full!," the phrase usually occurs in reference to the excessive consumption of alcohol, but it can be extrapolated to mean excessive consumption in general.

24. "Lieder und Songs aus dem Roxy/NF-Film *Das Mädchen Rosemarie*," 4–5.

25. "Prüfverfahren betr.: Spielfilm 'Das Mädchen Rosemarie,'" 3, in file on *Das Mädchen Rosemarie*, Schriftgutarchiv, Stiftung deutsche Kinemathek, Berlin.

26. "Prüfverfahren," 1. This objection was raised by the overruled minority of censors, and though it appeared in the censorship documents, it did not become a primary criterion in the censorship or rating of the film.

27. Eva Kolinsky, *Women in West Germany: Life, Work, Politics* (Oxford, 1989), 37.

28. Klaus-Jörg Ruhl, ed., *Frauen in der Nachkriegszeit: 1945–1963* (Munich, 1988), 8.

Chapter 10

GENDER AND THE NEW WAVE: HERBERT VESELY'S *THE BREAD OF THOSE EARLY YEARS* (1962) AS TRANSITIONAL FILM

The year 1962 has generally been understood as a caesura in postwar filmmaking,[1] in large part due to the notorious "Oberhausen Manifesto," the declaration of twenty-six young filmmakers who proclaimed "the collapse of the conventional German film" on February 28, at the Oberhausen Short Film Festival.[2] Already in decline for some time, attendance at the movies did experience a further sharp fall in popularity in 1962. Only 443 million tickets were sold that year, 75 million less than the year before, and down by almost 50 percent since 1956. Similarly, only sixty-four feature films were produced in West Germany, half the number in production at the height of cinema's popularity in the mid-1950s.[3]

However, the question of conventional cinema's decline is a bit more complicated than these numbers suggest. Notably, commercial German-language films continued to retain a large market share of domestic ticket sales. In the 1961/62 season, seven of the top ten films were German, Austrian, or Swiss, and in the 1962/63 season, five of the top ten were German and one was Austrian.[4] As Tim Bergfelder points out:

> A closer look at the 1960s … reveals that, despite the legendary declaration of the "Oberhausen Manifesto" in 1962 of the death of "Daddy's cinema", for most of the decade it was the commercial cinema of popular indigenous and European genre cycles that dominated West German screens and audience preferences, until it was eventually sidelined in the early 1970s, not by the internationally acclaimed films of the New German Cinema, but by Hollywood.[5]

Although subsequent scholars have certainly perpetuated the myth that pre-Oberhausen German cinema was a vast wasteland, the perception of a radical shift in postwar filmmaking practice in the 1960s is not merely the product of film historiography. Rather, the notion of staging a transformation in postwar cinema was pioneered already in the 1950s by German cinephiles whose vocal advocacy of a new wave contributed to what became a nearly obsessive public discourse about the necessity of rejuvenating the German film landscape and thus relegitimating German cinema once and for all. As we have seen, German filmmakers had already begun to experiment with new subject matter and formal innovations during the transitional period of the late 1950s. By the early 1960s, these nascent experiments had helped generate a climate of anticipation surrounding new wave films. In this climate, the "Oberhausen Manifesto" itself was greeted with acclaim as the final chance for German cinema's rebirth.

The first new wave film to be released after the "Oberhausen Manifesto," Herbert Vesely's *Das Brot der frühen Jahre* occupies a liminal space between the popular cinema of the 1950s and the later productions of the New German Cinema. Adapted from a novella by Heinrich Böll, the film sought to appeal to mainstream audiences with a narrative about contemporary issues that incorporated generic aspects of the detective story and the love story, while encoding this narrative within formal structures emblematic of the emergent new wave.

Like Böll's novella, the film version of *The Bread of Those Early Years* tells the story of Walter Fendrich (Christian Doermer), a washing machine repairman who is successful at his job, engaged to his boss's daughter, and well on his way to bourgeois bliss in the West German *Wirtschaftswunder*. This all changes one day in March, when he falls in love with Hedwig (Karen Blanguernon), a girl from his hometown whom he picks up at the train station when she moves to the city. Through the intensity of emotion he experiences in his immediate love for Hedwig, Walter is able to recognize his alienation and reject the life he has been living. He renounces that life, failing to report to work and breaking off his engagement to his fiancée Ulla (Vera Tschechowa). Throughout the day, he remembers the time in the immediate postwar years when he was plagued by a constant hunger for bread, which Ulla and her family never gave him. Though the desire symbolized by this bread is what propelled Walter into the alienated life he now leads, it has only been sublimated. Through Hedwig, the narrative suggests, Walter finds access to his desire once again. With several exceptions, Vesely's film remains true to the narrative of Böll's novella. The film transposes the action of the story from Cologne (the implied setting of Böll's narrative) to divided Berlin.[6] Aside from one flashback sequence that projects images of Fendrich's childhood and features a voiceover by his father, the narrative is compressed into one day in the life of Fendrich, the day when Hedwig comes to town and he ditches his job and his fiancée to be with her.

The viewer of the film only comprehends this narrative fully by piecing together its fragments bit by bit. *The Bread of Those Early Years* is set up almost as a detective story, in which various characters, and by extension the viewers in the audience, are engaged in a quest for knowledge about the motivations for Walter's strange behavior on this day. The film is characterized by a fragmentary, repetitive narrative style and a strong disjuncture between what viewers see and hear. Only slowly can viewers begin to discover who Walter is, what it is that he has done, and why it is of consequence. Little by little, we hear different versions of Walter's story in a montage of sound and image that at times resembles a documentary in the way it presents these accounts to viewers.

Despite its attempt to unite conventional generic elements with avant-garde filmmaking strategies, however, *The Bread of Those Early Years* was by all accounts a resounding failure. The film's inability to appeal to either mainstream audiences or critics invested in a rejuvenation of the German film caused the co-signers of the "Oberhausen Manifesto" to rethink their strategy for future film productions.[7] Had the film been more successful in its attempt to mediate between the popular film culture of the 1950s and the theoretical possibility of a new, experimental cinema in the 1960s, German film history might have turned out differently. Thus the film provides insight into the failure of a new generation of filmmakers to create a cinema that could be aesthetically innovative and politically relevant while still appealing to domestic audiences.[8]

The Bread of Those Early Years premiered at the Cannes Film Festival on May 18, 1962. Much fanfare surrounded the premiere of the film, which had been publicized for months as the first production of the recently proclaimed New German Cinema. Responses at Cannes were muted, however, and after the film opened in Germany on May 23, at Cologne's Lux am Dom cinema, it was panned. "A Dream Has Ended," mourned Munich's *Abendzeitung*, and other reviewers agreed.[9] While *The Bread of Those Early Years* was shown widely in West German cinemas and even went on to win several Federal Film Prizes, its popular and critical reception was characterized by a discourse of failure. Critics were receptive to the film's experimental visual style and fragmented narrative, but reviewers in both mainstream newspapers and in film journals agreed about the film's primary faults. Not only did its attempt to espouse a new wave, avant-garde style appear synthetic, but the film was too "cold" and failed to capture emotion or create any possibilities for identification. Incessant comparisons to recent French new wave films, in particular Alain Resnais's *L'Année dernière à Marienbad* (Last Year at Marienbad, 1961), not only fueled embarrassment over the continuing provincialism of German cinema and resentment over the reaction to the film at Cannes, but they also highlighted the inadequacy of the film's borrowed formal qualities in dealing with its uniquely German content.[10] As one reviewer said of Vesely, "Instead of bread, he gives us papier-mâché petit-fours."[11]

The massive popular and critical backlash against Vesely's film was not entirely surprising given the immense expectations whipped up by the media and by the publicity campaign engineered for the film by the vocal young film critic Joe Hembus, who stressed the film's popular appeal as much as its experimental, "artistic" aspects.[12] Anticipation about the film was already high in January 1962, when the journal *Filmkritik* published an article about the production of *The Bread of Those Early Years* that concluded: "We will know in March <the projected release date of the film>, then, if the German film, despite all skepticism, is in fact in the position to make a contribution to world cinematography after all."[13] Then, in February, as shooting of the film wrapped, the "Oberhausen Manifesto" was proclaimed. Director Herbert Vesely was among those who signed the declaration, as were the film's producer Hansjürgen Pohland, the cameraman Wolf Wirth, and the principal actor Christian Doermer.

While their film had gone into production long before the "Manifesto" was written, the film was nonetheless quickly cast as the vanguard in the attack against "Daddy's cinema."[14] As the publicity campaign emphasized, the film was made for a measly DM 400,000 at a time when most films cost at least five times that amount. The cast and crew were industry outsiders, none of whom was over the age of thirty-five, save for Heinrich Böll, who adapted the dialogue from his novella. Extensive newspaper coverage during production provided an "insider's look" at the glamorous young rebels of the cast and crew on the set of the film, which was shot on location in West Berlin (see figure 10.1). Given the drama and excitement surrounding the production itself, and the rumor that it would be a radical departure from the typical cinematic fare of the day, it was almost a foregone conclusion that the film could not fulfill these expectations. Nonetheless, the fact that the film generated high expectations does not account for the venom of the censure to which it was subjected, nor for the actual content of the criticism leveled against it. By 1962, film critics routinely denied the sentimentality and melodramatic affect of popular German cinema; it is thus all the more ironic that one of their chief qualms with *The Bread of Those Early Years* was its emotional detachment and "coldness." Agreeing that the film was an optical tour de force, critics in publications as diverse as the leftist journal *Filmkritik*, the film-evaluation organ of the Protestant Church *Evangelischer Film-Beobachter*, and the teen fan magazine *Bravo* suggested that the film's failure to address spectators clearly, and the absence of possibilities for spectator identification, left audiences with no access to the social and historical critique of West Germany that the film meant to articulate.[15] A reviewer for the *Beratungsdienst Jugend und Film* put it this way: "The epic form of theater, the new attempt in literature to substitute the 'stream of consciousness' for plot: these certainly constitute a new task for film. But it cannot be carried out in such a cold and bloodless manner. For in this film, the feelings of the spectator are hardly addressed."[16]

The Bread of Those Early Years was not wholly successful in its filmic project, but in hindsight it is noteworthy for its attempt to mediate between two polarized ideas of what the cinema can or should be. Both historically and aesthetically, Vesely's film is poised between the mainstream domestic cinema of the 1950s and the emergent European

Figure 10.1 German cinema's vanguard: The glamorous young rebels of the cast and crew of *The Bread of Those Early Years*. Source: Deutsche Kinemathek.

avant-garde cinema. Responding to postwar calls for cinematic realism as well as the formal innovations of the new wave, the film sought to reconcile disparate film forms, including elements of neo-realism and a highly fragmented, abstract narrative structure. At the level of content, the film's story addresses the alienation of a younger generation of Germans in the postwar climate of renewal characteristic of the

Wirtschaftswunder. As we have seen in the case of other postwar films, gender is implicated both in this film's attempts to offer resolution to social and representational problems and in its reception.

Reviewers of *The Bread of Those Early Years* were particularly disturbed by Walter Fendrich's lack of agency and impotence in the face of the events that befall him. Unlike the Fendrich of Böll's novella, the Fendrich of the film is only granted limited agency in the events that take place, and limited authority in the narrative interpretation of these events. As such, the film does not inscribe possibilities for spectator identification with him. This was particularly disturbing to critics who hoped for a New German Cinema featuring strong male characters who would provide a contrast to the passive and lacking male characters of early postwar cinema. The angry young men who confronted the problematic filmic legacy of the 1950s with their "Oberhausen Manifesto" were expected to present mimetic versions of themselves on screen: young, potent subjects brimming with agency. Instead, many of the early post-Oberhausen productions, like *The Bread of Those Early Years*, depicted young men who seemed to mirror their filmic fathers in their passivity, crisis, and subjective oblivion.[17]

Indeed, *The Bread of Those Early Years* failed with audiences and critics alike in large part because of its narrative and formal ambivalence, reflecting an instability of gender roles as well as confusion about the categories of the avant-garde and the modern in the cinema. The prolific public discourse surrounding Vesely's film is based on a complex set of repressions and elisions of what is truly at stake in its critical and popular rejection, namely anxiety that the film, like so many of its precursors, once again grants narrative authority to its female characters. This anxiety is not only emblematic of larger social and political anxieties at a moment when the conservative climate of the Adenauer Era had reached its peak and the upheaval of the 1960s was beginning to emerge; more importantly, inasmuch as Vesely's film employed strategies of women's cinema characteristic of its postwar precursors, it failed to live up to the aspirations of the cinephiles, whose hope for the renewal of German cinema was predicated on a transformation of its gender politics. As such, an analysis of Vesely's film and the anxieties it produced sheds light on the vexed relationship of the New German Cinema to its more popular predecessors.

I

By no means a spontaneous action, the "Oberhausen Manifesto" responded to longstanding criticisms leveled against postwar cinema since the 1950s by critics such as Joe Hembus and the collective that published the cinephile journal *Filmkritik*. Influenced by Siegfried Kracauer's account of the passive men of Weimar cinema—best epitomized by characters with their bowed and defeated heads in their wives' sheltering laps—these critics placed postwar cinema in a continuum with the aesthetically and politically problematic films of the Weimar and Nazi periods that thematized the ongoing crisis of German male subjectivity.[18] Already in the late 1950s, they began to call for a new mode of filmmaking that would break with this problematic continuum that they eventually labeled "Daddy's cinema."

Emblematic of the gendered discourse surrounding new wave film, the idea of "Daddy's cinema" itself effects an interesting assertion and displacement of male authority. Taken literally, "Daddy's cinema" refers to the cinema produced by the generation of the fathers; indeed, there were few young film directors or producers during the 1950s and many of the most popular directors and producers had been active in the film industry during the Third Reich. Declaring "Daddy's cinema" dead was thus an Oedipal gesture on the part of a younger generation of men, who in so doing sought to assert their own (male) subjectivity.

At the same time, however, the derogatory label "Daddy's cinema" refers to certain formal and functional qualities embodied by 1950s German films that have typically been gendered female. In a side bar entitled "Daddy's Cinema—A Definition" in the March 1962 issue, *Filmkritik* defined these qualities by reprinting an advertisement from the studio Ufa-Film-Hansa (the caption gleefully notes that the studio went broke several weeks after the appearance of the ad):

Was wir unter Film verstehen:	*What Film means to us:*
Format und Farbe: verschwenderisch	Format and color: extravagant
Inbegriff unbegrenzter Unterhaltung	Ideal of boundless entertainment
Lösung aus den eigenen vier Wänden	Liberation from one's own four walls
Mehrerlebnis weil Massenerlebnis	More experience through mass experience[19]

This definition of "Daddy's cinema" references a series of feminized traits (boundless entertainment that induces a loss of subjectivity and feelings of oneness with the diegetic space of the film, liberation from the domestic sphere into the "mass experience" of cinema) that are linked to the mass cultural realm of modernity.[20] These traits are also closely associated with the female viewer's experience of film, at least since Kracauer's description of "the little shop girls" at the movies.[21] In this sense, the concept of "Daddy's cinema" also responds to the postwar strategy of appealing to female spectators with elements of women's cinema. Indeed, the push for a New German Cinema in the early 1960s was predicated on a gender realignment: a rejection of the feminized qualities of popular cinema and its compromised, passive male characters and an embrace of the new wave, with its associations of virile masculinity. Signed by a cadre of angry young men, the "Oberhausen Manifesto" clearly reproduced this correlation of the avant-garde and masculinity and thus appeared to initiate a transition in both film authorship and representation.

Barton Byg has suggested a connection between the gendered development of new wave cinema and the emergent Cold War. Byg argues that in as much as postwar films set in Berlin clearly represented male subjectivity in crisis in the wake of World War II, they demonstrated the need for the Cold War and its culture. According to Byg, the Cold War recuperated masculinity both by reasserting a nonproblematic military prowess differentiated from Nazism and by promoting a rejuvenation of cinema:

> Regarding the latter <the rejuvenation of cinema>, a cultural recuperation of masculinity emerged through film noir and the subsequent renewal of the institution of cinema, propelled by male-oriented critical appreciations of noir and Italian Neo-Realism, and resulting eventually in the "new waves" of European cinema. In one sense, all these cinematic movements can be seen as narrative ways of restoring the vitality of a masculinity left vulnerable in the wake of the war and the abdication or disgrace of the "fathers." In another, as "modernist" movements within the popular context of the cinema, they are examples of the masculine impulse in art to resist the threats posed by the feminine aspects of modernity/modernism.[22]

Byg's analysis implies that the task of new wave films was indeed to effect a double displacement of the problematic masculinity represented by the notion of "Daddy's cinema" as well as of the feminized aspects of mass modernity epitomized by the popular cinema of the 1950s.

While in the U.S. film noir emerged as a strategy for confronting emasculated men and aggressive women in the aftermath of the war, in Germany, as we have seen, male subjectivity became so marginal that it could not stand at the authoritative center of any filmic narrative. As Byg points out, "In the German films, the women cannot be shown as either physically weak or aggressive; instead their threat resides in the fact that the male characters are the weak ones."[23] This attribution to female characters of the traits lacking in their male counterparts continued to structure the representation of gender roles in German films even after the emergence of the new wave. In contrast to the new wave films of other national cinemas, early German new wave films rarely portrayed strong, modern women or addressed the disruption of traditional, binary gender roles in ways that moved beyond the kind of inversion we have seen in so many postwar films beginning with *The Murderers Are Among Us*.[24]

Similarly, in the ongoing attempt to dispense with the Nazi past and its problematic cultural heritage in order to relegitimate German cinema, new wave German filmmakers (again in contrast to their counterparts in other countries) ultimately found that the most successful strategy was to reinstate the absolute incompatibility of the popular and the avant-garde, or of mass culture and autonomous art.[25] This is arguably what the New German Cinema ultimately did, sacrificing the possibility of truly transforming West German film culture and reaching out to wider audiences, and instead setting itself up in opposition to the popular cinema of the 1950s, which it saw as residually fascistic mass culture. But this strategy only emerged slowly.

In the early 1960s, film culture found itself at a turning point in many respects. In the 1950s, the cinema had still provided one of the primary (public) spaces in which West Germans were able to express emotion openly. The melodramatic and sentimental films of the era had thematized social problems that faced many people, in particular women. As such, they had presented a space where audiences could contemplate public and private histories, and do so with emotion at a time when affect was being slowly drained from the public and private spheres, especially within the realm of visual culture, as symbolized by the rise of abstract art. By the late 1960s, cinema would lose this role in society, as the student movement made history a subject of public confrontation and the countercultures provided new forums for the public and private expression of emotion. The "Oberhausen Manifesto" hinted at this transformation in the role of cinema by emphasizing its contested status already in 1962.

Within this complex constellation of gendered expectations surrounding the emergence of a triumphant new cinema, *The Bread of Those Early Years* debuted as the first great hope of the German new wave. In short, the film was charged with the tasks of displacing problematic masculinity and asserting a renewed masculine modernity that would shut out the threatening, feminized aspects of mass culture. The film failed miserably on both counts, almost embodying the very issues it was meant to resolve. It narrativized problematic male subjectivity in a highly self-conscious fashion, once again turning the tables of classical cinematic convention to vest female characters with authority while specularizing the male subject. In so doing, it provided identificatory possibilities only with its female characters, as had so many popular films in the 1950s. At the same time, it self-consciously attempted to merge the popular and the avant-garde. Finally, the film ended up displacing familiar formal qualities and staging gender inversions in ways that proved frustrating to critics and viewers alike.

II

Director Herbert Vesely explained *The Bread of Those Early Years* as an attempt to document contemporary reality by repeating certain narrative events from different perspectives, a device that he saw as creating an intensified mode of realism absent from German filmmaking in the 1950s.[26] Vesely's 1960 treatment for the film explains his conception of temporality and perspective as an attempt to portray visually a transformation of consciousness: "The past and the present permeate each other. The gaze is synchronous and everywhere. No plot with flashbacks, but rather synchronous occurrences: reflections, possibilities, realities. This interlacing of levels creates an expanding consciousness, the consciousness of Walter Fendrich, 23, electrical mechanic and specialist in washing machines, on this Monday, the 14th of March."[27] If, as Vesely's treatment suggests, "the gaze is everywhere," Walter is very much the object of that gaze, while the subject of the gaze is most often a woman. Notably, those characters who structure our knowledge about Walter by observing him and commenting on his behavior are almost exclusively women: Ulla, Hedwig, Walter's landlady, Frau Flink and the women who work in her laundromat, as well as the woman from the Kurbelstraße who has a washing machine that Walter repairs. In both form and content, the film grants an unusual amount of narrative authority to its female characters. In as much as they control the gaze and structure our knowledge within the context of the film's narrative, the female characters are also the characters with whom spectators are encouraged to identify. Once again, then, *The Bread of Those Early Years* returns to strategies of women's cinema, inverting conventional structures and appealing primarily to female spectators, in particular through the character of Walter's ditched fiancée Ulla.

Like other films of the European new wave, *The Bread of Those Early Years* invokes the model of the Hollywood film noir in its mood and structure. But while the narrative of the classic film noir is constructed around a quest (by the male protagonist, and by extension the male spectator) for knowledge about the mysterious and dangerous femme fatale, in Vesely's film, again, the tables are turned. Here it is the women who are engaged in a quest for knowledge about Walter, who takes on the structural role of the femme fatale in the film. As we have seen in chapter 4, Mary Ann Doane describes the femme fatale as a threat that must be deciphered, a figure who thus corresponds to "the epistemological drive of narrative, the hermeneutic structuration of the classic text."[28] This description is strikingly accurate as an explanation of the role Walter Fendrich plays in Vesely's film. Like the femme fatale, Walter turns out to be not at all as he had seemed, and he thus constitutes a threat not only to Ulla, whom he rejects, but also to Hedwig, whom he loves all too dangerously. Walter is the secret that must be aggressively uncovered by the female characters of *The Bread of Those Early Years*; as such, he becomes the epistemological drive of the narrative. As Doane maintains, sexuality—and sexual difference—are at the center of this narrative questioning of what can and cannot be known; but again, it is the women in Vesely's film who are vested with subjectivity and narrative authority, while Walter Fendrich is the object of their quest for knowledge. By extension, as the viewers of the film participate in this quest for knowledge that propels the film's narrative, they are encouraged to identify with the film's female characters.

The film's inversion of gender roles is accomplished on a formal level not only through the realignment of the gaze, but also through the use of disjunctive voiceover. As Kaja Silverman has argued, there are no instances within mainstream cinema of disembodied female voices, because the disembodied voice is a signifier of phallic, abstract power, of epistemological authority in the production of discourse. The woman, lacking phallic power, is obsessively specularized in mainstream films: if she is heard, she must be seen, though she may be seen without being heard. While even disembodied male voiceover is unusual in fiction film, when it does occur "the dis-embodied voice-over can be seen as 'exemplary' for male subjectivity, attesting to an achieved invisibility, omniscience and discursive power."[29] Invisibility is thus a representative trait for male subjectivity—most fully realized in the disembodied voiceover—while specularity, or visibility, is exemplary for female subjectivity as it is represented in dominant discourse. *The Bread of Those Early Years* inverts this model to a large extent: Walter Fendrich is highly visible, even specularized by the female gaze, and disembodied female voices vested with narrative authority comment upon and interpret his actions.

Because of the taboo against disembodied female voices within mainstream cinema, feminist cinema has often focused on the female voice as a site of aesthetic experimentation capable of reinvesting female subjectivity with agency. As Silverman suggests, a great deal is at stake in this disassociation: "the freeing-up of the female voice from its obsessive and indeed exclusive reference to the female body, a reference which turns woman—in representation and in fact—back upon herself, in a negative and finally self-consuming narcissism."[30] Feminist filmmakers have worked with a number of strategies to "challenge the imperative of synchronization": these include aligning the female voice with the male body (and thus challenging the reification of sexual difference), or presenting several female bodies to which voices, sounds, and stories could be attributed (thus frustrating cinematic codes by denaturalizing the voice–body alignment). *The Bread of Those Early Years* employs both of these strategies, in particular the latter. Ulla's voice is often matched to the landlady's image, and vice versa. Though Hedwig's voice is almost always aligned with her body, she and Ulla have such similar faces and voices that at times (when they are shot from a distance or behind glass) they seem almost indistinguishable.[31] The fact that the film was shot without sound, and only "synchronized" later in a sound studio, contributes further to the disalignment of voices and bodies and thus to the denaturalization of this semic link.

With this in mind, I do not mean to suggest that *The Bread of Those Early Years* can be read as an example of explicitly feminist cinema. On the contrary, the film does not grant agency and authority to its female characters by way of political intention. However, by inverting conventional codes, the film ends up displaying the fractured nature and instability of gender roles (both masculinity and femininity) in the cinema and in society in the postwar period. As such, the disjuncture of the female voice from the female body and the concomitant specularization of the male body constitute one explanation for the negative response to the film at a moment when critics hoped the new wave would reassert masculine authority.

III

The opening sequence of *The Bread of Those Early Years* structures the spectatorial relation to the subsequent disjuncture of sound and image by establishing an epistemological correspondence of images with narration despite their lack of an organic or naturalized connection. During the credit sequence, a train approaches Berlin's Gleisdreieck station, which itself functions as a metaphor for the love triangle between Walter, Ulla, and Hedwig, and for the tripartite structure of the narrative.[32] As the train arrives at the station, two female voices are heard in dialogue:

> "And then he went to the train station … at least that's what he says."
> "Which station was that?"
> "I don't know."

The camera cuts from the train to the Gleisdreieck station sign, and a male voice announces the arrival of the train from the station's loudspeaker. An extreme close-up of a lighted cigarette segues into a pan up to the loudspeaker, a pan that creates spatial confusion because it is subsequently clear that the cigarette smoker is not in the station. The camera zooms in on the loudspeaker in a shot that establishes the epistemological authority of the disembodied voice, which now directs passengers to board the train. The image now shifts to a shot of hands dialing a pay phone in the station, then cuts to a mouth smoking the same cigarette we have seen before. Women's voices discuss the disappearance of Walter Fendrich, attempting to reconstruct his actions over the course of the day. Through its metonymy with the loudspeaker as a transmitter of disembodied voices, the telephone here gives authority to the female voices that will construct our knowledge about Walter over the course of the film. Finally, we see a woman behind the glass of the phone booth (the glass functions as an obstacle to organic sound–image correspondence), followed by a full-face shot of the woman smoking the cigarette. While it is clear that the women we see are the women whose voices make up the soundtrack—the voices of the women, that is, are definitively linked to their bodies here—it is unclear which voice belongs to whom or even who these women who speculate on Walter's actions are. Nonetheless, in contrast to the classic film noir narrative, it is not the women about whom our curiosity is aroused but Walter Fendrich, the absent object of their speculations. The epistemological correspondence between voiceover narration and a series of divergent images that has been established throughout this sequence structures the spectatorial relation to the ensuing narrative, which is enunciated in an increasingly disjunctive fashion, albeit one that utilizes generic conventions in an attempt to offset the narrative fragmentation to some degree.

As in a detective story or film noir, we are drawn into the action by a set of mysterious occurrences about which we are given little information. Indeed, the impression of a detective narrative is confirmed shortly after the opening sequence ends, when the screen fades to black and a snappy jazz soundtrack accompanies images of Walter Fendrich in full face and profile that resemble mug shots. A male voice tells us that he is "Fendrich. Walter Fendrich, twenty-four years of age, refugee from the East." The images of Walter's face together with this voiceover foreground Walter's narrative centrality as object of the gaze and of inquiry in the film.

The narrative is subsequently divided into three overlapping and partially repetitive sections, loosely constructed around three parallel subjective sequences that record the perspectives of the three protagonists: Walter Fendrich, his fiancée Ulla Wickweber, and his new beloved Hedwig Muller. In these sequences, in which images are accompanied by voiceover narration, each protagonist projects a possible future life that is ultimately nullified by the events of this particular day. Walter imagines a regimented, bourgeois married life with Ulla. Ulla imagines herself as the accommodating and flexible, but proper wife for Walter, who would himself be stable and provide for her, even if he might have occasional affairs. Hedwig imagines a detailed future in a marriage to a man she has just met on the street. These circumscribed, "subjunctive" projections of a stable future stand in stark contrast to the fragmentary and uncertain events of the preceding and succeeding narrative, when the lives of all three characters are turned upside down almost despite themselves.

This present-day narrative, which parallels the three subjective sequences, is also tripartite in structure, though now marked by the "objective" perspectives of those who speculate on Walter's actions. The *Evangelischer Film-Beobachter* described this narrative in the following way:

> The spectator who is prepared to think it through can ascertain three clusters of experience: At the beginning stands Ulla's search for her fiancé, who roams the streets with a troubled face, and therein lies the story's search for its "hero". The comparison of the two women and Fendrich's decision between them constitutes the middle portion of the film. The new pair in the old environment is the end piece of the work.[33]

This description of events is accurate, though it is a stretch to suggest that Walter actually makes a choice between Ulla and Hedwig. Unlike Böll's novella, which suggests that Walter, after meeting and falling in love with Hedwig, is able to break out of the oppressive conditions of a bourgeois lifestyle for which he has never been suited, the film does not attribute such explicit agency to Walter. Instead, the film's narrative structure takes the events of the day as assumptions about reality, deconstructs them through visual and aural fragmentation and repetition, and reconstructs the events as a richer tapestry of reality through the perspectives of the various women who observe Walter. Reconstructed through the perspectives of these female characters (including Ulla and Hedwig), Walter's actions lack definitive meaning: they are invested with a multiplicity of meanings, all of which are subjectively determined by female perspectives. Although the film's ending, in which the camera circles around Walter and Hedwig embracing in the street, leaves little doubt that the two are united, the closure is arbitrary in both form and content. Not only does the episodic nature of the film make clear that this is just one moment in time (and things could change again in the next moment), but according to the film's narrative logic, Walter or Hedwig easily could have ended up with someone else instead.

Walter's lack of agency is confirmed on a formal level by his lack of narrative or epistemological authority. The first time he is allowed to speak at all in the film comes in the subjective sequence in which he imagines his future married life with Ulla. This sequence is sandwiched on both sides, and thus circumscribed, by Ulla's commentary on the events. As if this weren't enough to destabilize his authority, Walter says at the end of his subjective sequence, "I know nothing of this future, which will never be present. I don't see myself or hear myself, I don't smile or talk, shake hands, go to the movies or to visit people, open doors, nothing, nothing, I know nothing." Though the sequence is marked as subjective because of Walter's voiceover—it is indeed the first time we hear his voice—it ends with a statement that effectively disavows this subjectivity through the symbolic castration represented by his admission of "blindness" and "deafness" to the sounds and images of a future that spectators of the film can hear narrated and watch as they occur.

IV

Like the rubble films of the immediate postwar years, *The Bread of Those Early Years* uses real settings in Berlin as a backdrop. While the city is no longer in ruins, it now represents both the prosperity of the miracle years and the imminent threat of the Cold War, as embodied by the division of the Berlin Wall. Like the city of Berlin itself, Walter Fendrich is a divided subject who is pulled between the prosperity represented by Ulla and the desire represented by Hedwig, the woman who arrives from the East (see figure 10.2). Here too, the film disrupts conventional gendering, in that it departs from the particularly German tendency, beginning with the Weimar "street films," to equate the city with "Woman" in the cinema. Indeed, it is Walter who is equated with the city, while Hedwig is seduced by the streets of Berlin. Towards the end of the film she escapes the constricted space of Walter's car and, like a Weimar film hero, loses herself in the nighttime cityscape. It is here that she meets the man whom she considers marrying in the subjective sequence in which she imagines her future. Walter, afraid of losing Hedwig to the seductions of the city, rushes madly through the streets in pursuit of her. At the end of the film, the two are united, not in the secure domestic space that would ensure a happy ending, but under a streetlight, exposed in public.

To its credit, the film does not rely on the overdetermined symbolism of divided Berlin, nor does it evoke facile allusions to the Cold War politics for which Berlin was emblematic. Nonetheless, its subtle equation of the symbolically castrated Walter Fendrich with the symbolically castrated city of Berlin is revealing. If the ruined Berlin of the rubble films symbolized Nazism, which was embodied in these films, according to Barton Byg, by the femme fatale, here Berlin symbolizes the Cold War, which is in turn embodied by the "feminized" Fendrich.

Figure 10.2 Walter Fendrich (Christian Doermer) with Hedwig (Karen Blanguernon) in divided Berlin. Source: Deutsche Kinemathek.

It is this subtle invocation of Cold War politics and divided Berlin, in conjunction with the inversions and displacements the film effects in regard to male subjectivity, that helps to explain the seemingly paradoxical accusation against the film that it was too cold and failed to provide adequate structures of spectator identification. There is an inherent repression evident in the reviews of the film, which almost never mention the representation of Berlin except in passing.[34] Reviewers of the film had contradictory expectations: they hoped for an exemplary new wave film that would avoid sentimentality and expunge the feminized aspects of mass modernity from its formal canon, yet they continued to need the cinema as a forum for working through difficult emotions, as a site of mourning—in this case, mourning over the division of Berlin. Reviewers approached *The Bread of Those Early Years* as a work of autonomous art, but criticized it for not providing the structures of identification they expected from popular cinema. This double bind continued to plague the New German Cinema through the 1970s and 1980s, as directors increasingly developed formal strategies based on distantiation and alienation effects to mourn and work through the Nazi past that failed to address the emotions of spectators.[35]

Notably, however, it was primarily male critics and viewers who articulated this critique. By contrast, *Film und Frau* published one of the few positive reviews of the film, focusing on the strong female characters and the love story the film narrates as points of identification for female spectators.[36] The pictorial retelling of *The Bread of Those Early Years* in *Film und Frau* focuses as much on Ulla's subjective transformation as it does on the emergent love story between Hedwig and Walter. A close-up of Ulla is accompanied by the caption: "Ulla waits in front of the house in which <Walter> lives. She waits an entire night, and a transformation occurs in her as well. She sees how superficial her relationship with Walter was."[37] The accompanying article focuses on the ways in which Hedwig and Ulla shape Walter. As this *Film und Frau* review suggests, the film appealed to female spectators because it worked with the generic conventions of German popular cinema to challenge them in interesting ways.

Indeed, female viewers liked the film, in part due to the clear identificatory possibilities it offered them. An informal poll by one reviewer of responses to *The Bread of Those Early Years* found that the only viewers who had positive things to say about the film were women. The snide tone of the article uses the fact that only women liked the film as evidence of how bad it was: "In contrast, a few female voices: 'Wonderful photography', 'Deeply impressed by the images and words (!)'—Apparently men have worse nerves."[38] Nonetheless, the article offers one of the few attempts to gauge the actual responses of average viewers to the film, and it is notable that gender becomes a category of analysis as a result. The fact that the film was received positively by these female viewers and by a popular women's magazine (and almost nowhere else) suggests that gender is imbricated with definitions of the popular and the avant-garde that shaped the public discourse surrounding the film as well as with the conceptions of spectator address and identification at play in critiques of the film.

In both its narrative and its self-conscious form, *The Bread of Those Early Years* foregrounded the instability of gender roles in postwar Germany. But despite all the formal inversions it effects, the film does not really break with the ambivalent modes of representing gender that were so typical for postwar German cinema in general. In contrast to the female protagonists of other new wave cinemas—strong and unique modern women who often challenged traditional gender roles—the female characters in *The Bread of Those Early Years* are almost indistinguishable from one another, functioning more than anything as signifiers for male lack. In granting narrative authority to these female characters and in specularizing Walter Fendrich, the film inverts traditional gender dichotomies, but does not attempt to dismantle them.

Finally, the failure of Vesely's film cannot be attributed exclusively either to the inherent faults of the film itself or to a failure of reception. On the surface, *The Bread of Those Early Years* accomplishes what the new wave films of other national cinemas accomplish: it is self-reflexive about its construction; it makes a statement about the contested nature of reality as constructed through the cinematic process; it provokes both pleasure and discomfort in looking; in short, it puts into question both the process of filmmaking and the process of film spectatorship. In terms of content, too, the film addresses issues pertinent to the European new wave at large: it criticizes consumer capitalism, questions traditional values (such as the work ethic), problematizes love, marriage, and desire, and evidences discomfort with the liberal status quo of West German society in the Cold War era. Within the cinematic context of the postwar Federal Republic, the film also does meld certain aspects of popular cinema with new, experimental filmmaking strategies. What the film ultimately lacks in comparison with its new wave counterparts, however, is the dynamic energy that characterizes the successful fusion of the popular with the avant-garde, the novelty and vitality that exemplify popular modernity. Instead, *The Bread of Those Early Years* is marked by a feeling of exhaustion that manifests itself in the repetition of visual images, sound bites, and entire sequences. This cinematic fatigue is mirrored, and was perhaps in part provoked, by the endless repetition of public discourse surrounding the film, in the endless debates and commentaries that it inspired both before and after its release.

The conception of postwar West Germany as the site of an exhausted scopic regime has become commonplace. After the iconological ecstasy of fascism, the wealth of visual pleasure and the abundance of ideologically overburdened images of all kinds, visual culture in the postwar years, it is often argued, was completely bankrupt. This explanation is generally employed to vilify or dismissively excuse the provincial and frivolous cinema of the early postwar period. Yet that cinema, in all its provincialism and frivolity, was a dynamic, popular, and successful cinema, fueled by the national need for escapist entertainment tailored to the highly specific life experiences and visual frameworks of reconstruction-era West Germans. As the Federal Republic attained economic, political, and social stability towards the end of the 1950s, this cinema began to fade, in part because it was no longer needed to fulfill this purpose.

The Bread of Those Early Years attempted to fuse aspects of this fading popular German cinema with recent avant-garde filmmaking strategies appropriated from the French new wave. Precisely in foregrounding the instability of their project, which owed itself to the difficulty of reinstating an unproblematic, rejuvenated masculine modernity in the visual landscape of postwar West Germany, the film addresses both the promise and the curse of popular modernity as deployed in the German context. While the film failed, what remains compelling about *The Bread of Those Early Years* is Vesely's effort to present an innovative vision of what a new postwar film language might look like.

Notes

1. An earlier version of this chapter was published as "Negotiating the Popular and the Avant Garde: The Failure of Herbert Vesely's *The Bread of Those Early Years*," in *Light Motives: German Popular Film in Perspective*, ed. Randall Halle and Margaret McCarthy (Detroit, 2003), 171–96.
2. The "Oberhausen Manifesto" is reprinted in German in *Augenzeugen. 100 Texte neuer deutscher Filmemacher*, ed. Hans Helmut Prinzler and Eric Rentschler (Frankfurt am Main, 1988), and in English in *West German Filmmakers on Film*, ed. Eric Rentschler (New York, 1988).
3. See Hans Helmut Prinzler, *Chronik des deutschen Films 1895–1994* (Stuttgart, 1995), 234; and Elizabeth Prommer, *Kinobesuch im Lebenslauf. Eine historische und medienbiografische Studie* (Konstanz, 1999), 350.
4. See Joseph Garncarz, "Hollywood in Germany. Die Rolle des amerikanischen Films in Deutschland: 1925–1990," in *Der deutsche Film. Aspekte seiner Geschichte von den Anfängen bis zur Gegenwart*, ed. Uli Jung (Trier, 1993), 204.
5. Tim Bergfelder, *International Adventures: German Popular Cinema and European Co-Productions in the 1960s* (New York, 2005), 1–2.
6. The building of the Berlin Wall on August 13, 1961 had logistical consequences for Vesely's plans for the film and led both to narrative inconsistencies and to more fraught political meanings in the filmic narrative. The film was shot wholly on location in West Berlin streets, trains, and cafés, and in the apartments of friends of the film team. In the film, Fendrich is a refugee from the East who has emigrated to West Berlin years earlier. When Hedwig arrives from his hometown, it thus must be assumed that she is arriving from East Germany—the fact that she simply arrives at the Gleisdreieck station with no fanfare does not square with this assumption. On the other hand, the many shots in the film of empty S-Bahn trains rattling over elevated tracks constitute a subtle but omnipresent reminder of the situation in West Berlin during a time when the boycott of

the S-Bahn was still in effect. Similarly, Hedwig and Walter board a tram in the Tauentzienstraße labeled "Endstation Bernauer Straße," a tram leading directly to the new wall, to a street where people had jumped from buildings to land in the West and avoid separation from their families. Very few reviews of the film make mention of this backdrop, which, though not foregrounded, does lend direct contemporary political implications to an otherwise more subtly critical narrative. I will return to these issues below.

7. Indeed, future films associated with the New German Cinema could be much more easily aligned with either the "experimental camp" or the "popular camp." Examples of the former included Danielle Huillet and Jean-Marie Straub's two Böll adaptations *Machorka-Muff* (1962) and *Nicht versöhnt* (Unreconciled, 1965), as well as Vesely's own next attempt, *nicht mehr fliehen* (flee no more, 1965). These films had no pretension of addressing a mainstream audience and were aggressively fragmentary and avant-garde. It was not until around 1966 that New German films began to emerge that combined formal experimentation with a more straightforward narrative style that would prove successful with critics, if not with mass audiences. The two German submissions to the Cannes Film Festival in 1966, Ulrich Schamoni's *Es* (It) and Volker Schlöndorff's *Der junge Törleß* (Young Törleß) are exemplary of this group, as is Alexander Kluge's film from the same year, *Abschied von gestern* (Yesterday Girl). Nonetheless, all films associated with the New German Cinema were increasingly marginalized as both "difficult" and different from the popular cinema produced by the German studios and by Hollywood.

8. Many critics have sought to problematize the "break" between the popular German cinema of the 1950s and the new cinema that emerged in the 1960s and 1970s by adopting various descriptive terms to characterize different stages of the latter. Thomas Elsaesser's distinction between the Young German Film and the New German Cinema, with the *Autorenfilm* as a concept that mediates the two, has perhaps become the most accepted usage. See Elsaesser, *New German Cinema: A History* (New Brunswick, NJ, 1989), 2. I have chosen not to use this distinction in writing about a period during which it was as yet unclear how the various and sometimes competing notions of what the new cinema should or could be would evolve into specific styles, genres, or platforms. Instead, I refer to the "new wave" as a general designator for the various new films that sought to distinguish themselves from the popular cinema of the 1950s, and to the New German Cinema as the more programmatic agenda according to or against which these films developed.

9. Rev. of *Das Brot der frühen Jahre*, *Die Abendzeitung* (Munich), May 19/20, 1962. Other pithy headlines indicating the dominant response to the film included the following: "Der deutsche Film wurde noch nicht gerettet," *Der Tagesspiegel*, June 3, 1962; "Das Brötchen der frühen Jahre—Herbert Veselys Experiment rettet das deutsche Kino kaum," *Der Weser Kurier*, June 16, 1962; and "Ist Vater doch der Beste?," *Bravo*, July 24, 1962.

10. Critics quickly developed an ironic nickname for *The Bread of Those Early Years*: "Letztes Jahr atemlos in Mariendorf" (Last Year Breathless in Mariendorf), which punned on Godard's *À bout de souffle* (Breathless, 1960) and the Resnais film, while expressing through the substitution of "dorf" (village) for "bad" (spa) the provincialism of the German film in comparison with its cosmopolitan French counterparts.

11. Walter Kaul, rev. of *Das Brot der frühen Jahre*, *Kurier*, July 10, 1962.

12. Hembus was the author of a widely read pamphlet from 1961 ironically titled "The German Film Couldn't Be Better," and a contributor to the journal *Filmkritik*. See Joe Hembus, *Der deutsche Film kann gar nicht besser sein. Ein Pamphlet von gestern. Eine Abrechnung von heute* (Munich, 1981). Hembus's press book for the film is a brilliant attempt to convince potential exhibitors and audiences of the modernity of the film's style and to educate them about its meaning. He explains the plot in straightforward detail, and then goes on to explicate the formal style: "Independently of its relationship to its literary precursor, however, the film follows the legitimate principle of art:

decomposition of reality towards the composition of a world which matches the vision of the artists, or, to operate in filmic terms: a new montage of the elements of reality." See the *Presseheft: Das Brot der frühen Jahre*, in file on *Das Brot der frühen Jahre*, Schriftgutarchiv, Stiftung deutsche Kinemathek, Berlin.

13. Reinhold E. Thiel, "Mutmaßungen über Walter," *Filmkritik* 1 (1962): 16.
14. Reporting in *Filmkritik* on the events at the Oberhausen festival, Enno Patalas articulated the incredible expectations drummed up by the Manifesto: "A chance like this—the public bankrupting of all principles according to which films are produced and directed in this country—a chance like this will not return again so quickly. It will depend on the decisions of the next months as to whether a fourth decade of dominance by Philistines follows the three previous ones, or whether a new beginning can finally be risked." Enno Patalas, "Die Chance: Neubeginn im deutschen Film?" *Filmkritik* 4 (1962): 150.
15. See rev. of *Das Brot der Frühen Jahre, Filmkritik* 6 (1962): 262–64; rev. of *Das Brot der Frühen Jahre, Evangelischer Film-Beobachter* 14 (June 9, 1962): 257; and Heinz Martin, "Ist Vater doch der Beste?" *Bravo,* July 24, 1962.
16. Rev. of *Das Brot der frühen Jahre, Beratungsdienst Jugend und Film* 5 (1962): 2.
17. This can be said, for example, of the male characters in the next big New German Cinema productions to gain widespread attention, Ulrich Schamoni's *It* and Volker Schlöndorff's *Young Törleß*. Both films offer (very different) explorations of male subjectivity, but the male subjects evidence impotence and lack of agency in both cases.
18. See Siegfried Kracauer, *From Caligari to Hitler: A Psychological History of the German Film* (Princeton, 1947). On the crisis of masculinity in postwar cinema, see also Kaja Silverman, *Male Subjectivity at the Margins* (New York, 1992); Jaimey Fisher, *Disciplining Germany: Youth, Reeducation, and Reconstruction after the Second World War* (Detroit, 2007); Fisher, "On the Ruins of Masculinity: The Figure of the Child in Italian Neorealism and the German Rubble-Film," in *Italian Neorealism and Global Cinema,* ed. Laura E. Ruberto and Kristi M. Wilson (Detroit, 2007), 25–53; and Fisher, "Deleuze in a Ruinous Context: German Rubble-Film and Italian Neorealism," *iris* 23 (1997): 53–74.
19. "Papas Kino—Eine Definition,"*Filmkritik* 3 (1962): 98.
20. See Andreas Huyssen, "Mass Culture as Woman: Modernism's Other," in *After the Great Divide: Modernism, Mass Culture, Postmodernism* (Bloomington, 1986).
21. Siegfried Kracauer, "Die kleinen Ladenmädchen gehen ins Kino," *Das Ornament der Masse: Essays* (Frankfurt am Main, 1963). In English as "The Little Shop Girls Go to the Movies," *The Mass Ornament: Weimar Essays,* trans. and ed. Thomas Levin (Cambridge, 1995).
22. Barton Byg, "Nazism as Femme Fatale: Recuperation of Cinematic Masculinity in Postwar Berlin," in *Gender and Germanness: Cultural Productions of Nation,* ed. Patricia Herminghouse and Magda Mueller (Providence, RI, 1997).
23. Byg, "Nazism as Femme Fatale," 181.
24. Temby Caprio complicates this point in her "Women's Film Culture in the Sixties: Stars and Anti-Stars from *Papas Kino* to the German New Wave," *Women in German Yearbook* 15 (2000): 201–26. As she suggests, for cross-over audiences who saw the films of both "Daddy's cinema" and the New Wave, the transition from watching star actresses to watching the women featured in the new wave films (many of whom were not trained as actresses) would certainly have been an experience that disrupted traditional images of women on screen and traditional notions of authenticity in regard to film. Caprio mentions, for example, the career of Sabine Sinjen, who starred in both *Heimatfilme* and the new wave film *It*, where she played a woman who has an abortion. Most paradigmatically, she discusses the character Anita G. in *Yesterday Girl*, who was played by Alexandra Kluge, a physician by training and the sister of director Kluge. Anita G. was the most iconic character of new wave film, and certainly represented a departure from female characters of the past. Nonetheless, as Caprio writes, Anita G. "functions like a 'seismograph' (Kluge) of postwar German society, ricocheting between

paternalistic lovers and various other authority figures on her seemingly aimless journey through the legal, cultural, and educational institutions of the Federal Republic" (212). While Anita G., as many critics have argued, was a character with whom audiences could identify in multiple and complex ways, precisely this "seismograph" quality ultimately denies her a real subjectivity in the film. It could almost be argued, following Barton Byg, that Anita G. represents a departure from earlier depictions of women in German film primarily in the sense that, with *Yesterday Girl*, woman is once again able to structurally assume the role of the weak or passive character at the hands of paternalistic male authority figures. However, Caprio's reading, again, productively complicates any easy conclusions regarding the transformations of women's roles in new wave cinema, focusing as it does on the continuities and disruptions in star culture and the responses of (female) spectators to images of women on screen.

25. See Lutz Koepnick, *The Dark Mirror: German Cinema Between Hitler and Hollywood* (Berkeley, 2002).
26. See Volker Baer, "Heinrich Böll als Drehbuchautor," *Der Tagesspiegel*, December 24, 1961.
27. Joe Hembus, "Suche nach der verlorenen Zeit. Junger deutscher Spielfilm auf neuen Wegen," *Spandauer Volksblatt* (n.d.).
28. Mary Ann Doane, *Femmes Fatales: Feminism, Film Theory, Psychoanalysis* (New York, 1991), 1.
29. Kaja Silverman, "Dis-Embodying the Female Voice," in *Re-Vision: Essays in Feminist Film Criticism*, ed. Mary Ann Doane et al. (Los Angeles, 1984), 134.
30. Silverman, "Dis-Embodying the Female Voice," 137.
31. Reviewers commented uncomprehendingly on the astounding similarity between the two actresses. See for example Kaul, *Kurier*.
32. Gleisdreieck literally means "triangle of tracks," a place where three sets of train tracks converge and diverge again. The action of the film returns to this symbolic train station again and again.
33. Rev. of *Das Brot der frühen Jahre*, *Evangelischer Film-Beobachter* 14 (June 9, 1962): 257.
34. It was an Austrian reviewer who noted this fact: "Vesely elucidates the dividedness of German consciousness after August 13, 1961: the film is set in Berlin. Only the people don't seem to notice this. They don't see that an empty S-Bahn train goes by again and again (it's being boycotted still, and the public is supposed to take note of this)." Rev. of *Das Brot der Frühen Jahre*, *Profil* VII (1962).
35. This was of course the lesson brought home most explicitly by the success of the television mini-series *Holocaust* in 1979. See Andreas Huyssen, "The Politics of Identification: 'Holocaust' and West German Drama" in *After the Great Divide*. See also the articles on the subject collected in *Germans and Jews Since the Holocaust: The Changing Situation in West Germany*, ed. Anson Rabinbach and Jack Zipes (New York, 1986).
36. "Das Brot der frühen Jahre. Ein Film nach Heinrich Böll," *Film und Frau* 6 (1962): 106–8.
37. "Das Brot der frühen Jahre," *Film und Frau*, 106.
38. Ponkie, "Wie finden Sie Bubis Kino?," *Abendzeitung* (Munich), n.d.

Epilogue

ADAPTING THE 1950S: THE AFTERLIFE OF POSTWAR CINEMA IN POST-UNIFICATION POPULAR CULTURE

On December 23, 1996, the first film in the much-touted series "German Classics" debuted on the private television channel SAT.1. Showered with acclaim prior to its premiere and seen by 8.83 million viewers in Germany, this remake of *The Girl Rosemarie* constituted a success for Bernd Eichinger, the powerhouse producer who returned to the director's chair for the first time since his film school days to bring this adaptation to the small screen. Eichinger's own film was followed in the next weeks by three more remakes of popular classics from the 1950s, all produced by Eichinger and adapted by successful directors of the emergent popular cinema of the 1990s: Urs Egger's *Die Halbstarken* (The Rebels, orig. dir. Georg Tressler, 1956); Nico Hoffmann's *Es geschah am hellichten Tag* (It Happened in Broad Daylight, orig. dir. Ladislao Vajda, 1958); and Sönke Wortmann's *Charley's Tante* (Charley's Aunt, orig. dir. Geza von Cziffra, 1963).

Eichinger's return to 1950s cinema for this lavishly financed series was no accident. Unlike many of his colleagues in the world of post-Oberhausen German filmmaking, Eichinger had long been vocal about his admiration for the popular domestic cinema of the postwar period; indeed, his conscious recycling of elements from this period of German cinema has certainly contributed to his remarkable success as Germany's leading producer. Teaming up with a group of young directors whose careers were similarly inspired by the popular cinema of the early postwar period, Eichinger sought with the event "German Classics" to promote the new popular German cinema of the post-unification period while also capitalizing on the ongoing popularity of 1950s films with German television audiences.

In an interview about the "German Classics" series, Eichinger described the 1950s as "a great time, in which great dreams were dreamed, a time in which a new society was born."[1] Eichinger's statement at once caters to a nostalgic vision of the 1950s increasingly common among his jaded contemporaries and also suggests the hopes represented by the newly reunified Germany in the era of "normalization." The conscious exploration of parallels between these two eras of German reconstruction clearly informed the "German Classics" series. Yet Eichinger's nostalgic adaptations ultimately failed to satisfy post-Wall German critics or viewers, and after the initial success of *The Girl Rosemarie*, "German Classics" bombed. As it turned out, the remakes paled in comparison to the well-known originals, appearing trite and clichéd in terms of both film form and ideology.

Eichinger's "German Classics" series is only the most explicit example of what Georg Seeßlen has termed the "Neo-Adenauer style" of post-unification cinema.[2] As Seeßlen has argued, Eichinger's career is emblematic of the "reconciliation with Daddy's cinema" that has characterized contemporary film production, eclipsing the independent *Autorenkino* of the 1970s and 1980s. Seeßlen and other critics have noted a number of factors that link post-unification cinema with postwar cinema: its popularity with audiences; its domestic commercial success and general profitability; its return to generic formulas; and its lack of critical potential, producing what Eric Rentschler has called a "cinema of consensus."[3]

Strong similarities certainly exist between the Federal Republic of the 1950s and post-unification Germany. The social, political, and cultural preoccupations of both periods were essentially the same: these involved the projects of redefining national boundaries and national identity, reassessing the place of the political in the public sphere, reformulating gender roles and the function of the family unit—and thinking through the impact of shifting class structures and a new economy on all of these. It should therefore come as no surprise that German filmmakers in the post-unification period adopted similar strategies to those of their postwar precursors for addressing these concerns. These strategies, which sought to encourage the examination of social dilemmas and private destinies in an accessible context, included not only the return to genre cinema, but also the focus on a seemingly timeless and superficially ahistorical German landscape (often transformed in the 1990s into a cityscape), as well as a general repression of significant historical events in favor of highly encoded narratives that avoided direct reference to World War II, the Holocaust, or the fall of the Wall.

As in the late 1940s and 1950s, a resurgence of female-oriented films and the explicit attempt to appeal to largely female audiences also characterized the post-Wall cinema of the 1990s. Dickon Copsey has noted that, "Despite a general down-turn in the crucial under-25 cinema-going market, many films of this period <the early 1990s> were attracting audiences that were more than 75 percent female. Whatever the reasons, women have been recognized as an extremely important market for the <post-unification> German film industry, and this is reflected in film production and marketing strategies."[4] Among the most popular films of the 1990s were comedies such as Sönke Wortmann's *Der bewegte Mann* (Maybe … Maybe Not, 1993), Katja von Garnier's *Abgeschminkt!* (Makin'

Up, 1995), Doris Dörrie's *Keiner liebt mich* (Nobody Loves Me, 1996), and Rainer Kaufmann's *Stadtgespräch* (Talk of the Town, 1997), which, like their 1950s precursors, featured female protagonists (more often than not played by the immensely popular Katja Riemann) in narratives about contemporary social dilemmas—gender roles, family constructs, class differences, as well as issues of race and sexuality. These neo-*Heimatfilme* shared common strategies with non-comedic films—dramas like Wolfgang Becker's *Das Leben ist eine Baustelle* (Life Under Construction, 1997), action films like Tom Tykwer's *Lola rennt* (Run Lola Run, 1998), or historical melodramas like Max Färberböck's *Aimée und Jaguar* (1998)— that combined narratives about space and place with stars and genre conventions calculated to appeal to female spectators.

Filmmakers seeking to revisit questions of national identity in the 1990s thus turned to the popular films of the postwar period and adapted their strategies and conventions. Once more, their films often sublimated troubling issues of ethnicity and national identity into seemingly more harmless narratives about gender and sexual identity. And film viewers— raised on rebroadcasts of *Heimatfilme* on German television—sought popular representations that conformed to their genre expectations in times of national trauma. Along the way, these new genre films contributed to a revival of the domestic German film industry at the same time.

To return once again to the example of Bernd Eichinger's "German Classics," however, the failure of these remakes to live up to the quality of the originals also points to the limitations of the comparison between postwar cinema and post-unification popular culture. Eichinger's series certainly reveals the immense influence of the popular styles and themes of early postwar cinema on contemporary culture. But "German Classics" also highlights the dynamic qualities possessed by the once reviled films of the 1950s in comparison to their paler 1990s offspring.

As I have argued, postwar cinema presented a site of conflict and contradiction, epitomized by both the search for legitimate aesthetic forms and the attempt to imagine solutions for social problems, pursuits that are at the heart of so many films of the era. Characterized by ideological incongruity and aesthetic ambivalence, German cinema of the late 1940s and 1950s derived its vibrancy from the ongoing quest for a new film language in the postwar period.

Notes

1. Interview with Bernd Eichinger, *Sonntagsblatt*, December 13, 1996, qtd. in Andreas M. Rauch, *Bernd Eichinger und seine Filme* (Frankfurt am Main, 2000), 120.
2. Georg Seeßlen, "Der Neo-Adenauer-Stil," *die tageszeitung*, June 12, 1997.
3. Eric Rentschler, "From New German Cinema to the Post-Wall Cinema of Consensus," in *Cinema and Nation*, ed. Mette Hjort and Scott MacKenzie (New York, 2000), 260–77.
4. Dickon Copsey, "Women amongst Women: the New German Comedy and the Failed Romance," in *German Cinema Since Unification*, ed. David Clarke (London, 2006), 182.

BIBLIOGRAPHY

Books and Journal Articles

Alter, Nora, and Lutz Koepnick, eds. *Sound Matters: Essays on the Acoustics of German Culture*. New York: Berghahn Books, 2004.

Ascheid, Antje. *Hitler's Heroines: Stardom and Womanhood in Nazi Cinema*. Philadelphia: Temple University Press, 2003.

Baer, Hester. "From Riefenstahl to Riemann: Revisiting the Question of Women's Cinema in the German Context." In *The Cosmopolitan Screen: German Cinema and the Global Imaginary, 1945 to the Present*, ed. Lutz Koepnick and Stephan Schindler. Ann Arbor: University of Michigan Press, 2007.

Bandmann, Christa. *Es leuchten die Sterne: Aus der Glanzzeit des deutschen Films*. Munich: Heyne, 1979.

Bänsch, Dieter, ed. *Die fünfziger Jahre. Beiträge zur Politik und Kultur*. Tübingen: G. Narr, 1985.

Barthel, Manfred. *So war es wirklich: Der deutsche Nachkriegsfilm*. Munich and Berlin: Herbig, 1986.

———. *Als Opas Kino jung war: Der deutsche Nachkriegsfilm*. Frankfurt am Main: Ullstein, 1991.

Bazin, Andre. *What is Cinema?*, vol. 1., trans. Hugh Gray. Berkeley: University of California Press, 1967.

Bergfelder, Tim. *International Adventures: German Popular Cinema and European Co-Productions in the 1960s*. New York: Berghahn Books, 2005.

Bergfelder, Tim, Erica Carter, and Deniz Göktürk, eds. *The German Cinema Book*. London: British Film Institute, 2002.

Bessen, Ursula. *Trümmer und Träume. Nachkriegszeit und fünfziger Jahre auf Zelluloid*. Bochum: Brockmeyer, 1989.

Betts, Paul. *The Authority of Everyday Objects: A Cultural History of West German Industrial Design*. Berkeley: University of California Press, 2004.

Bliersbach, Gerhard. *So grün war die Heide ... Die gar nicht so heile Welt im Nachkriegsfilm*. Abridged ed. Weinheim and Basel: Beltz Verlag, 1989.

Bongartz, Barbara. *Von Caligari zu Hitler—Von Hitler zu Dr. Mabuse? Eine "psychologische" Geschichte des deutschen Films von 1946 bis 1960*. Münster: MakS Publikationen, 1992.

Brauner, Artur. *Mich gibt's nur einmal: Rückblende eines Lebens*. Munich: Herbig, 1976.

Burgess, Gordon. "The Failure of the Film of the Play. *Draussen vor der Tür* and *Liebe 47*." *German Life and Letters* 38.4 (1985): 155–64.

———. *The Life and Works of Wolfgang Borchert*. Rochester, NY: Camden House, 2003.

Burghardt, Kirsten. *Werk, Skandal, Exempel. Tabudurchbrechung durch fiktionale Modelle: Willi Forsts* Die Sünderin. Munich: Schaudig & Ledig, 1996.

Butler, Alison. *Women's Cinema: The Contested Screen*. London and New York: Wallflower, 2002.

Caprio, Temby. "Women's Film Culture in the Sixties: Stars and Anti-Stars from *Papas Kino* to the German New Wave." *Women in German Yearbook* 15 (2000): 201–25.

Carter, Erica. "Deviant Pleasures? Women, Melodrama, and Consumer Nationalism in West Germany." In *The Sex of Things: Gender and Consumption in Historical Perspective*, ed. Victoria de Grazia and Ellen Furlough. Berkeley: University of California Press, 1996.

————. *How German Is She?: Postwar West German Reconstruction and the Consuming Woman.* Ann Arbor: University of Michigan Press, 1997.

————. "Sweeping up the Past: Gender and History in the Post-war German 'Rubble Film.'" In *Heroines without Heroes: Reconstructing Female and National Identities in European Cinema, 1945–51,* ed. Ulrike Sieglohr. London: Cassell, 2000.

Clarke, David, ed. *German Cinema Since Unification.* London: Continuum, 2006.

Corrigan, Timothy. *New German Film: The Displaced Image.* Austin: University of Texas Press, 1983.

Crofts, Stephen. "Concepts of National Cinema." In *The Oxford Guide to Film Studies,* ed. John Hill and Pamela Church Gibson. Oxford: Oxford University Press, 1998.

Dachs, Robert. *Willi Forst: Eine Biographie.* Vienna: Kremayr & Scheriau, 1986.

Dalle Vacche, Angela. *Cinema and Painting: How Art Is Used in Film.* Austin: University of Texas Press, 1996.

Damus, Martin. *Kunst in der BRD, 1945–1990.* Reinbek bei Hamburg: Rowohlt, 1995.

Dannecker, Martin. "Der unstillbare Wunsch nach Anerkennung: Homosexuellenpolitik in den fünfziger und sechziger Jahren." In *Was heißt hier schwul? Politik und Identitäten im Wandel,* ed. Detlef Grumbach. Hamburg: MännerschwarmSkript, 1997.

Davidson, John. *Deterritorializing the New German Cinema.* Minneapolis: University of Minnesota Press, 1999.

————. "Working for the Man, Whoever That May Be: The Vocation of Wolfgang Liebeneiner." In *Cultural History through a National Socialist Lens: Essays on the Cinema of the Third Reich,* ed. Robert C. Reimer. Rochester, NY: Camden House, 2000.

Davidson, John, and Sabine Hake, eds. *Framing the Fifties: Cinema in a Divided Germany.* New York: Berghahn Books, 2007.

Delille, Angela, and Andrea Grohn. *Blick zurück aufs Glück: Frauenleben und Familienpolitik in den 50er Jahren.* Berlin: Elefanten-Press, 1985.

————. eds. *Perlonzeit: Wie die Frauen ihr Wirtschaftswunder erlebten.* Berlin: Elefanten-Press, 1985.

Dillmann-Kühn, Claudia. *Artur Brauner und die CCC: Filmgeschäft, Produktionsalltag, Studiogeschichte 1946–1990.* Frankfurt am Main: Deutsches Filmmuseum, 1990.

Doane, Mary Ann. *The Desire to Desire: The Woman's Film of the 1940s.* Bloomington: Indiana University Press, 1987.

————. *Femmes Fatales: Feminism, Film Theory, Psychoanalysis.* New York: Routledge, 1991.

Doane, Mary Ann, Patricia Mellencamp, and Linda Williams, eds. *Re-Vision: Essays in Feminist Film Criticism.* Los Angeles: American Film Institute, 1984.

Dyer, Richard. *Stars.* London: British Film Institute, 1979.

————. *Heavenly Bodies: Film Stars and Society.* New York: St. Martin's Press, 1986.

Elsaesser, Thomas. "The New Film History." *Sight & Sound* 55.4 (1986): 246–51.

————. *New German Cinema: A History.* New Brunswick, NJ: Rutgers University Press, 1989.

Elsaesser, Thomas, ed., with Michael Wedel. *The BFI Companion to German Cinema.* London: British Film Institute, 1999.

Fehrenbach, Heide. *Cinema in Democratizing Germany: Reconstructing National Identity After Hitler.* Chapel Hill: University of North Carolina Press, 1995.

————. *Race after Hitler: Black Occupation Children in Postwar Germany and America.* Princeton: Princeton University Press, 2005.

Feldmann, Erich, and Walter Hagemann, eds. *Der Film als Beeinflussungsmittel: Vorträge und Berichte der 2. Jahrestagung der Deutschen Gesellschaft für Filmwissenschaft.* Emsdetten: Lechte, 1955.

Fisher, Jaimey. "Deleuze in a Ruinous Context: German Rubble-Film and Italian Neorealism." *iris* 23 (1997): 53–74.

————. *Disciplining Germany: Youth, Reeducation, and Reconstruction after the Second World War.* Detroit: Wayne State University Press, 2007.

————. "On the Ruins of Masculinity: The Figure of the Child in Italian Neorealism and the German Rubble-Film." In *Italian Neorealism and Global Cinema,* ed. Laura E. Ruberto and Kristi M. Wilson. Detroit: Wayne State University Press, 2007.

Franklin, James. *New German Cinema: From Oberhausen to Hamburg*. Boston: Twayne, 1983.

Glaser, Hermann. *The Rubble Years: The Cultural Roots of Postwar Germany, 1945–1948*, trans. Franz Feige and Patricia Gleason. New York: Paragon House, 1986.

Gledhill, Christine. "Pleasurable Negotiations." In *Female Spectators: Looking at Film and Television*, ed. E. Diedre Pribram. London and New York: Verso, 1988.

Grasskamp, Walter. *Die unbewältigte Moderne. Kunst und Öffentlichkeit*. Munich: C.H. Beck, 1989.

Greenberg, Clement. *Clement Greenberg: The Collected Essays and Criticism*, vol. 1, ed. John O'Brian. Chicago: University of Chicago Press, 1986.

Greffrath, Bettina. *Gesellschaftsbilder der Nachkriegszeit: Deutsche Spielfilme 1945–1949*. Pfaffenweiler: Centaurus, 1995.

Gregor, Ulrich, and Enno Patalas. *Geschichte des Films*. Gütersloh: Sigbert Mohn, 1962.

Grohmann, Will, ed. *Neue Kunst nach 1945*. Cologne: M. Dumont Schauberg, 1958.

Groll, Gunter, Helmut Käutner, and Walter Talmon-Gros. "Every Audience, as Everybody Knows, Has the Films It Deserves," trans. Lance W. Garner. In *German Essays on Film*, ed. Richard W. McCormick and Alison Guenther-Pal. New York: Continuum, 2004.

Guilbaut, Serge. *How New York Stole the Idea of Modern Art: Abstract Expressionism, Freedom, and the Cold War*. Chicago: University of Chicago Press, 1983.

Habel, F.B. *Das grosse Lexikon der DEFA-Spielfilme*. Berlin: Schwarzkopf & Schwarzkopf, 2000.

Hagemann, Walter, ed. *Filmstudien: Beiträge des Filmseminars im Institut für Publizistik der Westfälischen Universität Münster*, vol. 3. Emsdetten: Lechte, 1957.

Hake, Sabine. *Popular Cinema of the Third Reich*. Austin: University of Texas Press, 2001.

Halle, Randall, and Margaret McCarthy, eds. *Light Motives: German Popular Film in Perspective*. Detroit: Wayne State University Press, 2003.

Hansen, Miriam. "Adventures of Goldilocks: Spectatorship, Consumerism, and Public Life." *Camera Obscura* 22 (1990): 51–71.

———. *Babel & Babylon: Spectatorship in American Silent Film*. Cambridge, MA: Harvard University Press, 1991.

Harlan, Veit. *Im Schatten meiner Filme*, ed. H.C. Opfermann. Gütersloh: S. Mohn, 1966.

Hauser, Johannes. *Neuaufbau der westdeutschen Filmwirtschaft 1945–1955 und der Einfluß der US-amerikanischen Filmpolitik. Vom reichseigenen Filmmonopolkonzern (UFI) zur privatwirtschaftlichen Konkurrenzwirtschaft*. Pfaffenweiler: Centaurus, 1989.

Hayward, Susan. *Key Concepts in Cinema Studies*. New York: Routledge, 1996.

Heibel, Yule F. *Reconstructing the Subject: Modernist Painting in Western Germany 1945–1950*. Princeton: Princeton University Press, 1995.

Heineman, Elizabeth. "The Hour of the Woman: Memories of Germany's 'Crisis Years' and West German National Identity." *American Historical Review* 101.2 (1996): 354–95.

Hembus, Joe. *Der deutsche Film kann gar nicht besser sein. Ein Pamphlet von gestern. Eine Abrechnung von heute*. 1961. Munich: Rogner & Bernhard, 1981.

Hermand, Jost. "Modernism Restored: West German Painting in the 1950s," trans. Biddy Martin. *New German Critique* 32 (1984): 23–41.

———. *Kultur im Wiederaufbau. Die Bundesrepublik Deutschland 1945–1965*. Munich: Nymphenburger, 1986.

Herminghouse, Patricia, and Magda Mueller, eds. *Gender and Germanness: Cultural Productions of Nation*. Providence, RI: Berghahn Books, 1997.

Herzog, Dagmar. *Sex After Fascism*. Princeton: Princeton University Press, 2005.

Higson, Andrew. "The Concept of National Cinema." *Screen* 30.4 (1989): 36–46.

Hoffmann, Hilmar, and Walter Schobert, eds. *Zwischen Gestern und Morgen. Westdeutscher Nachkriegsfilm 1946–1962*. Frankfurt am Main: Deutsches Filmmuseum, 1989.

Höhn, Maria. *GIs and Fräuleins: The German–American Encounter in 1950s West Germany*. Chapel Hill: University of North Carolina Press, 2002.

Huyssen, Andreas. *After the Great Divide: Modernism, Mass Culture, Postmodernism*. Bloomington: Indiana University Press, 1986.

Jacobsen, Wolfgang, and Hans Helmut Prinzler, eds. *Käutner*. Berlin: Edition Filme, 1992.

Joglekar, Yogini. "Who Cares Whodunit? Anti-detection in West German Cinema." Ph.D. diss., Ohio State University, 2002.

Johnston, Claire. "Women's Cinema as Counter Cinema." In *Movies and Methods I*, ed. Bill Nichols. Berkeley: University of California Press, 1976.

Jung, Uli, ed. *Der Deutsche Film: Aspekte seiner Geschichte von den Anfängen bis zur Gegenwart.* Trier: Wissenschaftlicher Verlag, 1993.

Kaes, Anton. *Kino-Debatte. Texte zum Verhältnis von Literatur und Film 1909–1929.* Munich: Deutscher Taschenbuch Verlag, 1978.

———. *From* Hitler *to* Heimat: *The Return of History as Film.* Cambridge, MA: Harvard University Press, 1989.

———. "German Cultural History and the Study of Film: Ten Theses and a Postscript." *New German Critique* 65 (1995): 47–58.

Kaplan, E. Ann. *Women & Film: Both Sides of the Camera.* New York: Methuen, 1983.

———. *Women in Film Noir.* Rev. ed. London: British Film Institute, 1998.

Klär, Karl. *Film zwischen Wunsch und Wirklichkeit: Gespräche mit den Freunden des Films und seinen Gegnern.* Wiesbaden-Biebrich: Der neue Film, 1957.

Knef, Hildegard. *The Gift Horse: Report on a Life,* trans. David Anthony Palastanga. New York: McGraw-Hill, 1971.

Knight, Julia. *Women and the New German Cinema.* New York: Verso, 1992.

Koepnick, Lutz. *The Dark Mirror: German Cinema Between Hitler and Hollywood.* Berkeley: University of California Press, 2002.

Kolinsky, Eva. *Women in West Germany: Life, Work, Politics.* Oxford: Oxford University Press, 1989.

Kracauer, Siegfried. *From Caligari to Hitler: A Psychological History of the German Film.* Princeton: Princeton University Press, 1947.

———. *Theory of Film: The Redemption of Physical Reality.* Oxford: Oxford University Press, 1960.

———. *Das Ornament der Masse: Essays.* Frankfurt am Main: Suhrkamp, 1963.

Kuby, Erich. *Alles über Rosemarie: Vom AA in Bonn bis Zensur.* Munich: Neue Film, 1958.

———. *Rosemarie—des deutschen Wunders liebstes Kind.* Stuttgart: H. Goverts, 1958.

Kuhn, Annette. *Women's Pictures: Feminism and Cinema* (1982). 2nd ed. London and New York: Verso, 1994.

Lack, Russell. *Twenty Four Frames Under: A Buried History of Film Music.* London: Quartet Books, 1997.

de Lauretis, Teresa. "Rethinking Women's Cinema: Aesthetic and Feminist Theory." In *Issues in Feminist Film Criticism,* ed. Patricia Erens. Bloomington: Indiana University Press, 1990.

Lawrence, Amy. *Echo and Narcissus: Women's Voices in Classical Hollywood Cinema.* Berkeley: University of California Press, 1991.

Linville, Susan E. *Feminism, Film, Fascism: Women's Auto/Biographical Film in Postwar Germany.* Austin: University of Texas Press, 1998.

Manvell, Roger, and Heinrich Fraenkel. *The German Cinema.* New York: Praeger, 1971.

Mänz, Peter, and Nils Warnecke, eds. *Die ideale Frau: Ruth Leuwerik und das Kino der fünfziger Jahre.* Berlin: Henschel, 2004.

Mayne, Judith. *The Woman at the Keyhole: Feminism and Women's Cinema.* Bloomington: Indiana University Press, 1990.

———. *Cinema and Spectatorship.* New York: Routledge, 1993.

McCormick, Richard W. *Gender and Sexuality in Weimar Modernity: Film, Literature, and "New Objectivity."* New York: Palgrave, 2001.

Meier, Gustav. *Filmstadt Göttingen: Bilder für eine neue Welt? Zur Geschichte der Göttinger Spielfilmproduktion 1945 bis 1961.* Hanover: Reichold, 1996.

Moeller, Robert G. *Protecting Motherhood: Women and the Family in the Politics of Postwar West Germany.* Berkeley: University of California Press, 1993.

———. "'The Homosexual Man is a "Man," the Homosexual Woman is a "Woman"': Sex, Society, and Law in Postwar Germany." *Journal of the History of Sexuality* 4.3 (1994): 395–429.

———. ed. *West Germany Under Construction: Politics, Society, and Culture in the Adenauer Era.* Ann Arbor: University of Michigan Press, 1997.

von Moltke, Johannes. *No Place Like Home: Locations of Heimat in German Cinema.* Berkeley: University of California Press, 2005.

Morton, David. *Off the Record: The Technology and Culture of Sound Recording in America.* New Brunswick, NJ: Rutgers University Press, 2000.

Mückenberger, Christiane, and Günter Jordan. *"Sie sehen selbst, Sie hören selbst ..." Eine Geschichte der DEFA von ihren Anfängen bis 1949.* Marburg: Hitzeroth, 1994.

Mulvey, Laura. *Visual and Other Pleasures.* Bloomington: Indiana University Press, 1989.

Noack, Frank. *Veit Harlan. "Des Teufels Regisseur."* Munich: Belleville, 2000.

Orbanz, Eva, and Hans Helmut Prinzler, eds. *Staudte.* Berlin: Edition Filme, 1991.

Penley, Constance. *Feminism and Film Theory.* New York: Routledge, 1988.

Perinelli, Massimo. *Liebe '47—Gesellschaft '49. Geschlechterverhältnisse in der deutschen Nachkriegszeit. Eine Analyse des Films* Liebe 47. Hamburg: LIT Verlag, 1999.

Petro, Patrice. "Mass Culture and the Feminine: The 'Place' of Television in Film Studies." *Cinema Journal* 25.3 (Spring 1986): 5–21.

———. *Joyless Streets: Women and Melodramatic Representation in Weimar Germany.* Princeton: Princeton University Press, 1989.

———. *Aftershocks of the New: Feminism and Film History.* New Brunswick, NJ: Rutgers University Press, 2002.

Peucker, Brigitte. *Incorporating Images: Film and the Rival Arts.* Princeton: Princeton University Press, 1995.

Pflaum, Hans Günther, and Hans Helmut Prinzler. *Film in der Bundesrepublik Deutschland.* Munich: Hanser, 1979.

Poiger, Uta. *Jazz, Rock, and Rebels: Cold War Politics and American Culture in a Divided Germany.* Berkeley: University of California Press, 2000.

Prinzler, Hans Helmut. *Chronik des deutschen Films 1895–1994.* Stuttgart: J.B. Metzler, 1995.

———. ed. *Das Jahr 1945: Filme aus fünfzehn Ländern.* Berlin: Stiftung deutsche Kinemathek, 1990.

Prinzler, Hans Helmut, and Eric Rentschler, eds. *Augenzeugen. 100 Texte neuer deutscher Filmemacher.* Frankfurt am Main: Verlag der Autoren, 1988.

Prommer, Elizabeth. *Kinobesuch im Lebenslauf. Eine historische und medienbiographische Studie.* Konstanz: UVK Medien, 1999.

Rabinbach, Anson, and Jack Zipes, eds. *Germans and Jews Since the Holocaust: The Changing Situation in West Germany.* New York: Holmes & Meier, 1986.

Rauch, Andreas M. *Bernd Eichinger und seine Filme.* Frankfurt am Main: Haag + Herchen, 2000.

Reimer, Robert C., and Carol J. Reimer. *Nazi-Retro Film: How German Narrative Cinema Remembers the Past.* New York: Twayne, 1992.

Rentschler, Eric. *West German Film in the Course of Time.* Bedford Hills, NY: Redgrave, 1984.

———. "Germany: The Past That Would Not Go Away." In *World Cinema Since 1945*, ed. William Luhr. New York: Ungar, 1987.

———. *The Ministry of Illusion: Nazi Cinema and Its Afterlife.* Cambridge, MA: Harvard University Press, 1996.

———. "From New German Cinema to the Post-Wall Cinema of Consensus." In *Cinema and Nation*, ed. Mette Hjort and Scott MacKenzie. New York: Routledge, 2000.

———. ed. *German Film and Literature: Adaptations and Transformations.* New York: Methuen, 1986.

———. ed. *West German Filmmakers on Film.* New York: Holmes & Meier, 1988.

Riecke, Christiane. *Feministische Filmtheorie in der Bundesrepublik Deutschland.* Frankfurt am Main: Peter Lang, 1998.

Riess, Curt. *Das gibt's nur einmal: Das Buch des deutschen Films nach 1945.* Hamburg: Nannen, 1958.

Ross, Kristin. *Fast Cars, Clean Bodies: Decolonization and the Reordering of French Culture.* Cambridge, MA: MIT Press, 1995.

Ruhl, Klaus-Jörg, ed. *Frauen in der Nachkriegszeit: 1945–1963*. Munich: Deutscher Taschenbuch Verlag, 1988.

Sandford, John. *The New German Cinema*. London: O. Wolff, 1980.

Schissler, Hanna, ed. *Miracle Years: A Cultural History of West Germany, 1949–1968*. Princeton: Princeton University Press, 2001.

Schmidt, Gary. *Koeppen—Andersch—Böll: Homosexualität und Faschismus in der deutschen Nachkriegsliteratur*. Hamburg: MännerschwarmSkript, 2001.

Schmieding, Walther. *Kunst oder Kasse: Der Ärger mit dem deutschen Film*. Hamburg: Rütten & Loening, 1961.

Schneider, Tassilo. "Reading Against the Grain: German Cinema and Film Historiography." In *Perspectives on German Cinema*, ed. Terri Ginsberg and Kirsten Moana Thompson. New York: G.K. Hall & Co., 1996.

Schnurre, Wolfdietrich. *Rettung des deutschen Films: Eine Streitschrift*. Stuttgart: Deutsche Verlags-Anstalt, 1950.

Schulz, Christian. *Paragraph 175. (abgewickelt): Homosexualität und Strafrecht im Nachkriegsdeutschland—Rechtsprechung, juristische Diskussionen und Reformen seit 1945*. Hamburg: MännerschwarmSkript, 1994.

Sedlmayr, Hans. *Der Verlust der Mitte: Die bildende Kunst des 19. und 20. Jahrhunderts als Symptom und Symbol der Zeit*. Salzburg: O. Müller, 1948.

Seeßlen, Georg. "Der Heimatfilm. Zur Mythologie eines Genres." In *Sprung im Spiegel: Filmisches Wahrnehmen zwischen Fiktion und Wirklichkeit*, ed. Christa Blümlinger. Vienna: Sonderzahl, 1990.

———. "Die andere Frau: Hildegard Knef." *EPD Film* 8.1 (1991): 15–19.

———. "Der Neo-Adenauer-Stil." *die tageszeitung*, June 12, 1997.

Seidl, Claudius. *Der deutsche Film der fünfziger Jahre*. Munich: W. Heyne, 1987.

Shandley, Robert. *Rubble Films: German Cinema in the Shadow of the Third Reich*. Philadelphia: Temple University Press, 2001.

Silberman, Marc. *German Cinema: Texts in Context*. Detroit: Wayne State University Press, 1995.

Silverman, Kaja. *The Acoustic Mirror: The Female Voice in Psychoanalysis and Cinema*. Bloomington: Indiana University Press, 1988.

———. *Male Subjectivity at the Margins*. New York: Routledge, 1992.

Smelik, Anneke. *And the Mirror Cracked: Feminist Cinema and Film Theory*. New York: St. Martin's Press, 1998.

Smith, Jeff. *The Sounds of Commerce: Marketing Popular Film Music*. New York: Columbia University Press, 1998.

Sobotka, Jens. "Die Filmwunderkinder: Hans Abich und die Filmaufbau GmbH Göttingen." Ph.D. diss., Westfälische Wilhelms-Universität-Münster, 1997. Düsseldorf, 1999.

Stacey, Jackie. *Star Gazing: Hollywood Cinema and Female Spectatorship*. New York: Routledge, 1994.

Stockhausen, Karlheinz. "Electronic and Instrumental Music <1958>," trans. Ruth Hein. In *Postwar German Culture*, ed. Charles E. McClelland and Steven P. Scher. New York: Dutton, 1974.

Stümke, Hans Georg. *Homosexuelle in Deutschland: Eine politische Geschichte*. Munich: C.H. Beck, 1989.

Westermann, Bärbel. *Nationale Identität im Spielfilm der fünfziger Jahre*. Frankfurt: Peter Lang, 1990.

Wilken, Waldemar. *Und Abends ins Kino*. Volksmissionarische Schriftreihe Heft 69. Gladbeck: Schriftsmissions-Verlag, 1959.

Williams, Christopher, ed. *Realism and the Cinema: A Reader*. London: Routledge and Kegan Paul, 1980.

Williams, Linda, ed. *Viewing Positions: Ways of Seeing Film*. New Brunswick, NJ: Rutgers University Press, 1995.

Wortig, Kurt. *Ihre Hoheit Lieschen Müller: Hof- und Hinterhofgespräche um Film und Fernsehen*. Munich: Kresselmeier, 1961.

Zielinski, Siegfried. *Veit Harlan: Analysen und Materialien zur Auseinandersetzung mit einem Film-Regisseur des deutschen Faschismus*. Frankfurt am Main: R.G. Fischer, 1981.

Newspapers, Periodicals, and Trade Journals

Abendpost
Die Abendzeitung
Badisches Tageblatt
Beratungsdienst Jugend und Film
Berlin am Mittag
Berliner Zeitung
Bravo
Christ und Welt
Deutsche Woche
Evangelischer Film-Beobachter
film 56: Internationale Zeitschrift für Filmkunst und Gesellschaft
Film und Frau
Film-Dienst
Film-Echo
Filmblätter
Filmdienst der Jugend
Filmkritik
Film Revue
Film Revue Sonderablage
Filmstudien: Beiträge des Filmseminars im Institut für Publizistik der Westf. Wilhelms-Universität Münster
Frankfurter Rundschau
Die Gegenwart
Handbuch für Filmclubarbeit
Hannoversche Allgemeine
Illustrierte Film-Bühne
Katholischer Filmdienst
Der Kreis
Die Kunst und das schöne Heim
Das Kunstwerk

Der Kurier
Lumiere. Zeitschrift der Film & Kino-Initiative Göttingen
Der neue Film
der neue ring
Neue Zeit Berlin
Die Neue Zeitung
Nordwest-Zeitung
Rheinischer Merkur
Rheinische Post
Rheinische Zeitung
Revue
Ruhr-Nachrichten
Die Sammlung
sie
Sonntag
Sonntagsblatt
Spandauer Volksblatt
Der Spiegel
Stuttgarter Zeitung
Süddeutsche Zeitung
Der Tagesspiegel
die tageszeitung
Telegraf
Time
Der Weg
Weltbild
Der Weser Kurier
Westfälische Rundschau
Die Wirtschaftszeitung
Die Zeit

INDEX

CPSIA information can be obtained at www.ICGtesting.com
Printed in the USA
BVOW021209050212

282170BV00004B/10/P